W9-BIG-359

# Java 2 Game Programming

Premier
Press

# Java 2 Game Programming

*Golley*

**Thomas Petchel**

Premier
*p*
Press

**Premier**

The Premier Press logo, top edge printing, and related trade dress are trademarks of Premier Press, Inc. and may not be used without written permission. All other trademarks are the property of their respective owners.

**Press**

**Publisher:** Stacy L. Hiquet

**Marketing Manager:** Heather Buzzingham

**Managing Editor:** Sandy Doell

**Acquisitions Editor:** Jody Kennen, Emi Smith

**Series Editor:** André LaMothe

**Project Editor:** Estelle Manticas

**Technical Reviewer:** Andre LaMothe

**Copy Editor:** Laura R. Gabler

**Interior Layout:** Scribe Tribe

**Cover Design:** Mike Tanamachi

**CD-ROM Producer:** Arlie Hartman

**Indexer:** Sharon Shock

Sun, Sun Microsystems, Java, and Java 2 are trademarks or registered trademarks of Sun Microsystems, Inc. in the United States and other countries.

All other trademarks are the property of their respective owners.

*Important:* Premier Press cannot provide software support. Please contact the appropriate software manufacturer's technical support line or Web site for assistance.

Premier Press and the author have attempted throughout this book to distinguish proprietary trademarks from descriptive terms by following the capitalization style used by the manufacturer.

Information contained in this book has been obtained by Premier Press from sources believed to be reliable. However, because of the possibility of human or mechanical error by our sources, Premier Press, or others, the Publisher does not guarantee the accuracy, adequacy, or completeness of any information and is not responsible for any errors or omissions or the results obtained from use of such information. Readers should be particularly aware of the fact that the Internet is an ever-changing entity. Some facts may have changed since this book went to press.

ISBN: 1-931841-07-1
Library of Congress Catalog Card Number: 2001096216
Printed in the United States of America

01 02 03 04 RI 10 9 8 7 6 5 4 3 2 1

*For Gloria and Tom—long live the Raccoon!*

# Acknowledgements

I'd first like to thank André LaMothe for his friendship and guidance over the past few years. He has always been there when I needed advice on anything—not just with game programming. It's amazing how much he's done to help amateur and hobbyist game developers break into the business. My internship with Xtreme Games was incredible. Our goal was just to write a few shareware games for the website. But by the time my internship was over, I had a full 3-D game on the shelves nationwide and a contract to write this book. That wouldn't have been possible without his support (and lots of caffeine, too).

I'd also like to thank my parents, Gloria and Tom, for feeding my computer and game addition ever since I got my first Commodore 64 at the ripe old age of six. Instead of making me play little league or take swimming lessons, they let me do my own thing, like studying karate and playing video games. They have always taught me that being an individual was one of the most important things in life.

My soul mate, Megan, has also been a source of inspiration and undying support. She has always been there in times of uncertainty and has always given me better perspective on things. Without her, I doubt I would have kept my sanity through the madness of school, work, and the other 10,000 projects I've had going on.

And of course, Jody Kennen, Emi Smith, Estelle Manticas, Laura Gabler, and all the other folks behind the scenes at Premier Press have been great throughout the entire writing process. They have made writing this book a relatively smooth and painless process.

I would like to give one final shout out to Art Bell (and Ian Punnett on weekends), hosts of *Coast-to-Coast AM.* Their discussions on the strange and paranormal, from Shadow People to Area 51, have kept me company many nights while I worked on this book.

Oh yeah, and the folks at Sun Microsystems—the developers of Java. I guess I had better thank them too—without them I wouldn't have had anything to write about!

# About the Author

**O**riginally hailing from parts unknown, **Tom Petchel** is no stranger to the world of video games. Through an aggressive video game playing campaign, Tom successfully completed more than 300 video games (mainly for the original 8-bit NES) by the time he was 12 years old, which might be even more impressive if he still had the pictures to prove it. Tom's enjoyment of object-oriented programming led to a natural switch to Java as his preferred language of choice. During his 2000 internship at Xtreme Games Tom successfully published his first video game title, *Mahjongg Empire*. At the 2000 Xtreme Games Developer's Conference (XGDC) in Santa Clara, CA, Tom gave a presentation entitled *An Introduction to Java Game Programming*.

Today, fresh out of Shippensburg University with his B.S. in Computer Science, Tom is a software developer at Wizard International, where he is working on the cutting-edge in innovative frame-shop software. He lives just outside Seattle with his fiancée, Megan, and his cats, Simon and Roxanne. Tom's future ambition is to become the most electrifying software developer in computer science history. Okay maybe not, but he *does* plan to continue working on the software that will entertain, and possibly improve, the lives of the masses of tomorrow.

# Contents at a Glance

# Contents

# Part Two
# Graphics Development with Java 2-D
# and the Abstract Window Toolkit .......... 139

## CHAPTER 5
## APPLET BASICS ............................... 141

# CHAPTER 6

# LISTENING TO YOUR USERS •••••••••••••••• 191

# CHAPTER 7

# RENDERING SHAPES, TEXT, AND IMAGES WITH JAVA 2-D, PART 1 ••••••••••••••••••209

# CHAPTER 8
# RENDERING SHAPES, TEXT, AND IMAGES
# WITH JAVA 2-D, PART II ................................. 259

# LETTER FROM THE SERIES EDITOR

Java has finally matured enough to make games! It's now a great way to create simple and mid-level games that can be played on many platforms. Moreover, Java's speed is getting better all the time, as is its support for other libraries you can use with it.

Java wasn't originally developed with game programming in mind. In fact, game programming was probably the last thing on the minds of its developers. What has hindered Java in the past is the environment in which it operates; the browser, along with the Java libraries, in essence dictated what kinds of applications you could write with Java, and high-speed games and graphics weren't included among them. This gave Java a bad reputation, as people were focusing not on the language, but on the environment in which it ran. Now that the browser isn't controlling everything anymore, it's time to give Java another chance as a game programming language. Java was a little before its time, and the marketing engine got a little carried away with it, but this time around Java can and will deliver.

*Java 2 Game Programming* will show you how to use the language and the libraries to create 2D games that include high speed, double-buffered graphics, animation, sound, media control, I/O and network support. Tom Petchel has a unique background—he was originally a C/C++ game programmer, and has created both 2D and 3D games for the PC in DirectX and Direct3D. This means that he isn't one of these Java fanatics who thinks it's the greatest thing in the world (even though they've never programmed any real games in C/C++); Tom has instead been legitimately swayed enough by Java to begin using it in his game programming. It's a ringing endorsement of the language when a C/C++ game programmer makes the transition to Java and actually likes it!

So what's this book about, exactly? Well, this book is really about how to make games with the Java language and how to think in the Java way. Although as languages Java and C++ are very similar, Java is the ultimate in object-orientation—*everything* is an object, and that takes a lot of getting used to. So does the lack of pointers and the memory management model. *Java 2 Game Programming* has a Java programming primer to get you started, so even a C/C++ programmer can pick this book up and immediately get use out of it. Once the basics are out of the way the book covers basic graphics, then animation and networking, and finally game-related topics.

The intent of the book, and this author, is to give you a solid foundation on how to do things the Java way, and to show you how to do them right. Tom's code is impressive—he really understands Java and how to use it properly. If you follow his examples and use his techniques in addition to learning the graphics, sound, and networking aspects you'll be in great shape. The book has a lot of code in it, lots of examples, and some really cool demos. Also, Tom decided to take a really generic approach to the code and examples in the book so they will all work with the straight Java runtime libraries from SUN, along with the applet viewer. This means you don't have to worry about browsers or IDE's.

This is the book for you if you're truly interested in learning about game programming and graphics using the Java platform.

Sincerely,

André LaMothe

# Introduction

These days the word *Internet* is practically synonymous with the word *computer*. More and more people are buying new computers just so they can surf the World Wide Web or keep in touch with friends and family through e-mail (or as your grandmother might say, "the e-mail"). Increased connectivity among users, as well as an exponential increase in the power of modern hardware and software, has created a gray area between where the personal computer ends and the network begins.

The cyber culture of the Internet has undoubtedly impacted our daily lives more than we imagine. Most of us browse the Web daily looking for information and news. Some of us use the Internet for academic research. Others use it to wreak havoc on others by spreading viruses or hacking into corporate websites. For me, the magic of the Web lies in the ability it affords one to play games online.

The video game industry is a multi-billion-dollar-per-year business. Most of this revenue comes from games for home consoles or shrink-wrapped PC games. I really think that online gaming is a largely untapped market—and that's very exciting, as it affords anyone the perfect opportunity to develop the "next big thing" in computer gaming. Whether it's a fresh new gaming genre geared towards online play or a new marketing scheme to help existing online games make money, opportunity abounds. Even if you don't end up being the next billion-dollar multimedia mogul, there is still plenty of room for you to make your mark on the gaming industry. Just remember, Java games often appeal to the 85 percent of computer users who aren't considered "hardcore" gamers, because Java games are usually simple, fun games that require minimal hardware requirements from the user. You can use this fact to spread your games to all types of gamers—not just the hardcore ones.

Whether you're a hobbyist programmer who likes to show off your games to your friends, or a seasoned professional looking to take advantage of the Internet to capitalize on the cutting-edge in gaming technology, this book will show you how to use the Java language to create robust, flexible gaming applications. Are you ready to take your skills to the next level? Read on, and maybe you'll be the one to write that next "killer game."

# Who Should Read this Book?

Computer programming is both an art and a science. It takes rigor as well as creativity to be able to take an idea and transform it into a complete product. I believe that anyone with at least some computer skills has the ability to become a computer programmer. The real question is: do you have the *interest* to become a computer programmer? Just picking up this book tells me that you do. But should you buy it?

You should probably buy this book if

- you're interested in game programming or are a beginning programmer and want to get the inside track on how you can use the Java language to create exciting Internet games.
- you already use packages such as DirectX or OpenGL, and would like to expand your skills into Java.
- you need a hefty book to prop up an uneven couch or chair.
- you are an avid Java programmer and want to see how you can expand your Java expertise to game development.
- you like books that contain no-frills source code and solid programming examples.
- you're interested in making games like the one shown in Figure 1.
- you have an empty slot on your bookshelf and can't resist filling it with one of the quality titles found in the Premier Press Game Development Series (shameless, *shameless* plug).

You should probably *not* buy this book if

- you like video games, but have little interest in actually *making* them.
- you were looking for a book about one of those *other* object-oriented languages.
- you're just pretending to read this book in the bookstore so others think you're a wicked game programming genius.
- you thought this would be a book about coffee, or possibly that little island off the coast of China.
- you were on the original Java development team and you're merely scoffing at my futile attempt at teaching the Java language.

With that in mind, we've come to a crossroads. If you feel that you fit into the first category and would like to learn about game programming with Java, go ahead and buy it (or try to sneak out of the bookstore with it). I guarantee you'll have loads of fun creating your own Java games. However, if you think you fit more into the second category, kindly hand this book to the next person who was waiting to see it. I know the psionic forces this book contains will draw you back next time.

# What You'll Get out of this Book

Like any journey into the unknown, it is always good to at least have *some* idea where you're going. That's why I've outlined the following list of goals to accomplish by the time we're done. Keep these ideas in the back of your mind. After finishing the final chapter, come back here and see just how far you've come.

By the end of this book, you should

- be able to write, compile, and run Java applications and applets.
- know the fundamental aspects and features of object-oriented programming, especially how they relate to Java and game programming.
- be able to use Java to create flexible, robust 2-D games and gaming tools.
- be able to add sound to your games.
- know how to utilize the more advanced features of the Java Abstract Window Toolkit and Java 2-D in your games.
- know what client-server architecture is, and how to implement it in your games
- have a solid understanding on how to create your own custom menuing and visual component system.
- be able to put all of the above concepts together into a single, reusable game development engine.

# How this Book is Organized

Learning game programming can seem overwhelming at first—especially to those new to the business. That's why I've broken everything down into distinct parts. That way, we can explore Java game programming in an organized fashion. Here's a brief roadmap of the topics we'll discuss throughout the book:

- **Part One—Entering the Java Jungle: Getting Started with the Java 2 API.** This part includes a brief history of the Java language, step-by-step instructions on how to set up Java on your system, and a full Java primer geared towards game programming. This section is great for the newbie programmer as well as C/C++ programmers looking at Java for the first time.

- **Part Two—Graphics Development with Java 2-D and the Abstract Window Toolkit.** Before we can start creating games, we should first investigate how a graphical Java program works. Part Two provides an overview on creating applets using the Java 2 API, as well as some of the common features found within the Abstract Window Toolkit (AWT). Part Two also discusses some more advanced graphical features using the Java 2-D package.

- **Part Three—Java Gaming for the Masses.** This is where the real fun begins. By building upon the concepts presented in Parts One and Two, you'll explore how to set up and manipulate game objects in a 2-D setting. This part also examines topics such as animation and game object manipulation. You'll also look at scene management and custom controls and menus, as well as how to set up a client-server network. Part Three culminates with the creation of a fully functional 2-D game development engine and a sample game.

# Tips for Programming Success

Following is a list of tips that will practically guarantee your success in just about any programming venture; although most of these tips are simple and intuitive, it can't hurt to keep them in the back of your mind.

- **Familiarize yourself with the Java language.** Although it may be tempting to dive right in, if you don't know Java's basic features you'll probably sink quickly. That's why I've included preface material geared towards game programming with Java. Even if you're an excellent C++ programmer, check out the features and structure of Java first before writing your first Java game.

- **Be open-minded.** Sometimes the best way to demonstrate a new concept or idea is by showing the longest way to do it. Therefore, some of my code examples may not be the most efficient way to accomplish what I'm explaining. I will try to point out instances where code can be improved or optimized. Feel free to make enhancements and changes to the code in this book, and remember that almost any piece of code has potential for improvement.

- **Be creative.** Although computer programming is mostly technical, what you decide to do with what you know is up to you. I'll give you the tools for creating games with Java; it's up to you to use those tools to create the next generation of innovative games.

- **Know what tools are available.** I wouldn't be caught dead not using an Integrated Development Environment (IDE), such as Microsoft® Visual Studio, for any large-scale C++ Windows application. However, for a Java project, I'm just as happy using a plain old text-editor and the command-line for compiling and running my Java programs. The decision of what tools to use is largely up to you. I have provided a copy of Forté 3.0 for Java on the accompanying CD-ROM, just in case you want to try it out. Tools such as the native Java packages and the `javadoc` utility will also help you write the most efficient code possible. Use the tools that will allow you to write your best code in as little time as possible. That's the name of the game.

- **Have plenty of caffeine available.** It's the key to those late-night coding sessions.  Personally, I'm trying to take it easy on my Mountain Dew consumption, but I still enjoy a bottle now and then to get me through those long nights of writing code.

- **Stay focused on the task at hand.**  There's nothing worse than being in the middle of coding a killer rendering routine when you suddenly think of a sound engine you want to write. Switching tasks mid-stream will cause you to lose focus, and you may not remember what you were doing when you come back. If you need to, takes notes when an idea pops into your head, but try to finish one thing at a time.

- **Most importantly, have fun!** Unless you're 15 minutes away from a deadline with two weeks of work left to do, don't panic if you get stuck at a particular stage of the development cycle. A good attitude will definitely shine through in the end product.

Well, that's it for the introduction.  Next, in Chapter 1, you'll see how to get started using Java.  We'll look at a brief history of the language, and how to set up the Java compiler and run Java programs. After that's out of the way, we'll start to look at the specifics of the Java language. So buckle your seatbelts, and prepare for an exciting ride ahead!

# Part One

# Entering the Java Jungle! Getting Started with the Java 2 API

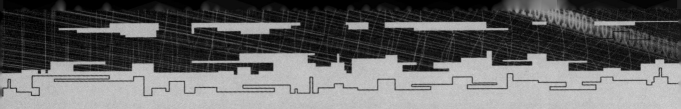

> **"Experience is a hard teacher because she gives the test first, the lesson after."**
>
> **-Vernon Lace**

So, you've decided to stick around and take the crash course; I hope you didn't forget your helmet! Those other guys (and gals) who are skipping this part won't know what they're missing. If you're familiar with C, the conversion to Java will be (somewhat) straightforward. If you're a C++ aficionado, Java will appear even more familiar.

Before we get into the details of programming the next great 3-D action thriller, let's first get acquainted with the specifics of the Java language itself. Game programming can be a tough subject to teach because there are people from all programming backgrounds who want to learn it. So as not to bore the programming geniuses but to still help the newcomer feel comfortable, I will try to balance thoroughness with brevity. I'll also try to gear our discussions toward how Java can be used for game programming wherever possible.

I suggest that if you're new to Java you take the time to review the next few chapters, so the material presented in later chapters won't seem so rough. If you're a seasoned Java veteran, you may want to just skim through the following sections. If you're an all-out Java guru, you can probably skip them altogether.

In the next few chapters, we'll look at the following topics:

- Installing Java and running Java programs
- General Java program structure
- Basic types, variable declarations, operators, and program flow
- The mysteries of classes, interfaces, and packages
- Getting around with commonly used Java classes

Keep in mind that this is not meant to be a complete guide to the Java language; that would take up an entire book! However, I hope it will give you enough information to become familiar with Java, if you aren't already. There will be exercises at the end of Chapters 2–13; I've made them as fun and painless as possible. In fact, I've made them so painless that I haven't provided answers—you can figure them out for yourself. So without further ado, let's get started!

# CHAPTER 1

# THE JAVA 2 SOFTWARE DEVELOPMENT KIT

# A (Very) Brief History of Java

"Write once, run anywhere" is the philosophy of the millions of Java developers all around the world.  In the past few years Java has become arguably the hottest and fastest-growing programming language available. How did this technological phenomenon come to be, and how has it become so popular so quickly?

The answer lies in the simple yet ingenious driving force behind the Java philosophy.  By focusing on abstraction and object-oriented principles, the creators of Java have formed a flexible, robust programming language whose applications can be run on virtually any platform.

The rest is history.  Actually, Java is still making history—everywhere you look, you see all types of developers creating new, exciting innovations using Java.  Java programs can be run on any platform that supports the Java platform.  From Windows to UNIX, from today's high-powered supercomputers all the way down to ordinary kitchen coffee makers (no pun intended), Java is being used everywhere.

Many people directly associate Java with the World Wide Web. Actually, the idea of Java existed before the Internet became so widely popular. According to one version of the Java FAQ, Bill Joy (co-founder of Sun Microsystems) was given credit for coming up with the brainchild known today as the Java language. His goal was to develop a "better" language for the tasks of the day. By 1991, Sun had developed a "Stealth Project" in order to investigate how such a technology could be created.

Sun began by looking at the C++ language, which remains to this day one of the most popular and powerful programming languages. However, after seeing many of the inherent flaws with C++, the company sought to do better. Sun then began developing a language that answered common complaints found in languages such as C++.  One of the intermediary results of Sun's work was called *Oak*.  The Oak language was improved upon and eventually renamed *Java*. (Although there have been many guesses at what the name might stand for, Java is not an acronym or an abbreviation for anything.  I suppose that since gourmet coffee had become so popular, "Java" would only be fitting for this popular new language.) Java was officially launched at SunWorld in 1995. Soon after, companies such as Netscape jumped to support Java in their products.

Unlike with most other languages, newer versions of Java become available every few months, as improvements and extensions are made. The name *Java 2* might be a bit misleading. The name was officially announced in December 1998 and it applies to versions of Java starting with 1.2. Versions 1.0.x and 1.1.x of Java were formerly known as the Java Development Kit, or JDK. As of the printing of this book, the current version of Java is version 1.4. I suggest that you make sure you're using the newest version of Java before getting started. The latest version of the Java 2 platform is recommended for development because of the latest advancements in core Java technology.

Since Java can be run on almost any of today's machines for almost any purpose, it did not take long before people began using Java to create games. Possibly the only drawback to using Java is its inherent lack of speed, as Java code is interpreted rather than fully compiled. Because of this relative lack of speed, it has been rare to see an industrial-strength computer game written with Java; Java is instead often seen as an amateur's tool to create Web-based games. However, with today's ever-increasing line of faster and better computer processors and technologies, Java's lack of speed is becoming less and less of an issue. In fact, Sun Microsystems has officially announced its support to game development companies at the 2001 Game Developers' Conference (GDC). Recent innovations using Java for game development include integration with consoles such as the Playstation 2, and a game development API written entirely in Java. We should expect to see many more enhancements geared specifically towards game development in the Java API in the near future.

Java has already proven itself as an industry standard with its networking and language capabilities. In fact, it is projected that professional Java users

## NOTE

Did someone say platform compatibility? Possibly not. Unfortunately for us programmers, politics has reared its ugly head in the world of platform-compatible software. After a legal wrangle with Sun Microsystems, Microsoft chose *not* to implement native support for Java in its latest edition to the Windows family, Windows XP. But all hope is not lost. Many Web sites that make heavy use of Java will allow you to automatically download and install Java-capable components. Equipment manufacturers may also opt to install these components. If you're upgrading from a previous edition of Windows to XP, then you will still have Java support. Since this book has hit the shelves so soon after Windows XP was released to the public, it may be too early to predict what impact, if any, this compatibility problem might have on the Java development community.

will outnumber those using C and C++ worldwide as early as 2002! Java is already the most popular development language outside the United States. If the game development community continues to follow current industry standards its members will, without a doubt, contribute to Java history by showing yet another way the language can be used to create innovative applications and program content.

# Why Use Java for Games?

Not totally convinced that Java is *the* premier language with which to write your next game? The decision whether to use Java over languages such as C or C++ is not always clear. There are situations where you may want to use one language and situations where another might be more appropriate. For instance, using Java to create today's latest and greatest first-person 3-D shooter may not be such a wise choice—at least not until more development tools are created. On the other hand, I guarantee that you object-oriented programmers out there can get that 2-D side-scroller done faster and more efficiently with Java than with practically any other language out there. Following are some reasons why you might choose Java for a particular game:

- **Platform Compatibility.** Practically all Java programs written on one system will automatically run on any other system that supports the Java platform. Therefore, the exact same code can be executed right out of the box on virtually any system, without any code changes needed. A game created with Java can be sold to someone running Windows XP just as it can to someone running an older edition of Linux. Try doing that with C or C++.

- **Internet Capabilities.** Much of the Java language is tailored for the Internet. Therefore, you can easily create and run games for the Web using Java. This includes everything from downloading simple games like checkers or blackjack and running them directly through your Web browser to playing multiplayer role-playing games online.

- **The Java API.** Java comes with a rather impressive number of data structures and other packages, saving the programmer from having to perform many menial, low-level tasks. The Java Abstract Window Toolkit (AWT), Java 2-D, and Java Project Swing are just a few Java technologies available to help you write better code faster. In short, the Java API allows you to focus on the problem at hand, rather than worrying about many of the underlying details.

- **Object-Oriented Design.** Reusable Java classes and packages are just one reason object-oriented design makes programming faster and easier. Large tasks can be broken down into smaller ones, and object-oriented programs are also generally easier to follow and manage than ones written using procedural languages. In the days when Basic and Fortran were most popular, it was practically impossible to maintain projects larger than 30,000–50,000 lines. Object-oriented languages allow for projects that are millions of lines long—many of today's large software ventures would not be possible without the advent of object-oriented design.

- **A Shallower Learning Curve.** Game programming requires knowledge of mathematics, physics, graphics programming, artificial intelligence, and so on. This can be quite intimidating to the new kid on the block. Using a language with so many built-in constructs allows newcomers to the field of game programming to feel comfortable more quickly, allowing them to break down projects into small, manageable steps.

I prefer Java for small to medium-sized games, but that doesn't mean Java isn't suitable for those large-scale online games as well. Once you get the hang of gearing Java to game development, you should be cranking games out in no time. In fact, many parlor-style games can be developed in less than a day. Figure 1.1 shows one such game I wrote in only a few hours. Check out this and the other sample games contained on the CD-ROM.

Of course, just because you develop a poker game in record time doesn't mean that the game is any good. That said, completing a few small games from start to finish will give you a good feel for the entire game development cycle. After you complete several quick and dirty Java games, you can slow down and start making some quality hits.

**Figure 1.1**

*Card games, such as* Xtreme Poker, *can be developed quite rapidly.*

# Preparing Your System for Java

One of Java's claims to fame lies within *platform compatibility*. This means you can create a Java program in just about any environment (Windows, UNIX, Solaris, and yes, even the Mac) and run it on any other environment without recompiling! To accomplish this, Java programs are not run directly through the operating system but are compiled into what's called *bytecode*, which is then interpreted by the Java Virtual Machine (JVM). To get started programming with Java, you'll need the following:

- **The Java Virtual Machine.** You must get and use the one written specifically for your operating system.
- **The Java Application Programming Interface (API).** This is a library of commonly used features that will save you time and effort.
- **The Java Compiler.** This converts your source files into a format readable by the Java Virtual Machine.

Luckily for us, the good folks at Sun have included all of these items in one package. You can either use the packages contained on the CD-ROM included with this book or go to Sun's Java Web site (http://www.java.sun.com) for an updated version.

## Installing the Java SDK

Getting Java up and running on your system is a fairly straightforward task. However, some fine points are involved in establishing your environment variables.

After obtaining the latest version of the Java 2 platform, go ahead and run the self-extracting executable. The on-screen directions should guide you through the installation. Some platform installers will ask you to reboot your system after installation so all updates to your system are accepted in full.

Now that you have the Java 2 platform installed, you can now set your PATH environment variable so the system knows where the Java compiler and run-time executables are found. By setting the PATH variable permanently, your PATH variable will persist even after rebooting.

Steps for permanently setting the system PATH variable differ from Windows 95/98 to Windows Millennium to Windows 2000 and XP to UNIX and Solaris platforms. Since you will most likely be using one of the various Windows platforms for your Java development, I have included the steps you'll need to take to permanently set your system's PATH configuration in a sidebar. If you're using a non-Windows operating system, I suggest reading the readme file found under the directory in which you installed the Java 2 platform. Since there are so many different configurations to discuss, this file will be the best place to get the most accurate information.

After you have the correct PATH set, you should set your CLASSPATH variable. This variable tells your Java programs where to find the .class containing Java bytecode. Platform-specific instructions on how to set this variable can be found directly after the instructions for setting your PATH environment variable. For Windows users, you can use the batch (.bat) file I have included with the example programs. Each of these files contains a line similar to the following, which will set the CLASSPATH variable for you:

```
SET CLASSPATH=.
```

Most integrated development environments (IDEs) out there take care of these steps for you, so the choice is up to you.

As I mentioned, since Windows is such a popular operating environment I have included Windows batch (.bat) files for compiling the source code examples contained within this book. These files also contain statements to temporarily set your PATH and CLASSPATH variables during the execution of each program.

# Compiling and Running Java Programs

If you choose to use an IDE to write your Java applications, all of the tools needed to edit your source code and to compile and run your programs are already supplied. If you're not going to use an IDE, you can edit your programs using your favorite text editor. In Chapter 2, you'll be presented with your first Java program. For now, let's look at how to compile Java programs. Feel free to come back here later for reference.

## Using the Command Line

I like using the command line to compile and run my Java applications. Both Windows and UNIX environments have shell environments that accept commands one line at a time. It's a no-frills, straightforward way to test and run your programs.

Once you have a complete source file, you can compile it from your user shell using the `javac` utility, such as the following:

```
javac HelloWorld.java
```

Multiple files can be compiled by separating them with a blank space:

```
javac File1.java File2.java File3.java
```

## Permanently Setting the PATH Variable (Windows)

Contained herein are the steps to permanently set your PATH variable so your system knows where to find the various utilities to compile and run Java programs. Of course, you can use the Java 2 SDK without setting the PATH variable every time. To do this, you would simply type in the full path of the location of the desired Java utility program, like as follows:

```
C:> \jdk1.4\bin\javac HelloWorld.java
```

Yuck! That's too much typing! So with each example program found on the CD-ROM, I have included a Windows batch (.bat) file that sets the PATH variable automatically before the statements to compile and run the program. This statement will look much like the following:

```
PATH=.;C:\JDK1.4\bin;%PATH%
```

This works great for times when you don't want to bother permanently setting the PATH variable for your operating system. If you still wish to set your PATH variable permanently, however, follow the steps that go along with your current operating system below.

- **Windows NT and 2000**. Choose Settings under Control Panel, then select System. On Windows NT, select the Environment tab; on Windows 2000 machines, select the Advanced tab. Look for "Path" in the User Variables and System Variables. You can add the path to the right end of the "Path" found in the User Variables like the following:

  ```
  C:\JDK1.4\BIN
  ```

  Capitalization does not matter. Once you're finished, click "Set," "OK," or "Apply."

- **Windows 95/98**. Open the Autoexec.bat file found under C:\ either manually or by running the `sysedit` utility from Start/Run on the taskbar. Look for the PATH statement (or add it to the top of the file if one does not already exist). Append ";C:\JDK.4\BIN" to the end of the PATH statement, like this:

  ```
  PATH C:\WINDOWS;C:\WINDOWS\COMMAND;C:\JDK1.4\BIN
  ```

  Capitalization does not matter. Save and close the file once you're finished.

- **Windows ME**. From the Start Menu, choose Programs, Accessories, System Tools, and then System Information. This brings up a window titled "Microsoft Help and Support." From here, choose the Tools menu, and then select the System Configuration utility. Click the Environment tab, select PATH and press the Edit button. Now add the SDK to your path as described in for Windows 95/98. After you've added the location of the SDK to your PATH, save the changes and reboot your machine when prompted.

After updating your PATH variable, reboot your machine (if you haven't already been prompted to), or type

```
C:> C:\AUTOEXEC.BAT
```

within a console window to update your PATH. To view the PATH variable at any time, simply type

```
C:> PATH
```

at the command prompt.

If you want to compile all of the source files within the current directory, you can use the asterisk (*) character to compile them all at one time, like in the following:

```
javac *.java
```

After running the javac utility, you may be given a list of errors that were generated during compilation. Simply go back and fix any errors you encounter, then run the javac utility again. Repeat until you generate a clean compile with no errors or warnings.

After generating a clean compile, a number of .class files will be generated in the same directory as the source files. These files contain the bytecode that is readable by the Java Virtual Machine. You are now ready to run your program. Console applications can be run by executing the java utility, such as the following:

```
java HelloWorld
```

Note that you don't need the .class extension and that the file name is case-sensitive. Figure 1.2 shows the entire process of creating a Java program from start to finish.

**Figure 1.2**

*Compiling and running Java programs from start to finish*

The `java` utility works for programs that are not run within a Web browser. If you are running a Web-based program, such as a Java applet, you will need to first create an .html file containing a reference to your code. You can name the .html file anything you want. The following shows a simple .html file that will load a program called *MyApplet*, with a width and height of 300 pixels:

```
<html>
<body>
<applet code=MyApplet.class width=300 height=300>
</applet>
</body>
</html>
```

You can then view your applet in one of two ways. You can directly open the .html file using your favorite Web browser, or you can use the `appletviewer` utility. The following command runs the `appletviewer` with a file named MyApplet.html:

```
appletviewer MyApplet.html
```

## Using Integrated Development Environments (IDE's)

If you choose to use an IDE for Java development, the tools to edit, compile,

> **NOTE**
>
> I have presented you with the basic way to create tags for displaying Java applets within a Web browser. Applets written with the Java 2 API will run correctly within the `appletviewer` program but probably won't within a Web browser, even with the Java 2 plug-in. There is a better way to format your .html files so that Java 2 programs will run correctly within a Web browser. See Appendix D for more on how this is done.

and run your programs should already be included. Since all IDE's differ from one another, it is difficult to generalize how they work. A good IDE will have an intuitive interface and good documentation for its more advanced features. See the release notes for your IDE to find out how it works.

I have included Sun's Forte for Java on the CD-ROM. I think this is one of the best IDE's out there. It is free, it is relatively easy to start using right away, and it includes many powerful features to make development easier. Best of all, it's written by Sun (in Java!), so you know it will be updated each time a major Java technology break-through is made. Figure 1.3 shows a typical screen from the Forte editor.

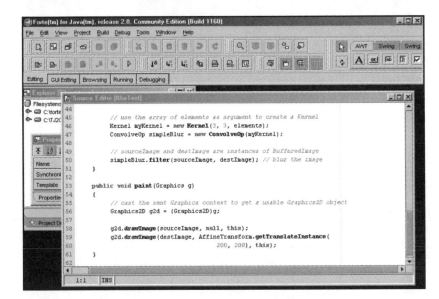

**Figure 1.3**

*Forte 2 for Java Community Edition (Windows Edition)*

## A Note about the Java 2 Documentation

Unfortunately, I was unable to provide the documentation for the Java 2 platform on the CD-ROM—it is a necessary tool for Java development. It includes reference material for the entire Java API, as well as many other techniques and standards used throughout the language. I mention it throughout the book, and I recommend it as a must-have for anyone serious about Java development. You can view the Java 2 documentation for version 1.4 online at

> http:/www.java.sun.com/j2se/1.4/docs/index.html

I'd recommend downloading the entire thing from the java.sun.com Web site, so it will always be available to you for offline viewing.

## Conclusion

That about wraps up our introduction to Java. By now, you should be familiar with the origins of the Java language and know why it's a good language to use for developing games. You should also be familiar with the steps for setting up the Java 2 platform on your system and know how to compile and run your Java programs. Be sure to visit this chapter again if you're having trouble doing any of those things.

Next, we'll delve into the specifics of the Java language. I suggest that you have Java installed and ready to go on your machine before proceeding. Actually working with any programming language is by far the best way to learn it. So what are you waiting for? Let's get our hands dirty and write some Java code!

# CHAPTER 2

# Priming the Pump! Learning the Java 2 API

A sk any Java programmer what Java is like and he or she will probably say something like, "It's *kinda* like C++, but not really." As with any programming you've done so far, you first need to know the basics of the language you're going to use. That's why I'm including a few primer chapters before getting into actual game code. In this chapter, we'll look at the following topics:

- The overall structure of a Java program
- Basic Java types, including `String` and array types
- Arithmetic as well as conditional operators, along with the operator order of precedence
- Conditional statements, including control statements and looping
- Exception handling using the `throws` statement along with `try-catch` blocks

I tried to balance this chapter so that it will be pertinent to both novice and more experienced programmers alike. Since most game programmers are experienced with C++, I will attempt to point out as many differences and similarities as I can. I suggest becoming familiar with the syntax of the Java language before proceeding to the later chapters of this book.

The first thing we'll look at in this chapter is a sample Java program and how its component parts all fit together.

# Game Over, Amigo!

Let's get started by examining a groundbreaking achievement in Java technology: the *Game Over!* program. First we'll look at the code, line by line, then we'll talk about what each part means and how you can relate it to other languages you may have worked with.

```
// The Game Over! program
   import java.lang.*;

   /*
    * file:   GameOver.java
    * author: Thomas Petchel
    * date:   xx-xx-20xx
```

```
    */

    public class GameOver
    {
        public static void main(String[] args)
        {
            System.out.println("Game Over, You Lose!!!");
        }
    }    // GameOver
```

Fascinating, isn't it? Try typing it into your text editor, or you can just pull it off the CD-ROM (you can find it under the Source/Chapter1/ directory). Keep in mind that Java is case-sensitive.

After you finish typing in the *Game Over!* program, go ahead and save it. Remember, the file must be named GameOver.java (the file name is case-sensitive as well). If you haven't already, create a directory in which to save your Java programs. A directory like C:\JavaDev or C:\J2GP works fine for Windows platforms; UNIX users can just save the file under the default user directory.

Okay, you've got the code typed in and saved to your work directory. So far so good. Now let's compile and run it. Launch a console shell and bring up the directory where you saved GameOver.java. Assuming your system's all configured to compile and run Java programs, the following command should compile your program:

```
javac GameOver.java
```

If you get any errors like "Bad command or file name," "javac: not found," or "could not find Java 2 Runtime Environment," then your system may not be set up to compile or run Java programs. Refer to the section called "Compiling and Running Java Programs" in Chapter 1 for more information on setting up your system.

If you receive any compiler errors that complain about your syntax or anything related to the program itself, go back and fix your program; the Java compiler is rather straightforward in its error reporting.

By now you should have a clean compile. Now it's time to run the application. Just as a reminder, here's how to run the *Game Over!* program:

```
java GameOver
```

Note that you don't need to include the .class extension to the program name. If the program executes correctly, you should see the words "Game Over, You Lose!!!" printed on the console, with the program terminating immediately afterward. If not, you have probably run into what's known as a *runtime error*. In that case, you may have left something out. Go back and correct the program if it did not execute correctly.

If you've made it this far, I commend you. You've properly set up the Java compiler and run your first program. Believe me, getting set up is the hard part! Now all you have to do is figure out what each part of the program means and you can begin to write your own programs. Let's begin by looking at the `import` statement.

# The import Statement

The `import` statement tells the compiler which libraries you want to use. The Java `import` statement is similar to the C++ `#include` directive. If you'll remember from the above program, we used the following `import` statement:

```
import java.lang.*;
```

Java objects are organized into categories called *packages*. Packages contain related classes for easy organization. For example, the `java.lang` package includes classes that relate to the fundamental design of the Java language. The `System` class is contained in the `java.lang` package. The `java.net` package includes classes for creating network applications. The `java.util` package includes utilities such as a random-number generator and date and time utilities. Currently, the barebones Java API contains over 75 packages (containing almost 2,000 classes in all), but we will only need to concern ourselves with a handful of those.

You C++ programmers out there know how difficult it can be to remember which header files go with which functions or classes. Luckily for us, the Java 2 documentation contains the package name with the class name. That way you can quickly obtain the proper package to import within your programs. A general rule of thumb about packages is to use what I call the *guess-and-check method*. If you know the package name for a particular class you wish to use, great—just type it in. Otherwise, take a logical guess. If that fails, look up the class name in the

> **C++**
>
> Recall that the Java `import` **keyword is analogous to the** `#include` **directive in C++. The only difference is that Java makes no distinction between header and source files. Both the declaration and implementation for Java classes are contained in a single .java file.**

online documentation; this only takes a minute and the name of the package for the class is printed right at the top of the page. Simple.

One more note about imports. For the above example, you could have imported the System class directly, that is:

```
import java.lang.System;
```

This is perfectly fine. However, each time you need to use a different class from the java.lang package, you must add an additional import statement so the class can be found. I generally import the entire package because most programs will use several classes from commonly used packages.

## Commenting Java Code

Immediately following the initial import statement, the *Game Over!* program contains the following lines of text:

```
/*
 * file:   GameOver.java
 * author: Thomas Petchel
 * date:   xx-xx-20xx
 */
```

C programmers will recognize this as a comment. Java, like most other programming languages, allows you to add inline comments to your code. Comments allow you to highlight important code, note changes, or explain what is going on at greater length. They are especially useful when you (or someone else) look at your code six months later and have no clue what you intended it to do. Comments are for the sole benefit of the programmer; the compiler simply ignores them. Therefore, you can add as many comments as you like without bloating the size of your compiled code.

Java supports three types of comments: C-style, C++ style, and Javadoc comments. Here's the skinny on each:

- **C-style comments.** C-style comments begin with /* and end with */. They can contain anything in between them, except an extra */ symbol.
- **C++ style comments.** This style is just a shorthand version of the first. These are great for when you have single-line comments. C++ style comments take on the following form:

  ```
  // I'd rather not comment on this comment.
  ```

  With this in mind, you can rewrite the above example like the following:

  ```
  // file:   GameOver.java
  // author: Thomas Petchel
  // date:   xx-xx-20xx
  ```

- **Javadoc comments.** This style is suitable when used with the javadoc utility. It's similar to the C-style comment, only this style uses an extra "*" for the comment header, as follows:

```
/** See Appendix A for more on the javadoc utility */
```

Be sure to comment your work, but don't go overboard. Avoid superfluous comments; these just clutter your code and can greatly overstate the obvious. Also be sure to fully explain the intent of each comment, without being overly verbose. Finally, note that C-style comments do not nest. The first instance of */ disables the most recent instance of /*. For example, the following will cause a compiler error:

```
/* Comments totally rule - /* just be sure not to nest them! */ */
```

Using an IDE that highlights comments with a different color will help you avoid nested comments.

# Java Class Declarations

A Java class is a structure that houses data for a program to use, as well as the operations that can act on the data. Our simple (um, I mean *ingenious*) Game Over! application contains only one class: the GameOver class. We could have defined more, but for this example we only needed one. The GameOver class can also be called our *application class,* since it acts as the startup point for our program.

The *scope,* or visibility, of a class can be defined in two different ways. For this example, the GameOver class is defined as public. Public classes are available to other classes outside their resident package. All public classes must be defined in a file called *<Classname>.java.* That's why the GameOver class must be defined in a file called GameOver.java.

The alternative form of the class would be to leave out the public keyword, leaving us with just class GameOver. The removal of the public keyword leaves the class available only to other classes within the same package. Nonpublic classes can be defined in a file with any name. Classes that are not declared as public are usually dependent or utility classes that are only used by other classes within the same package.

All classes have the same general structure, as follows:

```
{ public } class <Classname> { extends    <Classname> }
                              { implements <Interface1>,
                                           <Interface2>,
                                           [..],
```

```
                                  <InterfaceN> }
{
     // class body
}
```

The curly braces (except for the ones surrounding the class body) contain optional declaration options, so class declarations can range from the fairly simple to the complex. We'll talk a lot more about classes in Chapter 3. For now, just think of them as containers for data and data operations.

# Java Method Declarations

Our GameOver class contains one operation, or method: the main method. A typical application class would contain many methods, but one thing always remains true: every Java application class must contain a defined main method. (Java applets, on the other hand, are slightly different—you'll see how they're defined in Chapter 5.)

The main method is the definitive starting point for any application. If you'll recall, we ran the *Game Over!* application with the following command:

```
java GameOver
```

This implicitly commands the Java interpreter to make a call to GameOver.main. Every main method that exists in Java has the exact same syntax, as follows:

```
public static void main(String[] args)
{
     // method body
}
```

As long as you can remember—or can refer to—this syntax, you'll be in fine shape. There are some more fine points to note about the main method, and we'll discuss them in Chapter 3. But for now, all I want you to know is that this is where your programs begin (and end).

# Code Blocks in Java

One final aspect of our *Game Over!* program you should know about is *code blocks*. Code blocks are defined by a

---

**C++**

The main method in Java should look similar to the main function typically found in a console C or C++ application. Note that the Java version must be defined within a class, whereas the C and C++ versions must be defined globally. Furthermore, the main method in Java always returns void, unlike a C or C++ main function, which can have multiple return types.

number of statements sandwiched between a pair of braces. The entire body of the main method is one single code block. Let's take one final look at our main method:

```
public static void main(String[] args)
{
    System.out.println("Game Over, You Lose!!!" );
}
```

I make note of code blocks for those new to programming. As you can see, code blocks aid you in controlling program flow. Think of it as the glue that holds the code together.

## Key Points to Remember about Java Program Components

- You use the import statement to let the compiler know which libraries you wish to use.
- Comments can aid the programmer in many ways, but remember that improper use of them can do more harm than good.
- Everything you write in Java is encapsulated in a class, even your main startup point, the main method.
- A block of code contains related statements driven toward accomplishing a specific task. Code blocks keep your programs structured and easy to read and write.

## Bits and Bytes: Primitive Java Types

OK, so far you've taken a quick glance at how Java programs are structured. Great, but now what do you put *inside* your program? Programs need data. Programs love data. Programs can't live without data. Especially games.

Games are memory hogs. In the following subsections, you'll investigate the different mathematical and string types available in Java, as well as their associated memory requirements. Variables in Java can take up considerably more memory than within equivalent C++ programs, so knowing these memory requirements will help you avoid writing bloated code.

As you already know, Java is an object-oriented language. However, Java is not 100 percent object-oriented (many will argue this point, I know). This is because Java supports eight primitive types: byte, short, int, long, float, double, boolean, and char. Since these basic types are not objects, I say Java is not purely object-oriented.

In this section, you'll learn how Java defines primitive data types as well as examine the commonly used String class. In addition, you'll see how Java implements arrays as well as learn how modifiers can shape the meaning of your variables. Let's begin by looking at the primitive integer types.

# Basic Integer Types

Mathematically speaking, an integer is any whole number ranging from negative infinity to positive infinity. Some examples of integers are 5, 0, and –128,456. Since computers are finite machines and require memory to store variables, you must define your quantities accordingly. In Java, there are four defined integer types: byte, short, int, and long. Table 2.1 lists each type along with its storage requirements and associated minimum and maximum values.

How did I arrive at these values? I used each type's storage size as a guide. For example, I know that the int type takes up 32 bits. That makes $2^{32}$ (or 4,294,967,296) different values for an int variable. Since all Java variables are signed (meaning they all must implicitly carry a positive or negative value), the valid ranges become $-2^{32}$ (–2,147,483,648) through $2^{32}-1$ (2,147,483,647). The maximum value for int is 2,147,483,647 and not 2,147,483,648, since zero is included as a valid value.

**Table 2.1    Integer Types and Their Storage Requirements**

| Type | Storage | Minimum Value | Maximum Value |
| --- | --- | --- | --- |
| long | 64 bits | around $-9.2e+10^{18}$ | around $9.2e+10^{18}$ |
| int | 32 bits | –2,147,483,648 | 2,147,483,647 |
| short | 16 bits | –32,768 | 32,767u |
| byte | 8 bits | –128 | 127 |

The following examples illustrate some examples of how to initialize integer variables:

```
short numLives = 3;
int counter = 0;
long population;
byte currHealth;
```

As with all types, you should initialize variables before you use them. Even though the compiler will usually catch you on this, it is good practice to do it on your own anyway.

Typically, for game development you'll want to use int types for whole numbers and just ignore long, short, and byte types. Since the int type has a range of over 4 billion, you'll usually be safe with them. However, if you have an exceptionally generous scoring system or you want to count the number of people on earth, you'll have to go with the long type. Using short and byte types is usually reserved only for times when memory is limited or you are dealing with large arrays. So, for whole numbers, go with int most of the time, but be aware of times when you might need to use a different type.

# Floating-Point Types

Sometimes whole numbers just aren't enough. Values such as those used in math and physics are often expressed as decimal values. Java, like C++, supports two such decimal types: float and double. Table 2.2 shows the storage requirements and valid ranges for both of these types.

Rather than going into a laborious discussion on how these values can be obtained, let's just take them at face value. Here are some quick examples of how floating-point variables are declared:

```
double pi = 3.141592653589793d;
float velocity = 30.65f;
double gravity = 9.81;
```

Note that for a value to truly be considered a float, it must end with the f (or F) suffix. Otherwise, it is considered a double. It is optional to supply the d (or D) suffix for doubles.

From what I have seen, the jury's still out on which type should be typically used to store floating-point values. Doubles give us, in essence, double the precision of floats. However, this comes at a cost—typically memory consumption. Most method return types and data members found in the Java API use the double type. So I say why fight it? The pros like doubles, so I like doubles as well.

**Table 2.2    Floating-Point Types and Their Storage Requirements**

| Type | Storage | Minimum Value | Maximum Value |
|------|---------|---------------|---------------|
| double | 64 bits | around 4.9e–324 | around 1.79e+308 |
| float | 32 bits | around 1.4e–45 | around 3.4e+38 |

# The char Type

In Java a character (represented as char) represents a single entry from what is known as the *Unicode character set*. Unicode characters consist of 16 bits. Therefore, there are $2^{16}$ (65,536) different Unicode characters available—a huge difference from the standard 128 ASCII characters available in languages like C++! The Unicode character set gives us great flexibility in that it can contain characters from all different written languages, plus common symbols used in mathematics, science, and art.

Characters are represented by a single character surrounded by single quotes. Characters are often written in hexadecimal format, within the range of '\u0000' through '\uFFFF' (the 'u' tells the compiler you are indicating a Unicode character, along with 4 bytes [16 bits] of information about the character). The following are both examples of valid character use:

```
char letter;
char lastInitial = 'R';
```

**C++**

Note that in Java, unlike C++, an array of characters does not necessarily make a string. The Java API defines its own String type, which you'll see in just a moment. Treating arrays of characters is generally only done when sensitive information is needed, such as within a password field. This is because Java objects reside in memory until the Java Virtual Machine cleans up unreferenced objects. Leaving sensitive data laying around in memory can pose a dangerous situation if a shrewd hacker is lurking within the system.

**NOTE**

For more on the Unicode character set, including a complete listing of characters, refer to http://www.unicode.org.

# The boolean Type

The boolean type (aptly named after 19th-century mathematician George Boole) gives the programmer the ability to set truth values to variables. You've undoubtedly used Boolean variables in your programming past. However, many languages don't include it as a separate data type. In Java there are only two valid values of any boolean variable: true and false. The boolean type has no numeric equivalent, and no type conversions are permitted. Also, note that all if and while statements evaluate to a boolean result. The following is a valid use of the boolean type:

```
boolean isAlive = true;
while (isAlive)
{
     // program code
}
```

# The String Type

The Java String type is not really a primitive type at all. However, it is so intrinsic to the language I've decided to include it here anyway. The String type is actually a Java class. You'll learn all about objects and classes in Chapter 3. But for now, let's focus on how to define and manipulate strings in Java.

## Declaring Strings

Declaring strings in Java is actually quite straightforward. It is much more intuitive than in some other languages, such as C++. The following examples should give you the basic idea on how strings are declared:

```
String string = "Strings are a wonderful thing!";
string = "No String lives forever...";
```

## Manipulating Strings

Once you declare a String object, what can you do with it? Technically, you can't do much to modify the variable itself. This is because the Java String is an example of what is called an *immutable object;* that is, there are no operators defined to alter the contents of the object itself. However, there are operations defined on String objects that return new String objects themselves. Here's an example to make this point clearer:

```
String s1 = "I am the original String";
String s2 = s1.toUpperCase();
```

```
System.out.println(s1);
System.out.println(s2);
```

As you might have guessed, the content of s2 is "I AM THE ORIGNAL STRING." However, the original contents of s1 were not changed; the String toUpperCase method returned a new String object and assigned it to the variable named s2. Figure 2.1 shows a similar example of String assignment.

In Figure 2.1, you can see that s1 initially points to the original string. After reassignment, however, s1 now points to a different string of characters. The original data, "I am the original String," still resides in memory, but nothing references it. It has gone to the String graveyard, never to be heard from again.

Another way to manipulate Strings is by *string concatenation*. Basically, you can just "add" strings together to build new ones. Here's a quick example:

```
String s1 = getFirstName();
String s2 = getLastName();
System.out.print(s1 + " " + s2);
```

Realistically, you might not need to store the first and last names into separate variables, but you get the picture. You could just as easily store the entire name into a third variable, such as the following:

```
String s3 = getFirstName() + " " + getLastName();
```

The possibilities are endless. String concatenation will doubtlessly come in handy when reading input from the user or sending data across a network.

There are many, many different operators defined on String objects. The above examples are just a few ways String objects can be manipulated. Check out Chapter 4 or the Java 2 documentation for more on String manipulation.

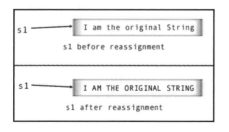

**Figure 2.1**

*Referencing a new*
*String object*

# Arrays

We'll wrap up this discussion on primitive types with a type that allows you to add more ordered structure to your data: the *array* type. An array in Java is more or less the same as you've encountered in languages such as C or C++. If arrays are new to you, just think of them as an ordered list of elements, indexed *0* through *n–1*, where *n* is the number of elements in the list.

For you array newbies out there, consider the following situation: You wish to keep a count of the ammo remaining for a number of weapons. You might develop the following list of counter variables to hold your values:

```
int ammo0 = 0;
int ammo1 = 0;
int ammo2 = 0;
int ammo3 = 0;
int ammo4 = 0;
```

Yuck! It will take a lot of tedious coding to initialize and manipulate just these five variables—imagine having 100,000 or more to deal with! However, by using arrays, you can reduce the declaration to one line:

```
int[] ammo;
```

The [] operator tells the compiler that the variable is of an arrayed type. Still, this doesn't do much. To actually create the array of variables, use:

```
int[] ammo;
ammo = new int[5];
```

Or, more compactly:

```
int[] ammo = new int[5];
```

Voilà! You've just created an array of integers containing five elements. Now let's fill in the array with some data:

```
for (int i = 0; i < 5; i++)
{
    ammo[i] = 0;
}
```

> **NOTE**
>
> In these examples, you're declaring arrays of type int. Remember, you can declare arrays of any type: long, float, String, Alligator...whatever.

Now we're getting somewhere. Note that the indexing starts at 0 and, in this case, ends with 4. While we're on the topic of indexing, Java supports a nifty operator on arrays: the `length` member. Rather than keeping track of how large your arrays are, you can use the `length` variable instead, like the following:

```
for (int i = 0; i < ammo.length; i++)
{
        ammo[i] = 0;
}
```

## Referencing Arrays

Arrays are all fine and good, but you can run into some problems if you're not careful. For example, consider the following code:

```
int[] a = { 1, 2, 3, 4, 5 };
int[] b = { 6, 7, 8, 9 };
```

> **C++ NOTE**
>
> There are two ways to declare arrays in Java. The first you've already seen:
>
> ```
> int[] prices;
> ```
>
> However, here's a slightly different way that may be more familiar to C++ programmers:
>
> ```
> int prices[];
> ```
>
> This all may seem rather trivial, but it is interesting to note. The folks who designed Java allowed both ways to keep C++ sticklers happy. I prefer the first way, since the [] operator directly next to the type declaration makes it very clear that you're declaring an array. In the end, however, it's a matter of personal preference; the choice is up to you.

The first line creates an integer array containing five elements; the second line creates an integer array containing four elements (note the shorthand notation for initializing an array). Now suppose you do the following:

```
b = a;
int x = b[2];
```

What is the value of x? Before saying for sure, let's look at the graphical representation (see Figure 2.2) of what's happening when you declare your two arrays.

Here you see each array referencing its respective set of data, just as you'd expect. Now examine what happens when you set b = a (see Figure 2.3).

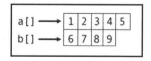

**Figure 2.2**

*Arrays referencing separate memory locations*

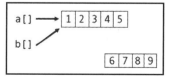

**Figure 2.3**

*Arrays referencing the same memory location*

As you can see, b now points to the same physical set of data as a does. Therefore, you can conclude that your x variable is equal to 3. Similarly, setting b[0] = 8 will also cause the value of a[0] to be 8. Both variables reference the same values, so when one changes, so does the other. Keeping this clear will save you headaches in the future.

## Copying Arrays

The previous example may not be of the greatest help, but it illustrates how the use of the = operator can lead to unwanted side effects. What do you do if you want to copy the contents of the first array into the second? In other words, you want two independent data sets containing the same information, such as seen in Figure 2.4.

Of course, only enough memory was allocated for four integers in the second variable, but we can live with that. So if you want to change the a array, like

```
a[2] = 721;
```

the value of b[2] will remain at 3. You can set up your own loops to copy the data, or you can use the predefined arrayCopy method from the System class. The syntax is as follows:

```
System.arrayCopy(Object src, int src_position,
                 Object dst, int dst_position,
                 int length);
```

Here, src refers to the source array to copy *from,* src_position refers to the starting index to copy from, dst refers to the array we want to copy *to,* dst_position refers to the start index of the array we want to copy to, and length specifies the number of array elements to copy. So, to copy the contents of a into b, write

```
System.arraycopy (a, 0, b, 0, b.length);
```

Now you have two arrays, each of which references different memory locations. Try typing in and running the entire example if this is not immediately clear to you. Remember to import java.lang.* so the compiler knows you are using the System class.

You can see from the arraycopy method that arrays can be sent as parameters to methods. Incidentally, arrays can also be the return type of a method. Chapter 4 goes into more detail on the operations available for use on arrays such as searching and sorting.

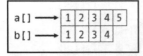

**Figure 2.4**

*Copying the contents of*
*one array to another*

## Multidimensional Arrays

Although Java does not physically store multidimensional arrays as such, you can still code as though it does. Take the following example: You want to design a game to play checkers. You might mentally visualize your checkerboard like that shown in Figure 2.5.

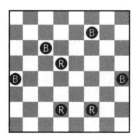

**Figure 2.5**

*An 8 x 8 checkerboard*

Right away, you should notice the layout of the board itself; it has eight rows and eight columns. Each square can be mapped (or indexed) by its row and column number. For example, the square in the first row and the third column would be mapped as (0, 2). This situation is perfect for a two-dimensional array. For this checkerboard, let the following hold true:

- The board has eight rows and eight columns.
- Each square is either shaded or plain.
- If any particular square on the board has a checker on top of it, the checker is black, red, black (king), or red (king).

For the sake of example, let's ignore the actual checkers for now and concentrate on the board layout itself. The following program, *CheckerBoardTest*, sets up a standard checkerboard and prints it out to the console:

```java
import java.lang.*;

public class CheckerBoard
{
    // constant value for the width and height of the board
    public static final int  SIZE  = 8;

    // character that represents a blank square
    public static final char PLAIN = ' ';

    // character that represents a shaded square
```

```java
public static final char SHADED = 'S';

// 2-D array of character data for the checkerboard
private char[][] board;

// fills in the board with shaded and plain square values
public CheckerBoardTest()
{
    // create an array of 9 values for one row of squares
    // this array will be copied from 0-7 or 1-8
    final char[] values = { PLAIN, SHADED, PLAIN, SHADED,
            PLAIN, SHADED, PLAIN, SHADED, PLAIN };

    // allocate memory for the checkerboard
    board = new char[SIZE][SIZE];

    // copy the array of square values to each row of squares
    // even rows will start at 0; odd rows will start at 1
    for(int i = 0; i < SIZE; i++)
    {
        System.arraycopy(values, i%2, board[i], 0, SIZE);
    }
}

// prints the state of the game board to the console
public void print()
{
    for(int i = 0; i < SIZE; i++)
    {
        for(int j = 0; j < SIZE; j++)
        {
            System.out.print(board[i][j]);
        }
        // print blank line between rows
        System.out.println();
    }
}

// creates a CheckerBoard object and prints it to the console
```

```
public static void main(String[] args)
{
    new CheckerBoardTest().print();
}
}   // CheckerBoardTest
```

Again, you can either copy the code into your favorite text editor or you can just copy the source file from the CD-ROM. The *CheckerBoardTest* program should output eight lines of text, each line containing alternating 'S' and blank characters, much like a checkerboard. It might not be the most visually stunning program, but it illustrates the concept of multidimensional arrays quite well.

Of course, multidimensional arrays do not have to be square, as in the above example. A two-dimensional array can be 3 x 2, 3 x 3, 1 x 10, 500 x 1,000, etc. Furthermore, you can also have what are known as *ragged arrays*. For example, you can have a 2-D array with five rows, but each row can have a different number of columns. Exercise 2.6 poses a situation in which ragged arrays might be useful.

## Casting Variables

Java uses C-style casting when a conversion is needed from one type to another. For instance, say you're using floating-point variables to track the x- and y-coordinates of an alien creature on the screen. However, the method to actually draw the alien to the screen takes integers for the x- and y-screen positions. All you need to do to perform a cast is to

**TIP**

**Arrays can make life a lot easier or—if used incorrectly—they can make your life miserable. The following tips might help you if you're having trouble deciding whether or not to use an array to solve a particular problem:**

- **Sketch an abstraction of the problem on a sheet of paper. If your data cannot be organized in terms of rows and columns, using an array might not be the best solution.**

- **Check the Java API before writing your own array utilities, such as sorting and searching routines. The** `java.util.Arrays` **package is always a good place to start. Java packages will inevitably save you time, plus it is very difficult to write more efficient code than what's supplied in the API.**

- **Although you can define arrays with three, four, five, or more dimensions, things can get a bit hectic after you leave the second dimension. If you need to go much past the third dimension, examine whether you can design or find another data structure, such as a tree, that will more elegantly solve your problem.**

declare the new data type in parentheses before the variable. The following illustrates how this is done:

```
// create an Alien, named harry, at position 40.0, 40.0
Alien harry = new Alien(40.0f, 40.0f);

// draw harry to the screen; the draw method takes integers for the
// position, so we need to cast the alien's position as int's
draw(harry, (int)harry.getX(), (int)harry.getY());
```

Java allows us to do what are called *widening conversions* without an explicit cast. A widening conversion occurs when you convert from one data type to a "larger" one. For example,

> **NOTE**
>
> Keep casting in the back of your mind; it will become extremely useful when we talk about inheritance throughout the book.

```
byte narrow = 16;
int wide = narrow;
```

is permitted since the contents of `wide` will still be 16. There is no possibility of data loss or loss of precision. An `int`-sized variable will always be able to hold the contents of a `byte`-sized variable; hence, no cast is explicitly required. On the other hand,

```
int wide = 32654312;
byte narrow = wide;
```

would cause a compiler error; since the `byte` type only holds 8 bits, it obviously won't hold the contents of a 32-bit integer. Therefore you need a cast, like the following:

```
int wide = 32654312;
byte narrow = (byte)wide;
```

> **C++ NOTE**
>
> Remember, unlike C++, the Java `boolean` type has no numeric equivalent. Therefore, there is no way to directly convert a `boolean` to an `int`. The quickest way to convert a `boolean` value to another type might be like the following:
>
> ```
> boolean gameStarted = true;
> int gameState = gameStarted ? 1 : 0;
> ```
>
> Although there is no cast being placed, the conversion can still be done in one line.

This lets the compiler know that you know that the contents of narrow will be truncated and that you are aware that possible side effects will occur. In this case, the value of narrow would be –24. While such side effects are predictable, they are not always particularly useful. Use casts with caution, and be aware of the side effects that may arise.

> **C++ NOTE**
>
> Here's a final note on variables. In Java there is no typedef operator, nor is there an equivalent to the #define preprocessor directive. Although this may take some getting used to for some, it will help eliminate errors and make your code look much cleaner. So, those of you who enjoy writing more "cryptic" code I'm sorry, but you will no longer be able to define an int as something like fa26b9.

## Key Points to Remember about Java Data Types, Arrays, and Modifiers

- The eight primitive types in Java—byte, short, int, long, float, double, boolean, and char—are not Java classes themselves, but rather the building blocks of our classes.

- Arrays in Java can be coded much like as in C and C++, but the Java implementation supplies an additional length field for accessing the number of elements of the array.

- Casting is a good way to convert variables from one type to another, but beware of potential side effects along the way.

- In the movie *Pulp Fiction,* there are bullet holes in the apartment walls before any shots are even fired.

# Operators in Java

Now that you know how to declare variables of a given type, you can look at what operations you can perform on them. As you know, an *operator* is simply a symbol that defines the behavior of a given set of *operands,* such as variables, classes, and methods. Most of the operators defined in Java are self-explanatory, but others may require some special attention. First we'll look at the assignment operator, then some numeric operations, Boolean operations, and finally an operator known as the *dot operator.*

## The Assignment Operator

This one should be a no-brainer for everyone. Whether you're an experienced programmer or not, this operator is very intuitive. The assignment operator first evaluates the expression on the right-hand side of the = symbol and then assigns that value to the variable on the left. For example:

```
int x = 10;  int y = 20;  int z = 30;
int sum = x + y + z;
```

The value of sum will (obviously) be 60, while the values of x, y, and z will remain at 10, 20, and 30, respectively.  Remember that the = operator does not imply equivalence, and such statements should not be interpreted as Algebraic statements.

C++ programmers know how to concatenate assignment expressions into a more compact form. To add 100 to the sum variable, write

```
sum = sum + 100;
```

This can be written more compactly as

```
sum += 100;
```

## Comparison Operators

Here's another easy construct from elementary math class. I'm including it just in case you're coming from a language that uses a different syntax. In Java, comparison operators help determine whether a given condition is true or false. Here's just a quick rundown of each operator along with example usage:

> **NOTE**
>
> Java supplies a special null value for objects that you are not yet ready to initialize or want to reference nothing. The null value is referenced to memory location zero and specifies that the object has not yet been created. The following shows how this is done:
>
> ```
> Robot roger = null;
> ```
>
> The roger variable, in essence, references nothing. Therefore, you cannot yet perform any manipulation on the robot variable. It is good practice to initialize all of your object instances to null if you do not immediately give them an explicit value. You'll get to examine memory allocation in greater depth in the next chapter.

- Less than (<)

```
if(a < b)    // true if a is less than b
```

- Less than or equal to (<=)

```
if(a <= b)    // true if a is less than or equal to b
```

- Greater than (>)

```
if(22 > 99)    // uh... looks false to me
```

- Greater than or equal to (>=)

```
if(a >= b)    // you get the picture
```

- Equivalence (==)

```
String s1 = "hello";
String s2 = "hello";
System.out.println(s1 == s2);    // prints false!!!
```

- Not equivalent (!=)

```
if(isReady != true) initialize();
```

- Logical *and* (&&)

```
if(a == 5 && b == 6)    // true if a is 5 and b is 6
```

- Logical *or* (||)

```
if(a == 5 || b == 6)    // true if either a is 5 or b is 6
```

- Ternary conditional operator (?:)

```
// if the condition (ammo > 0) is true, hasAmmo is assigned to true,
// otherwise, it is assigned to false
boolean hasAmmo = (ammo > 0) ? true : false;
```

So why did (s1 == s2) evaluate to false? Because for objects, conditional operators look at the memory addresses, not the values of the objects themselves. Even though the two String variables contain the same data, they are not stored at the same memory location. So how do you determine conditions such as equality for objects? Classes that provide an equals method help us determine if the state of two classes are equivalent. If you wish to determine if two String objects contain the same data, you would type the following:

```
String s1 = "hello";
String s2 = "hello";
System.out.println(s1.equals(s2));    // prints true!!!
```

That's better. As a general rule, look for methods such as compare, compareTo, and equals when you need to determine whether a given condition exists between objects. We'll examine these methods more closely before finishing Part One.

# Numeric Operators

There are a number of operators available to all numeric types, whether they are integers or floating-point numbers. Even if you are new to programming, you are surely familiar with the four basic numeric operators: addition (+), subtraction (–), multiplication (*), and division (/). Here is an example of each, just to give you a look at the syntax:

```
int oneThird = 100 / 3;        // result is 33
return (health - 5);           // returns 95 if health is 100
value = 2 * 2;                 // result is 4
value = 2 + 2;                 // result is also 4! Amazing!
```

Remember that an integer divided by an integer always gives an integer result. That's why 100 / 3 evaluates to 33 in the land of integers. If your program requires a decimal answer, you will need to store the result in a float or double.

You are probably familiar with a fifth numeric operator that is only defined for integer types: the modulus (%) operator. This operator gives you the remainder result from division of two integers. Modulus division comes in handy if you need to test a number as being even or odd or to see if one number is evenly divisible by another. Here are some examples:

```
int mod = 100 % 3;      // mod is 1
if(value % 2 == 0)      // tests if value is even
if(value % 7 == 1)      // tests if value equals 8, 15, 22, etc
```

## Increment and Decrement Operators

The increment and decrement operators are two commonly used operators taken directly from C++. These operators are defined for all numeric types. All they do is provide a shortcut to add or subtract one from a given variable. We use the ++ and -- notation to do this. For instance,

```
i++;
```

is equivalent to

```
i = i + 1;
```

Similarly, the -- operator does just the opposite. There is, however, a subtle yet important side effect with these operators. This effect is due to what is called the *prefix* and *postfix* placement of these operators. If the increment or decrement operator is placed before the variable name, the operation is done before evaluation of an expression. Conversely, if the operator is placed directly after the variable name, the operation is performed after the evaluation of an expression. Compare the following code snippets:

```
int x = 10;
int y = 7 + x++;
```

```
System.out.println(«y = « + y + « x = « + x);

int a = 10;
int b = 7 + ++a;
System.out.println("b = " + b + " a = " + a);
```

In both examples, the end values of x and a are both 11. However, you can see that y is 17 and b is 18. This is because the incrementing of x is suppressed until after the expression is evaluated, whereas the value of a is incremented before the expression is evaluated. Be sure to consider any potential side effects when using the increment and decrement operators within expressions.

# More Integer Operators

Besides the numeric operations mentioned above, there are a few more operators defined only on integers: the *bitwise* and *shift* operators. These operators can really make your code slick, but first you must understand what they mean. If you're a C++ programmer, you still might not be familiar with these operators, so I'll go over them here just in case.

## Bitwise Operators

Java defines four operators known as *bitwise operators* to manipulate integer values. These operators are named as such because they can manipulate the individual *bits* of a number. To fully understand these operators, let's look at the binary representation of the number 95 in `int` format:

```
00000000 00000000 00000000 01011111
```

The number 95 isn't very large, so it can be fully represented in the first 8 bits of the sequence. So to save trees, I'll ignore the first 24 bits and focus on the right-most 8 bits. The first bitwise operator you'll look at is the bitwise *and* (&) operator. To *and* two numbers together, compare the two numbers bit by bit. If a column contains only "one" bit, then the result for that column is one. Otherwise, the result is zero. The following illustrates how you can *and* the numbers 95 and 88:

```
    01011111     // 95
&   01011000     // 88
    01011000     // result is 88
```

Bitwise operations work much like simple addition; you start from the right and work your way left, comparing each column of bits. Your final result is the result of each column comparison of bits from the two numbers you are comparing.

Another important bitwise operation is the bitwise *or* (|) operation. As opposed to the bitwise *and* operation, if at least one of the two column bits is a 1, the result is 1. Let's *or* the same two numbers as above and compare the result:

```
    01011111    // 95
|   01011000    // 88
    01011111    // result is 95
```

Interesting. The logical *or* operation between the same two numbers gives 95 as the result. Bitwise operations do not always give one of the operands back as the result, however. Take the *exclusive or* (^) operator, for example. Also referred to as the *xor* operator, it sets the result bits to one *if and only if* the two column bits are *different;* one column bit must be a 0 bit and the other must be a 1 bit. Again, we'll use the same two numbers and compare the result:

```
    01011111    // 95
^   01011000    // 88
    00000111    // result is 7
```

As you might have noticed, only the last three column bits differ, giving a result of 7.

The fourth and final bitwise operator, called the *not* (~) operator, simply "inverts" the bits and stores them into the result. So the *not* of 95 becomes:

```
~ 00000000 00000000 00000000 01011111
= 11111111 11111111 11111111 10100000
```

or more specifically, -96, since integers are stored in two's complement form.

You might think all this is fine and dandy, but what good are the operators in the real world? I like them for storage of properties or attributes of an object. Let us define the following attributes for a simple monster object:

> **NOTE**
>
> Since it's not directly related to the subject, I won't go into the ins and outs of two's complement form here. But I will say that it allows us to denote both positive and negative numbers in binary format. Since we don't have the convenience of placing a negative sign before numbers stored in binary format, two's complement form does this for us. Usually, the left-most bit will denote the sign of the number; here, the left-most bit is a "I", giving us a negative number.

```java
public final static int ALIVE  = 1;
public final static int HUNGRY = 2;
public final static int ANGRY  = 4;
public final static int HAIRY  = 8;
```

Notice that I use a distinct power of two to represent each attribute. This way, the bit farthest to the right represents whether the monster is alive or dead, the second bit from the right represents whether the monster is hungry, and so on. There is no need to define alternative attributes for what is defined, such as DEAD or NOT_HUNGRY. A 1 bit will represent a truth for a specific attribute, a 0 bit represents otherwise. Let's create an int variable, named attributes, initialized to have no specific properties:

```
int attributes = 0;
```

To set attributes for the monster, say ALIVE and HUNGRY, use the bitwise *or* operator, as follows:

```
attributes = ALIVE | HAIRY;
```

To make the monster angry, just *or* the ANGRY property to the attributes variable:

```
attributes |= ANGRY;
```

To access individual properties, use the bitwise *and* operator. The following code snippet tests for the existence of each attribute:

```
if((attribute & ALIVE) > 0)
    System.out.println("I am alive!");
if((attribute & HUNGRY) > 0)
    System.out.println("I am hungry!");
if((attribute & ANGRY) > 0)
    System.out.println("I am angry!");
if((attribute & HAIRY) > 0)
    System.out.println("I am hairy!");
```

For this example, the output would be

```
I am alive!
I am angry!
I am hairy!
```

Setting attributes is fine, but what if you want to reset a particular attribute? To do so, use the bitwise *and* along with the *not* operator. The following shows how you can reset the HAIRY property from the attribute variable:

```
attribute &= ~HAIRY;    // same as attribute = attribute & ~HAIRY;
```

Of course, if you simply want to reset *all* of the attributes of the monster, simply set the attribute variable to zero, such as the following:

```
attribute = 0;              // no more monster!
```

As you can see, when used correctly, the use of bitwise operators can save you a lot of work. You do not need individual `boolean` variables for each attribute of the monster. Furthermore, you'll see in future chapters how this construct works nicely within a chain of class inheritance.

> **TIP**
>
> Okay, I lied a bit. The bitwise *or, and,* and *xor* operators not only work with integers, but they also work on `boolean` variables as well. For simplicity I decided not to introduce them formally, but they are still valid operations should the need arise.

## Shift Operators

*Shift operators* are similar to bitwise operators in that they both manipulate individual bits within an integer. The left (`<<`) and right (`>>`) shift operators shift the bit pattern to the left or right. Figure 2.6 shows the effects of shifting the number 95 to the left by one, two, three, and four bits.

The right shift operator works much the same way, except that it shifts the bits to the right. The right shift operator also extends the sign bit into the answer. There is also a third shift operator (`>>>`) that does not exist in C++. The `>>>` operator ignores the sign bit and just fills in the top bits with zero. Which one you use will depend on the task you wish to accomplish.

# Using the Dot Operator

Those of you who know C or C++ are certainly familiar with the *dot* operator (`.`). In Java the dot operator is used to separate package names from classes, as well as class names from their public method and field names. You've seen examples of this already. Take the following:

```
int[] array = { 4, 99, 32, 11, 0, 75, 6 };
java.util.Arrays.sort(array);
```

Here you have an array of integers that is sent to the `sort` method of the `Arrays` utility class. The dot notation separates the package name (`java.util`) from the class name (`Arrays`). Also, the dot operator separates the `Arrays` class name from the `sort`

| original value | shift value | binary representation | resulting value |
|---|---|---|---|
| 95 | 0 | 0000000001011111 | 95 |
| 95 | << 1 | 0000000010111110 | 190 |
| 95 | << 2 | 0000000101111100 | 380 |
| 95 | << 3 | 0000001011111000 | 760 |
| 95 | << 4 | 0000010111110000 | 1520 |

**Figure 2.6**

*Shifting a number to the left*

method name. Remember, you don't need the `java.util` part if you imported the package at the top of your program, but I include it here for demonstration.

# The instanceof Operator

The final operator you'll look at in this section is the `instanceof` operator. Since there are times when you might wish to know the run-time instance state of a particular variable, this operator comes in handy. The following example might give you some feel for how this operator works:

```
Creature creature = getNextCreature();
if(creature instanceof Dragon)
{
      creature.attack(human);
}
```

The above code makes some assumptions about the nature of the `Creature` hierarchy, but you get the picture. There will be times when this operator will guard your code and protect you from those vicious run-time errors, such as with the `clone` method, which we'll discuss in Chapter 4.

# Order of Precedence

It is important to be familiar with the order in which Java executes arithmetic statements within an expression. Since Java defines its own set of order precedence rules, you are guaranteed to be able to obtain the same, predictable results each time a program is run.

---

**C++ NOTE**

One feature that I've always disliked in C++ has been totally removed in Java. That feature is operator overloading. There's nothing worse than trying to figure out someone else's crazy C++ operator scheme. Therefore, you must stick with the native operators that go along with Java's basic types.

As a side note, you have probably seen the plus (+) operator used to concatenate `String` objects. This may lead some to believe that Java does allow overloaded operators to exist. Actually, the Java compiler allows this as a special operation performed through the `StringBuffer` **class.**

For all other object types, you'll need to provide methods to perform all of your operations, which is fine by me. I've found this rule forces one to write cleaner, better code.

The order of precedence in Java is similar to what you've learned in grade school. For example, multiplication and division come before addition and subtraction. Things in parentheses come even before all that.

Since game programming can be very math intensive, it is important that your code matches your intent. I use the following general guidelines when writing arithmetic code:

- Use parentheses to distinguish the intended order of precedence to the compiler. This will force you to think about what exactly you want your code to do.

- Break up tricky or complex statements into separate, simpler ones. There's nothing better than readable code, although your hacker friends might not be so impressed.

- If you absolutely need to combine several operators into one statement, use Table 2.3 on the next page to determine which operations will be performed first.

It never hurts to make your code a bit more verbose for the benefit of code clarity and readability. The Java compiler can usually optimize your code to be as efficient as possible. Remember, readable code is good code!

## Key Points to Remember about Operators

- Operators are the gears that make your programs run. The key is to know what operators are available and how each operator is used.

- Although use of bitwise operators isn't considered to be a very "organic" way to program, they are fast and succinct enough to be a game programmer's best friend.

- If you don't want to memorize the 14 levels of operator precedence, remember to use parentheses or break up large expressions into smaller ones.

## Conditional Statements

You know that if you are going to make your programs super flexible, you must allow them to be able to make decisions. These decisions can be based upon user input, file input, random variables, or whatever. The Java language uses the *if-then-else* structure of flow control, just like you've done in C++. Just in case you're not a C++ programmer, here's the general format of the if-then-else structure:

```
if(<condition>)
{
    // statements
```

## Table 2.3    The Operator Hierarchy Table

| Operator Type | Examples |
| --- | --- |
| Method operators, array subscripts | () . [] |
| Signing and casting variables, not, Increment/decrement operations, new | + – () ~ ! ++ — new |
| Multiplication operations | * / % |
| Addition operations | + – |
| Shift operations | << >> >>> |
| Comparison operations | < > <= >= instanceof |
| Comparison operations | == != |
| Bitwise *and* | & |
| Bitwise *xor* | ^ |
| Bitwise *or* | \| |
| Logical *and* | && |
| Logical *or* | \|\| |
| Conditional operator | ?: |
| Assignment operators | = += –= *= /= %= \|= ^= <<= >>= <<<= |

```
}
else if(<another condition>)
{
    // statements
}
else
{
    // statements
}
```

There can be as many else clauses to an if statement as you'd like, or none at all. It totally depends on the situation.

# The switch Statement

Multiple if-then-else statements are fine for most cases, but there are times when they are included *ad nauseam*. Take the following fictional setVideoModeA method, which might set the video mode based on the sent color depth:

```
public void setModeA(
    int mode  // the display mode, in bits-per-pixel
    )
{
    if(mode == 8)
    {       // do something
    }
    else if(mode == 16)
    {       // do something
    }
    else if(mode == 24)
    {       // do something
    }
    else if(mode == 32)
    {       // do something
    }
    else
    {       // do something
    }
}
```

For illustrative purposes, the above example only has five clauses. But you can very well imagine one that could have 20 or more! There is another way to write the if-then-else structure when you generally will have many alternative clauses. C++ programmers will know this as the switch statement. With it, you can rewrite the above method as follows:

```
public void setVideoModeB(
    int mode  // the display mode, in bits-per-pixel
    )
{
    switch(mode)
    {
        case(8):
        {       // do something
```

```
            break;
    }
case(16):
{       // do something
        break;
}
case(24):
{       // do something
        break;
}
case(32):
{       // do something
        break;
}
default:
{       // do something
        break;
}
    }
}
```

There doesn't appear to be much of an advantage to using the switch statement, other than the fact that you'll probably save a bit of typing, plus your code will look much cleaner. Also, when someone else comes along later to look at your code and notices the switch statement, he or she will know right away that you're looking to compare a variable against a specific case value.

Note the break statement at the end of each case. This is a very important thing to remember. The break statement ends a switch block; if you do not include the break statement, processing will continue to the next case statement, and so on. This will undoubtedly give erroneous results.

**C++ NOTE**

**Rules for evaluating Boolean expressions in Java differ slightly from that of C++. In C++ there is no true** boolean **type; therefore, these expressions will evaluate to a numeric expression. Typically, 0 evaluates to false, and anything else evaluates to true. In Java there is a true** boolean **type, and such expressions** must **evaluate to a** boolean **result. Therefore, the C++ expression**

```
while(1)
```

**must be changed to**

```
while(true)
```

**in Java. This is good since it forces the programmer to "think Boolean," which will alleviate errors in the future. This is why there are no conversions permitted from the** boolean **type to any of the integer types.**

You should also include a `default` statement as your final `case` statement. This acts like the final `else` statement in the first example; it allows action to be performed if the variable does not match any of the above cases.

Note that a `switch` is a very specific if-then-else case structure. It only permits one element of comparison, and you can only compare the variable against constant values. However, the `switch` statement is actually used quite frequently and can help you write clean code in less time.

## Going Loopy with Java

You probably know a *loop* as any block of code in which a statement or set of statements is performed repeatedly. You can use loops to manipulate arrays, read files, parse strings, or just about anything that needs to be done iteratively.

The Java language contains three ways to help us perform iteration: the `while`, `do while`, and `for` statements. If you've ever programmed in a procedural language, you know how these statements work. For instance, the `while` statement takes on the following syntax:

```
while(<condition>)
{
    // statements
}
```

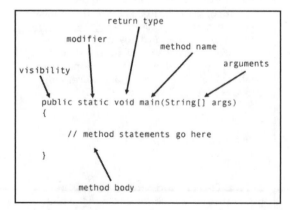

**Figure 2.7**

*The structure of a generic loop*

You also know that the for statement is just a more compact form of the while statement. The for statement looks like this:

```
for(<initial value>; <condition>; <action>)
{
    // statements
}
```

Okay, I'm itching for a code example. If you're not a looping connoisseur, pull the following program, *CoinTossTest,* from the CD-ROM, or simply type it in and run it. The *CoinTossTest* program simply simulates the flipping of a coin until the user decides to quit.

```
import java.io.*;

public class CoinTossTest
{
    // String representation of each side of a coin
    static final String[] faces = { "Heads", "Tails" };

    public static void main(String[] args) throws IOException
    {
        // create a reader to read user input
        BufferedReader reader = new BufferedReader(new
                                    InputStreamReader(System.in));

        // guarantees that we perform the loop at least once
        do
        {
            // generate a 0 or a 1
            int result = (int)Math.round(Math.random());

            // print the result
            System.out.print(faces[result] +
                            " it is! Toss again (Y/N)?  ");
        }
        // quit when user does not input "y" or "Y"
```

```
        while(reader.readLine().toUpperCase().equals("Y"));

    }      // main
}     // CoinTossTest
```

The do while statement works well in the above example, since we want to perform a coin toss once before asking the user if he or she would like to try again. Although this structure is not used quite that often, it does have its merit at times.

# Exiting Early with break, continue, and return

Besides failing the loop condition, there are other ways to break away from a loop. C++ programmers commonly use the break, continue, and return statements to end loops early. Java programmers use the same statements to break from loops as well. These statements offer more control over loops and can even give a slight performance boost as well.

For an example, suppose you are working on a space flight game in which you must destroy alien ships in order to save the universe. There are several types of alien ships; different ships are worth different point values when destroyed. At the end of each level, you want to give a bonus of 10 points for each ship worth at least 500 points that was destroyed. As you destroy alien ships, their point values are added to a list. At the end of a particular mission, you are left with the following set of point values:

```
500, 750, 100, 10, 10, 2000, 10, 10, 200, 500, 10, 500, 500, 100, 10, 500
```

You could easily traverse the list and give the 10-point bonus for each value worth at least 500, but what about missions where the player destroys 2,000 or more enemy ships? There would be a lot of time wasted rejecting all of those values that are less than 500.

A better way to calculate the bonus might be to keep the list of scores in a sorted list from high to low, like the following:

```
2000, 750, 500, 500, 500, 500, 500, 200, 100, 100, 10, 10, 10, 10, 10, 10
```

Now when you traverse the list, you can stop once you find a value lower than 500, since all values after that are guaranteed to also be less than 500. The following code snippet translates this into Java code:

```
// create some sorted data
int[] values = { 2000, 750, 500, 500, 500, 500, 500, 200, 100, 100, 10,
```

```
                    10, 10, 10, 10, 10 };

    int bonusEarned = 0;        // bonus counter

    for(int i = 0; i < values.length; i++)
    {
        // give a 10 point bonus for scores that are at least 500
        if(values[i] >= 500)
        {
            bonusEarned += 10;
        }
        // once we find a low score, break the loop
        else break;
    }
    // print out the final bonus
    System.out.println(bonusEarned);
```

If you run the above code, you'll find that 70 bonus points were earned using the data given. On the CD-ROM, you can find another example (named *BreakTest*) that is similar to the one above. It fills a very large array with random data and calculates the bonus based on the presorted array then the array after it is sorted. Note that the Arrays sort method naturally sorts integers from high to low; therefore, your loop must iterate the array from back to front.

# Handling Run-Time Exceptions

Everybody knows that Java is a great language, so it should be no surprise that it comes with a great error-handling system. It is the job of the compiler to catch any syntax errors you may have made while typing; but what about those vicious run-time errors that occur during the execution of your programs?

Run-time errors can rear their ugly heads at virtually any time. Attempting to access a method or operation of a null-referenced object, dividing by zero, and attempting to access an array index that's out-of-bounds are all types of run-time errors.

In Java we use the term *exception handling* when we refer to these run-time errors. This feature is also implemented in C++, but many people overlook it. Java, however, makes much greater use of exception handling. In general, when an exception occurs, it is "thrown" to the application, where the appropriate "catch" block will handle the error. Typically, a message will be printed to standard output stating the nature of the error and where it occurred. After that, processing can (usually) continue normally.

For now, we'll just focus on understanding how exceptions are used. Most exceptions that will arise in your programs are already defined within the Java API, but you will later see places where you can write your own.

There are two main ways you as a programmer can use exception handling. First, you can declare the throws clause in the method declaration. This is useful if you don't want to explicitly write code to handle the error yourself. You can also use the try and catch structure to handle the error explicitly. To ensure that the programmer handles errors that are commonly encountered, Java will generate compile-time errors to remind you that you must handle any potential run-time errors if you haven't already done so.

## Using try and catch Blocks

The first type of exception handling you'll look at is the use of try-catch blocks. Here, the application "tries" to execute a block of code. If there is a failure, an error is "thrown," and the error is "caught" by the nearest catch block, where it is handled. Before you look at an example of try-catch blocks, let's see what can happen if you don't attempt to handle an exception:

```
public static void main(String[] args)
{
    // declare an array of 5 integers
    int[] intArray = { 1, 2, 3, 4, 5 };

    // try to access the 100th member -- this should generate an exception
    System.out.println(intArray[100]);

    // we never get here, since the exception was never caught
    System.out.println("Exception handling is groovy!");
}
```

When you run the program, you should get something like the following as your output:

```
Exception in thread "main" java.lang.ArrayIndexOutOfBoundsException
        at ExceptionTest.main(ExceptionTest.java:12)
```

Since you do not explicitly handle the error, the attempt to access the array out of its bounds causes an exception to be thrown, and the program terminates. Therefore, the last `System.println` statement never gets executed. Let's rewrite the above code so that it makes use of the `try-catch` structure:

```
public static void main(String[] args)
{
    // declare an array of 5 integers
    int[] intArray = { 1, 2, 3, 4, 5 };

    // try to access the 100th member - this should generate an exception
    try
    {
        System.out.println(intArray[100]);
    }

    // catch any array indexing errors
    catch(ArrayIndexOutOfBoundsException e)
    {
        System.out.println("Attempt to access array out of bounds, " +
            "chowderhead!");
    }

    // now we'll get to this statement
    System.out.println("Exception handling is groovy!");
}   // main
```

Now when you run the program, you should get output similar to the following:

```
Attempt to access array out of bounds, chowderhead!
Exception handling is groovy!
```

Since you decided to handle the exception explicitly, the error was handled, and the program was allowed to continue to the end. Now, of course, this doesn't mean you have to use a `try-catch` block every time you want to access an array. Typically, when you do things such as arithmetic and array manipulation, the code is very controlled. If an array has five elements, you would be sure not to attempt to access anything beyond that. Therefore, you should consider using exception handling only in cases where your data can lose "control," such as when you process data from the user or need to add debugging statements to hunt down an elusive error.

Now let's look at a more concrete example of using exception handling in your code.

## Using the throws Clause

The second approach we'll take to exception handling is the use of the throws clause.  To use the throws clause, simply attach the throws keyword at the end of the method declaration, like the following:

```
public void myMethod() throws IOException
```

Rather than handling the error explicitly, the error will be propagated (sent back to) the calling method. The error will continue to propagate upward until there is a method that explicitly handles the error.

What's the advantage of using the throws clause over try-catch blocks? Oftentimes you'll find that you're writing the same error-handling routine over and over. Why not allow one base routine to cover an entire series of throws clauses? Figure 2.8 illustrates how this is done.

Think of it in terms of real life. Your boss asks you to perform a task. Halfway through, you come across a problem or an error you don't know how (or are too lazy) to deal with. You send the problem back up to your boss, figuring since he

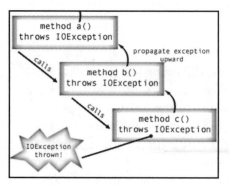

**Figure 2.8**

*Propagating an exception upward*

gave you the task, he better know how to fix any problems that come along. Your boss, in turn, sends the problem to his manager, and so on. This continues until someone knows how the heck to deal with the problem you came across. So yes, bureaucracy has found its way into modern computer languages as well. The following program, *PrimeFactorsTest,* illustrates multiple examples of exception handling, using both try-catch blocks and the throws clause. It reads numbers from the user and then prints out all of the prime factors associated with that number.

```java
import java.io.*;

public class PrimeFactorsTest
{
    // reads a String from the user and converts it to an int
    public static int readInt(String prompt) throws IOException
    {
        int result = 0;  // the value read from the user

        // create a new BufferedReader to read from standard input
        BufferedReader reader = new BufferedReader(new
                                    InputStreamReader(System.in));

        // print out the user prompt
        System.out.print(prompt);

        // attempt to read until valid input is entered
        while(true)
        {
            try
            {
                // parse the input into an integer
                result = Integer.parseInt(reader.readLine());
                return result;
            }
            catch(NumberFormatException e)
            {
                // ask the user to re-enter the data
                System.out.print("Bad number format, redo: ");
```

```
            }
        }
    }    // readInt


    // brute-force determination of whether a number is prime (has no
    // factors other than itself and one)
    public static boolean isPrime(int n)
    {
        for(int i = 2; i < n; i++)
        {
            // once we find a factor, we're done
            if(n%i == 0)
            {
                return false;
            }
        }
        // no factors!
        return true;
    }


    // brute-force method to find all of the prime factors of a number
    // not only must a number be a factor or n, but it also must be prime
    // as well
    public static void printPrimeFactors(int n, int start)
    {
        for(int i = start; i < n; i++)
        {
            if(n%i == 0 && isPrime(i))
            {
                System.out.print(i + " ");
            }
        }
    }


    public static void main(String[] args) throws IOException
    {
        // read in values until the user wants to quit
```

```
        int n = readInt("Enter a number, or -1 to quit: ");

        while(n > 0)
        {
            System.out.print(n + " : ");
            printPrimeFactors(n, 2);
            System.out.println();
            n = readInt("Enter a number, or -1 to quit: ");
        }
    }   // main

}    // PrimeFactorsTest
```

The above program illustrates exception handling in two ways. First, the BufferedReader readLine (used in the readInt method) method requires potential errors to be reported. In other words, the error must be propagated upward (via the throws clause in the method declaration) or be explicitly handled with a pair of try-catch statements. Since there is little I can do in the case of an IOException being thrown by the readLine method, I chose to let the error propagate upward. Since main calls the readInt method, which throws IOException, it therefore must throw IOException itself since it does not handle the exception explicitly. Try coding in the above program without the use of the throws clause—the compiler will catch it and warn you to include the missing code.

The second instance of exception handling in the *PrimeFactorsTest* program occurs within the readInt method. The Integer parseInt method attempts to parse the contents of a String into a numerical value. If the String contains any nonnumerical digits (except for a leading minus sign), a NumberFormatException is generated. The try-catch block is contained within an infinite while loop; therefore, all you need to do is ask the user to reenter the data until valid data is entered. Once valid data is entered, simply return the valid integer value.

There are lots of Exception classes available in the Java API. It often takes a little bit of analysis to determine if it is appropriate to add error handling and what the error-handling routine should do. Experiment with exception handling in your code until you know exactly when to use it. You can also look up Exception classes in the Java 2 API documentation if you get stuck.

## Key Points to Remember about Flow Control Statements

- All Java code is enclosed in some type of block. Flow control statements, such as conditional and loop statements, define the behavior of your programs.
- Exception handling helps you deal with those inevitable run-time errors. Both the `throws` statement as well as the `try-catch` block will help you hunt down and report these errors.
- Only YOU can prevent forest fires!

# Conclusion

I hope by now you have a good feel for many of the basic structures that make up a Java program. Although this chapter covers a lot of material, C++ programmers should be able to immediately catch on to the similarities and the differences between the two languages. Other programmers should also be familiar with the concepts presented in this chapter, leaving syntax as the only potential roadblock.

Try the following exercises. They should clear up any confusion you might have about the material covered in this chapter. In Chapter 3, we'll delve further into the Java language with object-oriented class design and use.

# Exercises

**2.1** What is the purpose of the Java import statement?

**2.2** Which of the following classes can be defined in a file called *Gunship.java?*
   a) public class Gunship
   b) public class Starship
   c) class Gunship
   d) class Spaghetti
   e) public class Battleship extends Gunship

**2.3** Which of the following is the proper way to declare the main method in Java? (Hint: The answer is *e*.)
   a) public static void main(String[] args)
   b) public static void main(String args[])

c)  public static void main(String args[])

d)  public static void main(String[] args)

e)  All of the above.

**2.4**  Suggest an appropriate primitive data type for the following variable descriptions:

a)   The value of *pi*

b)  The gross national product of Russia, in rubles

c)  The user's name

d)  The high score of a pinball game

e)  The number of hit movies starring Burt Reynolds

f)  An array containing 40,000 numeric values guaranteed to be between zero and 127

**2.5**  Based on your experiences with C++, describe why it might be good that Java does not permit conversions from the boolean type to any of the integer types.

**2.6**  (More difficult) Write a program that creates a "ragged" array containing all of the values found in the first five rows of Pascal's Triangle, then prints it to the screen. You can hard-code the values, but for bonus points try deriving the values algorithmically. Output should look similar to the following, but you don't necessarily need to center the text:

```
      1
     1 1
    1 2 1
   1 3 3 1
  1 4 6 4 1
```

(A solution to this problem can be found on the CD-ROM.)

**2.7**  Explain why comparing two String objects differs from comparing two variables of a primitive type. Write a small test program that compares two String objects and prints out the result.

**2.8**  If you are familiar with graphics packages such as DirectX, try this one: Write a program that builds up a 32-bit color using bit shifting. Color will be represented in ARGB order, that is, eight bits (values 0–255) for each of alpha, red, green, and blue. Output the result of the color value in hexadecimal by using the Integer.toHexString method.

**2.9** The following program creates a Random object with a seed of 21. It then saves the generator's next integer value from the range [0, 1,000,000) into n.

```
import java.io.*;
import java.util.*;

public class RandomExercise
{
    public static void main(String[] args)
    {
        Random r = new Random(21);
        int n = r.nextInt(1000000);
        System.out.println("number to generate is " + n);

        // your code goes here
    }
}
```

Complete the above program so that it counts the number of times it takes to generate the value of n again using the same random generator and sending the same parameter to nextInt. Print the result to the screen. (Hint: It will *always* take 122,963 times to find the same number again. Why?)

You can try the same program again, but *without* sending a parameter to the nextInt method (which will generate *any* number within the range of int). However, it takes a few billion tries to generate the same number again. Talk about uniform distribution!

**2.10** Declare a 2-D array of Point (don't forget to import java.awt.Point) objects, such as the following:

```
Point[][] points = new Point[10][10];
```

Now write a loop to fill each Point indexed by (*i*, *j*) with the values of *i* and *j*. You will need two loops, one for the rows and one for the columns. The code to actually create each Point object should look something like the following:

```
points[i][j] = new Point(i, j);
```

**2.11** Discuss some of the ways you can break out of an infinite loop, such as the following:

```
while(true)
{
    // program code here
}
```

What are some of the inherent dangers of this structure? Can you defend why this structure does not always have to be dangerous?

**2.12** One topic we didn't discuss in this chapter is that of *recursion*. Recursive algorithms solve a more complex problem by breaking it down into easier problems. A recursive method works by calling itself multiple times until reaching a *base case*. After the base case is found, the problem propagates back upward to each calling method. We won't get into the "magic" of how recursion works here, but you can at least look at a simple example.

The *factorial* of any given number, *n* (written as *n!*), is defined as the following:

```
n! = n * (n-1) * (n-2) * … * 1
```

Therefore, 5! = 5 * 4 * 3 * 2 * 1 = 120. You can write a method that calculates this value recursively, such as the following:

```
public int factorial(int n)
{
    if(n == 0 || n == 1)
    {    return n;
    }

    return n * factorial(n-1);
}
```

Note how this method repeatedly calls itself until it finds the base case, where n is either zero or one. Each active call to factorial can then send its answer to the corresponding instance of factorial that called it. Eventually, the process will work its way back up to the initial call and report the correct value.

Try writing a program that uses the above method and see if you can figure out how it works. Printing out values at each call to factorial might make things clearer. Then try writing the same procedure in a nonrecursive (iterative) fashion. For bonus points, explain under what circumstances the above code will fail and what you would do to fix it.

**2.13** Suppose you are to write a calculator program that calculates common arithmetic expressions. The following is a sample run of the program, where the user wants to divide two numbers:

```
Enter the numerator:    67
Enter the denominator: 13

67/13 = 5.1538463
```

Explain what conditions would cause an exception to be thrown, assuming the user will only enter valid numerical data. What might be a better method of safeguarding against arithmetic exceptions than using a try-catch block?

**2.14** Describe how shifting an integer left and right is related to division and multiplication operations on the same number. Assuming a shift operation is faster than multiplication and division, describe some situations where the shift operator might come in handy.

# CHAPTER 3

# A Language with Class! Object-Oriented Programming in Java

In Chapter 2, we looked at many of the individual components that make up a Java program, such as primitive data types, looping, and exception handling. In this chapter, we'll examine the object-oriented components of the Java language.

If you're an object-oriented C++ programmer, you know that object-oriented programming not only involves grouping data into structures but also defining the operations available to that structure. *Abstraction, information hiding, polymorphism,* and *encapsulation* are all words commonly associated with object-oriented programming.

As I mentioned before, object-oriented programming involves grouping together related entities into a single component. You might refer to these entities as *classes.* For you object-oriented newbies, instances of classes that are tangible or selectable are known as *objects.* The goal of the object-oriented programmer is to encapsulate related information into separate objects and create ways for these objects to interact with one another.

In the following sections, you will learn how to design and construct classes in Java—if you have no object-oriented experience. If you're already a C++ programmer, you will learn some more of the differences and similarities between the two languages. Let's begin with the design of a Java class.

# Designing a Java Class

A *class* is an entity that contains data as well as a set of operations to manipulate that data. This is what makes classes different than the primitive data types (`int`, `float`, `boolean`, etc.). We refer to variables of a given class as an *instance* of that class. After class instances are created, they can be manipulated by using their defined operators, called *methods.* A snapshot of an object at any single moment in time is known as the *state* of an object.

With these terms in mind, let's dig right in and design a simple class. Since we haven't covered how graphics are used in Java yet, let's focus on a game object class that can be expressed textually. Card games serve as an excellent example of text-based games. Let's start by creating a class to represent a single playing card. Before you lay down any code, let's take a quick look at the components that make up a card. Figure 3.1 shows the components that make up a physical playing card.

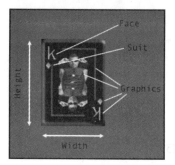

**Figure 3.1**

*Dissecting the components
of a playing card*

Since we're focusing on a text-based application, you can ignore certain physical attributes of a card: the width, height, and graphics components of the card in Figure 3.1 can all be discarded. To textually represent a playing card, all you need is its face and suit values.

You can make even further abstractions in this playing card analysis. In a standard deck of 52 playing cards, each card is distinct; that is, no two cards have the same suit and face combination. Therefore, you can assign a single index value to each card and then define operations that extract the face and suit value of individual cards. This excuses you from having to save the suit and face variables separately. And believe me, in an application that uses several hundred objects from the same class, you can save a nice chunk of memory by planning ahead.

There are several ways to extract the suit and face value from a single index, modulo division being one way. To do this, first create two arrays of String values that will textually represent all possible cards, like the following:

```
public static final String[] FACES = { "2", "3", "4", "5", "6", "7", "8",
                                        "9", "10", "J", "Q", "K", "A" };
public static final String[] SUITS = { "Hearts", "Spades",
                                        "Clubs", "Diamonds" };
```

You can now generate indexes to these arrays using modulo division. For example, to retrieve the index to the suit of a card, simply take the remainder of the card's value divided by the length of the suits array:

```
int index = cardValue % 4;
```

The same applies to the array of faces. To retrieve the actual name of the card's suit, just access the suits array with the value of your index:

```
System.out.println(SUITS[index]);
```

Okay, now that you've designed the base features of your Card class, let's code it out. If you want to try this in your editor, just copy the following code or pull the file named Card.java from the CD-ROM.

```java
public class Card
{
    // array representing all possible face values
    public static final String[] FACES = { "2", "3", "4", "5", "6",
                          "7", "8", "9", "10", "J", "Q", "K", "A" };

    // array representing all possible suit values
    public static final String[] SUITS = { "Hearts", "Spades",
                                        "Clubs",  "Diamonds" };

    // the maximum number of cards that can be indexed
    public static final int MAX_CARDS = FACES.length * SUITS.length;

    // the value assigned to this Card
    protected int value;

    // creates a default Card with a value of 0
    public Card()
    {
        value = 0;
    }

    // creates a Card indexed by n.  invalid indexes will cause the
    // program to terminate
    public Card(int n)
    {
        // rather than allowing errors to appear later, just terminate
        // the program with an error message if an invalid index is
        // specified
        if(n < 0 || n >= MAX_CARDS)
        {
            System.out.println("Error: Invalid Card Index (" +
                            n + "). Program terminating.");
            System.exit(0);
        }

        else
```

```
            {
                value = n;
            }
        }


        // returns the String representation of this Card's face value
        public String getFace()
        {
            return FACES[value%FACES.length];
        }


        // returns the String representation of this Card's suit value
        public String getSuit()
        {
            return SUITS[value%SUITS.length];
        }


        // returns the String representation of this Card
        public String toString()
        {
            return getFace() + " of " + getSuit();
        }
    }   // Card
```

Although the preceding Card class is rather basic in its functionality, it still covers a wide range of features Java has to offer. In Chapter 2, we discussed how to create the primitive data types found in the above code example. Variables that belong to class instances are known as class *members*. Now we'll continue our investigation of the Java language with the operators we can define on our data.

# A Method to the Madness

A *method* in Java is similar to a function in most procedural languages. A perfect method is designed to perform *a single specific task*. Java methods consist of several parts, including the following:

- Its visibility (public, private, or protected)
- Any modifiers it may have (such as static or final)
- Its return type (one of the eight primitive types, an object, or void)
- The name of the method (usually an action verb)

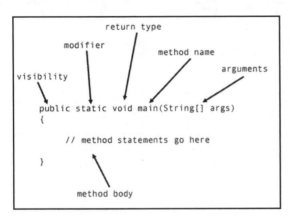

**Figure 3.2**

*Breaking down the main method into its component parts*

- An argument list (zero or more parameters passed to the method)
- A method body (zero or more statements surrounded by curly braces)

By now, you're surely familiar with the main method as it applies to Java. In fact, you can dissect the main method into the component parts as shown in Figure 3.2.

If you are familiar with other programming languages, you have undoubtedly used functions (or procedures) to implement your code. In Java, methods are nothing more than functions defined within a class. No global functions may exist outside a class in Java; all functions are defined as methods. The following few paragraphs detail some of the finer points of method design.

- Like C++, the accessibility of methods, as well as class member variables, to objects outside the class can be defined in three different ways: public, private, or protected. Entities declared as public are accessible from anyone outside the class. Otherwise, it is not directly accessible from outside the class. If you do not explicitly declare the accessibility of an entity, the default accessibility of private will be assumed. The distinction between private and protected class members will be discussed in the section on inheritance later in this chapter.

- Since data hiding is one of the cornerstones of object-oriented programming, data members are usually declared as private or protected. For methods that you wish to provide to objects outside the class, a public declaration will do. Methods that are meant to be accessed only within the class should be declared as either private or protected. It is generally acceptable to declare constant class data as public since that data cannot be modified.

- There are several *modifiers* you can impose upon your methods as well. Modifiers such as `static` and `final` both determine how a method will behave, as well as give it possible side effects. We will discuss these in detail in a later section.

- The *return type* of a method refers to the value it returns to its caller. A method's return type can be any of the primitive types or a Java object. If a given method need not return a value, the method is a `void` method.

> **C++**
>
> It's worth noting that Java objects serve as references; that is, there are no explicit pointer types in Java. Therefore, there's no distinction between the C++ dot operator ( . ) and the pointer access (->) operator. All Java objects reference data through the dot operator. You must also treat object method parameters the same way you would a C++ pointer. If an object is directly changed while inside a called method, the changes will be reflected throughout the entire program. Remember this only applies to mutable objects and not to Java primitive types or immutable objects such as `String` **objects.**

- The name of a particular method is of your choosing, just as long as it's not a Java reserved word. Method names are usually verbs and should describe what the method does. Be descriptive in your naming but not overly verbose. For example, `quickSort` is a fine name for a method, but `performSortUsingQuickSortAlgorithm` might be a bit too wordy.

- The argument list for a method is just the parameters you wish to send to the method. Arguments can be primitive types or Java objects. Not every method needs an argument list. In cases where a method takes zero parameters, all you need to supply is an empty pair of parenthesis.

# More on Methods

While we're at it, let's talk a bit about the types of methods you can write. I lump methods into four general categories: *constructor methods, access methods, class methods,* and what I affectionately call *other methods.*

## Constructor Methods

The *constructor method,* or just *constructor,* is a method called when memory for a particular object is allocated. The constructor method of a class allows the object to initialize its data members as needed. A class can have multiple constructors, each one with a different argument list. Generally, we call a constructor with no arguments the *default constructor.* The default constructor for your `Card` class just sets the `value` field to 0. It's included merely for illustration, but in a real application it probably wouldn't be needed. Only include default constructors when you want to provide a default way for objects to be created.

In addition to the default constructor, it is also helpful to define constructor methods that take one or more arguments. These arguments establish the initial state of the object. Your Card class contains one such constructor that takes a single parameter. This parameter represents the value of the Card with respect to the entire deck.

In addition, we call a constructor that takes an object of the same type as its argument the *copy constructor*. You will provide this type of method for times when you want to make a copy of an object rather than merely referencing multiple objects to the same memory location. For instance, the copy constructor for the Card class might look like the following:

> **NOTE**
>
> Remember, using the copy constructor is not the same as using the assignment operator. Therefore, the following statements are not equivalent:
>
> ```
> Card c2 = new Card(c1);
> Card c2 = c1;
> ```
>
> Simply assigning one Card object equivalent to another will cause both objects to reference the same physical object. So when one object's state changes, the other's changes as well. By invoking the copy constructor, you are creating an independent copy of the original Card object with the same initial state. You can now modify each object independently of one another.
>
> A common alternative in Java is to implement the clone method rather than defining a copy constructor. Refer to Chapter 4 for more on how to write a clone method for your classes.

```
public Card(Card other)
{
    value = other.value;
}
```

Since object creation requires memory to be allocated, simply sandwich the new keyword between the assignment operator and the call to the constructor, much like the following:

```
Card card1 = new Card();      // a plain vanilla Card object
Card card2 = new Card(39);    // the 2 of Diamonds!
```

## Access Methods

*Access methods* do nothing other than provide a safe way for private or protected class data to be accessed from outside the class. Access methods are commonly referred

> **C++**
>
> As you have seen, the `new` keyword allocates memory for the
> newly created object. C++ users undoubtedly have also used the
> `delete` keyword to clean up and destroy an allocated object. Java
> does not support an equivalent to the `delete` keyword. Rather, the
> Java Virtual Machine does what is known as *garbage collection*
> when the system has exhausted all available memory. Garbage
> collection frees up memory to objects that are no longer refer-
> enced or active. Therefore, it is not necessary for the Java pro-
> grammer to manually reclaim unused memory.

to as "get and set" methods, since they are usually prefixed as such. Using these
methods to access encapsulated data prevents you from modifying data accidentally.
Your `Card` class contains two access methods: one to get the card's suit value and one
to get the card's face value. If you want to allow `Card` object to be mutable, you can
define a method to set it to a new value, like the following:

```
public void setValue(int newValue)
{
     value = newValue;
}
```

You'll see plenty more access methods in subsequent chapters. Now let's switch
gears a bit and look at class methods.

# Class Methods

*Static,* or *class,* methods are methods that belong to the class as a whole and not to
any particular instance of the class. Class methods usually come in the form of
utilities or methods that act solely upon static class fields. You've seen a good example of class methods in Chapter 2: the `Integer` `parseInt` method. Recall that the
`parseInt` method parses a `String` object to an `int` value. The prototype for the
`parseInt` method is as follows:

```
public static int parseInt(String s) throws NumberFormatException
```

C++ programmers will be familiar with the use of the static keyword for declaring
class methods. Calls to the `parseInt` method are made by prefacing the method
name by the name of the class, like the following:

```
int number = Integer.parseInt("-328");
```

The functionality of the parseInt method is tied to the Integer class; however, it is not tied to any particular instance of the Integer class. It is merely a useful utility. The System and Math classes are just two other classes that contain useful static utility methods. You'll have a chance to learn about these classes in the following chapter.

## "Other" Methods

When I speak of "other" methods, I'm referring to methods that do not fall under any other category. Other methods perform operations on objects other than simply setting or retrieving values.

To illustrate other methods, I have designed a Deck class to go along with your lonely Card class. A Deck consists of a stack of Card objects and a List to store drawn cards. Cards can be drawn from the top of the deck's stack; a reference to each drawn card is added to the drawn list. The Deck class also provides a shuffle method to redistribute its contents. Try it out for yourself:

```
import java.util.*;

// represents a deck of cards of any size
public class Deck
{
    // a stack of Card objects
    protected Stack cards;

    // a collection of all drawn cards
    protected List drawnCards;

    // allows random retrieval of cards in the above List
    protected Random random;

    // creates a Deck of the given size
    public Deck(int size)
    {
        // push the sent number of Cards onto the stack
        cards = new Stack();
        for(int i = 0; i < size; i++)
        {
            cards.push(new Card(i));
```

```
        }

        // create a pool for drawn cards and our number generator
        drawnCards = new ArrayList();
        random = new Random();

        // shuffle the deck
        shuffle();
    }

// returns the number of cards associated with this Deck
public int getSize()
{
        return cards.size() + drawnCards.size();
}

// draws the top card from the deck
public Card draw()
{
        // if the stack is empty, fill it using the drawn pile
        if(cards.isEmpty())
        {
            shuffle();
        }

        // pop the top Card, add it to the pile, then return it
        Object card = cards.pop();
        drawnCards.add(card);
        return (Card)card;
}

// randomly shuffles the cards in this Deck
public void shuffle()
{
        // clear the stack
        while(!cards.isEmpty())
        {
            drawnCards.add(cards.pop());
```

```
        }

        // randomly draw cards from the drawn pile back onto the stack
        Object card = null;
        while(!drawnCards.isEmpty())
        {
            card = drawnCards.remove(
                        Math.abs(random.nextInt())%drawnCards.size());
            cards.push(card);
        }
    }
}    // Deck
```

As you can see, the Deck class contains Card objects as its private data. It also provides the operations to manipulate that data. If you are unfamiliar with the Stack, List, and Random classes, feel free to momentarily jump ahead to Chapter 4. Otherwise, let's finish this playing card example with a main class to tie it all together.

The following code listing is for a real quick and dirty test program for the Deck and Card classes. It simply creates a Deck object containing 52 cards and then prints them each to the console, one by one. To advance to the next card in the deck, just press the Enter key.

```
import java.io.*;

// prints the String representation of a deck of cards to standard output
public class CardTest
{
    public static void main(String[] args) throws IOException
    {
        // create a deck of 52 cards
        Deck deck = new Deck(52);

        // create a reader for entered keystrokes
        BufferedReader reader = new BufferedReader(new
                                    InputStreamReader(System.in));

        // display each card in the deck, allowing the user to pause
        // between each one
        for(int i = 0; i < 52; i++)
        {
            System.out.print("You drew the " + deck.draw());
```

```
                reader.readLine();
            }


        }
    }   // CardTest
```

> **NOTE**
>
> When working with multiple Java source files related to a single application, I prefer to use a batch or script file containing the necessary shell commands to compile and run the application. It saves me from typing the same things over and over. For instance, in Windows I would create a batch file named **CardTest.bat** that contains all of the commands needed to compile and run the *CardTest* program:
>
> ```
> javac Card.java Deck.java CardTest.java
> java CardTest
> ```
>
> Although my batch file only contains two lines, it saves me a lot of tedious typing, especially when I want to try a bunch of quick code changes. Just remember to save the changes to any dirty source files, or else you'll be scratching your head when your program doesn't seem to be working correctly. For Windows programmers, I have included Windows batch (.bat) files that contain the commands to compile and run each of the examples for you on the **CD-ROM**.

If you compile and run the *CardTest* program, you should be able to traverse through the entire deck of shuffled cards. All you need is a bit more processing in your application class and you've got a fully functional text-based game!

# Inheritance

Possibly my favorite aspect of object-oriented programming is that of *inheritance*. C++ programmers know inheritance as a very powerful construct that allows us to extend the functionality of our code. The basis of inheritance is simple: you can define simple, broad classes, called *base classes,* and then derive the functionality of these classes into specific, more complex classes, known as *derived classes*. Derived classes have all rights and privileges of the parent class, plus any additional privileges that are added.

Hardcore game programmers who swear by the C programming language will often tell you that using inheritance in C++ slows game code down too much to be usable. Although decreased throughput can be detected in C++ programs that make use of inheritance, today's optimized compilers and fast processors make such overhead negligible. As long as you don't abuse it, you should find that its benefits, especially decreased development time, greatly outweigh its shortcomings. Also, since Java forces you to program in an object-oriented fashion, you might as well take advantage of its greater features.

Here's an easy example for those who are new to object-oriented programming. The following class contains the magnitude component of a simple Vector object. As you look at the code, think about ways in which its functionality can be further extended.

```java
// a quick 'n' dirty class to represent a Vector object
public class Vector extends Object
{
    // the value of this Vector object
    protected int x;

    // creates a default Vector with a value of 0
    public Vector()
    {
        this(0);
    }

    // creates a Vector object with the sent value
    public Vector(int n)
    {
        setX(n);
    }

    // get/set access methods
    public final int getX()
    {
        return x;
    }

    public final void setX(int n)
    {
        x = n;
```

```
        }

        // translates the Vector by the sent value
        public void translate(int dx)
        {
            x += dx;
        }

        // returns the String representation of this Vector
        public String toString()
        {
            return "Vector [x=" + x + "]";
        }
    }    // Vector
```

First of all, note the use of the extends keyword. The extends keyword tells the compiler which class you're extending upon. It is analogous to the scope operator found in C++. Note that Java only supports single inheritance; that is, any given class can only extend upon a single base class. However, as you'll soon see, the chain of inheritance can continue as far as you need it to.

The above Vector class extends the functionality of the Object class. Object is the root of the entire Java class hierarchy. If you don't explicitly extend a Java class from another base class, the compiler will automatically extend it from the Object class. Therefore, all classes are indeed Objects. You'll see how you can use this to your advantage starting in Chapter 4.

Let's extend the functionality of the Vector class by adding an additional y component. The result will be defined within the Vector2d class. Again, this class is rather simple as well, so if you have never dealt with inheritance before you should be able to pick it up here.

```
    // extends the Vector class by adding a y component
    public class Vector2d extends Vector
    {
        // the added y value of this Vector2d object
        protected int y;

        // creates a default Vector2d with a value of (0,0)
        public Vector2d()
        {
```

```java
            this(0, 0);
    }

    // creates a Vector2d object with the sent values
    public Vector2d(int m, int n)
    {
        setX(m);
        setY(n);
    }

    // get/set access methods for the y component
    public final int getY()
    {
        return y;
    }

    public final void setY(int n)
    {
        y = n;
    }

    // translates the Vector2d by the sent value
    public void translate(int dx, int dy)
    {
        x += dx;
        y += dy;
    }

    // returns the String representation of this Vector2d
    public String toString()
    {
        return "Vector2d [x=" + x + ",y=" + y + "]";
    }
}   // Vector2d
```

Pretty straightforward. The Vector2d class inherits the x field from the Vector class and adds the additional y field. It also adds additional *set* and *get* methods, as well as overrides methods that need additional code to work properly. This is why the toString method has been modified, but the getX and setX methods were not. The result is a class that is based on the `Vector` class but adds additional components to make it more useful.

The chain of inheritance can reach as far as you need; the `Vector3d` class can be built upon the `Vector2d` class, the `Vector4d` class can be built from the `Vector3d` class, and so on. The `Vector3d` class has been provided on the CD-ROM in case you need another example.

Let's wrap up this vector example with a test program. The following program, *VectorTest*, creates various `Vector`, `Vector2d`, and `Vector3d` objects and prints out their values to the console. Try copying the following test program, or try creating one of your own:

```java
public class VectorTest extends Object
{
    public static void main(String[] args)
    {
        // print out the values of some Vector, Vector2d, and
        // Vector3d objects
        System.out.println(new Vector());
        System.out.println(new Vector(5));
        System.out.println(new Vector2d());
        System.out.println(new Vector2d(4, 9));
        System.out.println(new Vector3d());
        System.out.println(new Vector3d(-12, 25, 2));
    }
}   // VectorTest
```

Incidentally, when a class instance is sent to the `PrintStream` `println` method, its `toString` method is automatically invoked to attain a textual `String` representation of that object. That's why it's often handy to explicitly define the `toString` method for classes you anticipate needing a textual state representation of its instances.

You could add many more methods to the vector classes, such as rotation operations and dot and cross product calculations, but I've kept it simple here just to illustrate how inheritance is implemented in Java. The value of inheritance helps keep your projects manageable by reducing the amount of code needed to accomplish a given task. With a little planning, you can create powerful, reusable components for use in your games. You'll see inheritance used much more extensively in later chapters, especially when we talk about the Abstract Window Toolkit and Java 2-D.

> **NOTE**
>
> Remember to note the difference between the *is-a* and the *has-a* relationship among classes. It may initially look like inheritance is necessary when in fact the class you are designing is actually just a container for other classes. For instance, the `Deck` class we looked at previously does not extend the `Card` class; it merely contains `Card` objects. On the other hand, the `Vector2d` class must extend the `Vector` class because a vector *is* a vector with additional fields and operations. Don't let this distinction cloud your mind when designing classes for your programs.

# Abstract Classes

As you have already seen, the use of inheritance allows you to create a hierarchy of objects to meet the needs of an evolving, flexible application. In the above example, you extended a simple base class into a more complex one. Rather than redefining fields such as the x component of a vector, simply define them once and allow child classes to inherit them.

In the case of the `Vector` class, both it and its child classes can be useful. Your applications can define `Vector`, `Vector2d`, and `Vector3d` objects and have them do whatever you want. However, there are situations where you will wish to leave a parent class incomplete and allow child classes to fill in the cracks. This is where you can make use of *abstract classes*.

For example, suppose your project supervisor tells you that she needs a single class that defines a two-dimensional rectangle. However, due to varying requirements throughout the application, the rectangle class must be able to be expressed in terms of three different data types: `int`, `float`, and `double`.

Impossible, you might think. Maybe not. By creating an abstract class, you can create a generic, incomplete class skeleton and allow child classes to define the specifics. In fact, the Java 2 API does just that. The `Rectangle2D` class (found in the `java.awt.geom` package) is an incomplete, abstract class that only outlines the operations that can be performed by any 2-D rectangle. This class is then subclassed into the `Rectangle`, `Rectangle2D.Double`, and `Rectangle2D.Float` classes. These three classes concretely define a rectangle in terms of `int`, `double`, and `float` values, respectively. Figure 3.3 graphically shows how the `Rectangle2D` hierarchy is established.

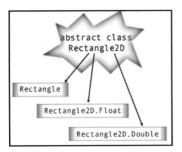

**Figure 3.3**

*Defining three rectangle classes from a single abstract base class*

In Java, we define an abstract class by placing the abstract keyword before the class name. C++ programmers define abstract classes by using pure virtual methods. The Rectangle2D class also defines several incomplete, abstract methods, such as createIntersection and createUnion, for its subclasses to define. So what's the advantage of defining an abstract base class? Since Rectangle, Rectangle2D.Double, and Rectangle2D.Float are child classes of Rectangle2D, instances of these classes are in fact Rectangle2D objects themselves. This allows you to declare variables of type Rectangle2D and redefine them any way you wish. For example, you can create a single Rectangle2D object and redefine it as follows:

```
Rectangle2D r;
r = new Rectangle2D.Double(4.0, 33.2);
r = new Rectangle(4, 3);
r = new Rectangle2D.Float(99.9f, 99.9f);
```

Here, flexibility is the key. A single declaration allows you to define several different types later to fit your needs. We'll look deeper into the various uses of this construct when we talk about the Java 2-D API.

Abstract classes are also commonly known as *class factories,* since we can quickly "crank out" child classes that fill in incomplete parent class methods. The following illustrates another example of how you can utilize abstract classes to easily calculate the area and perimeter of general geometric shapes:

```
abstract class AbstractShape
{
     public abstract double area();
     public abstract double perimeter();

     static double totalArea(final AbstractShape[] shapes)
     {
```

```java
                double total = 0.0;

                for(int i = 0; i < shapes.length; i++)
                {
                    total += shapes[i].area();
                }
                return total;
        }

        static double totalPerimeter(final AbstractShape[] shapes)
        {
                double total = 0.0;

                for(int i = 0; i < shapes.length; i++)
                {
                    total += shapes[i].perimeter();
                }
                return total;
        }
}    // class AbstractShape

class Circle extends AbstractShape
{
        private double radius;

        public Circle(double r)
        {
            radius = r;
        }
        public double area()
        {
            return Math.PI * radius * radius;
        }
        public double perimeter()
        {
            return (2.0 * Math.PI * radius);
        }
}
```

```
    }

class Rectangle extends AbstractShape
{
     private double width;
     private double height;

     public Rectangle(double w, double h)
     {
          width  = w;
          height = h;
     }
     public double area()
     {
          return (width * height);
     }
     public double perimeter()
     {
          return (2.0 * (width + height));
     }
}

public class ShapeTest
{
     public static void main(String[] args)
     {
          AbstractShape[] myShapes =
          {
               new Rectangle(10.0, 20.0),
               new Circle(5.5),
               new Rectangle(0.1, 0.2)
          };
          System.out.println(AbstractShape.totalArea(myShapes));
          System.out.println(AbstractShape.totalPerimeter(myShapes));
     }
}
```

As you can see, the AbstractShape class is declared as abstract. Any methods that cannot yet concretely be defined are also declared as abstract. Obviously, these methods will have no method body. Using the abstract keyword tells the compiler that it's all right to have an incomplete class and that derived classes will need to fully define these methods. With this in mind, here are a few other features associated with abstract classes that are important for you to know:

- Abstract classes cannot directly be instantiated, since their definitions are not complete. You can, however, create arrays of abstract objects, as long as each member is an instance of one of its derived classes (such as in the above example).

- A class that contains any number of abstract methods must itself be declared as abstract. Abstract classes can contain methods with defined bodies. However, only the incomplete methods should be prefaced with the abstract keyword.

- Classes derived from an abstract class must define method bodies for each of its parent's abstract methods in order to be instantiated. Otherwise, the class must also be declared abstract, where only its children that define these abstract methods can be instantiated.

Although abstract classes are generally not overly used, they can come in handy when groups of related objects all have the same "abstract" parent. As a general rule of thumb, when an object's parent is simply an idea or an intangible object, then the use of abstract classes might be a good idea. If any of this still seems confusing to you, try running the *ShapeTest* program. You will be using abstract classes more in the future.

# Class Modifiers

One thing that confused me while learning the Java language were some of those funny little keywords I would see prefixing member, class, and method names. We've already looked at modifiers such as abstract, public, private, and protected. Now let's take a look at two more keywords that have powerful influences over your code, the final and static keywords.

The static keyword is used in Java much as it is in C++. The static keyword allows us to define what are known as *class members* and *class methods*. Class members and methods are those that belong to the class as a whole, but not to any one particular class instance. For example, say you want to write a class where each instantiated member will receive a globally unique integer identifier. You can create a static class member field, called uniqueId, that will belong to the class as a whole; individual identifiers will belong to each instance of the class. You can also create a static class method, getNextUniqueId, which will allow objects to access the current value of the static uniqueId field. The following program, *IdTest*, demonstrates how you can use static class members and methods:

```
class IdObject
{
    // the next globally unique identifier for a newly created IdObject
    private static int uniqueId = 0;

    // the unique identifier for a single IdObject
    private int id;

    // creates a new IdObject with the next unique integer identifier
    public IdObject()
    {
        // assign the next unique identifier to this object's id
        id = uniqueId++;
    }

    // returns this object's unique identifier
    public int getId()
    {
        return id;
    }

    // returns the next available unique identifier for IdObjects
    public static int getNextUniqueId()
    {
        return uniqueId;
    }
}

public class IdTest
{
    public static void main(String[] args)
    {
        // create 10 IdObjects, print their unique id's, then print the
```

```
            // next available IdObject id

            IdObject[] objects = new IdObject[10];
            for(int i = 0; i < 10; i++)
            {
                objects[i] = new IdObject();
                System.out.println("id = " + objects[i].getId());
            }

            // now call the static getNextUniqueId method from the
            // IdObject class to get the next available id
            System.out.println("Next id = " + IdObject.getNextUniqueId());
        }
    }   // IdTest
```

As you might expect, the output to the *IdTest* program is as follows:

```
    id = 0
    id = 1
    id = 2
    id = 3
    id = 4
    id = 5
    id = 6
    id = 7
    id = 8
    id = 9
    Next id = 10
```

The AbstractShape class that has already been defined also contains static methods for calculating the area and perimeter of an array of AbstractShape objects. Therefore, static methods can be used for general utilities, such as you've seen in the AbstractShape class, or they can serve as access methods for a class's static variables, such as in the above IdObject class. Note that the static keyword is not associated with class definitions, just class fields and methods.

The second class modifier we will look at is the final modifier. The final keyword behaves slightly differently among classes, methods, and fields. Like the C++ const keyword, the final keyword generally denotes that an entity cannot be modified or changed in any way. It is the *final* value the member will hold.

For classes, prefixing the class name with the `final` keyword tells the compiler that this class may not be extended by any other class. So, if you declare the fictional `Monster` class as

```
final class Monster
```

then you will not be permitted to extend the `Monster` class to any other class, be it the `Ogre` class, the `Ghost` class, or whatever. That's it. The definition of this `Monster` class would be as far as it goes.

Just about now you may be thinking, "I thought the whole point of object-oriented programming was to use inheritance." Although inheritance is a very useful tool, there are times when you will want to avoid it. Utility classes are one instance of where inheritance is often avoided. For example, you have already seen and used the Java `System` class. The `System` class includes access to standard input, output, and error streams, as well as general system utilities and an array copy utility. The designers of this class felt that its implementation should not be flexible or extendable; therefore, they declared it as `final`. When a class is defined as `final`, its designer is trying to tell you that the implementation of the class is complete and extending its functionality would cloud the true meaning and purpose for which the class was created.

For methods, the `final` keyword is treated similarly. In this case, the `final` keyword tells the compiler that no further subclass is able to redefine or alter this method. If you'll recall, the three `Vector` classes contain access methods to set and retrieve vector components. These methods were declared `final` because their implementation is complete and should never be overridden.

The third way the `final` keyword can be used is to modify variables and fields. When the `final` keyword is used to modify a variable, the compiler is told that once the variable is given an initial value, it can never be changed. This is useful when you want to define constant values that you don't want to accidentally be changed. In the preceding shapes example, the need may arise to define the unit circle as follows:

```
final Circle unitCircle = new Circle(1.0);
```

A unit circle *always* has a radius of one unit; therefore, by declaring the `unitCircle` variable as `final`, you will never accidentally change its value, which ultimately enhances the integrity of your code.

Not only can you create methods and variables that are `static` or `final`, but you can also create entities that are *both* `static` *and* `final`. Class constants found throughout the Java API are often defined this way, such as the value of *pi* (the ratio of the circumference of a circle to its diameter) in the `java.lang.Math` class.

Since Java does not contain the #define precompiler directive as found in C++, the use of static final variables is the best way to define constant values within an application. Note that even though it defies the object-oriented principle of data hiding, constant class data members are usually defined to be public. This is usually just as a convenience to the programmer.

> **C++ NOTE**
>
> Don't confuse the C++ const keyword with the Java final keyword. C++ has been criticized for allowing const to be used in too many different ways, resulting in unwanted side effects and ambiguous code. The developers of Java have adopted the final keyword to denote constant, or unchangeable, values and definitions. The const keyword does exist in Java, but it is currently reserved for future use and has no meaning at this time.

# Interfaces

If you were previously unacquainted with classes and inheritance, that should no longer be the case. You have also learned how to use abstract classes as an incomplete base class from which concrete subclasses can be derived. Java also provides another programming construct—the ominous *interface*—that allows you to add flexibility to your applications. Even if you are an experienced C++ programmer, you may not be familiar with how interfaces are used. Simply put, a Java interface is an entity that contains incomplete methods but allows the programmer to "interface" an existing class with a separate, external class.

Interfaces are not classes and therefore cannot be instantiated. Furthermore, an interface contains no data members other than field constants. Like an abstract class, however, the methods contained within an interface are incomplete; it is up to the implementing class to provide definitions for these methods. All methods declared within an interface are public and abstract by default, so you do not need to specify these modifiers explicitly.

After an interface is created, you must create classes that implement it. In Java, use the implements keyword in the class declaration. It will then be that class's responsibility to define all methods contained within the implemented interfaces. As you'll see in later chapters, a class is permitted to implement more than one interface as well. The following demonstrates how to implement an interface:

```
public class MyClass implements MyInterface1, MyInterface2
```

Since the focus will mostly be on using predefined interfaces rather than writing your own, let's look at an example of a class that implements an existing Java interface. The Integer class is a good example. It implements the *Comparable* interface (found in the java.lang package). The *Comparable* interface allows classes to be grouped by what's called their *natural ordering*. This interface contains a single method, the compareTo method. Logical operators such as > and < are not applicable to objects; therefore, the compareTo method allows these comparisons to be made.

A bit of code should make this crystal clear. The following program, *SortTest,* sorts an array of Integer objects according to their natural ordering. The program then displays the sorted array to the console.

```java
import java.util.*;

public class SortTest extends Object
{
    public static void main(String[] args)
    {
        // create some Integer values
        Integer[] values = { new Integer(670), new Integer(90),
                             new Integer(-23), new Integer(0),
                             new Integer(2),   new Integer(659),
                             new Integer(1),   new Integer(-40) };

        // sort the values
        Arrays.sort(values);

        // print the sorted array to the console
        for(int i = 0; i < values.length; i++)
        {
            System.out.println(values[i]);
        }
    }
}    // SortTest
```

The Arrays sort method only accepts objects that implement the *Comparable* interface. The sort method invokes the compareTo method as defined by the array of objects passed to it. As you might expect, the above program will then print the sorted Integer values from low to high.

Interfaces are a great way to connect your classes with other external classes. Interfaces may at first resemble abstract classes, but they differ from abstract classes in three major ways. First, interfaces can only contain methods and constant fields. Therefore, an abstract class may be necessary if nonconstant class fields are required. Similarly, each method within an interface *must* be declared as abstract. Abstract classes must have at least one incomplete method; the others can all be defined within the class. In our shapes example, we defined `totalArea` and `totalPerimeter` methods within the `AbstractShape` class, something we could not do using an interface.

Interfaces do provide one major advantage over abstract classes. Recall that Java does not permit multiple inheritance. However, you are permitted to implement several interfaces under a single class. Therefore, you can code as though multiple inheritance does exist, to a point. For now, think of interfaces as a way to have your cake and eat it too.

# Creating Classes on-the-Fly

Now suppose you have an array of `String` objects that you wish to sort. Assume each member of the array is guaranteed to be in the format *<last name, first name>*, with a comma separating the last name from the first name. Additionally, you wish to sort the data in reverse alphabetical order by the first name. The `Arrays` class offers a second `sort` method that takes two parameters, an array of type `Object[]`, as well as a class that implements the *Comparator* interface.

In order to invoke this `sort` method, you could build a new class, called something like `ReverseAlphabeticalNameSort`, which implements the *Comparator* interface. Within this new class, you would need to define the *Comparator* `compare` method. You would then send an instance of this newly created class to the `Arrays` `sort` method, such as the following:

```
// assume strArray refers to an array of String objects
Arrays.sort(strArray, new ReverseAlphabeticalNameSort());
```

That gets the job done, but it is time consuming and complex. Not only do you have to define a new class to do this rather specific task, but you are also defining a class that you are most likely only going to use once and will never use again.

Fortunately, there is a better way. For times where you need to define a class to accomplish a specific task, you can use what is known as an *anonymous inner class*. To implement an anonymous inner class, all you need to do is specify the body of your class on the fly; that is, define it where it's used. To better understand this, check out the following example:

```
import java.util.*;

public class NameSortTest
{
```

```java
public static void main(String[] args)
{
    // create an array of Strings
    String[] strArray = {
     "Ward, Bill", "Osbourne, Ozzy", "Butlet, Geezer", "Iommi, Tony"
    };

    // print out the unsorted String array
    System.out.println("String array before sort:");
    for(int i = 0; i < strArray.length; i++)
    {
        System.out.println(i + ": " + strArray[i]);
    }

    Arrays.sort(strArray, new Comparator()
    {
        public int compare(Object a, Object b)
        {
            // cast a and b to String objects
            String s1 = (String)a;
            String s2 = (String)b;

            // since we're comparing by first name, parse the
            // first name from the strings
            s1 = s1.substring(s1.indexOf(",")+1);
            s2 = s2.substring(s2.indexOf(",")+1);

            // trim off any leading or trailing whitespace
            s1 = s1.trim();
            s2 = s2.trim();

            // let the String compareTo method compare the first
            // names
            return s2.compareTo(s1);
        }   // compare
    } );

    // print out the newly sorted String array
    System.out.println("\nString array after sort:");
```

```
            for(int i = 0; i < strArray.length; i++)
            {
                System.out.println(i + ": " + strArray[i]);
            }
    }     // main
}    // NameSortTest
```

The output of the NameSortTest program is as follows:

```
String array before sort:
0: Ward, Bill
1: Osbourne, Ozzy
2: Butlet, Geezer
3: Iommi, Tony

String array after sort:
0: Iommi, Tony
1: Osbourne, Ozzy
2: Butlet, Geezer
3: Ward, Bill
```

Voilà! With a minimal amount of code, the four original members of Black Sabbath are now sorted in reverse alphabetical order according to first name. You are now the true Iron Man!

What you've actually done is defined an unnamed (anonymous) class that implements the *Comparator* interface *inside* of another class. Again, this is great for times when you only need a particular instance of a class once. Should you need to use the functionality of this unnamed class throughout your program, then go ahead and declare it as an official class. In the next section, you'll see how you can organize your classes so they can be reused with minimal effort.

# The Package Deal

Since Chapter 2, you've seen how to use the Java import statement to include specific Java packages into your program. All Java packages are organized into groups by their type; the java.io package includes classes relevant to input and output, java.applet contains classes related to applet development, java.util gives us general utility classes, such as data structures and timers, and so on.

You can follow this pattern to create your own packages. For instance, for my senior-year Operating Systems project I wrote a simple operating system in Java that served as an overlay to the parent operating system, which I named *MOSES* (for Multiplatform Operating System Emulation Simulator). While designing the system, I noticed that it contained four main parts: the kernel, command interpreter, file system, and process manager. Therefore, I put code related to each of these four components within its own package. The advantage to this is that it keeps projects organized. In addition, all classes that are declared as `public` are automatically visible to all other classes within the package, which alleviates having to import each related class into each separate source file.

To create a package, you only need to do two things. First, you need to include the `package` statement at the top of your source listing, typically right before the `import` statements. For example, in my Java operating system I had a file named VirtualProcess.java. The header of the file looks something like the following:

```
/** VirtualProcess.java
 *    Defines a base structure for all further derived processes.
 */
package moses.process;

import java.io.*;
import java.lang.Thread;

public abstract class VirtualProcess implements Disposable
```

Note the `package` keyword near the top of the file. The `VirtualProcess` class is now part of the `moses.process` package. The `VirtualProcess` class also implements the `Disposable` interface, which is also part of the same package, so it does not need to be imported explicitly.

Putting related files into the same package gives you a clean, organized work space, both physically and logically. The second step to create a package is to copy your compiled source files into a directory that matches the package name. All you need to do is create a directory that replaces the "." with a path name separator within the package name. So, on a machine running Windows, you can copy the compiled process .class files to a directory named *\moses\process\VirtualProcess.class* (or *…/moses/process/VirtualProcess.class* on UNIX machines). Not only will your programs then look cleaner, but the file organization will be clean and organized as well. Figure 3.4 illustrates this structure as I used it for my Java operating system.

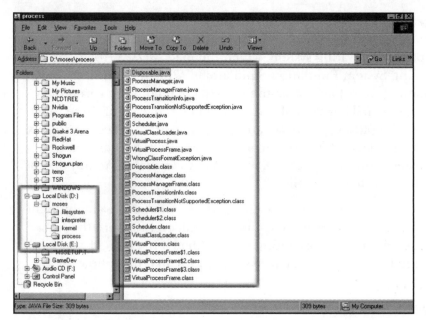

**Figure 3.4**

*The MOSES file and package structure*

Using packages is also great for reusable classes, such as those contained in a game engine, which we'll talk about in Part III. Once you write a package full of reusable goodies, all you need to do is set your CLASSPATH and import the package. Now your packages are ripe for the picking. Remember, you'll most likely need to update your CLASSPATH variable if you plan to use any custom packages. If you need a refresher on setting your CLASSPATH environment variable, refer back to Chapter 1.

# Conclusion

There you have it—an overview of object-oriented programming in about 30 pages! There are entire schools of thought devoted to object-oriented programming, so treat this as an introduction. We'll fill in any gaps as we go along.

Keep the principles of basic class construction, inheritance, and abstract classes in the back of your mind. If you're not already a seasoned C++ or Java programmer, it's not important that you master the ins and outs of object-oriented programming. Familiarity is the key; the concepts covered in this chapter will be reinforced throughout the rest of this book.

Give the following exercises a try to check your understanding of object-oriented programming thus far. In the final chapter of this section, we'll take a closer look at the Java API and how these predefined objects can make our lives a lot easier.

# Exercises

**3.1** Describe the difference between the following code snippets in terms of how memory is allocated to each object:

```
// snippet A
Card c1 = new Card(21);
Card c2 = c1;

// snippet B
Card c1 = new Card(21);
Card c2 = new Card(c1);
```

**3.2** Extend the Vector2d class to define the Vector3d class, a vector containing three dimensions. Use the Vector2d class as a template if you need to. For bonus points, implement operations that calculate the cross and dot products of two Vector3d objects.

**3.3** Using the Java 2 documentation, investigate the StringTokenizer class. From where does this class inherit its functionality? Does it have a parent base class? What are the default delimiting characters? Write a small test program that parses elements from a comma delimited list.

**3.4** Explain why the following would not be a valid instantiation of a fictitious abstract Product class:

```
Product x = new Product("Acme Inc.", 431);
```

# CHAPTER 4

# At Your Service with the Java 2 API: Commonly Used Java Classes

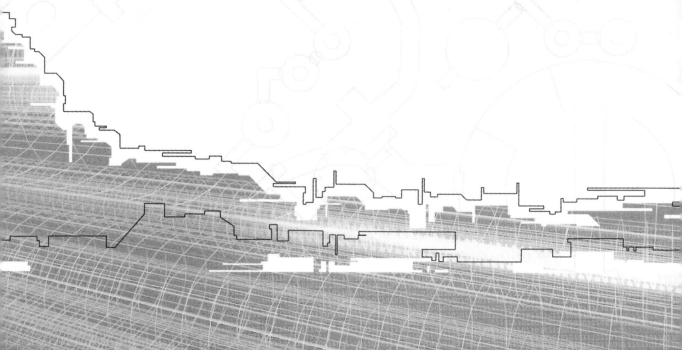

The Java API comes with literally hundreds of ready-to-use classes right out of the box. These classes can perform everything from basic input and output to playing sound to drawing windows and buttons. Many of these classes perform very specialized functions; others you'll use every day. With all of these classes at your disposal, it's good to know what's out there so you don't end up reinventing the wheel. In this chapter, we'll look at some of the more commonly used classes provided by the Java API. We'll discuss them by package, starting with classes contained in the java.lang package. You might also want to have your Java 2 documentation handy so you can follow along and catch any details I might not cover.

# The java.lang Package

The java.lang package contains the classes that are fundamental to the Java language. This includes system utilities, wrapper classes to primitive types, math utilities, and thread management. The first class from this package we'll look at is the Object class, which sits at the top of the Java class hierarchy.

## java.lang.Object

As mentioned above, the Object class is the base class from which all further Java classes are derived. This makes Java a *single typed* language; that is, all defined types derive from a single common ancestor. All classes derive from Object whether it is explicitly stated or not. For example, consider the following class declarations:

```
public class AquaMonster
public class AquaMonster extends Object
```

Both declarations declare an AquaMonster class; and, yes, both inherit their functionality from the Object class. The two declarations are semantically identical. If a class does not explicitly extend any other known class, then the compiler will automatically insert extends Object in the class declaration.

Classes that extend classes other than the Object class are still of type Object themselves. For example, here is the header for a fictitious Hydra class:

```
public class Hydra extends AquaMonster
```

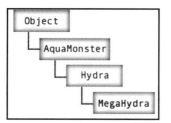

**Figure 4.1**

*Yes, Virginia, a*
`MegaHydra` *is an*
`Object`.

Therefore, you can see the "is-a" relationship reaches up the entire ladder of inheritance. Figure 4.1 shows an entire hierarchy of the water monster family.

So, who cares that the is-a relationship extends up the hierarchy ladder? Well, it makes a world of difference when you want to write generic, flexible code. For example, recall that in the previous chapter you used the `Arrays` `sort` method to sort an array of `String` objects. The `sort` method took a *Comparator* object as its second argument. The *Comparator* interface, in turn, has one method, the `compare` method. The `compare` method then takes two `Object` parameters to compare, as the following header shows:

```
public int compare(Object a, Object b)
```

Since *every* class you write extends `Object`, you can send *any* class type to the `compare` method (you'll see how to make this work with primitive types later). If you didn't have `Object` as a root base class, then you would have to define a different compare method for every conceivable class you can think of: `String`, `Dog`, `Cigar`, `ReflectPermission`, `Hydra`—the list goes on forever. In short, the removal of the `Object` class from the Java language would drastically cut down on its ability to allow for rapid, flexible development.

Now that you know that the `Object` class is the supreme king over all other objects, let's talk about some of the methods the `Object` class has to offer.

## The clone Method

No, the `Object` `clone` method has nothing to do with Episode II of the *Star Wars* series. What it does is create what is known as a *deep copy* of the object calling it and returns a copy back to the main program. The `clone` method has the following prototype:

```
protected Object clone() throws CloneNotSupportedException
```

The `clone` method performs an action similar to that of a class's copy constructor, but it is becoming a more preferred way of creating an exact copy of an object.

We'll look at the inner workings of the clone method when we talk about the Cloneable interface toward the end of this section.

## The equals Method

The equals method returns a value of true or false depending on whether or not the sent Object is logically "equal" to the calling Object. It has the following prototype:

```
public boolean equals(Object obj)
```

Recall that I mentioned that the Java == operator only determines if two nonprimitive objects occupy the same memory location. It literally determines if two objects reference the same thing. The equals method can help determine if two objects are *logically* equivalent.

Suppose you're designing a shoot 'em up game involving various types of tanks. Tanks that are on the same team will be of the same color and size; both color and size are expressed using int values. You don't want tanks on the same team to be able to damage one another. Therefore, for any two tanks to be logically equivalent, they have to be the same color and size. You could then implement the Tank equals method as follows:

```
// determines if two Tank objects are logically equal
public boolean equals(Object other)
{
    Tank temp;

    // the objects are equal if they refer to the same object
    if(this == other)
    {
        return true;
    }

    // the objects are not equal if the other object is null or is not
    // an instance of the Tank class
    if(other == null || !(other instanceof Tank))
    {
        return false;
    }

    // cast the incoming Object as a Tank
```

```
        temp = (Tank)other;

        // return based on the equality of the colors and sizes
        return(getColor() == temp.getColor() &&
               getSize()  == temp.getSize());
    }    // equals
```

Your main processing code can then easily determine if two Tank objects can attack one another:

```
// assume tank1 and tank2 reference two valid Tank objects
if(! tank1.equals(tank2))
{
    // allow Tanks to fight
}
```

Each equals method you write should pass several trivial rejections before determining if the two objects are equal. If the two objects reside at the same memory address, then of course they are equal. If the sent Object is null or isn't even an instance of the Tank class, then the two objects are not equal. Finally, if the incoming Object is not trivially rejected, you must cast it to a valid Tank object before determining whether they are equal.

Feel free to override the equals method as needed. If you don't anticipate ever needing to determine equivalence among objects of the same class, then you don't have to bother overriding this method.

## The hashCode Method

A *hash code* is a code that distinctly identifies an object. This is often useful when you wish to organize data by mapping object values to distinct "key" values. Java defines the header of the Object hashCode method as follows:

```
public int hashCode()
```

You can see that the hashCode method always returns an int value, which will give you more than enough distinct hash values for just about any application.

The Java API suggests the following guidelines when designing a custom hashCode method:

- **The method must be consistent.** Invoking the hashCode method on an object any number of times should produce the exact same integer result, provided the object has not been modified between calls. This preserves the paradigm of mapping an object with a distinct hash value.

- **Equivalent objects produce equivalent hash codes.** If two objects are logically equivalent (according to their equals method), then they should return the same hash code value.

- **Nonequivalent objects can produce equivalent hash codes.** Not all distinct objects have to produce distinct hash code values, but the closer you come to having unequal objects produce distinct values, the better performance your programs will have (and you'll see exactly why later).

If you're familiar with data structures such as hash tables, then you already know how an object's hash code might be useful. If you plan on adding objects to structures such as a Map, consider implementing this method. For more on hashing, check out the section titled "java.util.Hashtable" toward the end of this chapter.

## The toString Method

You've seen this one before. The toString method builds and returns a String to represent the current state of an object. A String representation of objects is great for general purpose debugging and error handling. Just as a refresher, the Vector2d toString method is defined as follows:

```
// returns the String representation of this Vector2d
public String toString()
{
    return "Vector2d [x=" + x + ",y=" + y + "]";
}
```

The Java 2 documentation suggests that each class override this method. Just keep in mind that if you choose not to override this method, the Object toString method returns the class name of the object along with the hash code associated with it.

Like the toString method, the Object class defines several more methods; these are just a few of the more common methods you'll use. We'll look at some of the others you should be aware of as we progress through the book. Again, the Java 2 documentation is another great resource for finding out more about any given native class.

## java.lang.String

We've already looked at the String type when we looked at primitive types. There are, however, many more methods that the String class provides. The following sections discuss just a few of the commonly used ones.

## The length Method

The `String` length method returns the number of characters contained within the `String`. So the following code snippet would return 27 to the main program:

```
String str = "Not ANOTHER String example!";
return str.length();
```

## The charAt Method

The `charAt` method returns the character at a specified index. Its prototype looks like this:

```
public char charAt(int index)
```

To extract the second character from a String object, use the following:

```
String str = "abcdefg";
char ch = str.charAt(1);
```

This will assign the character "b" to the `ch` variable. Indexing for `String` objects works the same as arrays; indexing starts at zero and ends at (length of `String`)−1.

## The endsWith and startsWith Methods

The `String` endsWith method has several nifty uses; one in particular is for determining whether a given file name is valid. The following example checks to see if a given file name is a valid Windows text file:

```
if(filename.endsWith(".txt"))
{
    // open and process the file
}
else
{
    // invalid format: report error message
}
```

There is also a `String` startsWith method that works in the same general fashion.

## The substring Method

The `String` substring method does as you would expect—it extracts a substring from a `String` object given a set of indices. There are two flavors to this method. One takes both starting and ending indices. It has the following prototype:

```
public String substring(int beginIndex, int endIndex)
```

The other only takes the beginning index and assumes the end index is the end of the string. The following code concatenates two substrings and prints the result:

```
String str = "Polygon".substring(0,4) + "whirlpool".substring(0,5);
System.out.println(str);
```

This would print the word "Polywhirl" to the console. Notice that the string literals "Polygon" and "whirlpool" are automatically considered String objects as they are created.

## The toLowerCase and toUpperCase Methods

The String toLowerCase method returns a new String object that converts each character to its lowercase equivalent according to the default Locale (a Locale represents a geographic, political, or cultural region). So in my current Locale,

```
String str = "I LiKE CaRROtS AnD STrIngBeaNS";
System.out.println(str.toLowerCase());
System.out.println(str);
```

would output

```
i like carrots and stringbeans
I LiKE CaRROtS AnD STrIngBeaNS
```

to the console. Notice that the toLowerCase method does not change the contents of str; it instead returns a new String containing the lowercase representation of the original String. There is also a toUpperCase String method that works in much the same way. Consult the Java documentation for converting strings of a different Locale to upper- or lowercase.

## The trim Method

For times when you need to remove white space from the beginning and/or the end of a String, the trim method will save you much time and effort. Let's see it in action:

```
String str = "       whitespace BAAAAAAD   !!!";
str = str.trim();
System.out.println(str);
```

Like you might imagine, the output will be "whitespace BAAAAAAD!!!" Obviously, only leading and trailing white space is removed; the rest stays where it is.

## The valueOf Method

There are several `valueOf` methods defined within the `String` class, one for each primitive type. This method is useful for when you wish to convert a numerical or other primitive type to a `String`. The general prototype for these methods looks like the following:

```
public static String valueOf(<primitive> p)
```

The following demonstrates how to use the `valueOf` method to convert primitives into `String` objects:

```
int value = 54;
double pi = Math.PI;
String str = String.valueOf(value) + String.valueOf(pi);
System.out.println(str);
```

The above code concatenates two new `String` objects into a third one. The `String` literal "543.141592653589793" is what is printed to the screen.

# java.lang.StringBuffer

Unlike the Java `String` type, the `StringBuffer` type is a *mutable* object; that is, its contents can be modified directly. Let's look at a few of the more useful `StringBuffer` methods, starting with the `insert` method.

## The insert Method

The `insert` method from the `StringBuffer` class inserts the sent `String` into the buffer at the given offset and then returns a reference to itself to the main program. The following example demonstrates how you can convert a swine into a critter from the prickly *Erethizontidae* family:

```
StringBuffer sb = new StringBuffer("Porcine");
sb.insert(4, "up");
System.out.println(sb);
```

The above example prints the word "Porcupine" to the console. Now *that's* Kosher!

## The delete and deleteCharAt Methods

Now that you've filled your `StringBuffer` full of data, you can now start to delete characters from it. The `StringBuffer` `delete` and `deleteCharAt` methods allow you to do this. The `delete` method has the following prototype:

```
public StringBuffer delete(int start, int end)
```

Similarly, the `deleteCharAt` method looks like this:

```
public StringBuffer deleteCharAt(int index)
```

These methods work much the same as the `insert` method, so I won't torture you with an example.

## The append Method

Although you might not make great use of it, it might be interesting to note the way `String` concatenation works in Java. The Java compiler uses the `StringBuffer append` method to implement the binary + operator for strings. For example,

```
String s = new StringBuffer().append("card").append("inal").toString();
```

is equivalent to

```
String s = "card" + "inal";
```

The `StringBuffer` class contains several other methods, including `substring`, `toString`, `reverse`, and `replace`. They're pretty self-explanatory, so I'll leave these methods up to you to explore on your own.

## Wrapper Classes

The `java.lang` package also contains a number of classes known as *wrapper classes*. Each wrapper class "wraps" one of the eight Java primitive types. Wrapper classes contain a primitive type, as well as provide a number of operations on it. `Integer`, `Long`, `Short`, `Byte`, `Boolean`, `Float`, `Double`, and `Character` are all Java wrapper classes. Figure 4.2 illustrates how the `Integer` class wraps a single `int` value and provides operations on it.

If you already have the eight primitive types available to you, then doesn't the existence of wrapper classes add unneeded complexity to your programs? Yes and no. It would be silly to use the wrapper classes to carry out basic operations, such as the following:

```
Integer i = new Integer((new Integer( 5).intValue()) +
                        (new Integer(20).intValue()));
System.out.println(i.toString());
```

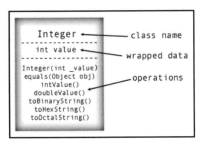

**Figure 4.2**

*Wrapping an int value within an Integer object*

Boy, that's a whole lot of work just to get the number 25 on the screen! It makes me glad to still have primitive types available. However, if you think about it you'll realize a strong point about wrapper classes, which is that each wrapper class extends the Object class. This means that you can still incorporate primitive types in data structures that ordinarily only accept objects. Take the Stack class, for instance. Since you can only place Object types on a stack, you must use an appropriate wrapper class to push primitives on it. The following example pushes a number of primitives on a stack and then unwinds the stack until it is empty:

```java
// create a new Stack object
Stack s = new Stack();

// throw some values on the stack
s.push(new Integer(5));
s.push(new Character('X'));
s.push(new Float(5.5));
s.push(new Integer(10));
s.push(new Double(Math.PI));
s.push(new Boolean(true));

// unwind the stack, printing each value along the way
while(!s.empty())
{
    System.out.println(s.pop());
}
```

Here's the output, which prints the stack in the exact opposite order as it was assembled:

```
true
3.141592653589793
```

```
10
5.5
X
5
```

Not only can wrapper classes be used with data structures, but they also provide a number of conversions and utilities as well. The following shows some utilities provided by the Integer class:

```java
// here's a utility to convert an existing Integer's value to a double
Integer i = new Integer(2);
System.out.println(i.doubleValue());

// now let's show off some static methods available in the Integer class

// conversion of a String to an Integer
String str = "567";
int value = Integer.parseInt(str);

// conversion from base 10 to base 2, 8, and 16, respectively
int decimalValue = 516;
System.out.println(Integer.toBinaryString(decimalValue));
System.out.println(Integer.toOctalString(decimalValue));
System.out.println(Integer.toHexString(decimalValue));
```

Try it yourself to see what the output is. Before you embark on writing a standard utility for your program, check the Java API first—chances are they've already thought of it.

# java.lang.Math

Another class you'll refer to often, especially when programming games, is the Math class. Rather than instantiating this class, you'll want to use its static methods to perform many different mathematical operations.

The Math class provides two handy constant values for use in your programs: the natural logarithm base *e* and the value of *pi*—the ratio of the circumference of a circle to its diameter. The following illustrates how you can use *pi* to calculate the area of a circle:

```java
double radius = 4.5;
double area = Math.PI * radius * radius;
```

```
System.out.println("The area of a circle with radius " +
                    radius + " is " + area);
```

The output would be

```
The area of a circle with radius 4.5 is 63.61725123519331
```

Other utilities found within the Math class include basic trigonometry and degree conversion methods. This includes the sine, arcsine, cosine, arccosine, tangent, and arctangent of an angular measurement in radians. You can also quickly convert a degree measurement to radians and vice versa using the toRadians, and toDegrees methods, respectively:

```
double degrees = 45.0;
double radians = Math.toRadians(degrees);
System.out.println(degrees + " degrees = " + radians + " radians");
System.out.println("So, " + radians + " radians = " +
                    Math.toDegrees(radians) + " degrees!");
```

This will output

```
45.0 degrees = 0.7853981633974483 radians
So, 0.7853981633974483 radians = 45.0 degrees!
```

OK, maybe that wasn't the most fascinating example, but it is a useful construct nonetheless. A possibly more interesting method found in the Math class is the random method. Granted, there is no such thing as a truly random number on digital computers since on computers random numbers are computed algorithmically with deterministic algorithms and their sequences can be predicted and reproduced. However, the way in which Java pseudorandomly calculates random numbers is sufficient for your needs.

The Math random method generates a double value greater than or equal to 0.0 and less than 1.0. Its magnitude is always positive, and the values it chooses generally fall within a uniform distribution of that range. The following code snippet generates 25 Integer objects whose values range between 50 and 100:

```
Integer[] values = new Integer[20];
for(int i = 0; i < values.length; i++)
{
    values[i] = new Integer((int)(50.0 + (Math.random()*51.0)));
}
System.out.println(Arrays.asList(values));
```

I chose to use Integer objects so that I could use the Arrays asList method to neatly print out the list. If you feel that the code that chooses the random value looks too congested, feel free to break it up into several steps. Output for this code might look like the following:

```
[87, 65, 99, 67, 62, 65, 95, 69, 96, 92, 50, 98, 53, 100, 69, 51, 95, 54, 76, 55]
```

There are also a number of other Math routines, summarized by the following:

- **Math.abs.** Returns the absolute value of the sent number.
- **Math.ceil.** Returns the ceiling of the sent double value.
- **Math.exp.** Returns the value of *e* raised to the sent double value. This is equivalent to

```
System.out.println(Math.pow(Math.E, value));
```

- **Math.floor.** Returns the floor value of the sent double.
- **Math.max.** Returns the greater of the two sent parameters.
- **Math.min.** Returns the lesser of the two sent parameters.
- **Math.pow.** Returns the first value raised to the power of the second.
- **Math.round.** For float types, returns the closest int value. For doubles, returns the closest long value.
- **Math.sqrt.** Returns the rounded positive square root of the sent double value.

# java.lang.System

The Java System class is a final, uninstantiable class that contains several useful methods and utilities, many of which you'll see later. For now, let's examine a few of the important ones.

## The println Method

Thus far, we've focused our attention solely on console applications. Undoubtedly, you're familiar with the following System command:

```
System.out.println("println rules!");
```

Here, out is a public instance of the PrintStream class. The current environment dictates its use. For your console applications, it is defined to print sent text to "standard output," or directly to the console.

## The arraycopy Method

The next System feature we'll look at is the arraycopy method. It copies a portion of a source array into a destination array. It is prototyped by the following:

```
public static void arraycopy(Object src, int src_position,
                             Object dst, int dst_position, int length)
```

Here, src_position refers to the index to start copying from the src array; dst_position refers to the position of the dst array to start copying to. Finally, length refers to the number of members that should be copied to dst. Here's an example of how it's used:

```
// build our initial source and destination arrays
String[] src = { "1", "2", "3", "4", "5", "6", "7", "8", "9", "A" };
String[] dst = { "0", "0", "0", "0", "0", "0", "0", "0", "0", "0" };

// copy 5 members from index 3 in the source array into 5 members
// from index 4 in the destination array
System.arraycopy(src, 3, dst, 4, 5);

// print out the dst array as a list
System.out.println(Arrays.asList(dst));
```

Alas, here's the output:

```
[0, 0, 0, 0, 4, 5, 6, 7, 8, 0]
```

Be cautious when using the arraycopy method; your run-time environment will throw an error if you supply indices that are out of bounds or if the length parameter causes the routine to overstep either array's bounds.

## The currentTimeMillis Method

The next System utility, currentTimeMillis, is very useful for when you wish to update objects at a regular interval or if you just want to know the current time. The currentTimeMillis method returns the current time in milliseconds. The following code snippet creates a Date object with the current system time and prints it to the console:

```
System.out.println(new Date(System.currentTimeMillis()));
```

Try it out to see how it works.

## The exit Method

A final System utility we'll look at is the System exit method. It's a good idea to use this method when you encounter a serious or unrecoverable error. The following demonstrates how you could write a rudimentary routine to read in input from the keyboard:

```java
// create a new String to hold the input, as well as a temporary character
// variable to hold keystrokes
String s = new String();
char ch = '\0';

// loop until the user hits Enter
while(true)
{
    // attempt to read a character from standard input
    try
    {
        ch = (char)System.in.read();
    }
    // exit the program if an IOException is thrown
    catch(IOException e)
    {
        System.out.println("IOException thrown: " + e);
        System.exit(-1);
    }

    // break the loop if input was the Enter key (character code 13)
    if(ch == 13)
    {
        break;
    }

    // add the character to the end of our String
    s = s.concat(String.valueOf(ch));
}

// print the final String back out
System.out.println(s);
```

In the above example, a value of –1 was passed as the error code. If the program becomes unable to accept user input, there's no sense in continuing the program.

An error code of zero signifies that the program exited cleanly and without error, so use a nonzero error code if your applications need to terminate abnormally.

# java.lang.Cloneable

The *Cloneable* interface is a public interface that we implement in our classes if we wish to override the Object clone method. The *Cloneable* interface contains no methods, but implementing it indicates that it is legal for a class to implement the clone method. If you'll recall, the clone method creates a full copy of the calling object and returns it to the main program.

Also remember that Java objects are all reference values; that is, they are referenced by their current memory location. So using the assignment operator on objects merely assigns them to the same memory location. For instance, think about a fictional Alien class that takes its x, y screen coordinates as parameters to its constructor method. You declare two Alien objects then later assign the second Alien object to the first, like the following:

```
Alien a1 = new Alien(50, 150);
Alien a2 = a1;
```

Conceptually, Figure 4.3 shows what you've created.

Now, say you want to change a2's position, like the following:

```
a2.moveTo(300, 300);
```

Figure 4.4 shows the result.

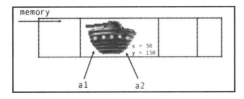

**Figure 4.3**

*Assigning two Alien objects to the same memory location*

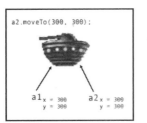

**Figure 4.4**

*Altering one Alien reference affects the other.*

That's fine and dandy if you wish to have two references to the same object. But what if you want two independent copies of the same object so that changing one will not change the other? The answer lies in creating a clone of `a1` and assigning it to `a2`.

Assume that the `Alien` class only contains primitive data fields, such as

```
int health;
double shields;
int x;
int y;
int type;
```

The following code illustrates how you can write the `Alien` clone method to produce a full copy of an `Alien` object:

```
// clones an Alien; throws an error if the clone is unsuccessful.
public Object clone()
{
    try
    {
        return(super.clone());  // call Object.clone()
    }

    catch(CloneNotSupportedException e)
    {
        // should never happen, since we declared ourself Cloneable
        throw new InternalError();
    }
}
```

The call to `super.clone` takes care of the "magic and voodoo" involved in creating a member-by-member copy of the calling `Alien` object. If your program requires internal clones to be created (such as if each Alien object contains references to other `Alien` objects), the clone method should explicitly make calls to their `clone` methods as well.

In order to guarantee that the `CloneNotSupportedException` is not thrown, you must remember to implement the *Cloneable* interface in your class header so the compiler knows it's okay to clone, as follows:

```
public class Alien implements Cloneable
```

The Java `clone` method is preferred over using the copy constructor to create copies of objects. Now you can create a copy of `a1` by invoking its `clone` method:

```
a2 = a1.clone();
```

Don't forget to cast, since the `clone` method always returns an `Object`. Predict what will happen now when you execute the following:

```
a1 = new Alien(50, 150);
a2 = (Alien)a1.clone();
a2.moveTo(300, 300);
```

> **TIP**
>
> If one class contains an instance of another class, it is important that it too provides its own `clone` method so that a full copy of the object is made. Otherwise, what is known as a *shallow copy* is made, and your data is most likely going to be corrupted very soon.

That's right—`a1` and `a2` initially contain the same data but reside at their own memory locations. When you change the position of `a2`, it will remain independent of `a1`. Figure 4.5 shows how cloned objects maintain their data independence.

## java.lang.Thread

The final `java.lang` class I'd like to look at is the `Thread` class. Threading is an important aspect of Java, especially once you begin looking at graphical user applications. Java provides a much simpler way to implement threading than languages such as C or C++. If you are familiar with threading using a Java release before 1.2, you should note some of the differences in thread use under Java 2.

Most operating systems today allow more than one program to run concurrently. Each concurrently running program is known as a *process*. You can run as many simultaneous processes as will fit into memory. Since the CPU can only do one thing at a time, the operating system must load each process into memory and allow it to run briefly before switching to the next one. It is also the job of the operating

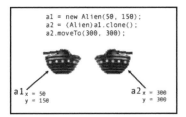

**Figure 4.5**

*Cloning an object retains each copy's data independence.*

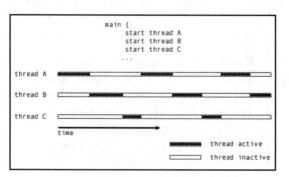

**Figure 4.6**

*Using multiple threads within a single application*

system to manage these processes as well as process resources. This rapid "swapping" of programs in and out of memory is what makes it appear as though all of the programs are running simultaneously.

Unlike a process, a *thread* is an instance of execution *within* a program. Every Java program is guaranteed to contain at least one thread. The execution of the main method is one thread of execution. Once a thread is started, it is scheduled to run concurrently alongside other threads. It is the job of the Java Virtual Machine to prioritize and execute active threads much like the operating system manages processes.

As threads are added to an application, processor time is given to individual threads via finite time slices. Figure 4.6 shows how multiple threads are assigned time slices over the course of an application's life cycle.

Figure 4.6 does not demonstrate the time slices allocated to the thread containing the main method, but you can see how time slices are allocated among multiple threads.

## An Example

The following program creates and runs a thread that calculates the Fibonacci sequence. This sequence of numbers starts with {1, 1}; each subsequent number is the sum of the previous two. So {1, 1, 2, 3, 5, 8, 13} are the first seven numbers in the sequence.

```java
// Thread to calculate and print out the Fibonacci sequence of numbers
class Fibonacci extends Thread
{
    // the minimum time to wait before updating
    private static final long WAIT_TIME = 500;

    // the previous number in the sequence
```

```java
private long previous;

// the current number in the sequence
private long current;

// an identifier for this sequence
private char ident;

// constructs a new Fibonacci sequence
public Fibonacci(char id)
{
    // set the identifier for this sequence
    ident = id;

    // initialize the first two numbers in the sequence
    previous = 1;
    current = 1;
}

// prints the next number in the sequence
private void printNext()
{
    System.out.print("(" + ident + ") " + current + ", ");
}

// calculates the next number in the sequence; it is calculated as
// the sum of the last two numbers in the sequence
private void update()
{
    long temp = current;
    current = previous + current;
    previous = temp;
}

// execution code for the thread; this method is inherited from the
// Thread class
public void run()
{
    // print the first two numbers in the sequence
```

```
            printNext();
            printNext();

            // get a reference to this thread
            Thread t = Thread.currentThread();

            // loop while the thread is active
            while(t == this)
            {
                // update the sequence
                update();

                // once the current sequence value exceeds the largest long value,
                // it will wrap around to negative values.  once current is
                // negative, terminate this thread of execution
                if(current < 0L)
                {
                    System.out.println("\nNo more long values! " +
                                            "Thread terminating...");
                    t = null;
                    return;
                }

                // print out the next Fibonacci number
                printNext();

                // pause a bit
                try
                {
                    Thread.sleep(WAIT_TIME);
                }

                catch(InterruptedException e) { }
            }
        }    // run
    }
```

If you have used the Thread class under Java releases before 1.2, you might want to note some changes. The Thread methods suspend, resume, and stop have all been depreciated in Java 2. *Depreciated methods* are methods that are still implemented for backward compatibility but are not recommended for current or future use. In this case, the depreciated Thread methods are either unsafe or inconsistent or are otherwise prone to deadlock. The above program illustrates one way in which a Thread object can be properly implemented under Java 2.

Also note how you can synchronize the *Fibonacci* program to output the next value at a regular interval. Each instance of the *Fibonacci* program is assigned its own character identifier; by running the program, you'll see how output is interweaved among the three Thread objects created. If you're feeling ambitious, try altering the above program to output values from another mathematical sequence, such as the prime number sequence. Maybe you'll be the one to discover the 39th Mersenne prime!

## The Runnable Interface

Alternatively, threads can also be created by implementing the *Runnable* interface rather than inheriting the Thread class. This allows you to give classes the ability to thread off from the main program yet not be locked in to inheriting the Thread class. You can thread off a *Runnable* object by passing it to a new Thread object. Assuming the Fibonacci class implemented *Runnable* rather than extending Thread, you could have started a Fibonacci thread as follows:

```
// creates a new Fibonacci sequence generators to test multi-threaded
// applications
public class ThreadTest
{
     public static void main(String[] args)
     {
         // start a few Fibonacci threads
         new Fibonacci('A').start();
         new Fibonacci('B').start();
         new Fibonacci('C').start();
     }
}
```

This way, if the Fibonacci class needed to inherit its functionality from a class other than Thread, it would be free to do so.

All this talk about threads brings us to an interesting point: What happens if two threads attempt to access and manipulate a memory address or value at the same relative time? The terms *dirty read* and *lost update* both come to mind. Consider the following situation:

Multiple threads are permitted to access the user's score. These threads can both read from and write to the user's current score. Thread A allocates points when enemy planes are destroyed. Thread B updates the score when bonus items are collected. Let's say the user currently has 5,000 points. Thread A comes along and reads in the user's score, then adds 500 to it for a total of 5,500. Before Thread A can write the final score back to the main program, it is interrupted (or *preempted*) by Thread B, which now also reads the score as 5,000. Immediately after Thread B gains control and reads the score, it quickly adds 1,500 bonus points to the score and updates the main program, giving the user 6,500 points in total. Control is now given back to Thread A. Thread A proudly completes its job by writing what it thinks is the proper score of 5,500 points back to the main program. Control is then passed to another thread. Figure 4.7 shows how one thread can step on the toes of another.

What just happened? The user just got ripped out of 500 points! In other words, a lost update has just occurred.

How can you keep threads from stepping over each other's feet? The answer lies in the *synchronization* of objects. Using the `synchronized` keyword with class methods or code blocks, you can put a "lock" on objects. When an object is locked, no other thread can access the object until the code block or method has completed. In the preceding example, if you'd had Thread A lock the score, then Thread B would not have been able to alter it until Thread A had completed. We'll look more at synchronization later in the book, but I just wanted to throw the idea out to you now so you'll be familiar with it.

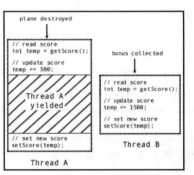

**Figure 4.7**

*The dangers of a lost update*

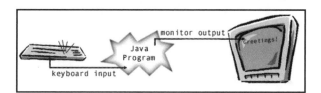

**Figure 4.8**

*Standard I/O from the keyboard to the monitor*

# The java.io Package

Package java.io contains a number of uniform input and output (I/O) operations that allow you to send and receive data. The source or destination of this data can be virtually anything—input from the keyboard, output to the monitor, files, even server-client architectures. The magic behind Java I/O is achieved through what are called *streams*. A stream is simply a sequence of characters or bytes that is either read from a source or written to a destination.  Figure 4.8 shows how strokes from the keyboard are caught by a Java program and then sent to the monitor.

Java I/O begins with two abstract classes called java.io.Reader and java.io.Writer. All further I/O operations are implemented in subclasses that extend their functionality. Rather than going into the nitty-gritty on how these classes work, let's look at an example of how you can use them.

One way you can input information from the user is by using the BufferedReader class. Buffering input saves Java from converting each character as it is read, therefore increasing throughput. You can use the BufferedReader class, for instance, to read information from the monitor or from a file. The following illustrates how you can use the BufferedReader class to input an integer from the user:

```
// create a new BufferedReader that takes input from standard input
BufferedReader reader = new BufferedReader(new InputStreamReader(System.in));

boolean validInput = false;    // flags "good" input

// prompt the user to enter an integer
System.out.print("Enter an integer value: ");

// loop until the user enters valid input
while(!validInput)
{
    // assume input will be valid until we prove otherwise
```

```
        validInput = true;
        try
        {
                String input = reader.readLine();
                try
                {
                    // if parseInt cannot properly parse the String, a
                    // NumberFormatException is thrown
                    int i = Integer.parseInt(input);
                    System.out.println("You typed the number: " + i);
                }
                catch(NumberFormatException e)
                {
                    // set our valid flag to false and prompt for input
                    validInput = false;
                    System.out.print("Invalid, redo: ");
                }

        }
        catch(IOException e)
        {
                // if reading from standard should fail, print an error message and
                // terminate the program
                System.out.println("IOException caught- Program terminating");
                System.exit(-1);
        }
    }
```

The above routine prompts the user to input an integer until he or she enters valid data. The following might be a sample run of this routine:

```
Enter an integer value: integer
Invalid, redo: value
Invalid, redo: huh?
Invalid, redo: 873!!!!
Invalid, redo: -2
You typed the number: -2
```

As you can see, the above code contains lots of exception handling. That's why it is always a good idea to methodize such utilities. It will save you lots of coding in the future (do I smell a chapter exercise?).

Later, we'll look at streams that handle sounds, images, files, and network communication. Since GUI applications handle user input differently than console applications, you don't have to be a wizard at writing Java console input routines. But for now it's a good topic to look at while you're still familiarizing yourself with the Java language. So, keep on writing those console applications! Before you know it, you'll be dishing out streams left and right.

# The java.util Package

The `java.util` package contains a number of utilities, including those for date and time functions, tokenizing strings, and generating random numbers. The `java.util` package also provides a number of data structures, or collection classes, that allow you to store and organize data efficiently. We'll begin our investigation of the `java.util` package by looking at the `StringTokenizer` class.

## java.util.StringTokenizer

The `StringTokenizer` class allows you to break up `String` objects into what are known as *tokens*. Tokens are separated by what we call *delimiters*. The `StringTokenizer` class is handy when you need to break apart a list of data items that are assumed to be in a specific format. For example, consider the following list of names:

```
Suzy, Yetti, John, Mary, Rover, Ezekiel
```

A comma followed by a space character separates each item in the list. Suppose you want to parse only the names from the `String` and print them out. The following code constructs a `StringTokenizer` object to parse the names and print them to the console:

```
String names = "Suzy, Yetti, John, Mary, Rover, Ezekiel";
String delimiter = ", ";
StringTokenizer st = new StringTokenizer(names, delimiter);
while(st.hasMoreTokens())
{
    System.out.println(st.nextToken());
}
```

The `StringTokenizer` constructor I chose to use takes two `String` arguments: the `String` to tokenize and a list of delimiter characters. Notice that the delimiter `String` contains both the space character as well as the comma character. These characters do not need to be found sequentially in order to be delimited; all the tokenizer needs is to find *at least one* of the characters found in the delimiter String to work. Therefore, you would expect the program to print the following:

```
Suzy
Yetti
John
Mary
Rover
Ezekiel
```

## java.util.Random

As we have seen, the Math random method generates a random number between 0.0 and 1.0. The first time this method is invoked, it creates a new java.util.Random object, with the current system time as its seed. Subsequent calls to the Math random method return the next generated number from the same Random object.

Use of the Math random method works well for most cases. However, there are times when you will wish to have more control over the random values produced. For example, when the Random class is seeded with the same value, it will produce the same output. You may want to specify a particular seed (a long value) so that you can control and monitor your results to ensure you attain the same output each time. You may also want to give specific objects their own Random object to ensure that each object obtains its own unique distribution of random values, rather than having them all feed from the same Random instance.

Another advantage of using the Random class over the Math random method is that you can obtain values of different primitive types. The following code snippet illustrates how you can obtain random values of type float, boolean, long, and double:

```
// create a new Random object with an initial seed of 200
Random random = new Random(200);

// print out the next random int value
System.out.println(random.nextInt());

// print out the next random int, restricting output to numbers between 0 and 20
System.out.println(random.nextInt(20));

// print out the next random boolean value
```

```java
System.out.println(random.nextBoolean());

// print out the next random float value
System.out.println(random.nextFloat());

// print out the next random double value
System.out.println(random.nextDouble());

// change the generator's seed to 100
random.setSeed(100);

// print out the next random long value
System.out.println(random.nextLong());
```

The above program will always, *always,* print out the same set of values each time it is run. If it ever doesn't, then I'll eat this book (or make the person who designed the Random class eat it for promising it would). If you require different random results each time your program runs, just invoke the Random default constructor without any arguments. This will seed the generator with the current system time. Since it is never the same time twice (at least within one millisecond of polling), this class will produce different results each time. Just in case you're curious, the above code will always produce the following results:

```
-1133938638
1
true
0.74504864
0.7007618335887928
-5128016860359238732
```

# The Java 2 Collections Framework

The final topic we'll talk about in this chapter is *data structures*. In Java 2, data structure classes are part of what's called the *collections framework*. Simply stated, a data structure is a container for other objects. Its purpose is to abstract the data in question, represent objects, allow efficient access, and to preserve the order that objects are inserted in some predictable manner. If you're familiar with data structures in C++, you've undoubtedly used pointers when working with data structures. Since Java does not support pointers, this somewhat clouds the way common data structures are implemented. However, at this point, you're not interested in developing data structures; Java provides several ready-to-go data structures for you to use in your programs.

Although there have been hundreds of data structures developed over the years, there are a few fundamental ones I feel are important for game programming. In the following sections, we'll look at the Vector, Stack, LinkedList, and Hashtable classes and how you can gear them toward game development. Let's start with the Vector class.

## java.util.Vector

A Java Vector is simply an expandable array. That is, unlike an array, a Vector can expand beyond its initial capacity. Like arrays, objects contained within a Vector are accessed through an integer index.

New Vector objects can be created through an assortment of constructor methods. You can pass an argument to allocate an initial size of the Vector. The plain vanilla constructor creates a Vector with a default size of 10. You can also pass a capacity increment to the Vector constructor. The capacity increment is the amount by which a Vector grows each time its capacity overflows. The default capacity increment is zero; in this case, the capacity doubles each time the Vector overflows.

There are several methods for altering the contents of a Vector object, such as insertion and deletion methods. One nifty way to cycle through the contents of a Vector is through an Enumeration object. An Enumeration represents a series of elements; the next element in the series is accessed through the nextElement method. The following program, *VectorTest,* shows a quick and easy example of how to extract the highest value out of a Vector of Integer objects:

```
import java.util.*;

class VectorTest extends Object
{
    public static Vector getRandomScores()
    {
        // create a random number generator
        Random rand = new Random();

        // generate between 500 and 1000 random scores
        int numElements = 500 + Math.abs(rand.nextInt())%501;

        // create a new Vector and fill it in with a bunch of random scores
        Vector v = new Vector(numElements);
```

```
        while(numElements > 0)
        {
            // add an Integer between 0 and 2000
            v.add(new Integer(Math.abs(rand.nextInt())%2001));
            numElements--;
        }

        return v;
    }

    // finds the greatest score within a vector of random scores
    public static void main(String[] args)
    {
        int highestScore = 0;    // the highest score we've seen so far

        // generate some random scores
        Vector scores = getRandomScores();

        // cycle through the enumeration of the scores and pick out
        // the highest one
        for(Enumeration e = scores.elements(); e.hasMoreElements(); )
        {
            Integer score = (Integer)(e.nextElement());

            if(score.intValue() > highestScore)
            {
                highestScore = score.intValue();
            }
        }

        // print out the highest score
        System.out.println(highestScore);
    }
}   // VectorTest
```

A real-life application of the above code would probably use a Vector to hold an actual series of scores. Since it would be handy to have an expandable rather than a static array to hold the score data, a Vector might be a good choice to use.

If you want to use Vector objects in your games, check out the Java 2 documentation for a more detailed list of the methods available to you within this class.

## java.util.Stack

As you may already know, a *stack* is a last-in-first-out (LIFO) data structure. This means that the object that was inserted last will be the first to be removed. The Java Stack class defines five methods: push, pop, peek, empty, and search.

Think of a Java Stack as you would a stack of everyday objects, such as a stack of cards or newspapers. The push method allows you to place an item on the top of the Stack. Conversely, the pop method removes the top item of the Stack and returns it to the calling program. The Stack peek method returns the top item without removing it from the Stack. To determine if the Stack contains any items on it, use the empty method; it returns a value of true if there are no more items remaining on it. Finally, the search method returns the 1-based position of where an item is placed within the Stack. So if an item is found directly at the top of the Stack, this method will return 1. If the item is not contained on the Stack, −1 is returned. Figure 4.9 shows some of the major Stack operations in action.

As a simple example, let's push a bunch of Integer objects on a stack, then pop them off and print their values:

```
// create a new Stack object
Stack integerStack = new Stack();

// push 10 Integer objects onto the stack
for(int i = 0; i < 10; i++)
{
     integerStack.push(new Integer(i));
}

// pop off all the stack's values and print them out
while(! integerStack.empty())
{
     System.out.println(integerStack.pop());
}
```

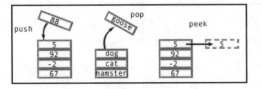

**Figure 4.9**

*The Stack push, pop, and peek operations*

Notice that as we pop objects off the stack, they will appear in the reverse order in which they were inserted. Here's the output of the above code:

```
9
8
7
6
5
4
3
2
1
0
```

Pretty cool. One of my favorite uses for a stack is for handling my own custom menu objects. We'll actually look at how to write a custom menu handler in Part Three.

## java.util.LinkedList

Unlike a stack, a linked list is a first-in-first-out (FIFO) structure. The Java implementation of the LinkedList class contains methods that allow inserts and retrievals at either end of the list. Such a linked list is often known as a *double-ended queue,* or *deque.* Figure 4.10 shows how linked list items are connected within a list.

At first, it might not be obviously apparent why this structure would be used over an array. A LinkedList should be used when we wish to work with an indefinite number of list elements. Assessing the data structures necessary for your programs is a crucial step in the software design process. For example, consider the following line of code:

```java
Object[] objects = new Object[10];
```

This is fine, assuming that you will never need to store more than 10 objects. But what if you don't know how many objects you will need to store, such as in a database situation? You could adjust the above declaration to store 1,000 objects, as follows:

```java
Object[] objects = new Object[1000];
```

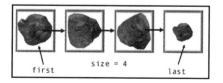

**Figure 4.10**

A *LinkedList* with first *and* last entries

It might appear that this would solve your problems, but it too has its disadvantages. If you never need to store more than, say, 200 objects, you're fine. But what a waste of memory! On the other hand, what if you need to store 1,001 objects? The array is still too small, and there is no way you can "squeeze" any more objects into your array.

There can be even more disadvantages to using arrays over linked lists. For example, what if you need to remove an item from the array? Say you are done with a particular object and you null out that array entry, like the following:

```
objects[230] = null;
```

Now you will have a "hole" in your array. If you wish to keep your array compact, it will take extra code to search for a null value when you want to add an item to the array. You could opt to write a routine to compact arrays after items are removed, but this will most likely be too time consuming. In many situations, using a linked list is a better way.

Linked lists already provide the operations for inserting, removing, and searching for data within a collection. There is no additional code for you to write. Figure 4.11 offers a conceptual example of how an item within a linked list can be removed.

As you can see, the linked list in Figure 4.11 fills in the "hole" by relinking the list to account for the removed item. Another great property of a linked list is that it can expand or contract as much as you need it to. Therefore, there is no wasted memory. Using such a predefined structure will make life much easier for you.

The structure shown in Figure 4.11 can be coded in Java like the following:

```
// add some asteroid objects to a linked list
LinkedList list = new LinkedList();
list.add(a1);
```

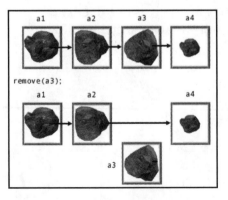

**Figure 4.11**

*Removing an entry from a linked list*

```
        list.add(a2);
        list.add(a3);
        list.add(a4);

        // print out the list
        System.out.println("Original list: " + list);

        // bye-bye, a3!
        list.remove(a3);

        // print out the list again
        System.out.println("List without a3: " + list);
```

With minimal code, you are able to focus on the problem and forget the riffraff. In short, there are times when arrays are fine and other times when a linked list is more appropriate. When you have a collection that needs to be regularly searched or updated, consider using the LinkedList class. As always, examine the problem before diving in; the choice to use an array or linked list should be relatively clear.

## java.util.Hashtable

The final collection class we'll look at in this section is the Java Hashtable class. If you've ever implemented a hash table in C++, you know it can take a lot of work to get a good table scheme up and running. The beauty of the Java Hashtable class is that you can set up a simple database with a very minimal amount of code.

Entries added to a Hashtable consist of two components: the Object value of the entry along with its associated Object key value. A value added to the table can later be retrieved with its associated key. Although the key values can be of any type, they must implement the hashCode and equals methods to be useful. (For more on these methods, refer to the section entitled "java.lang.Object" earlier in this chapter.)

Suppose you are implementing a tile engine for an overhead-view game. You want to contain all of your tiles within a single container and access them by the file name that contains the image data for each tile. A Hashtable would be the perfect choice to implement this scheme. The images for the tiles would be added as the data items, and their associated String representations would be the key values. Figure 4.12 shows how these mapped values might be stored internally.

Now that you have a clear idea of how your images are going to be stored, let's write a test program to try it out. Since you're dealing with graphics, creating an applet will be an ideal way to try out the Hashtable class. The following applet, *HashTest,*

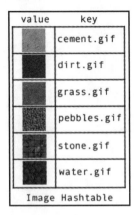

| value | key |
|-------|-----|
| | cement.gif |
| | dirt.gif |
| | grass.gif |
| | pebbles.gif |
| | stone.gif |
| | water.gif |
| Image Hashtable | |

**Figure 4.12**

*Mapping Image values
to their key String
representation*

loads images and their keys into a Hashtable object and allows the user to select one
from a drop-box. Each time a different image is chosen, the selected image will be
tiled on the applet window. If you don't want to type in the source code, just pull
the source from the CD-ROM.

```java
import java.applet.*;
import java.awt.*;
import java.awt.geom.*;
import java.awt.event.*;
import java.util.*;

public class HashTest extends Applet implements ItemListener
{
    // Hashtable to add tile images
    private Hashtable imageTable;

    // a Choice of the various tile images
    private Choice selections;

    // assume tiles will have the same width and height; this represents
    // both a tile's width and height
    private int imageSize;

    // filename description of our images
    private final String[] filenames = { "cement.gif",  "dirt.gif", "grass.gif",
                                "pebbles.gif", "stone.gif", "water.gif" };

    // initializes the Applet
```

```java
public void init()
{
     int n = filenames.length;

     // create a new Hashtable with n members
     imageTable = new Hashtable(n);

     // create the Choice
     selections = new Choice();

     // create a Panel to add our choice at the bottom of the window
     Panel p = new Panel();
     p.add(selections, BorderLayout.SOUTH);
     p.setBackground(Color.RED);

     // add the Choice to the applet and register the ItemListener
     setLayout(new BorderLayout());
     add(p, BorderLayout.SOUTH);
     selections.addItemListener(this);

     // allocate memory for the images and load 'em in
     for(int i = 0; i < n; i++)
     {
          Image img = getImage(getCodeBase(), filenames[i]);
          while(img.getWidth(this) < 0);

          // add the image to the Hashtable and the Choice
          imageTable.put(filenames[i], img);
          selections.add(filenames[i]);

          // set the imageSize field
          if(i == 0)
          {
               imageSize = img.getWidth(this);
          }
     }
}    // init

// tiles the currently selected tile image within the Applet
public void paint(Graphics g)
```

```java
        {
            // cast the sent Graphics context to get a usable Graphics2D object
            Graphics2D g2d = (Graphics2D)g;

            // save the Applet's width and height
            int width = getSize().width;
            int height = getSize().height;

            // create an AffineTransform to place tile images
            AffineTransform at = new AffineTransform();

            // get the currently selected tile image
            Image currImage =
(Image)imageTable.get(selections.getSelectedItem());

            // tile the image throughout the Applet
            int y = 0;
            while(y < height)
            {
                int x = 0;
                while(x < width)
                {
                    at.setToTranslation(x, y);

                    // draw the image
                    g2d.drawImage(currImage, at, this);
                    x += imageSize;
                }
                y += imageSize;
            }
        }    // paint

        // called when the tile image Choice is changed
        public void itemStateChanged(ItemEvent e)
        {
            // our drop box has changed-- redraw the scene
            repaint();
        }
    }    // HashTest
```

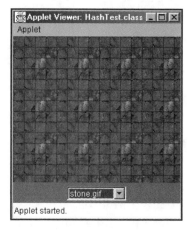

**Figure 4.13**

*Tiling images with the*
*HashTest applet*

Figure 4.13 shows a run of the *HashTest* applet.

Although you saw how to compile and run applets in Chapter 1, I'll go over it again since this is the first applet we'll look at. Compiling the source code is the same as always:

```
javac HashTest.java
```

Once you get a clean compile, running the *HashTest* applet is as easy as the following:

```
appletviewer HashTest.html
```

If the source listing for the *HashTest* applet seems intimidating, don't panic! I'll go over each of the components presented in Part Two. But I felt this was the perfect opportunity to show how the Java `Hashtable` class can help you gear your code toward game development with as little code as possible. For now, focus on how the methods involved in inserting and retrieving values from your table are used. You might also want to open the tile images with your favorite image editor and imagine how they can be tiled over the entire applet window. The magic lies in creating images that visually "lock" together when drawn one after another.

We'll look at another `Hashtable` example in Part Three, when we talk about creating a custom font class. If you understand this example and the table exercise presented in this chapter's exercises, consider yourself ready.

# Conclusion

Please don't treat this as a complete discourse on what Java makes available to you; there are literally hundreds more Java classes available in the standard edition of the API. I just want you to be familiar with some of the more commonly used features that Java provides. In your own Java endeavors, always check the Java API before writing a utility from scratch—chances are there is already a class that provides the functionality you desire, or at least an existing base class to build upon.

In all, Java provides many classes, interfaces, and utilities, such as threads, that allow you to develop powerful applications more quickly, simply, and elegantly than most other languages. I hope that once you understand all the details and levels of extendability behind the Java language, you'll appreciate its beauty and ability to aid the programmer in focusing on problem solving rather than on basic operations.

Try the following exercises and imagine how easily they could be solved in other languages such as C++. I think you'll agree that the classes provided with Java are an invaluable way to get your programs up and running more quickly and efficiently.

# Exercises

**4.1** Write code that reverses the order of a linked-list. (Hint: The Java `LinkedList` is a FIFO structure—which classes do you know that have a LIFO structure?)

**4.2** Would the code from Exercise 4.1 differ greatly to reverse the contents of a `StringBuffer` object?

**4.3** Write a utility class that wraps the `BufferedReader` class and reads various types of information from the keyboard, such as `float` values, `int` values, `boolean` values, etc. You'll want to write methods such as `readInt`, `readFloat`, and so on. Make sure that each component only accepts valid input and prompts the user to reenter the data should it not be valid.

**4.4** Write a program (using the `BufferedReader` class) to read `Strings` from a file named file.txt. The reader should read sequentially throughout the file. File input should be immediately redirected back to standard output. Output an error message if the file does not exist or cannot be opened. (Hint: Use the `FileReader` class found in the `java.io` package.)

**4.5** Rewrite the `Fibonacci` program so that it uses the `Timer` and `TimerTask` classes found in the `java.util` package. I suggest you keep the `Fibonacci` class framework but provide an anonymous inner class to do the timing.

**4.6** Create a `Hashtable` that maps holidays to their calendar dates. Use `java.util.GregorianCalendar` objects as the table values and `String` objects as the keys. For example, to add my favorite holiday to the table, I might write the following:

```
Hashtable ht = new Hashtable();
Calendar c = new GregorianCalendar();
c.set(Calendar.MONTH, Calendar.NOVEMBER);
c.set(Calendar.DAY_OF_MONTH, 3);
ht.put("Tom's Birthday", c);


System.out.println(ht.get("Tom's Birthday"));
```

Try adding some of your own favorite holidays and make sure you can retrieve them from the table.

**4.7** This one is more of a project-style question, so put on your thinking caps. We haven't yet looked at how to create and draw graphics, but you can still write a simple game that uses object-oriented concepts for use on the command line. Write a program that plays the game of blackjack for one player. You will need (at the very least) five classes: a `Card` class, a `Deck` class, a `Hand` class, a `Player` class, and finally, a `Blackjack` class. We've already looked at the `Card` and `Deck` classes in Part I.

The `Blackjack` class will do most of the major game processing. A `Card` will contain just one integer variable to describe which of the 52 cards it is. Refer back to Chapter 3 for more on this class. Your `Deck` will consist of 52 `Card` objects and should call its `shuffle` method before each game. A `Deck` object must also be able to deal the next card in the deck to a specified hand. For the sake of flexibility, the `Hand` class should be able to contain any number of `Card` objects; that way you can reuse the `Hand` class for virtually any card game. The `Player` class should contain the number of games played, as well as the number of games won. It will also contain one `Hand` variable to hold the player's cards. However, make sure that your `Blackjack` class does most of the processing specific to the overall game.

Keep the following details in mind:

- Aces can represent either 1 or 11, depending on which gives a better "fit." For example, A A 2 5 would total 19 points; A A A Q would total 13 points; and A K would be blackjack.
- You might want to ask the user if he or she would like to view the rules of blackjack before play begins.

- If the player can draw five cards without going over 21, he or she automatically wins.

If you need help with this project, feel free to sneak a peek at my source code contained on the CD-ROM. Bonus points will be given for a clean interface and addictive game play.

The toughest part of this program for a newcomer to Java might be making everything work together. I suggest drawing what you want on paper before doing any coding. Also, don't be afraid to provide any methods you feel necessary that I did not specify above. Remember to keep data members private (or protected), and access them only with the proper access methods.

Is blackjack not enough for you? Using the same Card, Deck, and Hand classes, extend the Blackjack program to play a game of five-card draw poker for one player. I'll leave the details up to you. Have fun and good luck!

# Where We Are and Where We're Going

Part Two can seem like a lot to take in all at one time—especially if you're a newcomer to Java or object-oriented programming. It's difficult to compact the specifics of the entire Java language into a few chapters; I doubt a thorough investigation of the entire language could be done in fewer than 1,000 pages. Therefore, if you still feel uncomfortable with what we've covered so far, it might be worth going over again. Try doing the exercises at the end of each chapter or writing some basic programs of your own before moving on. You don't have to be a Java expert to start making games, but having a solid understanding of the basics of Java will allow you to digest the rest of this book more easily. Java is full of quirks and fine points, but it isn't exactly rocket science either (that is, unless you're using it to program rockets).

If you really want to get into the guts of how the Java language works, check out *The Java Language Specification*, which is found within the Java 2 documentation or online at http://java.sun.com/docs/books/jls/second_edition/html/j.title.doc.html.

With that said, you're almost ready to start programming some games. Next we'll take a look at creating graphical user interfaces, along with how to use input devices to really tell your applications who's boss.

# Part Two

# Graphics Development with Java 2-D and the Abstract Window Toolkit

# "I'm not dumb. I just have a command of thoroughly useless information."

## —Calvin, of Calvin and Hobbes

There are numerous ways to deliver the content of your games to others. As you already know, Java applications can be run within any environment that supports Java. Such environments include not only Solaris or Windows, but handheld and "smart" devices as well. Heck, you can even program a blender to function as a game! However, the most popular way of running games is from an applet, either running within a Web browser or Sun's `appletviewer` utility. We'll begin Part Two with a look at the Java `Applet` class and how we can develop visual programs with very little code.

By now, you should have much of the knowledge required to start making games. You know the fundamentals of the Java language and how to use pre-defined Java classes to your advantage. In Part Two, we'll begin our investigation into actual 2-D game programming. To do so, we'll take a look at the Java Abstract Window Toolkit (AWT) and one of its main extensions, Java 2-D. Specifically, we'll examine the following topics:

- **Applet Basics.** What exactly an applet is, as well as applet structure and use.
- **AWT Components.** Including using buttons, drop-boxes, text boxes, and layout managers to provide interaction with the user.
- **Event Handling.** Including how to catch events generated by the mouse and keyboard and respond to these events appropriately.
- **Java 2-D.** A two-chapter overview on modeling, rendering, and filling shapes, loading and drawing images from file, as well as manipulating and rendering text. I'll also discuss topics such as geometry addition, collision-testing, and image enhancement operations.

So turn to Chapter 5, "Applet Basics," and get ready to learn how to create an interactive visual application framework on which to build your Java games.

# CHAPTER 5

# APPLET BASICS

In this chapter we'll look at the components that make up an applet, see how an applet differs from an application, and check out a few applet examples. Since a greater part of this book focuses on developing games within an applet, it is good to first know the basics of how applets work.

We'll also look at how you can put some of the Java Abstract Window Toolkit (AWT) components to use in your applets. The Java AWT contains a set of classes and interfaces for drawing visual components within a window. I find it easiest to think of the AWT in terms of two separate categories: *containers* and *components*. A container represents an object capable of holding other objects. Components refer to the visible objects that the user can interact with. Buttons, radio buttons, and text labels are just a few examples of component objects.

The root of the AWT lies within the `Component` class, located in the `java.awt` package. The `Component` class is an abstract class intended to be extended to create specific controls. All AWT classes, even the container classes, extend the `Component` class. Figure 5.1 illustrates the class hierarchy under the `Component` class. Note this illustration does not show all of the AWT classes; it only shows those that extend the `Component` class.

Before we look at these classes, let's see what exactly an applet is and then set up and run a simple example.

# What Is a Java Applet?

A Java *applet* is simply a piece of software that is embedded within another application. In other words, applets are not stand-alone applications; they are dependent on other software to run. An *applet context* refers to the software that runs an applet. This can be anything from a Web browser to Sun's `appletviewer` utility.

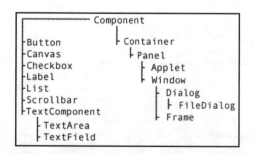

**Figure 5.1**

*Extensions of the Component class*

Applets are great because virtually anyone with a computer and an Internet connection already has the software required to run them. Typically, when a user loads a Web page containing an applet, the applet content is transmitted across the network and loaded into the user's Web browser. An applet's content can be anything from text to graphics to sound and music files.

Another great thing about applets is that they do not have to be downloaded again each time a user wishes to access them. Applets can be permanently downloaded for offline viewing, either within a Web browser or within the `appletviewer` utility.

Applets are a convenient way to deliver game content to your users. Applets are by nature contained within a window and can be easily programmed to respond to user events such as mouse clicks and keystrokes. In languages such as C++, you know it can take a while to get just the window up and running. Applets already contain the skeleton graphical user interface (GUI) for your games; all you need to do is fill it with exciting gaming content.

# Applets Versus Applications

A Java applet is *not* the same as a Java application. Until now, most of our examples have been written as applications. Applications are written to run independently of any software except the Java Virtual Machine. The applications you've seen thus far were console programs, which were run on the command line.

However, there are other ways to deliver application content, such as through the Java Swing classes. Packages such as Swing produce a dedicated window and are not run through applet contexts. However, I find Swing programs to be too bulky to use for games. I prefer to use Swing for "productivity" software rather than gaming software. Additionally, it is not as convenient for the end user to load and run Swing programs as it is applets. That is why I usually choose to use applets for my games. If you prefer application programming to applet programming, be my guest. Most of the concepts we'll cover can be applied to both program paradigms.

# The Structure and Life Cycle of an Applet

Now that you know what an applet is, you should know how an applet actually works. The Java `Applet` class contains the methods needed to initialize and run an applet. Your job is to use inheritance to override the `Applet` class and fill in these

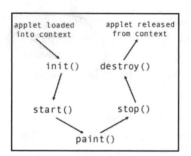

**Figure 5.2**

*The life cycle of a Java applet*

methods as needed. When an applet is loaded into its applet context, certain applet methods are called in a specific order. At the scope of the Applet class, these methods don't actually do anything. However, they are not declared as abstract either, so you don't *have* to override them. Nonetheless, they are provided as empty skeleton methods for your applets to follow.

According to Figure 5.2, after an applet has been loaded into its context its init method is called. Within the init method you should provide the code to initialize your applet. This includes initializing your game objects as well as loading any images or sound your applet may use.

The next method to be called is the start method. It simply informs the applet that it is ready to begin execution. You can use the start method to do things such as begin animation sequences and threads.

After the start method has completed, the paint method is called. This is where the visible applet content is rendered to the window. It passes to it the applet's Graphics context, which is used to present graphic material to the window. Don't worry too much about the Graphics class right now; we'll look at it in greater depth in Chapters 6 and 7.

What happens next is up to you. This is where you'll want to add interactivity between the user and the applet. We'll look at this more in the following chapters. When the user is finished with the applet and either goes to another Web page or closes the browser altogether, the stop and destroy methods are called. The stop method stops the execution of the applet. So if you started an animation within the start method, this is the time to end it. The final method called within an applet is the destroy method. It is here that you should terminate live objects, such as threads, created during the life of the applet.

## Hey, What Happened to main?

In our discussion on applets thus far, there has been no mention of the main method. Actually, Java applets do not contain a main method. Applets are started automatically by their applet context; therefore, there is really no need for a main method. At the API level, all you need to concern yourself with is the fact that the init method is called first, then start, and so on. Later on, you'll see how you can implement the main method to allow your programs to behave as either an applet *or* an application.

# A Sample Applet

Here's the part you've been waiting for—a solid code example of how an applet works. The following program, *ManyShapes*, extends the Applet class and defines only one method: the paint method. The paint method draws 10,000 shapes to the window. Within each iteration of the loop, a random number chooses the shape to be drawn.

```
import java.applet.*;
import java.awt.*;
import java.util.*;

public class ManyShapes extends Applet
{
    // this method overrides the paint method from the Applet class
    public void paint(
        Graphics g  // the Graphics context to draw with
        )
    {
        // create a new number generator
        Random r = new Random();

        // draw 10000 shapes
        for(int i = 0; i < 10000; i++)
        {
            // generate random values for our shape
            int x = r.nextInt()%300;
            int y = r.nextInt()%300;
            int width  = r.nextInt()%300;
            int height = r.nextInt()%300;

            // set a random color
```

```java
        g.setColor(new Color(r.nextInt()));

        // generate a positive number between 0 and 4
        int n = Math.abs(r.nextInt()%5);

        // draw a shape based on the value of n
        switch(n)
        {
            case(0):
                g.draw3DRect(x, y, width, height, true);
                break;
            case(1):
                g.drawRect(x, y, width, height);
                break;
            case(2):
                g.drawOval(x, y, width, height);
                break;
            case(3):
                g.fillRect(x, y, width, height);
                break;
            case(4):
                g.fillOval(x, y, width, height);
                break;

            // this shouldn't happen; but if it does, print a message
            default:
                System.out.println("Invalid case: " + n);
                break;
        }   // switch
    }   // for
}   // paint

}   // ManyShapes
```

Again, you only had to define a single method for your program. Don't define methods such as the init method because you have no class members to initialize. Try running the code above if you haven't already. If you need a refresher on compiling and running applets, see the next section.

# Running Java Applets

Here's a refresher on how to compile and run your newly created applet from the command line. If you haven't already, type the code listing above into a file named ManyShapes.java. Now you must create an .html file containing the `applet` tag that loads your applet. The following .html code loads the *ManyShapes* applet with a width and height of 300 pixels. I also added a horizontal rule (`<hr>`) tag before and after to applet to set it off from the rest of the file. Include it if you wish.

```
<html>

<head>
<title>ManyShapes</title>
</head>

<body>
<hr>
<applet code=ManyShapes.java width=300 height=300></applet>
<hr>

</body>
</html>
```

You can now save the .html file to any name you want; for a lack of creativity, I named mine ManyShapes.html.

Now you can compile your source code. As always, use the `javac` utility as such:

```
javac ManyShapes.java
```

Fix any errors that may occur, and then recompile. Once you get a clean compile, you can simply open the .html file using your favorite (Java-enabled) Web browser, or use the `appletviewer` utility:

```
appletviewer ManyShapes.html
```

Congratulations! Your first Java applet. A sample run of the *ManyShapes* applet is shown in Figure 5.3.

**Figure 5.3**

*The* ManyShapes *applet*

# Common AWT Components

A handy way to get input from your users is with some of the commonly found AWT components, such as buttons and text fields. In the next few sections, we'll look at several of these components and how they can help your applets take shape.

Adding AWT components to your applets is fairly simple. First of all, if you antici-pate using a visual AWT component in your programs, you must first implement an *EventListener* interface in the class definitions that are interested in receiving messages from your component. The EventListener class is located within the java.util package, but its subinterfaces that you'll typically use are located in the java.awt.event package.

C++ programs can equate implementing the *EventListener* interface to adding a callback function to receive system messages. Typically, it will be your applet class that will receive component messages, hence it will implement an *EventListener*.

After implementing the proper *EventListener* interfaces you can define which AWT controls your program needs. Each control will usually reside as a private (or protected) class member within your applet. After allocating memory to your AWT controls you must register them with the applet so that their events will be caught. Figure 5.4 illustrates how you can attach a button to your applet and catch any action events that occur.

To solidify this in your mind, I offer the steps needed to add AWT components to your applets:

- Implement your applet class as a subinterface of *EventListener*.
- Define the methods required by implemented *EventListener* interfaces; you can leave these methods empty for now.

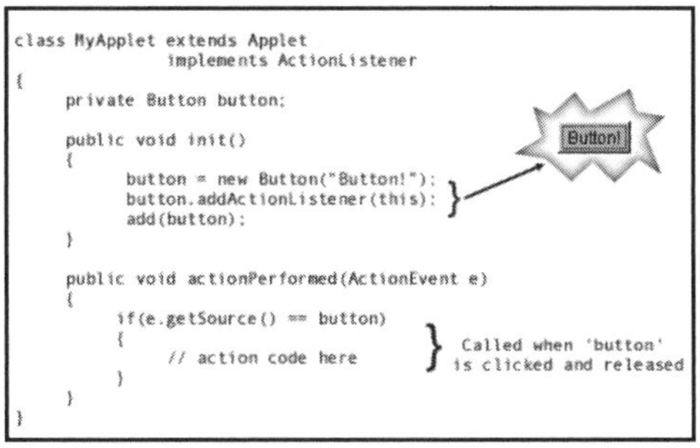

```
class MyApplet extends Applet
             implements ActionListener
{
    private Button button;

    public void init()
    {
        button = new Button("Button!");
        button.addActionListener(this);
        add(button);
    }

    public void actionPerformed(ActionEvent e)
    {
        if(e.getSource() == button)
        {
            // action code here
        }
    }
}
```

**Figure 5.4**

*Interaction with a
Button object*

- Add private or protected AWT class members to your class.
- Initialize, register, and add your newly created AWT components to the container.
- Fill in the methods defined by your *EventListener* interfaces.

In the following sections, we'll look at more concrete examples of using AWT components within your applets.

# Buttons

*Buttons* are a quick and easy way to allow your users to make choices inside your applets. Figure 5.4 showed us a simple model of button usage. Let's jump right into a more complex example that will actually allow a button to generate an action. The following program, *ButtonTest*, contains a single Button object. When the button is pressed, the window's background color will change. The program cycles through four different background colors.

```java
import java.applet.*;
import java.awt.*;
import java.awt.event.*;

public class ButtonTest extends Applet implements ActionListener
{
    // a single, lonely Button
    private Button button;

    // background colors used by the applet
    private final Color bgColors[] = new Color[] {
        Color.RED, Color.BLUE, Color.GREEN, Color.YELLOW
```

```java
      };

      // index to the current background color
      private int currentColor;

      // this method overrides the init method from the Applet class
      public void init()
      {
          // create a new Button object, register it with the applet, then add
          // it to the applet
          button = new Button("Press me!");
          button.addActionListener(this);
          add(button);

          // initialize the index for background coloring
          currentColor = -1;
          changeWindowColor();
      }

      // this method overrides the paint method from the Applet class
      public void paint(Graphics g)
      {
          // set the window's background color based on the current index
          setBackground(bgColors[currentColor]);

          // set the foreground (text) of the button to the background color
          button.setForeground(bgColors[currentColor]);

      }   // paint

      // increments the current background color index
      private void changeWindowColor()
      {
          currentColor++;
          if(currentColor == bgColors.length)
          {
              currentColor = 0;
          }
```

```
    }

    // implementation of the actionPerformed method from the ActionListener
    // interface
    public void actionPerformed(ActionEvent e)
    {
        // if button fired the event, change the window's background color
        if(button == e.getSource())
        {
            changeWindowColor();
            repaint();
        }
    }

}    // ButtonTest
```

As you can see, the Applet class implements the *ActionListener* interface in order to register itself as an object capable of receiving button events. *ActionListener* defines a single method, actionPerformed, which takes an ActionEvent object as its parameter. When an event occurs (such as clicking and releasing a button), an ActionEvent object that describes the event is built and sent to the actionPerformed method. This is where you can define the actual action that occurs.

You should also note the use of the getSource method from the ActionEvent class. It returns the Object that triggered the event. This is helpful when you have multiple components that register with the same *ActionListener*. Notice that for the above example, you don't necessarily need to check the source because the applet contains only a single Button object.

Examine each method in the *ButtonTest* applet from top to bottom to understand exactly what's going on. You might also want to type it in and try it for yourself. Your friends and family will enjoy hours of fun cycling through the four different colored backgrounds. Check out a screenshot of the *ButtonTest* applet in Figure 5.5.

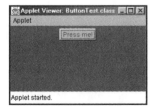

**Figure 5.5**

*The* ButtonTest *applet*

# Radio Buttons

There will be times when you'll want the user to select among several values, or you'll want to keep track of "on" and "off" values for a specific attribute. This is where *radio buttons* (you might call them *check boxes*) come in handy. Radio buttons differ from regular buttons in that interaction with radio buttons is not caught by the *ActionListener* interface. Instead, your applet must implement the *ItemListener* interface. Much like the *ActionListener* interface, the *ItemListener* interface defines a single method, in this case the itemStateChanged method, which takes an ItemEvent as its parameter.

Radio buttons can be added to your applets singularly or within *button groups*. To allow the user to toggle the sound on or off, you might use a single radio button. To create such a labeled radio button initially set to "on," type the following:

```
Checkbox sound = new Checkbox("Enable Sound", true);
```

To access the state of a radio button, you can use the getState method, such as the following:

```
boolean soundEnabled = sound.getState();
```

Another way to use radio buttons is within button groups. Button groups preserve the idea of a single selection within the group. When a member of the group is toggled "on," all other buttons within the group are automatically toggled "off." Use this when your applet requires *only one* of a group of items to be active. The Java CheckboxGroup class is used to hold a group of radio buttons.

The following program, *CheckboxTest*, uses a CheckboxGroup to hold a number of selections. Each time a different item is selected, a message is printed to the console (see Figure 5.6).

```
import java.applet.*;
import java.awt.*;
import java.awt.event.*;

public class CheckboxTest extends Applet implements ItemListener
{
    // a CheckboxGroup to hold a number of items
    private CheckboxGroup cbg;

    // selections used by the applet
    private final String selections[] = {
```

```
                "Pepsi", "Coke", "Mountain Dew", "Tab"
    };

    private Checkbox createCheckbox(
         String label,          // label for Checkbox
         CheckboxGroup group,   // group Checkbox belongs to
         boolean enabled        // true to set this Checkbox "on"
         )
    {
         Checkbox cb = new Checkbox(label, group, enabled);
         cb.addItemListener(this);
         return cb;
    }


    // this method overrides the init method from the Applet class
    public void init()
    {
         cbg = new CheckboxGroup();
         for(int i = 0; i < selections.length; i++)
         {
              add(createCheckbox(selections[i], cbg, false));
         }
    }


    // implementation of the itemStateChanged method from the ItemListener
    // interface
    public void itemStateChanged(ItemEvent e)
    {
         // print out a message about the selection
         System.out.println("Yes, I certainly agree, " +
                             cbg.getSelectedCheckbox().getLabel() +
                          " is very delicious!");
    }


}   // CheckboxTest
```

Note the use of the *ItemListener* interface and the addItemListener method. I also created a createCheckbox method to aid in creating Checkbox objects. Evil, indeed.

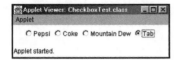

**Figure 5.6**

*Testing the*
CheckboxTest *applet*

# Making Important Choices

Another component you might find useful is the easy-to-use Choice class. Microsoft
Foundation Classes (MFC) programmers will probably know these objects as *combo
boxes*. Either way, a *choice* simply provides the user with a drop-down box of items to
select from. Items maintained within the list are kept as String objects.

Much like the Checkbox class, Choice objects register themselves to *ItemListener* classes
that wish to receive events about them. *ItemListener* classes must implement the
itemStateChanged method. Again, this method takes an ItemEvent as its parameter.

Let's jump right into an example. The following applet listing, *ChoiceTest*, creates a
Choice object with the very scientific and technical names of several parts of our
skeletal system. When the state of the Choice box is altered, an informative message
about our skeletal system is printed to the console.

```java
import java.applet.*;
import java.awt.*;
import java.awt.event.*;

public class ChoiceTest extends Applet implements ItemListener
{
    // technical names of some skeletal bones
    public final String[] BONES =
            { "foot", "leg", "knee", "hip", "rib", "shoulder", "neck" };

    // a drop-down box containing the above String array
    private Choice choice;

    public void init()
    {
        setBackground(new Color(125, 0, 225));

        // create our Choice and register it as an item listener
        choice = new Choice();
        for(int i = 0; i < BONES.length; i++)
```

```
            {
                // add a String to describe each choice
                choice.add(BONES[i]);
            }
            choice.addItemListener(this);
            add(choice);
        }


        // called when the state of a registered listener is changed
        public void itemStateChanged(ItemEvent e)
        {
            // generate a different index than the one currently selected
            int index;
            do
            {
                index = (int)(Math.random()*BONES.length);
            } while(index == choice.getSelectedIndex());

            // print out an important fact about the human anatomy
            System.out.println("The " + choice.getSelectedItem() +
                               " bone is connected to the " + BONES[index] +
                               " bone...");
        }

    }   // ChoiceTest
```

Figure 5.7 shows us the *ChoiceTest* applet in action.

Not only is the *ChoiceTest* applet a great example of how to use Java `Choice` objects, but it is rather informative as well.

Now let's switch directions and try something a little more practical; let's develop an applet that will allow the user to play and loop different audio files.

**Figure 5.7**

*The* ChoiceTest *applet*

## Playing and Looping Audio Files

I thought this would be a good time to jump topics and look at something just about every game needs: sound. I remember when I was in second grade and I had to play *The Legend of Zelda* on mute late at night on school nights. It wasn't nearly as fun.

In the ancient days when MS-DOS games were all the rage, developers had to write separate drivers to make games work on different sound cards. As more and more different types of sound cards became available, the harder it was for game developers to keep up. Luckily for us, today there are easier ways to play audio files, such as with Microsoft's DirectSound package. But even with DirectSound it can take a while to get a good sound engine up and running. Heck, DirectSound doesn't even have a standard way to load audio files. What a pain!

Although playing sound within a Java applet is a rather trivial task, I'd first like to make a few points about playing sounds in Java. First of all, I suggest using the Sun .au format for all of your sound files. It's a good format that is guaranteed to work across platforms. Although other formats might work well within Windows, they might not be valid formats on other systems such as Linux or the Mac.

In this section, we'll focus on how to load and play audio files from within a Java applet. The packages related to `java.sound` contain a lot more as far as manipulating and sampling audio files; however, since some of it requires manual installations and security access that may be inconvenient for the user to adjust, using it might not be the best idea for games. But feel free to refer to these packages anyway if you're still curious about the deeper features of sound manipulation under Java.

For now, let's focus on the most direct way to load audio files within an applet. The `Applet` class provides several ways to load and play audio files. There are two methods for direct audio playback, both named `play`; one takes a `URL` (Uniform Resource Locator) object along with a `String` object, and the other just takes a `URL`. These methods create a temporary *AudioClip* object and immediately stream its data to audio output. No errors are generated if the audio file cannot be found or is otherwise unavailable.

The `play` method wastes memory and can potentially slow down applets since the audio data is read and played on the fly. A better way to handle audio for games is to cache the audio data ahead of time. This way if a sound is requested for playback over and over, it can be read from a single source that is already loaded into memory. For this, Java provides the *AudioClip* interface for playing, looping, and stopping audio playback. Although *AudioClip* is an interface, all versions of Java for varying platforms define their own internal class implementations that define this interface. Since you're programming generically, all you need to worry about is the *AudioClip* interface at this scope.

To create an *AudioClip* object, use the Applet getAudioClip method. Like the play method, this method takes either a URL object or a URL object along with a String object. I prefer using the version that takes two parameters when my audio content is stored at the same location as my applet bytecode. For instance, the following will load a file named bang.au:

```
AudioClip ac = getAudioClip(getCodeBase(), "bang.au");
```

The getCodeBase method returns the URL from where the applet code is located. So whether you decide to run the applet remotely or locally, the above method call will work properly.

A third way to load an audio clip is with the Applet newAudioClip method. It comes in a single flavor that takes a URL object that points directly to the audio file. Since this is a static method, it is useful for when you want to load an AudioFile but you do not have a reference to a valid Applet object.

The following code listing, *AudioChoiceTest*, loads in several AudioClip objects from file and uses a Choice to allow the user to select a clip. There are also buttons that allow playback, looped playback, and termination of playback for the clips. As always, this applet is available on the CD-ROM for those who don't feel like typing it in.

```
import java.applet.*;
import java.awt.*;
import java.awt.event.*;

// allows the user to choose from several audio clips to play
public class AudioChoiceTest extends Applet implements ActionListener
{
    // audio names for this program
    public final String[] AUDIO =
            { "ping", "pop", "return", "salvation", "shuffle", "squish" };

    // a drop-down box containing the above String array
    private Choice choice;

    // the actual audio clip data
    private AudioClip[] clips;

    // control buttons to play or stop sounds
```

```java
private Button playClip;
private Button loopClip;
private Button stopClip;
private Button stopAllClips;

// tracks which clips are currently being played
private boolean[] clipsPlaying;

public void init()
{
    setBackground(new Color(48, 255, 0));

    // create the drop-down box and AudioClip objects
    choice        = new Choice();
    clips         = new AudioClip[AUDIO.length];
    clipsPlaying = new boolean[AUDIO.length];
    for(int i = 0; i < AUDIO.length; i++)
    {
        // add a String to describe each choice
        choice.add(AUDIO[i]);
        // add pathname and extension to the audio clip name
        clips[i] = getAudioClip(getCodeBase(), "audio/"+AUDIO[i]+".au");

        // a value of false means that the clip is not playing
        clipsPlaying[i] = false;
    }
    add(choice);

    // create the buttons to play or stop audio clips
    playClip = new Button("Play clip");
    playClip.addActionListener(this);
    add(playClip);

    loopClip = new Button("Loop clip");
    loopClip.addActionListener(this);
    add(loopClip);

    stopClip = new Button("Stop clip");
    stopClip.addActionListener(this);
```

```
            add(stopClip);

            stopAllClips = new Button("Stop all clips");
            stopAllClips.addActionListener(this);
            add(stopAllClips);

            // gray-out the stop buttons if there is nothing to stop
            stopClip.setEnabled(false);
            stopAllClips.setEnabled(false);
        }


    // stops all playing audio clips
    public void stop()
    {
            for(int i = 0; i < AUDIO.length; i++)
            {
                if(clipsPlaying[i])
                {
                    clips[i].stop();
                }
            }
    }


    // allows the user to play, loop, or stop the audio clips
    public void actionPerformed(ActionEvent e)
    {
            int clipIndex  = choice.getSelectedIndex();
            AudioClip clip = clips[clipIndex];

            // play the selected clip
            if(e.getSource() == playClip)
            {
                clip.play();
                stopClip.setEnabled(true);
                stopAllClips.setEnabled(true);
                clipsPlaying[clipIndex] = true;
            }

            // loop the selected clip
```

```
else if(e.getSource() == loopClip)
{
    clip.loop();
    stopClip.setEnabled(true);
    stopAllClips.setEnabled(true);
    clipsPlaying[clipIndex] = true;
}

// stop the selected clip
else if(e.getSource() == stopClip)
{
    clip.stop();
    stopClip.setEnabled(false);
    stopAllClips.setEnabled(false);

    clipsPlaying[clipIndex] = false;

    // enable stop buttons if at least one clip is playing
    for(int i = 0; i < AUDIO.length; i++)
    {
        if(clipsPlaying[i])
        {
            stopClip.setEnabled(true);
            stopAllClips.setEnabled(true);
            break;
        }
    }
}

// stop all playing clips
else if(e.getSource() == stopAllClips)
{
    for(int i = 0; i < AUDIO.length; i++)
    {
        if(clipsPlaying[i])
        {
            clips[i].stop();
            clipsPlaying[i] = false;
```

```
                    }
            }

            stopClip.setEnabled(false);
            stopAllClips.setEnabled(false);
        }
    }

    }     // AudioChoiceTest
```

Figure 5.8 gives you an inside look at the *AudioChoiceTest* applet.

I threw in a liberal amount of inline documentation, so the above code should be pretty self-explanatory. Try looping several sounds all at once. Java allows several sounds to be played simultaneously and produces a composite of all simultaneously playing streams. This enables you to produce some nice effects with minimal effort.

One final word of caution: The *AudioChoiceTest* is bound to annoy both friends and foes alike. So make sure your speakers are on all the way and try this one out late at night when everyone is asleep. Try adding in your own annoying sounds and setting them for loop playback next time you leave the house.

> **NOTE**
>
> If you wish to provide an interface where the user can make several selections from the same group of data, consider using a `List` object. For more on the `List` class, see your Java 2 documentation.

I hope you have a good feel for playing sounds within an applet. Now we'll move on and talk more about the Java AWT, starting with text fields.

# Text Fields

*Text fields* are a very easy way to read string input from your users. When creating a text field, you will typically want to specify the maximum number of characters the

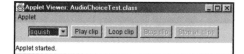

**Figure 5.8**

*The* AudioChoiceTest *applet*

field can contain. You can also specify optional default text within the field. The following illustrates two ways to create text fields and add them to your applet:

```
TextField tf1 = new TextField("I am TextField tf1!", 30);
add(tf1);
TextField tf2 = new TextField(22);
add(tf2);
```

Another useful method in the TextField class is the getText method. It returns a String object containing the field's text. The following prints out the contents of tf1 to the console:

```
System.out.println(tf1.getText());
```

You do not need any listeners to retrieve text from a text field. The next section shows an example of how to use a TextField object in your applets.

## Labels

A Java *label* is simply a single line of static text painted to the screen. Labels are great for adding titles to components or to request user input. The following creates a simple label, as well as a text field and an "OK" button to retrieve the user's name. You can see the output for this code in Figure 5.9.

**NOTE**

In addition to adding listeners to your objects, you can remove them as well. For instance, the Button class has a removeActionListener method that will remove the action listener from the object. Use this method if you ever want to disable components or you need to cease listener feedback. Methods that remove listeners may also be called when the applet's stop method is invoked. However, since all child threads are killed once their parent thread is killed, removing listeners when your applet stops is not completely necessary.

```
Label label = new Label("Enter your name (15 chars max.): ");
add(label);
TextField field = new TextField(15);
add(field);
Button button = new Button("OK");
button.addActionListener(this);
add(button);
```

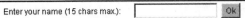

**Figure 5.9**

*Prompting for the user's name*

# Layout Management

Thus far, it might appear as though the components layout has been added haphazardly or randomly to the applet windows. Actually, there *is* a method to the madness. So how does an applet know how to place its components? The answer lies within the use of *layout managers*. `LayoutManager` is an interface implemented by classes that know how to place components within a container. There are several classes within the `java.awt` package that implement the *LayoutManager* interface. We'll start by looking at the `FlowLayout` class.

## The FlowLayout Class

The `FlowLayout` class is perhaps the simplest of all of the `java.awt` layout classes. It simply lays out components from left to right, in the order in which they were added to the applet. This is the default layout manager, so it is used automatically even if you do not specify one directly. All of the applet examples you've seen thus far have been using it implicitly, so you've seen how it works.

However, if you want to specify use of the `FlowLayout` class (or any other layout manager) directly, you would typically call the `setLayout` method within your container's `init` method, such as the following:

```
setLayout(new FlowLayout());
add(new Button("Layout"));
add(new Button("Managers"));
add(new Button("Rule!"));
```

Why would you ever want to explicitly specify a `FlowLayout` if it is the default? You can send parameters to the `FlowLayout` constructor to specify both the layout's alignment as well as the horizontal and vertical gaps between components.

Other than the default constructor, there are two other `FlowLayout` constructor methods. The first takes an `int` value describing the alignment of the layout. There are five values that can be sent as the parameter: `LEFT`, `CENTER`, `RIGHT`, `LEADING`, and `TRAILING`. The following shows how to create a left-justified `FlowLayout` with horizontal and vertical gap size of 10:

```
setLayout(new FlowLayout(FlowLayout.LEFT, 10, 10));
```

If no parameters are sent to the constructor, the default alignment is `FlowLayout.CENTER` and the default gap size is set to five pixels. Figure 5.10 shows a right-justified `FlowLayout` with three options to put the hurt on your opponent.

**Figure 5.10**

*A right-justified*
`FlowLayout`

# The GridLayout Class

The `GridLayout` class represents a second type of layout manager. A `GridLayout` places components within a grid with a specified number of rows and columns. All components within the grid are of equal size.

Creating a `GridLayout` is similar to creating a `FlowLayout`, except that it has different constructor methods. The default constructor creates a layout containing a single component per column. The other two are listed below:

```
GridLayout (int rows, int cols);
GridLayout (int rows, int cols, int hgap, int vgap);
```

Use of these constructors should be self-explanatory. If you don't specify the gaps their values will default to zero. If you specify either the rows or columns value as zero, or you add more than *rows x columns* components, the layout manager will adjust its values so that the components still fit within the grid.

The following listing, *GridTest*, creates a 3 x 3 arrangement of labels. There is a five-pixel horizontal and vertical gap between the labels. Each label background color is green so you can see the gaps.

```
import java.applet.*;
import java.awt.*;

public class GridTest extends Applet
{
    public void init()
    {
        // create a String and a StringTokenizer to parse the String
        String string = "My Head Is My Only House Unless It Rains";
        java.util.StringTokenizer st = new java.util.StringTokenizer(string);

        // create a 3 by 3 grid layout with a 5 pixel gap between components
        setLayout(new GridLayout(3, 3, 5, 5));

        // for each String token, create a label with a green background and
        // add it to the panel
        while(st.hasMoreTokens())
```

```
            {
                Label label = new Label(st.nextToken(), Label.CENTER);
                label.setBackground(Color.green);
                add(label);
            }
        }

    }    // GridTest
```

Check out Figure 5.11 for output to the *GridTest* applet.

## The BorderLayout Class

The BorderLayout class is yet another type of layout manager. This class arranges components according to the four ordinal directions (north, south, east, west), plus a fifth "center" location.  Figure 5.12 shows how all five locations of a BorderLayout are established relative to one another.

The code to create a BorderLayout containing buttons similar to Figure 5.12 might look like the following:

```
setLayout(new BorderLayout());
add(new Button("North"),  BorderLayout.NORTH);
add(new Button("South"),  BorderLayout.SOUTH);
add(new Button("East"),   BorderLayout.EAST);
add(new Button("West"),   BorderLayout.WEST);
add(new Button("Center"), BorderLayout.CENTER);
```

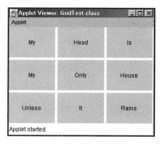

**Figure 5.11**

*The* GridTest *applet*

**Figure 5.12**

*Component arrangement according to the* BorderLayout *class*

Other than the default constructor, there is also a constructor that takes the horizontal and the vertical gap size, respectively, to separate the components.

## The CardLayout Class

The CardLayout class stacks components on top of one another like a deck of cards. The CardLayout class has two constructors: the default constructor as well as one that takes the horizontal and vertical gap sizes.

The following applet animates through 10 Button objects labeled "Card 1" through "Card 10." The next button in the set is presented every second. The *CardTest* applet uses the CardLayout for layout management and a Thread object to do the animation.

```java
import java.awt.*;
import java.applet.*;

public class CardTest extends Applet implements Runnable
{
    // a Thread to act as the timer
    private Thread timer;

    public void init()
    {
        // create a new CardLayout
        setLayout(new CardLayout());

        // create 10 buttons stacked within the CardLayout
        for(int i = 1; i <= 10; i++)
        {
            // the second parameter is a mandatory String representation
            // of the Button to add
            add(new Button("Card " + i), "Card " + i);
        }

        // register this applet as a Thread
        timer = new Thread(this);
    }

    public void start()
    {
```

```
        timer.start();
    }

    public void stop()
    {
        timer = null;
    }

    // define the run method as prescribed in the Runnable interface
    public void run()
    {
        CardLayout layout = (CardLayout)getLayout();

        // get a reference to this thread
        Thread t = Thread.currentThread();

        // loop while the thread is active
        while(t == timer)
        {
            layout.next(this);

            // wait one second between updates
            try
            {
                timer.sleep(1000);
            }
            catch(InterruptedException e) { return; }
        }
    }   // run

}   // CardTest
```

Figure 5.13 shows a sample *CardTest* applet run.

There are some notable methods contained within the CardLayout class that were not used in the above code listing. The first and last methods display the first and last component in the layout, respectively. In addition to the next method, there is also a previous method, which displays the previous component in the layout. Each of these four methods takes a Container as its parameter; in this case, it's the applet itself. We will look more at the Container class in the next section.

**Figure 5.13**

*Execution of the
CardTest applet*

A fifth `CardLayout` method worth looking at is the `show` method. It takes a `Container` as its first parameter and a `String` as its second. The `String` should match one of the `String` objects sent as a parameter to the add method when creating the layout. For example, when adding buttons to the layout I associated the button labeled "Card 1" with the string "Card 1," the button labeled "Card2" was associated with the string "Card 2," and so on. Therefore, the following code would display the card labeled "Card 5":

```
layout.show(this, "Card 5");
```

# Containers

Thus far, you have mostly looked at component classes and how they can be arranged within an applet. Now let's look at container classes.

Recall from our definition that a container can contain another component—even another container. Containers are separated into two main categories: those that can be moved freely and those that remain in a fixed position. In Figure 5.14, the left-hand branch of the `Container` hierarchy (`Window` and its child classes) contains the containers that can be moved freely; they exist as dedicated windows. The right-

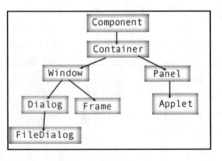

**Figure 5.14**

*The `Container` class
hierarchy*

hand branch stemming from Container (Panel and Applet) contains those that are attached to another surface, such as a Web browser or appletviewer.

Let's extend our discussion of applets by looking at the Panel class before looking at the left-hand side of the Container class hierarchy.

## The Panel Class

If you look at the Java documentation, you'll see that the Applet class is a subclass of the Panel class. Panel, in turn, is a subclass of Container. An important property of the Container hierarchy is the fact that it's the Container class that actually defines methods such as setLayout. Therefore, you can make the call to setLayout at any level in the hierarchy. This becomes important when you wish to embed several layout managers within the same Applet window.

You've already learned how to set up a few different layout managers within you-applets. When you set up a layout manager within a panel (such as an applet), i controls the *entire* panel. So, what if you want to set up several *different* layouts withi the *same* window

The answer lies within a very special property of panels. Unlike classes derivin from Window, which can be moved independently, Panel classes must be attached t another surface. The applets that you write are attached to a Web browser or th appletviewer utility. You can actually embed several Panel or Container objects to parent Container object. Each object that is attached to the parent Container can hav its own layout manager. Using this model, you can create some rather elaborat layouts within your applets. Figure 5.15 shows how you can combine panels with different layouts to create a more complex layout.

The following code, *PanelTest*, illustrates a panel layout similar to that shown in Figure 5.15. Here, two Panel objects are created, each with a different layout. Several Button objects are added to each panel, and then the panels are added to the applet. The applet will use the default FlowLayout manager to display the two panels.

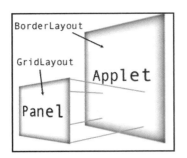

**Figure 5.15**

*Embedding one Container within another*

```java
import java.awt.*;
import java.applet.*;

public class PanelTest extends Applet
{
    public void init()
    {
        // set the applet's layout to the default FlowLayout
        setLayout(new FlowLayout());

        // create a Panel with a 2x2 GridLayout and attach 4 buttons
        // to it, then attach the panel to the parent applet
        Panel p1 = new Panel();
        p1.setLayout(new GridLayout(2, 2));
        p1.add(new Button("B1"));
        p1.add(new Button("B2"));
        p1.add(new Button("B3"));
        p1.add(new Button("B4"));
        add(p1);

        // create a second Panel with a BorderLayout and attach 5 buttons
        // to it, then attach the panel to the applet
        Panel p2 = new Panel();
        p2.setLayout(new BorderLayout());
        p2.add(new Button("North"),  BorderLayout.NORTH);
        p2.add(new Button("South"),  BorderLayout.SOUTH);
        p2.add(new Button("East"),   BorderLayout.EAST);
        p2.add(new Button("West"),   BorderLayout.WEST);
        p2.add(new Button("Center"), BorderLayout.CENTER);
        add(p2);

    }   // init

}   // PanelTest
```

Since the above code does not save references to each button, there is no way to catch events fired by them. Of course, a *real* applet would implement *ActionListener* and hold references to the buttons as private members; the above code merely serves as a simple example. The result of the above code is shown within a 150 x 125 window in Figure 5.16.

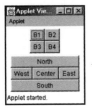

**Figure 5.16**

*The* PanelTest *applet*

# Creating Custom Components

To get more power out of your applets, you can extend component or container classes to behave any way you want them to. We'll start out with a simple example that uses a single form, then build up to a more complete example.

Suppose you are developing a role-playing game where the user can customize his or her character. An important aspect of role-playing character development is skill allocation. Given an initial number of "skill points," your user can allocate points towards different skills. The more skill points an attribute has, the greater that skill is for the character. You've undoubtedly seen this before in games you've played.

The *AttributeTest* applet allows the user to allocate 10 skill points among four skill types: Strength, Wisdom, Agility, and Magic. The code for this applet introduces two classes that extend basic AWT components to add functionality to your program: AttributeButton and AttributePanel. The AttributeButton class extends the Button class and adds a way to link itself to an AttributePanel and update its contents. The AttributePanel class contains a description of an attribute along with the points allocated to that attribute. It also contains two AttributeButton objects for reallocating attribute points. The user can "tweak" allocated points among the attributes until he or she is satisfied with the final allocation.

Enough of my babble—go ahead and dig into this somewhat lengthy example, then check out the screenshot in Figure 5.17.

```
import java.applet.*;
import java.awt.*;
import java.awt.event.*;

// allows an attribute value to be adjusted
class AttributeButton extends Button
{
    // the Panel that owns this button
```

```java
private AttributePanel parent;

public AttributeButton(String label, AttributePanel ap)
{
    super(label);
    parent = ap;
}
 // updates the parent attribute's valu
 public int updatePanel
     int pointsRemaining  // points left to allocat


     // allocate a point for 'plus' button
     if(getLabel().equals("+")

         // only allocate if there's points remainin
         if(pointsRemaining > 0

             parent.allocatePoints(1)
             return -1

         else return 0


     // otherwise, deallocate a poin
     els

         // don't allow negative allocatio
         if(parent.getPointsAllocated() > 0

             parent.allocatePoints(-1)
             return 1

         else return 0

     }
```

```
    }

}    // AttributeButton
// allows the value for single character Attribute to be adjuste
class AttributePanel extends Pane

    // text description of the attribut
    private String attribute

    // Label holding the points allocated to this attribut
    private Label pointsAllocated

    public AttributePanel(String attr, ActionListener l

        attribute = attr

        pointsAllocated = new Label("0", Label.CENTER)

        // set the panel layout within a 3x1 gri
        setLayout(new GridLayout(3, 1))

        setBackground(Color.GREEN)

        // add Labels to describe attribut
        add(new Label(attr, Label.CENTER))
        add(pointsAllocated)

        // attach the +/- buttons to the parent ActionListene
        Button incr = new AttributeButton("+", this)
        incr.addActionListener(l)
        Button decr = new AttributeButton("-", this)
        decr.addActionListener(l)

        // add another Panel with the plus/minus button

    Panel p = new Panel();
```

```java
            p.add(incr);
            p.add(decr);
            add(p);
    }


    // updates the pointsAllocated label
    public void allocatePoints(int n)
    {
        int value = getPointsAllocated() + n;
        pointsAllocated.setText("" + value);
    }
      // returns the points allocated to this attribut
      public int getPointsAllocated(

           return Integer.parseInt(pointsAllocated.getText())


      public String toString(

           // return a verbose description of the attribut
           return attribute + ": " + getPointsAllocated()


}       // AttributePane

public class AttributeTest extends Applet implements ActionListene

      // overall points remaining to allocat
      Label pointsRemaining

      // the attributes for this apple
    private final String ATTRS[] = { "Strength", "Wisdom", "Agility", "Magic" }

      public void init(

           pointsRemaining = new Label("Points remaining: 10", Label.CENTER)


           // set the applet's layout to a FlowLayout
```

```
        setLayout(new FlowLayout(FlowLayout.CENTER, 5, 10));

        // add the components to the layout
        for(int i = 0; i < ATTRS.length; i++)
        {
            add(new AttributePanel(ATTRS[i], this));
        }
          add(pointsRemaining)

    }     // ini

    /
    public void actionPerformed(ActionEvent e

        // get the points left to allocat
        int n = Integer.parseInt(pointsRemaining.getText().substring(18))

        // update the Button's Panel and the main Labe
        n += ((AttributeButton)e.getSource()).updatePanel(n)
        pointsRemaining.setText("Points remaining: " + n)



    }     // AttributeTes
```

Graphically, the *AttributeTest* applet may not be the most elegant applet ever created but you get the point. After we talk more about graphics and imaging in Chapters and 8, you'll be able to spruce it up quite nicely. For now, focus on how th `AttributeButton` and `AttributePanel` classes extend basic AWT components and ho the classes can communicate with one another

The last section of this chapter extends the*AttributeTest* applet into a more complet way to define a character in a simple role-playing game.

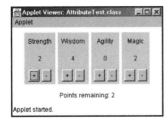

**Figure 5.17**

*Using custom components in the* AttributeTest *applet*

# A Complete Example

It is now time to put what you know about components and containers together and create an applet that can actually do something quite useful.

Our previous example demonstrated how to use basic applet components to create a character profile for a role-playing game. Although it was pretty snazzy for a beginning applet, there are a few things that can be done to improve upon it, such as:

- **Adding more attribute panels.** It might also be nice to allow the user to enter his or her name, choose a profession and gender, as well as review a summary of selected attributes.

- **Increasing flexibility.** If you want to have multiple attribute menus, it might be nice to allow them to extend from a single base class with methods common to all attribute menus. This way you can program more flexibly, which will allow you to add and change your applet more easily.

Okay, great. So let's improve upon the *AttributeTest* applet and allow the user to create a more complicated character. By using the improvements stated above, you can create a much more useful application.

The idea for the *CharacterBuilder* applet is to create a CardLayout that can be traversed by a set of buttons. Each card in the layout will consist of a panel containing options for a single character attribute. The user can visit each card and select his or her preferences, such as name, profession, and gender. The user will also be able to allocate skills given a finite number of allocation points, as seen in the original *AttributeTest* applet. Figure 5.18 shows the basic layout for this extended layout.

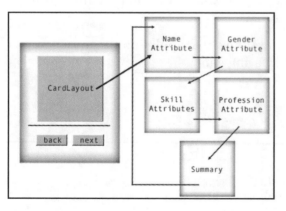

**Figure 5.18**

*Designing the CharacterBuilder applet*

To add flexibility to the applet, let's define an abstract AttributePanel class to serve as the base class for all panels that display character attributes. To get you started, here's the source listing for the AttributePanel class:

```java
// file: AttributePanel.java
import java.awt.*;

// Panel for holding character attributes
public abstract class AttributePanel extends Panel
{
    // text description of the attribute
    protected String attribute;
    public AttributePanel(String attr

        attribute = attr


    public final String getAttribute(

        return attribute


    // force subclasses to override the toString metho
    public abstract String toString()

}      // AttributePane
```

The abstract AttributePanel class serves two main purposes. First, it allows you t associate several properties to all panels that contain character attribute options Each defines a String attribute to describe the panel, as well as the ability to define String representation of the attribute itself. Another advantage is that you ca define AttributePanel objects without having to know their final run-time type ahea of time. Remember that the following are legal ways to create AttributePanel objects

```java
AttributePanel[] panels = new AttributePanel[3]
 panels[0] = new TextFieldPanel("Name", "Enter your name: ", 20)
 panels[1] = new CheckboxPanel("Gender", new String[] { "M", "F" }, "M")

panels[2] = new SkillPanel("Skills", new String[] { "Strength", "Magic" }, 10);
```

Since the AttributePanel class is declared as abstract, you can't instantiate AttributePanel objects directly, but that's okay; it was designed it to be incomplete on purpose so that it can be extended by the needs of specific character attributes.

Now on with the subclasses. As I said, you want to allow the user to define a name, profession, and gender to a character in addition to distributing points among various skills. You can also create a panel containing a summary of defined character attributes. The following class listing, TextFieldPanel, creates a TextField and a Label to allow the user to input his or her name:

```java
// file: TextFieldPanel.java
import java.awt.*;

// holds a String attribute within a Panel
public class TextFieldPanel extends AttributePanel
{
    // the TextField for the attribute
    private TextField textField;
      public TextFieldPanel(String attr, String prompt, int textLength

        super(attr)

        setLayout(new FlowLayout(FlowLayout.CENTER, 15, 0))

        // add a Label if the prompt is a valid Strin
        if(prompt != null

            add(new Label(prompt, Label.LEFT))


        // create and add the TextField to the Pane
        textField = new TextField(textLength)
        add(textField)


    public String toString(

        // return the attribute, a "not specified" messag

        if(textField.getText().trim().equals(""))
        {
```

```
                return attribute + ": not specified";
        }

        return attribute + ": " + textField.getText().trim();
    }
}       // TextFieldPanel
```

The CheckboxPanel class allows the user to choose a single attribute from a number of selections, such as gender and profession. Here's the code:

```
// file: CheckboxPanel.java
import java.awt.*;

public class CheckboxPanel extends AttributePanel
{
    // a CheckboxGroup to hold our Checkboxes
    protected CheckboxGroup cbg;

    // this method overrides the init method from the Applet class
    public CheckboxPanel(String attr, String[] items, String selectedItem)
    {
        super(attr);

        setLayout(new GridLayout(items.length+1, 1, 5, 5));

        add(new Label(attribute, Label.CENTER));

        // create the CheckboxGroup
        cbg = new CheckboxGroup();
        for(int i = 0; i < items.length; i++)
        {
            add(new Checkbox(items[i], cbg, items[i].equals(selectedItem)));
        }
    }

    public String toString()
    {
        return attribute + ": " + cbg.getSelectedCheckbox().getLabel();
    }

}       // CheckboxPanel
```

Finally, here's the last listing for attribute selection panels. The `SkillPanel` class allows the user to allocate points toward different skills. It does much the same thing that you did in the *AttributeTest* applet shown earlier.

```java
// file: SkillPanel.java
import java.awt.*;
import java.awt.event.*;

// Represents a button capable of adjusting the value of a skill
class SkillButton extends Button
{
    // Label referencing the points allocated to this skill
    private Label pointsAllocated;

    public SkillButton(String desc, Label label)
    {
        super(desc);
        pointsAllocated = label;
    }
      // parses the value from the Labe
      public int getPointsAllocated(

            return Integer.parseInt(pointsAllocated.getText())


      // updates the pointsAllocated labe
      private void allocatePoints(int n

            int value = getPointsAllocated() + n
            pointsAllocated.setText("" + value)


      // updates the parent attribute's valu
      public int update
          int pointsRemaining  // overall points left to allocat


      {
          // allocate a point for 'plus' buttons
          if(getLabel().equals("+"))
```

```
        {
            // only allocate if there's points remaining
            if(pointsRemaining > 0)
            {
                allocatePoints(1);
                return -1;
            }
        }
        // otherwise, deallocate a poin
        els

            // don't allow negative allocatio
            if(getPointsAllocated() > 0

                allocatePoints(-1)
                return 1



        // de/allocation faile
        return 0


// holds numerical values for various character skill
public class SkillPanel extends AttributePanel implements ActionListene

    // points allocated to each skil
    Label[] pointsAllocated

    // overall points remaining to allocat
    Label pointsRemaining

    // the attributes for this apple
    private String[] skills


    public SkillPanel(String attr, String[] sk, int alloc)
    {
```

```java
        super(attr);

    skills = sk;
        // create the pointsRemaining Labe
        pointsRemaining = new Label("Points remaining: "
                                    alloc, Label.CENTER)

        // set the applet's layout to a FlowLayou
        setLayout(new FlowLayout(FlowLayout.CENTER, 5, 10))

        // add the components to the layou
        pointsAllocated = new Label[skills.length]
        for(int i = 0; i < skills.length; i++

            pointsAllocated[i] = new Label("0", Label.CENTER)
            addSkill(skills[i], pointsAllocated[i])


        add(pointsRemaining)


    private void addSkill(String skill, Label label

        Panel p = new Panel()

        // set the panel layout within a 3x1 gri
        p.setLayout(new GridLayout(3, 1))

        p.setBackground(Color.GREEN.darker())

        // add Labels to describe attribut
        p.add(new Label(skill, Label.CENTER))
        p.add(label)

        // attach the +/- buttons to the parent ActionListene

    Button incr = new SkillButton("+", label);
    incr.addActionListener(this);
    Button decr = new SkillButton("-", label);
```

```
            decr.addActionListener(this);

            // add another Panel with the plus/minus buttons
            Panel buttonPanel = new Panel();
            buttonPanel.add(incr);
            buttonPanel.add(decr);
            p.add(buttonPanel);
              add(p)


    public String toString(

            // return a String containing the allocation for each skil
            String s = ""
            int points = 0
            for(int i = 0; i < skills.length; i++

                points = Integer.parseInt(pointsAllocated[i].getText())
                s = s + skills[i] + " (" + points + ")       "


            return s


    public void actionPerformed(ActionEvent e

            // get the points left to allocat
            int n = Integer.parseInt(pointsRemaining.getText().substring(18))

            // update the Button's Panel and the main Labe
            n += ((SkillButton)e.getSource()).update(n)
            pointsRemaining.setText("Points remaining: " + n)


    }       // SkillPane
```

I also promised you a panel that shows a summary of user input. It contains
reference to each of the main applet's AttributePanel objects and allows thei
toString method to define the summary text displayed

```java
// file: SummaryPanel.java
import java.awt.*;
 // Panel containing a summary of the attribute
 public class SummaryPanel extends Pane

     // a Label to describe each attribut
     private Label[] summaries

     // reference to array of AttributePanels for the attribute
     private AttributePanel[] panels

     public SummaryPanel(AttributePanel[] ap

         super()

         panels = ap

         setLayout(new GridLayout(panels.length+1, 1, 5, 5))

         add(new Label("Summary:", Label.CENTER))

         // add the Labels to the Pane
         summaries = new Label[panels.length]
         for(int i = 0; i < panels.length; i++

             summaries[i] = new Label("", Label.LEFT)
             add(summaries[i])


    // since we don't know exactly which panel has been updated, let eac
    // AttributePanel update its Labe
    public void update(

        for(int i = 0; i < panels.length; i++)
        {
            summaries[i].setText(panels[i].toString());
        }
```

```
        }

    }    // SummaryPanel
```

You can now put it all together and start building some characters. The following *CharacterBuilder* applet brings the design shown in Figure 5.18 to life. It defines four attribute selection panels and a summary panel within a CardLayout. Pressing the Back and Next buttons will traverse the layout. Here's the code for the main *CharacterBuilder* class:

```java
import java.applet.*;
import java.awt.*;
import java.awt.event.*;

// the CharacterBuilder class consists of a number of Panels arranged within
// a CardLayout along with associated "back" and "next" buttons
public class CharacterBuilder extends Applet implements ActionListener
{
    // selects the next and previous cards in cardPanel
    private Button back;
    private Button next;

    private Panel       attributePanel;
    private SummaryPanel summaryPanel;

    // final String arrays representing various attribute selections
    private final String[] GENDERS = new String[] { "Male", "Female" };
    private final String[] SKILLS = new String[]
                        { "Strength", "Wisdom", "Agility",  "Magic" };
    private final String[] PROFESSIONS = new String[]
        { "Knight", "Ranger", "Archer", "Wizard", "Smith",  "Druid" };
    // this method overrides the init method from the Applet clas
    public void init(

        // create a GridLayout to hold our Cards and Button

        setLayout(new GridLayout(2, 1));

        // get the number of skill points to be allocated to the character
        int skillPoints;
```

```java
try
{
    skillPoints = Integer.parseInt(getParameter("SkillPoints"));
}
catch(NumberFormatException e)
{
    skillPoints = 10;
}

// create an array of panels for our attributes; one for the name,
// gender, skills, and profession of the character
AttributePanel[] panels = new AttributePanel[] {
    new TextFieldPanel("Name", "Enter your name: ", 20),
    new CheckboxPanel("Gender", GENDERS, GENDERS[0]),
    new SkillPanel("Skills", SKILLS, skillPoints),
    new CheckboxPanel("Profession", PROFESSIONS, PROFESSIONS[0])
};

// create a Panel to place our CardLayout
attributePanel = new Panel();
attributePanel.setLayout(new CardLayout());

// add the AttributePanels to the main Panel
for(int i = 0; i < panels.length; i++)
{
    attributePanel.add(panels[i], panels[i].getAttribute());
}

// create the SummaryPanel and add it to our CardLayout
summaryPanel = new SummaryPanel(panels);
attributePanel.add(summaryPanel, "Summary");

// add the attributePanel
add(attributePanel);

// create and add our "back" and "next" buttons
Panel p = new Panel();

back = new Button("back");
```

```
        back.addActionListener(this);
        p.add(back);

        next = new Button("next");
        next.addActionListener(this);
        p.add(next);

        p.setBackground(Color.BLACK);

        add(p);
    }

    // called when the "back" or "next" button is clicked
    public void actionPerformed(ActionEvent e)
    {
        CardLayout cardLayout = (CardLayout)attributePanel.getLayout();

        if(e.getSource() == back)
        {
            cardLayout.previous(attributePanel);
        }
        else if(e.getSource() == next)
        {
            cardLayout.next(attributePanel);
        }

        // update the Summary after each change
        summaryPanel.update();
    }

}   // CharacterBuilder
```

Figure 5.19 shows the Profession selection screen from the *CharacterBuilder* applet.

Whew! This lengthy example demonstrates the major features discussed in this chapter: component and container use, layout managers, listeners, and custom components. The *CharacterBuilder* applet is the longest we've seen yet. Just take it line by line and visualize what each step is trying to accomplish.

There is one more point I'd like to mention. Notice at the top of the init method under the CharacterBuilder class the use of the getParameter method. Parameters can

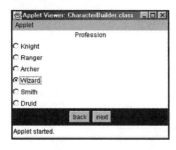

**Figure 5.19**

*A glimpse at the final*
CharacterBuilder
*applet*

be sent to an applet much like they can to console programs run on the command line. This is useful when you want to send information to an applet without having to recompile. The above code listing reads one parameter representing the number of skill points to allocate. The following code shows how to include parameters from within your .html documents:

```
<applet code=CharacterBuilder.class width=350 height=160>
<param name="SkillPoints" value="15">
</applet>
```

To access the "SkillPoints" parameter from within your applet, simply use

```
int skillPoints = Integer.parseInt(getParameter("SkillPoints"));
```

Since the point value is an integer, I embedded the above code within a try/catch block just in case some wise guy tries to insert invalid data into the Web document. Applet parameters are a great way to make quick changes to your code without wasting time having to recompile. They are also handy for times when you want the end user to be able to define parameters for the applet quickly and easily. One of this chapter's exercises asks you to define an applet parameter for the default character name.

# Conclusion

Remember, a Java applet is simply a piece of software that is embedded within another application. Applets are a very convenient and popular way to deliver content to your users.

Not all of the AWT components were presented in this chapter. I wanted to use this chapter mainly as an introduction to components and containers; we'll pick up the slack with topics such as the Graphics class coming up in the next chapter. Using AWT components is a very quick and easy way to present interactive content to the user. Components such as buttons, check boxes, and labels can be attached to your applets with just a few lines of code. However, I feel the AWT does come with a few restrictions. Although it is great for designing software independent of window resolution, I would like to have a bit more control over the placement of my components. I would also like a way to create more attractive components that fit within the "feel" of my games rather than using the default windowing and drawing styles. But don't discount the native AWT components entirely; their flexibility and ease of use will surely come in handy in the future.

You have had just a glimpse of the power of the Applet class. With just a few lines of code, you can embed buttons, text fields, and labels to an applet window. But it doesn't end there. In Chapter 7, we'll look at ways to draw lines, shapes, and text within our applets.

# Exercises

**5.1** Predict the output of the following code snippet:

```
class B extends Applet
{
        public static void main(String[] args)
        {
                    System.out.println("I am a Java guru!");
        }
}    // B
```

**5.2** Why is it important for Applet classes to implement *EventListener* interfaces when using components such as Button objects? If you're not sure, look at the prototype for the Button addActionListener method and it should become clearer.

**5.3** Describe the differences and similarities between a *component* and a *container.*

**5.4** Modify the ButtonTest applet so that it contains a separate Button for each color in the Color array. The Button associated with the color red should be labeled "Red," the blue one labeled "Blue," and so on. A simple way to do this would be to create parallel arrays all indexed by the currentColor variable. A more robust way would be to extend the Button class so that it changes the color internally. You can associate a Color with your custom Button in its constructor and have the actionPerformed method allow the Button to update the window.

**5.5** Change the *AudioChoiceTest* applet so that it implements a List object to hold the audio file names. Your list should be capable of having multiple selections at any time, so be sure to adjust your audio control code accordingly.

**5.6** Describe how multiple Panel objects can be used to create more elaborate layouts.

**5.7** What is the air-speed velocity of an unladen swallow?

**5.8** Sketch how a group of five buttons can be arranged given the following layout managers: FlowLayout, GridLayout, CardLayout, BorderLayout.

**5.9** Write an applet that displays the current date and time within a Label object. The applet should update itself regularly so that the date and time display looks continuous.

**5.10** Modify the CharacterBuilder class so that it reads an applet parameter describing the default character name. You'll have to either adjust the constructor of the TextFieldPanel class or add a method to set the text field's value. You'll also have to add a parameter tag to your .html file like the following:

```
<param name="DefaultName" value="Merlin">
```

# CHAPTER 6

# LISTENING TO YOUR USERS

In Chapter 5, you saw two interfaces that extend upon the *EventListener* interface: *ActionListener* and *ItemListener*. You used the *ActionListener* interface to catch events associated with interacting with components such as buttons, and you used the *ItemListener* interface to catch selection changes within components such as check boxes.

In this chapter, we're going to cover several more listener interfaces. I hope to plow through each of these interfaces with a brief explanation and an example; that way you'll be familiar enough with them to write some killer applets.

# The *EventListener* Interface

As you saw in Chapter 5, the *EventListener* interface is the super interface for all further event listener interfaces. Although the listener interfaces we will discuss reside within the java.awt.event package, the *EventListener* interface comes from the java.util package.

The *EventListener* interface contains no methods; it is merely an empty tagging interface that all listeners must extend. Figure 6.1 offers a refresher on how listener interfaces work.

When registering an applet (or any component) with a listener, pass a reference to the listener object. That way, the listener knows who to refer back to when an event is generated.

Here's an analogy that might help you visualize this process. Suppose Joe owns a local pawnshop. Every day, Joe has people coming in looking for various items

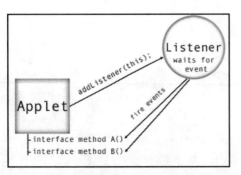

**Figure 6.1**

*Interfacing a listener with an applet*

(such as furniture, guns, whatever). On Tuesday, Bob comes in looking for a gold watch. Not having any on hand, Joe promises to call Bob when he receives one. Two weeks later, an ominous individual comes in and trades in his gold watch for a rare copy of *Recursive Programming Techniques,* by W.H. Burge. After securing the watch, Joe immediately calls Bob on the phone to tell him a gold watch has arrived. Bob then rushes over to the pawnshop to check out the watch.

In the above case, Bob acted as the component capable of handling events. Joe acted as the listener. Basically, Bob registered himself with Joe to sit around and wait for a gold watch to arrive. Once Joe had one, he reported the event back to Bob. Bob was then able to take action and run to the pawnshop to buy the watch. Listener interfaces act in much the same way.

Now we'll take a look at some real-life listener interfaces, starting with the *MouseListener* interface.

## The *MouseListener* Interface

The *MouseListener* interface listens for many of the events associated with the mouse. This includes listening for when the mouse pointer enters or leaves a component, when a mouse button is pressed or released, and when a mouse button is clicked (a combination of being pressed *and* released).

The *MouseListener* interface defines five methods: mouseClicked, mouseEntered, mouseExited, mousePressed, and mouseReleased. They are all void methods and take a single MouseEvent object as their parameter. Keep in mind that you must define all five of these methods; otherwise, your class must be declared as abstract. The *MouseListener* interface does not track events such as the explicit movement of the mouse. For that, see the *MouseMotionListener* interface below.

I remember once seeing a nifty sample applet that registers a Panel with a mouse listener and sends events generated by the listener to a TextArea. The following program accomplishes much the same thing; try it out for yourself.

```
import java.applet.*;
import java.awt.*;
import java.awt.event.*;

// appends come common MouseEvents to a TextArea
public class MouseTest extends Applet implements MouseListener
{
    // the TextArea to receive MouseEvents
```

```java
private TextArea textArea;

// this method overrides the init method from the Applet class
public void init()
{
    setLayout(new GridLayout(2, 1));

    // set up a new Panel object that will fire mouse events to the applet
    Panel p = new Panel();
    p.setBackground(new Color(0, 127, 255));
    p.add(new Label("I LOVE Mouse Events!"));
    p.addMouseListener(this);
    add(p);

    // now add the TextArea to the applet
    textArea = new TextArea();
    add(textArea);
}

// appends the sent String, the component fired upon, and the point where
// it happened to the TextArea
private void reportMouseEvent(String s, MouseEvent e)
{
    String point = "(" + e.getX() + ", " + e.getY() + ")";
    textArea.append(s + e.getSource().getClass() + " at " + point + "\n");
}

// methods implemented in the MouseListener interface; their usage should
// be self-explanatory

public void mouseClicked(MouseEvent e)
{
    // for this method, differentiate between left and right clicks
    if(e.getModifiers() == MouseEvent.BUTTON1_MASK)
    {
        reportMouseEvent("Mouse left-clicked on ", e);
    }

    if(e.getModifiers() == MouseEvent.BUTTON3_MASK)
```

```
        {
            reportMouseEvent("Mouse right-clicked on ", e);
        }
    }

    public void mouseEntered(MouseEvent e)
    {
        reportMouseEvent("Mouse entered ", e);
    }

    public void mouseExited(MouseEvent e)
    {
        reportMouseEvent("Mouse exited ", e);
    }

    public void mousePressed(MouseEvent e)
    {
        reportMouseEvent("Mouse pressed over ", e);
    }

    public void mouseReleased(MouseEvent e)
    {
        reportMouseEvent("Mouse released over ", e);
    }

}    // MouseTest
```

Figure 6.2 shows the *MouseTest* applet in action.

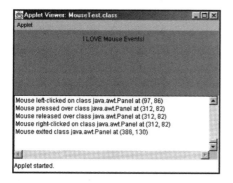

**Figure 6.2**

*The* MouseTest *applet*

The *MouseTest* applet is a fun program to try out for yourself. Notice that it is the blue panel at the top of the applet that is registered to fire mouse events, not the entire applet itself. However, it is a reference to the applet that is sent to the addMouseListener method; the applet will be informed of mouse events and print these events within the text field.

Now let's take a look at a related interface, the *MouseMotionListener* interface.

## The *MouseMotionListener* Interface

As previously mentioned, the *MouseMotionListener* interface generates action events caused by the movement of the mouse. It defines two methods: mouseDragged and mouseMoved. Again, both are void methods that take a single MouseEvent parameter.

The following program, *Scribble*, mimics the classic GUI example program. Note the use of the ColorDescription class; I used it to ease the coding required to associate a Color with its associated String description (such as associating the constant, Color.BLACK, with the String "Black"). To make the program simpler (yet more difficult to modify and maintain), you can eliminate the ColorDescription class and hard-code all of the values directly.

```java
import java.applet.*;
import java.awt.*;
import java.awt.event.*;


// the ColorDescription class stores a Color as well as its String description.
// this class is provided purely as a convenience for associating a Color with a
// String
class ColorDescription
{
    // associates a Color with a text String, declared public for convenience
    public Color color;
    public String text;

    public ColorDescription(Color c, String s)
    {
        color = c;
        text  = s;
    }


    public boolean matches(String s)
```

```
        {
            return text.equals(s);
        }
    }    // ColorDescription


// the Scribble applet allows the user to draw points and lines with
// the mouse, as well as choose the current pen color.
public class Scribble extends Applet implements ItemListener, ActionListener,
                                        MouseListener, MouseMotionListener
{
    private Choice colorChooser;  // a combo-box to store colors
    private Color  currentColor;  // the current pen color

    // an array of Colors with their associated String names
    // all you need to do is edit this list to add or remove choices
    // from the applet
    private final ColorDescription[] colors = new ColorDescription[] {
        new ColorDescription(Color.BLACK,  "Black"),
        new ColorDescription(Color.RED,    "Red"),
        new ColorDescription(Color.GREEN,  "Green"),
        new ColorDescription(Color.BLUE,   "Blue"),
        new ColorDescription(Color.YELLOW, "Yellow"),
        new ColorDescription(Color.ORANGE, "Orange"),
        new ColorDescription(Color.GRAY,   "Gray"),
        new ColorDescription(Color.CYAN,   "Cyan")
    };

    // the source and destination points for drawing lines
    private Point p1;
    private Point p2;

    // this method overrides the init method from the Applet class
    public void init()
    {
        p1 = null;
        p2 = null;

        setBackground(Color.WHITE);

        // remember to register ourself to receive mouse events
```

```java
        addMouseListener(this);
        addMouseMotionListener(this);

        // set the cursor to something snazzy
        setCursor(new Cursor(Cursor.CROSSHAIR_CURSOR));

        currentColor = colors[0].color;

        // create a "sidebar" containing applet commands
        createSidebar();
    }

    // this method overrides the init method from the Applet class
    public void destroy()
    {
        // release any listeners added during the applet's lifecycle
        removeMouseListener(this);
        removeMouseMotionListener(this);

        colorChooser.removeItemListener(this);
    }

    // creates a Frame containing the drop-down box of Color choices
    // and a button to clear the applet window
    private void createSidebar()
    {
        // for each ColorDescription in the colors array, extract the text
        // component and add it to the choice listing
        colorChooser = new Choice();
        for(int i = 0; i < colors.length; i++)
        {
            colorChooser.add(colors[i].text);
        }
        colorChooser.addItemListener(this);

        // create a "clear window" button
        Button b = new Button("Clear Window");
        b.addActionListener(this);

        // create the frame
```

```java
        Frame f = new Frame();
        f.setLocation(getX() + getSize().width + 8, getY());
        f.setLayout(new GridLayout(3, 1, 5, 5));
        f.setBackground(Color.YELLOW);
        f.add(new Label("Pen Color:", Label.CENTER));
        f.add(colorChooser);
        f.add(b);
        f.pack();
        f.show();
    }


    // draws points connecting points p1 and p2 using the current pen color
    private void drawPoints()
    {
        Graphics g = getGraphics();
        g.setColor(currentColor);
        g.drawLine(p1.x, p1.y, p2.x, p2.y);
    }


    // called when the sidebar's "clear window" button is pressed
    public void actionPerformed(ActionEvent e)
    {
        repaint();
    }


    // called when the drop-box is changed
    public void itemStateChanged(ItemEvent e)
    {
        String color = colorChooser.getSelectedItem();

        // match the current pen color with the selected item
        for(int i = 0; i < colors.length; i++)
        {
            if(colors[i].matches(color))
            {
                // set the color
                currentColor = colors[i].color;
                break;
            }
```

```java
        }
    }

    /** methods implemented in the MouseMotionListener interface */

    public void mouseMoved(MouseEvent e)
    {
        // do nothing...

    }

    public void mouseDragged(MouseEvent e)
    {
        // set the points if they are not yet set
        if(p1 == null)
        {
            p1 = new Point(e.getX(), e.getY());
        }
        if(p2 == null)
        {
            p2 = new Point(e.getX(), e.getY());
        }

        // update the points and draw the point
        p1.x = p2.x;
        p1.y = p2.y;

        p2.x = e.getX();
        p2.y = e.getY();

        drawPoints();
    }

    /** methods implemented in the MouseListener interface */

    public void mouseClicked(MouseEvent e)
    {
        // do nothing...
```

```
        }

        public void mouseEntered(MouseEvent e)
        {
              // do nothing...
        }

        public void mouseExited(MouseEvent e)
        {
              // do nothing...
        }

        // allows a point to be drawn when the mouse button is down but
        // the mouse is not necessarily being "dragged"
        public void mousePressed(MouseEvent e)
        {
              mouseDragged(e);
        }

        // release the points to allow non-continuous drawing
        public void mouseReleased(MouseEvent e)
        {
              p1 = null;
              p2 = null;
        }

    }    // Scribble
```

Figure 6.3 shows my contribution to the modern art world using the *Scribble* applet (okay, so I'm not an artist).

Although it's a simple program, the *Scribble* applet implements both the *MouseListener* as well as the *MouseInputListener* interfaces. It also implements the *ActionListener* and *ItemListener* interfaces, which you've already seen. With a few lines of code, you can get a useful application up and running rather quickly. There are *lots* of enhancements that can be made to this applet (smells like a chapter exercise to me). Just imagine what goes into those thousand-dollar graphics suites out there!

Also note the use of the Frame class to open up a separate window. This is handy when you want to include extra controls or options but you don't want them to get

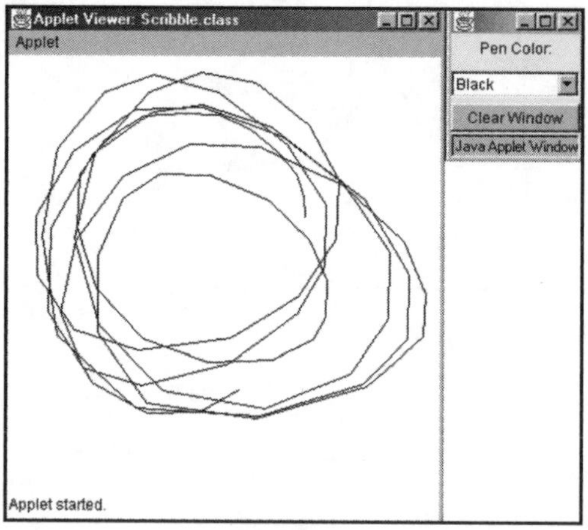

**Figure 6.3**

*The* Scribble *applet*

in the way. Try using the Frame class when you want a separate menu to be readily available to your users at any time.

It is important to nail down the use of mouse listener interfaces. The games you will be creating will inevitably use mouse input that requires the position of the mouse as well as which button was pressed. After you get the *Scribble* applet up and running, read on to see how to capture keyboard events with the *KeyListener* interface.

> **NOTE**
>
> If you plan on reusing any of the classes you write, you can always put the it in its own file. But remember, you must declare the class as public for it to compile correctly. For simplicity, I just added the ColorDescription class to the Scribble.java file. Since it might be handy to use again one day, you can always declare the ColorDescription class as public and add it to ColorDescription.java.

# The *KeyListener* Interface

As you might expect, the *KeyListener* interface listens for events associated with the keyboard. It is analogous to the *MouseListener* interface. It listens for when a key is pressed or released, and when a key is typed (a combination of being pressed *and* released).

The three methods implemented by the interface are keyPressed, keyReleased, and keyTyped. Again, these methods should be self-explanatory. They are all void methods that take a single KeyEvent object as their parameter.

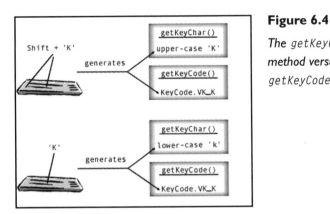

**Figure 6.4**

*The* `getKeyChar`
*method versus the*
`getKeyCode` *method*

One distinction should be made about the `KeyEvent` class. When determining which key was pressed, you can examine the actual character type, or its virtual key code. When you are interested in the actual character generated (such as "a" versus "A"), use the `getKeyChar` method, which returns a `char`. However, when you are merely interested in which key on the keyboard was typed, use the `getKeyCode` method, which returns an `int`. So for example, if the user holds down the Shift key and types the 'G' key, then `getKeyChar` will generate a "G." However, if just the "G" key is pressed, then `getKeyChar` will generate the character "g." In both cases, `getKeyCode` will generate the integer constant `VK_G`.

All key codes are prefixed by `VK_`. Since there are about 200 virtual key codes defined in the `KeyEvent` class, I won't show them all here. A full list can be found within the Java 2 documentation. Figure 6.4 shows some of the subtle differences between the `getKeyChar` and `getKeyCode` methods.

The following applet, *KeyTest*, demonstrates use of both the `getKeyChar` and the `getKeyCode` methods. As you skim the source code or type it into your text editor, think about the advantages and disadvantages of both methods.

```java
import java.applet.*;
import java.awt.*;
import java.awt.event.*;

// this applet allows the user to move a black rectangle using the arrow keys.
// the user can also change the applet's background color with the
// 'R', 'G', 'B', and 'W' keys.  It also shows the different ways a KeyEvent
// object can be interpreted.
```

```java
public class KeyTest extends Applet implements KeyListener
{
    // moveable black rectangle
    private Rectangle r;

    // current background color for the applet
    private Color backColor;

    // this method overrides the init method from the Applet class
    public void init()
    {
        r = new Rectangle(0, 0, 20, 10);

        backColor = Color.WHITE;

        addKeyListener(this);
    }

    // paints the rectangle at the updated position
    public void paint(Graphics g)
    {
        setBackground(backColor);
        g.fillRect(r.x, r.y, r.width, r.height);
    }

    /** methods implemented in the KeyListener interface */

    public void keyPressed(KeyEvent e)
    {
        // for this method, use the key code to generate movement
        int keyCode = e.getKeyCode();

        // move the rectangle
        if(keyCode == KeyEvent.VK_LEFT)
        {
            r.x -= 5;
            if(r.x < 0) r.x = 0;
            repaint();
        }
```

```
            else if(keyCode == KeyEvent.VK_RIGHT)
            {
                r.x += 5;
                if(r.x > getSize().width-r.width)
                {
                    r.x = getSize().width-r.width;
                }
                repaint();
            }
            else if(keyCode == KeyEvent.VK_UP)
            {
                r.y -= 5;
                if(r.y < 0) r.y = 0;
                repaint();
            }
            else if(keyCode == KeyEvent.VK_DOWN)
            {
                r.y += 5;
                if(r.y > getSize().height-r.height)
                {
                    r.y = getSize().height-r.height;
                }
                repaint();
            }
    }

    public void keyReleased(KeyEvent e)
    {
        // do nothing...
    }

    public void keyTyped(KeyEvent e)
    {
        // for this method, use the actual key char to call action
        char keyChar = e.getKeyChar();

        // change the background color
        switch(keyChar)
        {
```

```
                    case 'r':
                    {
                            backColor = Color.RED;
                            repaint();
                            break;
                    }
                    case 'g':
                    {
                            backColor = Color.GREEN;
                            repaint();
                            break;
                    }
                    case 'b':
                    {
                            backColor = Color.BLUE;
                            repaint();
                            break;
                    }
                    case 'w':
                    {
                            backColor = Color.WHITE;
                            repaint();
                            break;
                    }
            }
        }

    }    // KeyTest
```

Check out Figure 6.5 for a look at the *KeyTest* applet in action.

**Figure 6.5**

*The* KeyTest *applet*

Don't forget that in addition to moving the rectangle around with the arrow keys, you can also change the applet's background color to red, green, blue, and back to white. If the keyboard doesn't seem to move the block around the screen, make sure that the window is the currently focused window on the desktop (this can be done by clicking the mouse anywhere in the *KeyTest* window).

## Other *EventListener* Interfaces

There are many, many other `EventListener` interfaces out there: `WindowListener`, `FocusListener`, `MenuListener`, the list goes on and on. Most of them you won't ever use. Just look up the `EventListener` interface in the Java 2 documentation and you'll find a complete list of its subinterfaces. Although it would take a modest amount of work, you can even write your own listeners if you need to.

## Conclusion

The collection of `EventListener` interfaces is a great example of what an interface should do, and that is to provide a bridge between two components. The interfaces discussed in this chapter bridge the gap between visual components and user input.

As far as the specific listener interfaces discussed in this chapter, both mouse and keyboard listeners are pretty safe to

**CAUTION**

One word of caution: Not all keyboards are capable of generating all of the virtual key codes. Furthermore, no attempt has been made to allow artificial generation of these codes. So if you're trying something tricky and you fear that all keyboards are not capable of generating the event, try using the `getKeyChar` method. Many games allow multiple keyboard actions to generate the same event; this way, nobody gets left out. You can also create a menu to allow the user to map which keys correlate to which functions. It all depends on how you want your users to interact with your games.

**NOTE**

As an alternative to implementing listener interfaces, you can extend their equivalent adapter classes. For example, rather than implementing the `MouseListener` interface, you can extend the `MouseAdapter` class instead. An advantage to this is that you can override and define only those methods of interest; remember that the interface implementation forces you to define all of its methods. However, the principle of single inheritance states that you can only directly inherit one class. But it has its use, and like most things, there are certain advantages as well as disadvantages.

use, as long as you keep compatibility in mind. Remember, since Java is cross-platform compatible, there is always a good chance that someone from across the world will be playing your games. Chances are, that user will have a keyboard layout that is different than yours. As for mouse listeners, remember that mice come in many different flavors: three-button mice are popular, two-button mice are even more popular, and yes, there are even those systems that use the one-button mouse as well (sigh). So remember to program your games so that just about anyone on any system will be able to interact and use your programs. Designing games that allow custom keyboard and mouse configuration is a good way to guarantee that everyone will be able to enjoy the games you make.

# Exercises

**6.1** Write an applet that implements several different listeners. Choose "basic" listeners that are able to fire events even in an empty applet window, such as *MouseListener*, *MouseMotionListener*, *KeyListener*, and *WindowListener*. For each event fired, just log the event to standard output by invoking its toString method, such as the following:

```
public void mouseMoved(MouseEvent e)
{
        System.out.println(e);
}
```

**6.2** If you're feeling ambitious, try writing the program presented in exercise 5.1 to send the event information to a TextArea field rather than standard output.

**6.3** Write an applet that implements the *MouseListener* as well as the *MouseMotionListener* interfaces in order to improve upon the *Scribble* applet. Use the mouseReleased method to allow the pen to be picked "off" of the paper. Also, define the right mouse button to change the pen color to a random color. (Hint: Use a random number generator and the setColor method from the Graphics class to change the color.) The applet should still set the cursor to the crosshair cursor just as the original did.

**6.4** Modify the *Scribble* applet to allow the user to adjust the width of the pen. You should include another text label and a combo box that includes various pen widths. Widths of one to six pixels should be fine, but you can adjust to suit your taste. If you're not sure how to approach this problem, come back after reading Chapters 7 and 8, and the solution should become clear.

# CHAPTER 7

# Rendering Shapes, Text, and Images with Java 2-D, Part 1

If you're a beginner to graphics programming, you're in luck. Because Java was designed to be platform-independent, you can program abstractly and allow the lower-level Java routines to do the actual rendering for you. Even if you do have experience with graphics packages such as OpenGL or DirectX, you'll appreciate the relative ease in which graphical components can be rendered in Java.

The overall visual presentation is the first thing your users will notice about your games. This can be the make-or-break aspect—if your games don't have pleasing graphics, your users may not stick around long enough to see the amazing game play, artificially intelligent entities, and killer sounds your game has to offer. The graphics you provide in your games don't have to be groundbreaking, but they should be pleasing enough to keep your users' interest. Java provides the tools necessary to create more than adequate scenes with little effort.

In the following chapters, you'll use the Java 2-D API class as the workhorse for rendering your graphical components. The components contained within Java 2-D can be found within the `java.awt` and `java.awt.image` packages, making Java 2-D part of the Java AWT.

Java 2-D contains classes and methods for rendering geometry, images, and even text. If you're already familiar with topics such as color blending, additive geometry, and collision testing in other graphics packages, rest assured that Java 2-D contains native support for these operations and a host of others. As of Java 2, release 1.4, there is also native support for hardware acceleration, which allows your games to gain lightning-fast frame rates.

An important part of Java 2-D is the `Graphics2D` class. But before we delve into the guts of this class, let's take a look at the coordinate system you will be working with.

# Coordinate Spaces

The Java 2-D system defines two coordinate systems for us: *user space* and *device space*. User space is an abstract, logical coordinate system used by all Java 2-D applications. User space works independently of any devices you wish to render to. So whether you wish to render an image to a window within a single monitor system, a dual monitor system, or even a printer, you use this coordinate system exclusively. User space has its origin at (0, 0), which exists in the upper left-hand corner of your rendering target.

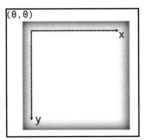

**Figure 7.1**

*User space as defined by Java 2-D*

Device space refers to the coordinate system contained within a specific device. A device can be anything from a monitor to a printer. Java 2-D supplies a three-tiered hierarchy for converting coordinates provided in user space to the actual device space coordinates. For our purposes, you do not need to go into the inner workings of how device spaces work, although you are able to access the device space of a particular rendering device. All you need to do is program in user coordinates, and the rest will be taken care of automatically. Figure 7.1 shows the coordinate system as defined under Java 2-D.

Note that with this system, x-coordinates get larger as you move to the right, and y-coordinates get larger as you move down.

# The Graphics2D Class

Early implementations of Java use the Graphics class to aid in the rendering of common components, such as line drawing and imaging. You may have noticed the use of the Graphics class in earlier chapters of this book. In addition to rendering components, the Graphics class also holds state attributes for rendering, such as the current color to draw with and the current transformation state. A snapshot of all of these state variables is known as the graphics *context*.

The designers of Java have extended the Graphics class by developing the Graphics2D class. The Graphics2D class contains many enhanced features not found in the Graphics class. For backward compatibility, all container classes, such as Applet, still pass the original Graphics context to its methods. Since the Graphics2D class directly extends the Graphics class, a plain-vanilla cast will give you a usable Graphics2D context, such as the following:

```
public void methodX(Graphics g)
{
    Graphics2D g2d = (Graphics2D)g;
    // do some killer stuff here[...]
}
```

What can the `Graphics2D` class do? In the following subsections, we will investigate the following `Graphics2D` features:

- Transformations
- Color models
- Draw and fill operations
- Drawing images
- Drawing text
- Using geometry
- Setting rendering hints

Now, let's take a look at transformations.

# Using Affined Transformations

In graphics, we use what is called a *transformation* to manipulate geometry and place it within a scene. Transformations can come in many forms, such as *translations* (movement along the x, y axis), *rotations* (angular movement about an anchor point), *flips* (mirroring geometry about a given axis or line), *scales* (uniform expansion/shrinking), and *shears* (distortion along an axis).

In Java 2-D, all transformations you will create come in the form of an *affine transformation*. In general, an affine transform can represent any combination of translations, rotations, etc. They also preserve the parallelism of lines and line segments. So although you can manipulate any given geometry, the nature of the geometry itself will not be affected. Affine transformations are also unique because they do not work with respect to an origin, as a vector transformation would. This way, the same affine transformation can be used to map coordinates within user space or a given device space. The operations needed to generate affine transformations are contained within the `AffineTransform` class.

The Java `AffineTransform` class uses what is called a *right-handed coordinate system*. It also uses a 3 x 3 matrix to store information about the transformation. This is where many beginners who don't have a good background in linear algebra often get stuck. Luckily, Java is object-oriented and practically all of the work has been done for you. The `AffineTransform` class is highly abstracted; therefore, you don't have to know how it works, just how to use it. With that in mind, we won't talk about matrix manipulation here, but instead we will look at some of the finer points of matrices as they come up.

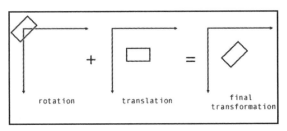

**Figure 7.2**

*Rotating and translating a rectangle*

rotation + translation = final transformation

When you build a new AffineTransform using its default constructor, it will represent what is called the *identity transformation*. The identity transformation does not affect the scene; that is, it does not affect any geometry it is applied to. Always call the AffineTransform setToIdentity method when you want to clear a transformation.

As I've already stated, an affine transformation is any combination of independent transformations. So how do you combine these transformations? The answer lies in *concatenation*. To concatenate transformations, all you do is specify the transformations in a specific order. The magic and voodoo contained within Java 2-D will then give your final transformation. Remember, you don't need to know how it's done, just how to use it.

Here's a quick example. Say you have a rectangle that you wish to rotate 45 degrees about the origin. You then want to move (translate) the rectangle 100 units along both the x- and y-axis. The result would look something like Figure 7.2.

Actually setting these transformations is fairly simple; however, there is one part that can be a bit tricky. The rule for concatenating transformations is that the *last* transformation specified is the *first* one applied. Think of it in terms of a stack: the last component pushed onto it will be the first one removed. Therefore, if you wish to first scale, then rotate, then translate an object, perform the steps in the following order:

1. Set the translation.
2. Set the rotation.
3. Set the scale.

In short, you will want to specify transformations in the *opposite* order than you want them to be logically applied. The actual code for this might look like the following:

```
Graphics2D g2d = (Graphics2D)g;
AffineTransform at = new AffineTransform();

at.setToIdentity();
at.translate(100, 100);
```

```
        at.rotate(radians);
        at.scale(10, 10);


        g2d.setTransform(at);
```

Does the order in which you specify your transformations really matter? You bet it does. For instance, suppose you have an object lying at the origin, (0, 0). You rotate the object 30 degrees and then translate it by (20, 40). The result will look something like Figure 7.2. On the other hand, suppose you perform the operations in the opposite order: you translate the object then rotate it. This will move the object by (20, 40) and then rotate the object about the origin. Although it may not be immediately obvious, this will produce a totally different result. To illustrate this, try running the following program, *AffineTest*. It allows you to specify the logical order you wish to transform the object. Check it out:

```java
import java.applet.*;
import java.awt.*;
import java.awt.event.*;
import java.awt.geom.*;
import java.util.*;

public class AffineTest extends Applet implements ItemListener
{
    // the rectangle to draw
    private Rectangle2D rect;

    // two checkboxes to allow us to specify the logical order in which
    // to apply the transformations
    private Checkbox rotateFirst;
    private Checkbox translateFirst;

    public void init()
    {
        // create a CheckboxGroup containing the two Checkboxes
        setLayout(new BorderLayout());

        CheckboxGroup cbg = new CheckboxGroup();
        Panel p = new Panel();

        rotateFirst = new Checkbox("rotate, translate", cbg, true);
```

```
        rotateFirst.addItemListener(this);
        p.add(rotateFirst);
        translateFirst = new Checkbox("translate, rotate", cbg, false);
        translateFirst.addItemListener(this);
        p.add(translateFirst);
        add(p, BorderLayout.SOUTH);

        // model our rectangle about the origin
        rect = new Rectangle2D.Float(-0.5f, -0.5f, 1.0f, 1.0f);
    }


    public void paint(Graphics g)
    {
        // cast the sent Graphics context to get a usable Graphics2D object
        Graphics2D g2d = (Graphics2D)g;

        // save an identity transform to clear the Graphics2D context
        final AffineTransform identity = new AffineTransform();

        // true if we wish to logically rotate first
        boolean rotate = rotateFirst.getState();

        // create a random number generator to produce random colors
        Random r = new Random();

        final double oneRadian = Math.toRadians(1.0);
        for(double radians = 0.0; radians < 2.0*Math.PI; radians += oneRadian)
        {
            // clear this Graphics2D's transform
            g2d.setTransform(identity);

            // remember, operations are performed in reverse order than we
            // logically prefer them!

            if(rotate)
            {
                g2d.translate(100, 100);
                g2d.rotate(radians);
            }
```

```
            else
            {
                    g2d.rotate(radians);
                    g2d.translate(100, 100);
            }

            g2d.scale(10, 10);

            g2d.setColor(new Color(r.nextInt()));
            g2d.fill(rect);
        }
    }

    public void itemStateChanged(ItemEvent e)
    {
        // a new Checkbox was selected, better repaint!
        repaint();
    }
}    // AffineTest
```

Figure 7.3 shows both transformation sequences offered in the *AffineTest* applet.

Notice in the code above that you did nothing to modify the rectangle itself. All you did was modify the transformation contained within the Graphics2D context. Also notice that the actual order the operations are performed in is reversed from the logical order. Don't forget this important fact, or else you'll end up with some oddly-behaving programs.

Next, we'll look into drawing geometry with Graphics2D.

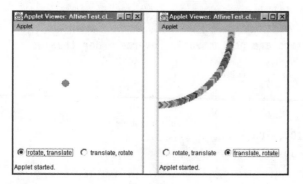

**Figure 7.3**

*The* AffineTest *applet*

# Drawing Shapes

Under the original `Graphics` class, there are several methods defined to draw lines and shapes, such as `drawLine`, `drawRect`, `drawRoundRect`, `drawOval`, `drawArc`, `drawPolyline`, and `drawPolygon`, as well as their associated fill methods, including `fillRect`, `fillRoundRect`, `fillOval`, `fillArc`, `fillPolygon`, and `clearRect`. Although these methods work fine, there were improvements that could be made. For example, suppose your program makes extensive use of the `Graphics` `drawRect` method. You later decide that you would rather draw rounded rectangles, that is, rectangles with rounded edges. It will take some tedious effort to change each instance of `drawRect` to `drawRoundRect`. Also, since both of these methods take a different number of parameters, the solution isn't as simple as doing a global find and replace with your text editor. Additionally, most of these methods take primitive types (namely integers) as their arguments, so it would be difficult to draw geometry created with instance modeling (which you'll see a little later in this chapter). This approach can make it difficult to keep track of your objects, where you'll often find yourself using parallel arrays or some type of "hacked" data structure to store your points.

> **NOTE**
>
> The `AffineTransform` **class contains a slew of methods for altering the state of your transformations. Be sure to look up the** `AffineTransform` **class in your Java 2 documentation. Some of the methods are convenient shortcuts to longer transformation operations. For instance, just call the** `setToTranslation` **method instead of manually clearing a transformation before creating a translation or even totally reallocating new memory for the object. It is important to know the shortcuts so your games don't get bottlenecked with unnecessary** `AffineTransform` **method calls.**

Fortunately, Java 2-D contains an enhanced `Graphics2D` class, which you know extends the original `Graphics` class. The draw and fill methods listed above have been replaced with a single `draw` and a single `fill` method. Both of these methods take a *Shape* object as their parameter. These methods also use the current `AffineTransform` contained within the `Graphics2D` context (you'll see why this is so great in just a bit). This way, all of your points are contained within their own data structures. This also allows you to change the geometry of your objects quite easily; basically, all you have to do is change the object's declaration and the `draw` and `fill` methods will still work.

We have just discussed how the `Graphics2D` draw and fill methods take *Shape* objects as their parameter. But what exactly is a *Shape* object? *Shape* is an interface that is implemented by classes that wish to represent some kind of geometric shape. The *Shape* interface contains methods for accessing a shape's boundaries and

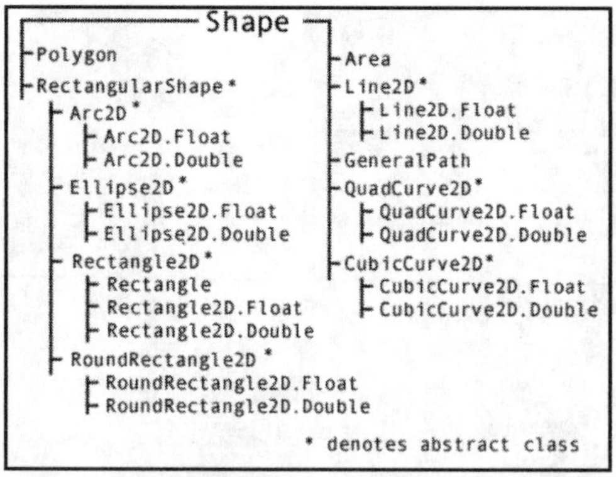

```
                    Shape
  Polygon                        Area
  RectangularShape *             Line2D *
      Arc2D *                        Line2D.Float
          Arc2D.Float                Line2D.Double
          Arc2D.Double           GeneralPath
      Ellipse2D *                QuadCurve2D *
          Ellipse2D.Float            QuadCurve2D.Float
          Ellipse2D.Double           QuadCurve2D.Double
      Rectangle2D *              CubicCurve2D *
          Rectangle                  CubicCurve2D.Float
          Rectangle2D.Float          CubicCurve2D.Double
          Rectangle2D.Double
      RoundRectangle2D *
          RoundRectangle2D.Float
          RoundRectangle2D.Double
                          * denotes abstract class
```

**Figure 7.4**

*Classes implementing the* Shape *interface*

detecting collisions. We'll examine the Shape methods more closely when we talk about animation and collision testing.

Since Shape is an interface, there has to be a class that implements it to be usable. Luckily, there are a number of classes that implement the Shape interface. All of these classes are fair game for use in the Graphics2D draw and fill methods. Figure 7.4 shows all known implementing classes of the Shape interface.

Most of the classes shown in Figure 7.4 are self-explanatory. We'll explore some of the more unique and interesting ones in later sections. For now, let's look at an example of drawing and filling shapes. The following applet, *MouseShapeTest*, fills a predefined Shape when the mouse cursor is within its bounds. Otherwise, only the outline of the Shape is drawn.

```java
import java.applet.*;
import java.awt.*;
import java.awt.event.*;
import java.awt.geom.*;
import java.util.*;

public class MouseShapeTest extends Applet implements MouseMotionListener
{
    // the Shape to draw
    private Shape shape;

    // flags whether or not the mouse cursor is over the Shape
    private boolean mouseOver;

    // the current draw and fill color
```

```java
private Color currentColor;

public void init()
{
    // the control points for the Shape
    int[] x = { 25, 55, 60, 75, 110, 130 };
    int[] y = { 65, 100, 133, 20, 115, 55 };

    // create a new Polygon to represent our Shape.  Remember, a Polygon
    // *is* a Shape since it implements the Shape interface
    shape = new Polygon(x, y, x.length);

    mouseOver = false;
    addMouseMotionListener(this);
}

public void paint(Graphics g)
{
    // cast the sent Graphics context to get a usable Graphics2D object
    Graphics2D g2d = (Graphics2D)g;

    g2d.setColor(currentColor);

    // fill the Shape if the mouse cursor is over it
    if(mouseOver)
    {
        g2d.fill(shape);
    }
    // otherwise, just draw the outline of the Shape
    else
    {
        g2d.draw(shape);
    }
}

public void mouseDragged(MouseEvent e) { /* do nothing */ }

public void mouseMoved(MouseEvent e)
{
```

```
            // save the previous value
            boolean prevValue = mouseOver;

            // update the mouseOver flag using the Shape contains method
            mouseOver = shape.contains(e.getPoint()) ? true : false;

            // repaint only if there is reason to
            if(prevValue != mouseOver)
            {
                // why not change the current color while we're at it
                currentColor = new Color(new Random().nextInt());
                repaint();
            }
        }
    }

}    // MouseShapeTest
```

I like to declare my geometry as *Shape* objects. It's more flexible that way. I can allocate a *Shape* to anything that implements the *Shape* interface and let polymorphism do the work for me.

# Instance Modeling

In the *MouseShapeTest* applet from the previous section, we defined the specific points that made up our Polygon object. The coordinates were arbitrarily placed within our window. Although the geometry of our shape suited that particular example well, it has its shortcomings.

> **NOTE**
> Although the Graphics2D **class defines new methods for drawing and filling shapes, the older** Graphics **methods have not been depreciated for reasons of backward compatibility. So, in order to keep with the newer, preferred way to draw shapes, try to stick with only those methods that rely on the context's current transform to manipulate the geometry. Many people also prefer to stay away from methods that directly take x, y coordinates as parameters.**

For example, what if you wanted to move the object? I suppose you could manipulate each of the points individually, but that would be much too tedious, especially for lazy programmers such as myself. You could certainly use an AffineTransform to move the object. The trouble with this is that if you have many objects you wish to manipulate, you will lose track of your scene very quickly.

A reasonable solution to this problem lies in *instance modeling*. Instance modeling involves two main ideas. First, your geometry is modeled, or defined, about the origin. This gives all objects the same frame of reference, which is helpful if you wish to manipulate an entire scene. It also allows you to rotate objects about themselves, such as was accomplished in the *AffineTest* applet.

The second principle of instance modeling lies in defining your geometry to be unit size. In other words, you should try to model all of your objects such that their dimensions are all a single unit long. You may recall from math class that the *unit circle* is a circle with a diameter of one. Possibly the biggest benefit of modeling to unit size is the fact that your objects are not bound to a specific size. By simply scaling your objects within an AffineTransform, you can create an object of any size. A unit size of one allows you to scale in a linear fashion.

To make instance modeling even more appealing, let's look at a counterexample. Suppose you have a rectangle whose coordinates are arbitrarily defined as (ordered counterclockwise) (102, 167), (102, 207), (152, 207), (152, 167). In order to rotate this object about itself, you would have to translate it back to the origin, perform the rotation, and then translate the object back to its original position. The logical steps required would be:

1. Translate by (−122, −187).
2. Rotate by theta degrees.
3. Translate by (122, 187).

If you don't immediately see where the above translation values come from, work it out on paper. You'll see that these values uniformly distribute the object about the

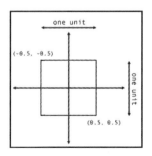

**Figure 7.5**

*Modeling an object about the origin*

origin. I hope you'll agree that this is a pain-in-the-neck way to go about rotating the object. The same thing goes for other transformations, such as scaling. Algorithms that can calculate ways to transform arbitrarily defined geometries will, in essence, waste many clock cycles and make things much more difficult than they need to be.

If that doesn't convince you, then try out the following applet, *InstanceTest*. Using a single *Shape* object, you can render as many instances as you want. This is just a quick and dirty example of instance modeling; if the mood strikes you, try generating different shapes or try building a complex shape by using a single, simple shape.

```java
import java.applet.*;
import java.awt.*;
import java.awt.event.*;
import java.awt.geom.*;
import java.util.*;

public class InstanceTest extends Applet
{
    // the Shape to draw
    private Shape shape;

    public void init()
    {
        // create a unit square modeled about the origin
        shape = new Rectangle2D.Float(-0.5f, -0.5f, 1.0f, 1.0f);
    }

    public void paint(Graphics g)
    {
        // cast the sent Graphics context to get a usable Graphics2D object
        Graphics2D g2d = (Graphics2D)g;

        // save an identity transform to clear the Graphics2D context
        final AffineTransform identity = new AffineTransform();

        Random r = new Random();

        int width = getSize().width;
```

```
int height = getSize().height;

// create 500 instances of the shape's geometry
for(int i = 0; i < 500; i++)
{
    // clear this Graphics2D's transform
    g2d.setTransform(identity);

    // randomly set up the transform
    g2d.translate(r.nextInt()%width, r.nextInt()%height);
    g2d.rotate(Math.toRadians(360*r.nextDouble()));
    g2d.scale(20*r.nextDouble(), 10*r.nextDouble());

    // draw the shape
    g2d.setColor(new Color(r.nextInt()));
    g2d.fill(shape);
    }
}

}    // InstanceTest
```

Figure 7.6 shows a unique run of the *InstanceTest* applet.

The moral of the story is that with a single set of geometry, you can easily generate an infinite number of instances of that geometry. Even though you will typically need at least one translation and scale operation per instance, this model far exceeds any haphazard attempts at modeling geometry as far as flexibility and simplicity are concerned.

In the next section, we'll switch gears a bit and learn how to load and render images.

**Figure 7.6**

*The* InstanceTest *applet*

# The Image Class

Thus far, we've looked at how to create and draw *Shape* objects to the screen. Although we'll make greater use of shape drawing later, let's turn our attention to drawing images.

You'll probably agree that an *image* refers to an *n* x *m* array of pixels that can be drawn to the screen. Such an array of pixels is also known as a *raster*. Images are typically stored within files located on disk. There are many programs out there for creating and manipulating image files, some of which you can find for free. Such programs are beyond the scope of this book, so I will leave it up to you to find one for your favorite development platform.

Undoubtedly, you are familiar with many of the popular image formats, such as .gif, .jpg, .bmp, and .pcx. We will focus our attention on the .gif image format, since Java will be able to render this format on any platform. Formats such as .bmp and .pcx are often platform-dependent; therefore, your programs may only run on a single platform. This would defeat the purpose of using Java, which is to create programs that are platform-independent! With that said, let's look at how to load and render an image to the screen.

In addition to the image format problem posed above, different platforms manipulate and render images in different ways as well. Therefore, you need a way to abstractly define an image and allow the operating system to do the low-level work. Luckily, Java provides an Image class. The Image class is an abstract class. It contains abstract methods that can (among other things) create a Graphics context as well as access the width and height of the image.

> **NOTE**
>
> Here are a few quick notes about .gif files. First, feel free to define a transparency layer within your .gif files; Java 2-D will preserve the transparency in your games. If you're an OpenGL or DirectX programmer, you'll appreciate the ability to embed transparency within your image files, practically giving you transparency without any work.
>
> Also, some people assume that since .gif files can only contain 256 different colors they all must be mapped to the same color lookup table. Don't worry about normalizing your .gif files to within a single 256-color table. As long as your overall desktop resolution is greater than 8-bit color, your images will look fine.

The Applet class defines two methods for loading an Image object, both named getImage. Much like creating *AudioClip* objects, we will concern ourselves with the one that takes two parameters: a URL and a String. The URL object contains information about the Internet location of the applet. Since applets were designed to run within a Web browser, the URL of the image is a necessary component. The String parameter refers to the actual file name of the image you want to load. The getImage method concatenates these two parameters together to create a path to the actual image file.

Since image files typically will not stray too far from our applet's Internet location, we can use the getCodeBase method from the Applet class to get the applet's URL location. This is the approach we will take with all of our examples. If your applet will load many images, you may want to save the code base into a URL object to avoid redundant method calls. Code to load an image named ship.gif may look like the following:

```
...
private Image ship;

public void init()
{
      ship = getImage(getCodeBase(), "ship.gif");
      ...
}
```

Since the Image class is abstract, it is up to the specific platform implementation to create the proper subclass instance of Image. For instance, the Windows implementation may load a sun.awt.windows.Wimage object that overrides the Image methods. However, you are programming abstractly, so all you need to know is how to use the base Image class and its operations.

You can also use the getImage method that takes a single URL as its parameter. This URL should contain the *absolute* location of the image, including the file name. We will focus on using the method that takes two parameters because it is generally more convenient.

> **NOTE**
>
> Windows users need to be courteous to users of other platforms! Since many non-Windows operating systems are case-sensitive with regard to file names, be sure not to mix and match case when referencing file names. For instance, if you have a file named **MYFILE.GIF** (all caps), then be sure not to reference it as myfile.gif (lowercase) in your code. Otherwise, you might end up scratching your head at why your UNIX buddies can't get your game to run.

Now that we have successfully loaded an Image object, let's draw it to the screen. The Graphics2D class defines a single drawImage method that takes an Image as one of its parameters. For legacy purposes, the (six!) drawImage methods from the original Graphics class can still be used, but I would suggest staying away from them.

The Graphics2D drawImage method we are interested in takes three parameters: the Image object that we wish to render, an AffineTransform object containing transformation information for the image, and an *ImageObserver* object. As a side note, *ImageObserver* is an interface for updating Image information. Since Applet implements the *ImageObserver* interface, it is itself an *ImageObserver* object. Therefore, when you call the drawImage method within an Applet method, you can simply pass this (a reference to the Applet object itself). Later, you'll see how to pass an explicit reference to the Applet when the drawImage method is *not* called within an Applet method.

The following applet, *ImageTest*, loads three Image objects from file. It then draws 100 images, each with a randomly generated affine transform. Check it out:

```
import java.applet.*;
import java.awt.*;
import java.awt.geom.*;
import java.util.*;

public class ImageTest extends Applet
{
    // the Images to render
    private Image[] images;

    // filename description of our images
    private final String[] filenames =
        { "simon.gif", "tj2gp.gif", "blade.gif" };

    public void init()
    {
        // get the base URL
        java.net.URL appletBaseURL = getCodeBase();

        // allocate memory for the images and load 'em in
        int n = filenames.length;
        images = new Image[n];
        for(int i = 0; i < n; i++)
        {
            images[i] = getImage(appletBaseURL, filenames[i]);
```

```
        }
    }

    public void paint(Graphics g)
    {
        // cast the sent Graphics context to get a usable Graphics2D object
        Graphics2D g2d = (Graphics2D)g;

        // save an identity transform
        final AffineTransform identity = new AffineTransform();

        // used to transform our images
        AffineTransform at = new AffineTransform();

        Random r = new Random();

        int width = getSize().width;
        int height = getSize().height;

        int numImages = filenames.length;

        // render 100 images, each with a random transformation
        for(int i = 0; i < 100; i++)
        {
            // clear the transformation
            at.setTransform(identity);

            // randomly set up the translation and rotation
            at.translate(r.nextInt()%width, r.nextInt()%height);
            at.rotate(Math.toRadians(360*r.nextDouble()));

            // draw one of the images
            g2d.drawImage(images[i%numImages], at, this);
        }
    }

}   // ImageTest
```

Figure 7.7 shows a fun image of the *ImageTest* applet. Note how it resembles the *InstanceTest* applet.

**Figure 7.7**

*The* ImageTest *applet*

I purposely designed the *ImageTest* applet to resemble the *InstanceTest* applet so we can discuss some of the differences (and similarities) between rendering images and shapes. First, both images and shapes use affine transformations to place them within the scene. In fact, any particular AffineTransform object will be applied the same to both images and shapes. However, there are some differences. The most obvious is the fact that the Graphics2D class uses different methods to render images and shapes. Another notable difference lies in the fact that shape drawing relies on the Graphics2D object's native AffineTransform, where the drawImage method requires a dedicated AffineTransform object to be sent as a parameter. Furthermore, there is little benefit in storing images as unit size. This is because images are less reusable; you will usually create your graphics with the size you wish them to be seen within your scene. However, you can apply the scale operation to your AffineTransform if you wish to resize an image. You'll soon see how you can encapsulate both concepts into a single class structure through abstraction.

Let's revert our attention to shapes a bit and look at some more draw and fill operations.

# More Draw and Fill Operations

In this section, we'll look at several ways to enhance our rendering output, including color blending and two enhancement interfaces: the *Stroke* and *Paint* interfaces. After setting up objects that implement these interfaces, they can be fed to the current Graphics2D context. The Graphics2D object then considers these attributes as subsequent *Shape* objects are rendered.

Let's begin by looking at the *Stroke* interface.

# The *Stroke* Interface

In general, *stroke* refers to attributes applied to lines as they are drawn. These attributes can be the line width as well as other relevant decorations that can be applied to a line. When drawing shapes, the Graphics2D class uses stroke attributes to draw the outline of shapes. We'll use the BasicStroke class to demonstrate how strokes can be used to enhance line and shape drawing in Java.

## The BasicStroke Class

The Java API provides the *Stroke* interface as a bridge between a Graphics2D context and a class that implements the *Stroke* interface. BasicStroke is the only class thus far that implements the *Stroke* interface. However, it can strongly define how shapes should be drawn. Specifically, the BasicStroke class allows you to define the following properties of lines:

- **Width.** The width, or thickness, of the pen.
- **End Caps.** The decoration that is applied to the end of line segments.
- **Line Joins.** The decoration applied where two line segments meet.
- **Dash Pattern.** Breaking up a line into transparent (invisible) and opaque (visible) segments.

Here, the *width* of a line can be any positive floating-point number. The *end caps* can be any one of the following int fields from the BasicStroke class:

- **BasicStroke.CAP_BUTT.** Ends line segments with no additional decoration.
- **BasicStroke.CAP_ROUND.** Ends line segments with a rounded decoration that has a radius that is half the width of the pen.
- **BasicStroke.CAP_SQUARE.** Ends line segments with square decoration extending a distance half the line width beyond the end of the line segment.

Similar to end caps, the *line joins* can be any one of the following BasicStroke class constants:

- **BasicStroke.JOIN_BEVEL.** Connects line segments with a straight line segment.
- **BasicStroke.JOIN_MITER.** Extends the outside edges of line segments until they meet.
- **BasicStroke.JOIN_ROUND.** Rounds off connecting line segments at the corner.

The *dash pattern* is perhaps the most complex of the four stroke attributes. An array of floating-point values is used to define the line size and gap size of individual line segments. For example, an array defined as

```
float[] dashPattern = { 3.0f, 10.0f, 6.0f, 2.0f };
```

would cause the first dash within a line to be 3.0 pixels long, the first gap will be 10.0 pixels long, the second segment would be 6.0 pixels long, and the second gap would be 2.0 pixels long. The pattern would then repeat for the third segment and gap, and so on.

BasicStroke attributes must be set within the constructor. Therefore, there are several constructor methods (with ranging complexity) to allow you to set a custom stroke. The following applet, *StrokeTest*, shows some of the attributes of a BasicStroke using the most complex constructor. It sets the pen width to 3.0 and uses no end cap decorations, a JOIN_MITER to connect lines at corners, and a simple dashing pattern. It then draws a line and a rectangle to show off the stroke's attributes.

```
import java.applet.*;
import java.awt.*;
import java.awt.geom.*;

public class StrokeTest extends Applet
{
    public void paint(Graphics g)
    {
        // cast the sent Graphics context to get a usable Graphics2D object
        Graphics2D g2d = (Graphics2D)g;

        // set the pen width to 3.0 pixels
        float penWidth = 3.0f;

        // set a plain end caps decoration and a join miter line join
        int endCaps = BasicStroke.CAP_BUTT;
        int lineJoins = BasicStroke.JOIN_MITER;

        // limit the miter join trim to 10.0 pixels
        float trim = 10.0f;

        // set the dash pattern
```

```
        float[] dashPattern = { 5.0f, 9.0f, 3.0f };

        // begin the pattern right away (with no pixel offset)
        float dashOffset = 0.0f;

        BasicStroke stroke = new BasicStroke(penWidth, endCaps, lineJoins,
              trim, dashPattern, dashOffset);

        g2d.setStroke(stroke);

        g2d.draw(new Line2D.Float(10.0f, 10.0f, 140.0f, 10.0f));
        g2d.draw(new Rectangle2D.Float(20.0f, 60.0f, 100.0f, 50.0f));
    }

}    // StrokeTest
```

If you don't want to try the *StrokeTest* applet for yourself, check out the nifty screenshot in Figure 7.8.

This was a rather long-winded example. Obviously, in a real applet, you wouldn't need to explicitly name each attribute, but I so did for purposes of demonstration. Once you get the hang of using strokes, the above code can be rewritten in only a few lines. Also, try different combinations of line widths, end caps, line joins, and dash patterns to see how they are all used.

Strokes give you a way to enhance the drawing of shapes. Now let's look at ways to *fill* your shapes using the `Paint` interface.

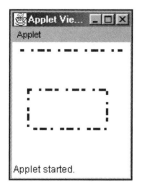

**Figure 7.8**

*The* StrokeTest *applet*

# The *Paint* Interface

Much like the `Stroke` interface, the Java API also defines a `Paint` interface. The `Paint` interface allows you to define how a shape should be filled. The `Color` class is one class that implements the `Paint` interface. When you call the `setColor` method from the `Graphics2D` class, you are essentially defining how a shape should be filled. The Java API also defines two other classes that implement the `Paint` interface: `GradientPaint` and `TexturePaint`. In this section, we'll focus on how to use these two classes to fill *Shape* objects.

> **NOTE**
>
> You already saw in **Chapter 6** how to use `Color` **objects to set the background color of the applet. The** `Graphics2D` **class also contains a method, called** `setColor`, **to set the current rendering color. In Java 2 releases, a** `setPaint` **method has also been added to the** `Graphics2D` **class. The** `setColor` **and** `setPaint` **methods are identical; either method call will yield the same result. So the choice of whether to use the** `Graphics2D` `setColor` **or** `setPaint` **method is entirely up to you.**

## The GradientPaint Class

A *gradient* refers to a colored strip with two defined endpoints. Both endpoints are defined with a different color, and all interior points are filled with colors "in between" the endpoints. The color of each interior pixel is interpolated based on its distance from the endpoints. Figure 7.9 shows a simple example of a black-to-white gradient fill.

As you can see, point *p1* is defined with black color, and point *p2* is defined with white color. All interior points are defined as some color "in between" the two. In this example, all interior points are some shade of gray.

The Java `GradientPaint` class allows you to set up gradient-filled shapes like the one shown in Figure 7.9. To use a `GradientPaint`, you must first have a *Shape* object and two points that will define what the endpoints of the paint will be.

Much like the `BasicStroke` class, the attributes for a *GradientPaint* object must be set when the object is allocated, that is, within one of its constructor methods. There are several constructor methods available for creating gradient paints that can be found in the Java 2 documentation.

The following applet, *GradientTest*, renders a star filled with a green-to-orange gradient paint.

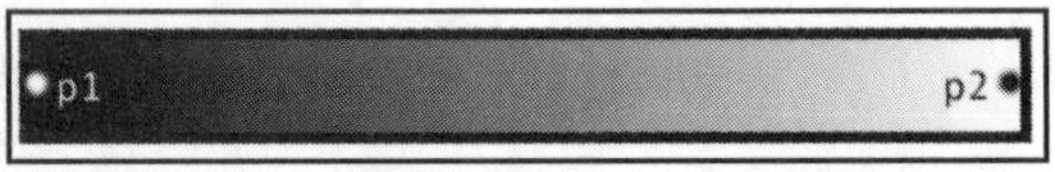

**Figure 7.9**

*A black-to-white gradient*

```java
import java.applet.*;
import java.awt.*;
import java.awt.geom.*;
import java.util.*;

public class GradientTest extends Applet
{
    // the Polygon to draw
    private Polygon poly;

    // the two points that will define the paint's endpoints
    private Point2D p1;
    private Point2D p2;

    public void init()
    {
        // the radius of two circles
        final float[] radii = { 10.0f, 20.0f };

        // the starting point and increment level for plotting points
        double radians = 0.0;
        final double increment = Math.toRadians(15.0);

        poly = new Polygon();

        // the shape will be determined by alternating between points on
        // the perimeters of two circles
        // since we are incrementing by 15 degrees, we can fit 24
        // points in our shape (360/15 = 24)
        for(int i = 0; i < 24; i++)
        {
            poly.addPoint((int)(radii[i%2]*Math.cos(radians)),
                          (int)(radii[i%2]*Math.sin(radians)));

            radians += increment;
        }

        // set the endpoints of our paint.  these values will be scaled
        // by the Graphics2D object
```

```
            p1 = new Point2D.Float(0.0f, +20.0f);
            p2 = new Point2D.Float(0.0f, -20.0f);
        }

    public void paint(Graphics g)
    {
        // cast the sent Graphics context to get a usable Graphics2D object
        Graphics2D g2d = (Graphics2D)g;

        AffineTransform at = new AffineTransform();
        at.translate(100,100);
        at.scale(5, 5);

        // draw the shape
        g2d.setTransform(at);
        g2d.setPaint(new GradientPaint(p1, Color.ORANGE, p2, Color.GREEN));
        g2d.fill(poly);
    }

}    // GradientTest
```

Figure 7.10 shows the *GradientTest* applet in action.

I purposely didn't model the polygon above as unit size. Polygon objects are defined using integers. Therefore, it is impossible to model most objects to unit size to scale later. This is because the only values we can use would be zero or one. It makes me wonder why most *Shape* objects are defined using float-point numbers and the Polygon class is defined by integers. Ho hum.

Also notice that the points that define the paint's endpoints get transformed along with the shape. In the above example, I defined the endpoints for the paint along

**Figure 7.10**

*The* GradientTest *applet*

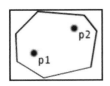

**Figure 7.11**

*Defining interior
endpoints for the paint*

the perimeter of the shape. But what if we define our paint's endpoints within the
interior of our shape, such as shown in Figure 7.11.

What color will the points exterior to *p1* and *p2* look like? The answer depends on
whether the paint is defined as *cyclic* or *acyclic*. If a paint is cyclic, the colors exterior
to points *p1* and *p2* will cycle back through the colors between *p1* and *p2*. Think of
it as a mirroring effect, where points equidistant of *p1* and *p2* will be the same. On
the other hand, acyclic paints use the color defined by the interior points to draw
exterior points. Therefore, points exterior to *p1* will use *p1*'s color, and points
exterior to *p2* will use *p2*'s color.

The following applet, *CycleTest*, demonstrates both cyclic and acyclic gradient
paints. It also draws a line perpendicular to the shape at the points the gradient
paint is defined.

```java
import java.applet.*;
import java.awt.*;
import java.awt.event.*;
import java.awt.geom.*;

public class CycleTest extends Applet implements ItemListener
{
    // the Rectangle to draw
    private Rectangle2D rect;

    // the line containing the points that will define the paint's endpoints
    private Line2D line;

    // checkboxes for selecting gradient cycle type
    private Checkbox cyclic;
    private Checkbox acyclic;

    public void init()
    {
        // create a unit square
```

```java
        rect = new Rectangle2D.Float(-0.5f, -0.5f, 1.0f, 1.0f);

        // set the endpoints of our paint.
        line = new Line2D.Float(-0.25f, 0.0f, 0.25f, 0.0f);

        setBackground(Color.ORANGE);

        // create checkboxes for selecting gradient cycle type
        CheckboxGroup cbg = new CheckboxGroup();
        setLayout(new BorderLayout());
        Panel p = new Panel();
        p.setBackground(Color.GREEN);
        cyclic = new Checkbox("cyclic", cbg, true);
        cyclic.addItemListener(this);
        p.add(cyclic);
        acyclic = new Checkbox("acyclic", cbg, false);
        acyclic.addItemListener(this);
        p.add(acyclic);
        add(p, BorderLayout.SOUTH);
    }

public void paint(Graphics g)
{
        // the scaled width of the rectangle
        final double scaleWidth = 100.0f;

        // cast the sent Graphics context to get a usable Graphics2D object
        Graphics2D g2d = (Graphics2D)g;

        // transform the shape
        g2d.translate(100,100);
        g2d.scale(scaleWidth, 50);

        // draw the shape
        g2d.setPaint(new GradientPaint(line.getP1(), Color.BLACK,
                                       line.getP2(), Color.WHITE,
                                       cyclic.getState()));
```

```
            g2d.fill(rect);

            // draw lines perpendicular to paint endpoints
            g2d.setPaint(Color.RED);

            g2d.setTransform(new AffineTransform());
            g2d.translate(100-0.25*scaleWidth, 100);
            g2d.rotate(Math.PI/2);
            g2d.scale(scaleWidth/2, 1);
            g2d.draw(line);

            g2d.setTransform(new AffineTransform());
            g2d.translate(100+0.25*scaleWidth, 100);
            g2d.rotate(Math.PI/2);
            g2d.scale(scaleWidth/2, 1);
            g2d.draw(line);
        }

        public void itemStateChanged(ItemEvent e)
        {
            // update the change!
            repaint();
        }

    }   // CycleTest
```

Figure 7.12 shows the "cyclic" view of the *CycleTest* applet. Try running the program to see how both views differ from each other.

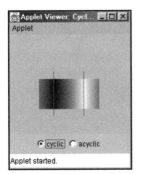

**Figure 7.12**

*The* CycleTest *applet*

Notice how the cyclic value is set in the constructor of the GradientPaint class. Try it for yourself to really see the difference between the two cyclic gradient paint styles.

## The TexturePaint Class

If you liked the GradientPaint class, you're sure to love the TexturePaint class. Just like the GradientPaint class, the TexturePaint class implements the *Paint* interface. With the TexturePaint class, you can fill a shape with a *texture,* or image. Figure 7.13 suggests what a textured paint might look like.

As a programmer, all you need to provide is a BufferedImage and an anchoring rectangle to a TexturePaint object and use the setPaint method from a Graphics2D context to set the paint. You then use the Graphics2D context to fill a specified shape with the texture.

Since we will talk at greater length about the BufferedImage class in Chapter 8, all I will say now is that a BufferedImage represents an accessible chunk of memory containing image data. You can create a BufferedImage of any size and render whatever you want to it. You then pass this image on to your TexturePaint object.

The second parameter sent to a TexturePaint object is an anchoring Rectangle2D object. This rectangle is replicated in all directions within the shape, and the desired texture is mapped to it. The repeating frequency of the texture is greater for small rectangles and lesser for larger rectangles.

Let's try an example. The following applet, *TextureTest*, allows the user to type in the name of a file he or she would like to use as the texture. The applet then attempts to load the image based on the file name and uses the loaded texture as the shape fill.

```
import java.applet.*;
import java.awt.*;
import java.awt.image.*;
import java.awt.event.*;
import java.awt.geom.*;


public class TextureTest extends Applet implements ActionListener
```

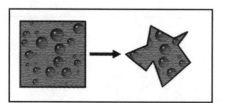

**Figure 7.13**

*Painting a* Shape *with a texture*

```
{
    // field for accepting a filename
    private TextField input;

    public void init()
    {
        // create a layout and add the text field and "OK" button
        setLayout(new BorderLayout());
        Panel p = new Panel();
        input = new TextField("", 20);
        p.add(input);
        Button ok = new Button("OK");
        ok.addActionListener(this);
        p.add(ok);
        add(p, BorderLayout.SOUTH);
    }

    public void paint(Graphics g)
    {
        // cast the sent Graphics context to get a usable Graphics2D object
        Graphics2D g2d = (Graphics2D)g;

        // just draw an outline of the shape and return if the text
        // field just contains white-space or the empty string
        if("".equals(input.getText().trim()))
        {
            g2d.translate(112, 15);
            g2d.rotate(Math.PI/4);
            g2d.draw(new Rectangle2D.Double(0, 0, 104, 104));
            return;
        }

        // load an image
        // we'll look at the MediaTracker class when we discuss animation

        MediaTracker mt = new MediaTracker(this);
        Image image = getImage(getCodeBase(), input.getText());
        mt.addImage(image, 0);
        try
```

```
        {
            mt.waitForAll();
        }
        catch(InterruptedException e) { /* do nothing */ }

        // the filename was probably invalid if the width or height of
        // the image created is <= 0
        if(image.getWidth(this) <= 0 || image.getHeight(this) <= 0)
        {
            // print error message and return
            input.setText(input.getText() + " : invalid filename.");
            return;
        }


        // create a new BufferedImage with the image's width and height
        BufferedImage bi = new BufferedImage(
                image.getWidth(this), image.getHeight(this),
                BufferedImage.TYPE_INT_RGB);

        // get the Graphics2D context of the BufferedImage and render the
        // original image onto it
        ((Graphics2D)bi.getGraphics()).drawImage(
                image, new AffineTransform(), this);

        // create the anchoring rectangle for the paint's image equal in size
        // to the image's size
        Rectangle2D bounds = new Rectangle2D.Float(
                0, 0, bi.getWidth(), bi.getHeight());

        // set the paint
        g2d.setPaint(new TexturePaint(bi, bounds));

        // transform and render!
        g2d.translate(112, 15);
        g2d.rotate(Math.PI/4);
        g2d.fill(new Rectangle2D.Double(0, 0, 104, 104));
    }


    public void actionPerformed(ActionEvent e)
```

```
        {
            // the "OK" button was pressed; update the changes
            repaint();
        }

    }    // TextureTest
```

Checkout Figure 7.14 to see the TextureTest applet in action.

A few items should be noted. BufferedImage objects should be kept as small as possible, since the Graphics2D context creates a full copy of the image data rather than just a shallow copy, or reference, of the data. So don't let large textures lock your programs down.

Other items of note lie within the actual rendering of the textures. First, the texture is transformed along with the geometry of the shape. Also, the texture is clipped at the shape's boundaries if it does not fit perfectly within the shape. Therefore, if either of these effects is undesirable, you must find a work-around to combat it.

> **NOTE**
>
> For now, don't worry about the MediaTracker **class. Just know that it makes sure that images are properly loaded before the application proceeds. We'll talk more about this class in Chapter 9.**

In Chapter 8, we'll look at how to render shapes to a BufferedImage object and use the modified image as a texture to create a paint. For now, let's turn our attention to how we can blend the colors of overlapping objects.

# Blending Operations

Although the "worlds" you create are actually two-dimensional objects being rendered to a two-dimensional plane, it is not entirely impossible to imagine these

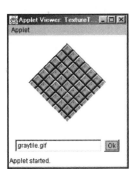

**Figure 7.14**

*The TextureTest applet*

objects "overlapping" one another. If you render objects in the same proximity, you can give the illusion of depth or even a mixing of objects. Wouldn't it be nice if you could make your objects appear *transparent,* or give your objects the appearance of light passing through them?

Well, you can. The Java API provides a `Composite` interface that allows objects such as text, shapes, and images to be blended with their underlying components. The composite is calculated according to what's called a *rule.* There is one class that implements the `Composite` interface: the `AlphaComposite` class. The `AlphaComposite` class allows you the programmer to specify an *alpha channel,* or transparency value for your objects. The rules for calculating these transparency values are based on the Porter-Duff rules for compositing images.

Alpha values are contained as floating-point numbers. They are normalized values ranging from 0.0 (totally transparent) to 1.0 (totally opaque, or devoid of transparency). If an alpha value is not specified, it is assumed to be 1.0. Mathematically, alpha blending works something like:

```
(final_pixelRGB) = (alpha)*(source_pixelRGB) + (alpha-1)*(destination_pixelRGB)
```

There is no explicit constructor method for creating `AlphaComposite` objects; rather, they are accessed through the `getInstance` method. The `getInstance` method is a static class method that returns a predefined `AlphaComposite` object. There are two `getInstance` methods: one that only takes the rule as its argument (and assumes an alpha value of 1.0), and one that takes both the rule and the alpha value (within the range of 0.0 to 1.0) as its arguments. The *rule* argument to the `getInstance` method is an integer and must be one of the defined fields from the `AlphaComposite` class. The most common rule to use is the `SRC_OVER` rule, but there are many other rules you can use, including `CLEAR`, `DST`, `DST_ATOP`, `DST_IN`, `DST_OUT`, `DST_OVER`, `SRC`, `SRC_ATOP`, `SRC_IN`, `SRC_OUT`, `SRC_OVER`, and `XOR`.

I'm sure you're anxious for a code example. I think alpha rendering is so much fun, I'm going to introduce you to some basic animation under Java. The following applet, *CompositeTest,* creates several squares and bounces them around the window. Try not to focus on the animation code itself, just the construction of the `AlphaBox` objects and how to apply their composite values. Pay special attention to the color generated when one square overlaps another.

```
import java.applet.*;
import java.awt.*;
import java.awt.geom.*;
```

```java
import java.util.*;

// A quick 'n' dirty approach to encapsulating the properties (position, size,
// etc) of a square so that it can be updated regularly
class AlphaBox
{
    // a random number generator for the class
    private static Random random = null;

    // all rendering will be based from a single unit square
    private static Rectangle2D square = null;

    // a class copy of the identity affine transform
    private static AffineTransform identity = null;

    // properties of our box
    private AlphaComposite alpha;
    private double xPos;              // x, y position
    private double yPos;
    private double xVel;              // x, y speed
    private double yVel;
    private double size;              // width and height
    private Color  color;             // color of this instance
    private Dimension windowSize;

    public AlphaBox(Dimension d)
    {
        windowSize = d;

        // define any null objects
        if(random == null)
        {
            random = new Random();
        }

        if(square == null)
        {
            square = new Rectangle2D.Float(-0.5f, -0.5f, 1.0f, 1.0f);
```

```
        }

        if(identity == null)
        {
            identity = new AffineTransform();
        }

        // all composites will be SRC_OVER and very transparent
        // play around with these values (try randomizing them)
        // to get some cool effects
        alpha = AlphaComposite.getInstance(
            AlphaComposite.SRC_OVER, 0.25f);

        // randomize the properties of the box
        xPos = windowSize.width*random.nextDouble();
        yPos = windowSize.height*random.nextDouble();
        xVel = 1+2*random.nextDouble();
        if(random.nextDouble() > 0.5) xVel = -xVel;
        yVel = 1+2*random.nextDouble();
        if(random.nextDouble() > 0.5) yVel = -yVel;
        size = 25+100*random.nextDouble();
        color = new Color(random.nextInt()).brighter();
    }

    // paints the box to the sent Graphics2D context according
    // to its current properties
    public void paint(Graphics2D g2d)
    {
        // bounce the box around the window

        xPos += xVel;
        if(xPos > windowSize.width)
        {
            xPos = windowSize.width;
            xVel = -xVel;
        }
        if(xPos < 0)
        {
            xPos = 0;
```

```
                xVel = -xVel;
            }

            yPos += yVel;
            if(yPos > windowSize.height)
            {
                yPos = windowSize.height;
                yVel = -yVel;
            }
            if(yPos < 0)
            {
                yPos = 0;
                yVel = -yVel;
            }

            // render the box
            g2d.setTransform(identity);
            g2d.translate(xPos, yPos);
            g2d.scale(size, size);
            g2d.setComposite(alpha);
            g2d.setPaint(color);
            g2d.fill(square);
        }

    }    // AlphaBox

public class CompositeTest extends Applet implements Runnable
{
    // a thread for animation--we'll talk about this later
    private volatile Thread animation;

    // an array of AlphaBox objects
    private AlphaBox[] boxes;

    public void init()
    {
        animation = new Thread(this);

        // create the boxes
```

```java
        final int n = 10;
        boxes = new AlphaBox[n];
        Dimension size = this.getSize();
        for(int i = 0; i < n; i++)
        {
            boxes[i] = new AlphaBox(size);
        }
    }

    public void start()
    {
        animation.start();
    }

    public void stop()
    {
        animation = null;
    }

    // override the update method so that it doesn't clear the window
    public void update(Graphics g)
    {
        paint(g);
    }

    public void paint(Graphics g)
    {
        Graphics2D g2d = (Graphics2D)g;

        // paint each AlphaBox
        for(int i = 0; i < boxes.length; i++)
        {
            boxes[i].paint(g2d);
        }
    }

    public void run()
    {
        // we'll talk about this stuff later!
```

```
Thread t = Thread.currentThread();
while (t == animation)
{
    try
    {
        t.sleep(10);
    }
    catch (InterruptedException e)
    {
    }
    repaint();
}
}
}    // CompositeTest
```

Figure 7.15 shows a snapshot of a sample run of the *CompositeTest* applet.

The default Applet update method clears the target rendering window before proceeding. Therefore, you need to override it so that window clearing does not occur.

> **NOTE**
>
> Remember, if you do not specify the composite for the Graphics2D context, the default is SRC_OVER with an alpha value of 1.0 (fully opaque).

Although the above listing is rather long, I feel that it is worthwhile to type it in and try it for yourself. It is also a good introduction to using live animation within your

**Figure 7.15**

*Bouncing around with the* CompositeTest *applet*

applets. There's also enough room for you to dig in and play around with some of
the values yourself.

# Manipulating Text

In Chapter 5, we looked at how to use the `Label` class to render static text on the
screen. The use of labels is fine for some purposes, but you don't get the exact
precision of your text layout that you might want. You can use the Java 2-D classes
when you want to place text at exact locations, such as within games. You can also
manipulate text through `AffineTransform` objects to create some cool effects. Java 2-D
also allows you to render text using a specified font.

You are probably familiar with the various fonts available on your computer. Arial,
Helvetica, and Courier are common fonts found under systems running Windows.
With regard to Java 2-D, fonts are nothing more than *Shape* objects that can be
transformed and rendered much like any other *Shape*. The shapes that make up
individual letters or groups of letters are known as *glyphs*. Therefore, a *font* is simply
a collection of glyphs representing all of the characters the font wishes to represent.

Additionally, you can have several variations on a particular font: regular, bold,
italic, and gothic are just a few. Such variations are known as *font faces*. The collection of variations on a particular font type is known as a *font family*.

How can you tell which fonts are available on any particular system? The following
program, *FontListing*, can do this for you. It uses a `GraphicsEnvironment` object to read
the names of all the font families available on a system. The names of the font
families are returned to an array of `String` objects. The program then prints out the
name of each font family.

```java
import java.io.*;
import java.awt.*;

public class FontListing
{
    public static void pause()
    {
        System.out.println("\nPress Enter to Continue");
        try
        {
```

```java
                System.in.read();
        }
        catch(IOException e)
        {
        }
    }

    public static void main(String[] args)
    {
        String[] availableFonts = GraphicsEnvironment.
            getLocalGraphicsEnvironment().getAvailableFontFamilyNames();

        for(int i = 0; i < availableFonts.length; i++)
        {
            System.out.println(availableFonts[i]);

            if(i%20 == 0 && i > 0)
            {
                pause();
            }
        }
    }

}   // FontListing
```

The pause method in the above listing merely allows the user to view the potentially large list of font names one page at a time. Otherwise, the listing might fly by too quickly to read. Remember, this is a console application, so be sure to run it with the java utility from the command line.

Okay, now that you have a good idea what fonts are available on your system, let's look at how to render fonts to the screen.

# Creating and Drawing Text

If you'll recall, a font is simply a collection of glyphs that are used to represent text. In Java, you can use the Font class available in the java.awt.Font package. To render text in Java 2-D, you must first create a Font object and then tell your Graphics2D context you wish to use that font. Creating a Font object is fairly easy. The Font class provides two constructor methods capable of creating a font. We'll focus on the constructor that takes three arguments, described as follows:

- **The name of the font.** It can either be a specific name of a font face or a predefined "logical" font. If you use a logical font name, it must be one of the following: Dialog, DialogInput, Monospaced, Serif, or SansSerif. If no value is specified (i.e., a null value is sent), then "Default" will be used as the font face.

- **The style for the font.** Common styles include Font.PLAIN, Font.BOLD, and Font.ITALIC. This parameter is an int value; therefore, if you wish to specify more than one style for the font, you can use the bitwise union operation, such as Font.BOLD | Font.ITALIC.

- **The point size for the font.** This can be any integer value, such as 8, 12, or 20.

The following creates a Font object using the font face Helvetica, with a bold style and a point size of one:

```
Font font = new Font("Helvetica", Font.BOLD, 1);
```

Then to set this font as the current font to draw with, use the Graphics2D setFont method. The font passed, including all of its attributes, will be used in subsequent text-rendering operations.

```
// assume g2d refers to a valid Graphics2D object
g2d.setFont(font);
```

Or, if you don't need a cached reference to your Font object, you can just set the font in one line, as follows:

```
// assume g2d refers to a valid Graphics2D object
g2d.setFont(new Font("Helvetica", Font.BOLD, 1));
```

Wait a minute. I mentioned that the Font construct takes a point size as its third parameter. So why specify a point size of one? The font would be tiny! Well, remember that Java treats font glyphs as *Shape* objects. Therefore, when you render text, it will render according to your Graphics2D context's current transformation. That means instead of locking yourself into a specific point size, you can specify a size of one and use an AffineTransform to scale the font. Additionally, you can translate, rotate, and shear your fonts as well. Also, font drawing will adhere to the current Graphics2D *Paint* object. All this gives you a lot of control for rendering text (did I hear someone say *instance modeling*?).

When you want to actually draw text, use the Graphics2D drawString method. This method takes three parameters: a String to draw, and the x- and y-positions to draw the text. There are two flavors of this method: one that takes int coordinates (vanilla) and one that takes float coordinates (chocolate).

Let's try an example. The following program, *FontTest*, renders colored text to the screen. It uses a transformation to move, scale, and rotate the text to various positions.

```java
import java.applet.*;
import java.awt.*;
import java.awt.font.*;

public class FontTest extends Applet
{
    // Color constants for rendering different colored text
    static final Color[] colors = {
        Color.RED, Color.BLUE, Color.ORANGE, Color.DARK_GRAY };

    // paints some text to the screen
    public void paint(Graphics g)
    {
        // remember to cast to a valid Graphics2D object
        Graphics2D g2d = (Graphics2D)g;

        // we don't need an explicit reference to the font, so we'll
        // just specify it in one line.  applets that use multiple fonts
        // would want to save a copy of each font.
        g2d.setFont(new Font("Helvetica", Font.BOLD, 1));

        // scale the font, then translate it to be centered on the screen
        g2d.translate(150, 150);
        g2d.scale(20, 20);

        // render "Fonts are FUN!" using each color,
        for(int i = 0; i < colors.length; i++)
        {
            // set the current color
            g2d.setPaint(colors[i]);

            // render the String at (0,0); g2d's transform will take care
```

```
                    // of the actual rendering position and orientation
                    g2d.drawString("Fonts are FUN!", 0, 0);

                    // rotate by 90 degrees
                    g2d.rotate(Math.PI/2.0);
            }
        }    // paint

    }    // FontTest
```

Figure 7.16 shows the FontTest applet.

Notice that you render the text at (0, 0) and allow the current Graphics2D transform to take care of the rest. You could alternatively set explicit values for placement of the text. However, if the current transform of the Graphics2D context is *not* the identity transform, it will further transform the text and possibly give unwanted results. So I prefer to take the safe route and specify transformations all in one single place.

## Deriving Fonts

You have seen how to create fonts with a given font name, style, and size. Suppose you wish to permanently manipulate or distort a font rather than repeatedly transforming your Graphics2D context. For example, suppose a given font has no native italic variation, but you still wish to display it in italicized form. It would appear that you're out of luck.

Well, you would be out of luck if it weren't for *derived fonts*. A derived font is simply a series of operations that replicates a given Font object and then applies new attributes to it. The result will be an entirely new Font object with the specified attributes.

**Figure 7.16**

The FontTest *applet*

Currently, the Font class provides six different deriveFont methods for deriving fonts. Each of these methods returns a newly created Font object. For the above problem with creating an italic font, you would use the method that takes a single AffineTransform object. Specifically, you would provide a transform that is sheared to the right by a given amount. (See Figure 7.17.)

The following code snippet creates a base font and a sheared AffineTransform. It then sets the current font to a derived font with the given transformation.

```
// create a base font
Font baseFont = new Font("Helvetica", Font.BOLD, 1);

// create a transformation for the font
AffineTransform fontAT = new AffineTransform();

// shear the base font to the right
fontAT.shear(-0.75, 0.0);

// create and set a derived font using the above transformation
Font derivedFont = baseFont.deriveFont(fontAT);
g2d.setFont(derivedFont);

// do some drawing here[...]
```

The other five deriveFont methods in the Font class can be quite useful as well. There are methods that derive fonts of given point sizes and given styles. Check out your local Java 2 documentation for more information.

## Retrieving Font Metrics

Other than creating and rendering fonts, you can find out a lot about a particular font through what are called *font metrics*. This includes a font's ascent (the typical maximum height of individual letters, such as capital letters), descent (the typical distance letters may dip below the baseline, such as j, g, and y), and the bounding rectangle that encloses a string of text.

**Figure 7.17**

*Using a shear transformation to create italic text*

Possibly one of the most interesting and useful font metrics you can query is a text string's *bounding rectangle*. A string's bounding rectangle is simply the smallest rectangle that still encompasses a specified string. To retrieve the bounding rectangle of your text, you will need a `FontRenderContext`, a `TextLayout`, and a `Rectangle2D` object.

A `FontRenderContext` object contains information on how text is measured. Rather than creating instances of this class yourself, allow your `Graphics2D` class to do it for you. This way, you are guaranteed that the `FontRenderContext` will properly represent text information on a particular system. To get the context for font rendering, simply call the `getFontRenderContext` method from the `Graphics2D` class, as follows:

```
// assume g2d refers to a valid Graphics2D object
FontRenderContext frc = g2d.getFontRenderContext();
```

Now to get the actual metrics for your font, use a `TextLayout` object. The `TextLayout` class provides the actual font metrics information for your text. You can create a useful `TextLayout` object by specifying a `Font` and `FontRenderContext`, as well as the text string whose capabilities you are interested in, in your constructor method:

```
// assume font refers to a valid Font object
TextLayout layout = new TextLayout("TextLayouts are your friend", font, frc);
```

Now your `TextLayout` object contains your font metrics information regarding the above string, font, and render context. You can now directly receive metric information from your layout. Again, since you are interested in the bounding rectangle, you can call the `getBounds` method from your `TextLayout`, like the following:

```
Rectangle2D textBounds = layout.getBounds();
```

Note that the position of the bounding rectangle of a text string is based relative to the `TextLayout` and not any screen position. Therefore, if you wish to draw the bounding rectangle around your text, you must translate the rectangle to the same position as your text string.

The following applet, *FontBoundsTest*, renders a sample `String` object along with its bounding rectangle:

```
import java.applet.*;
import java.awt.*;
import java.awt.font.*;
import java.awt.geom.*;

public class FontBoundsTest extends Applet
{
```

```java
    private final String MESSAGE = "Trapped!";

    public void paint(Graphics g)
    {
        Graphics2D g2d = (Graphics2D)g;

        // create a Font Object.
        Font baseFont = new Font("Helvetica", Font.PLAIN, 50);

        // get the FontRenderContext for the Graphics2D context
        FontRenderContext frc = g2d.getFontRenderContext();

        // get the layout of our message and font, using the above
        // FontRenderContext
        TextLayout layout = new TextLayout(MESSAGE, baseFont, frc);

        // get the bounds of the layout
        Rectangle2D textBounds = layout.getBounds();

        // draw the message and the bounding rectangle at (45, 50)
        g2d.setFont(baseFont);
        g2d.setPaint(Color.BLACK);
        g2d.drawString(MESSAGE, 45, 50);

        g2d.translate(45, 50);
        g2d.setPaint(Color.RED);
        g2d.draw(textBounds);
    }

} // FontBoundsTest
```

See Figure 7.18 for an illustration of the FontBoundsTest applet.

Alternatively, you can also render the contents of your TextLayout object directly to your Graphics2D context. Depending on the situation, drawing text in this manner

**Figure 7.18**

*The* FontBoundsTest *applet*

may prove useful. You can render text directly to your Graphics2D context like the following:

```
layout.draw(g2d, 45, 50);
```

There's a lot more you can do with fonts, such as creating editable text, highlighting selections, and performing hit testing on text characters. We'll look at some more rendering techniques for fonts when we look at clipping paths in Chapter 8.

> **NOTE**
>
> Remember, not all fonts are available on all systems. Therefore, you should be careful when deciding which fonts to use. Obviously, fonts that are commonly available on the widest number of systems are good to use. If you specify a font that does not exist on a particular system, Java will select a default font to use.

# Conclusion

In this chapter, you learned a lot of the basics to help you get up and running. Understanding how coordinate systems, transformations, shape drawing and filling, and text rendering are used in Java will give you a great head start on becoming a master at Java 2-D. When developing the graphics for your games, you'll have a lot of different things to keep in mind. That's why I hope this chapter will serve as a useful reference for developing the visual components of your games.

I can't think of any other graphics package that puts so much power behind the use of primitive shape and line drawing. Using strokes, paints, and fills are all great ways to enhance primitive shape and text rendering. Using these techniques to their fullest will certainly help you pull off some great-looking graphics in your games without having to rely solely on prerendered images pulled from file.

I felt that plowing through the entire Java 2-D API in one chapter could possibly overload one's circuits. So to break up the insanity of Java 2-D, I have decided to end here and save topics such as collision detection, additive geometry, rendering hints, and image enhancement operations for the next chapter. So get your bearings and try the following exercises before moving on, and I'll see you in Chapter 8 when we continue with Part II of the Java 2-D API!

# Exercises

**7.1**  Discuss some of the benefits the Graphics2D class has over the Graphics class.

**7.2**  Discuss why components rendered within a FlowLayout (such as buttons, labels, etc.) are largely resolution-independent operations, whereas Java 2-D rendering operations can be considered more dependent on the window resolution. Defend why resolution-dependent operations are okay for game programming.

**7.3** Rewrite the *MouseShapeTest* to use instance modeling. Be sure to use the techniques for normalizing the width of a line stroke for drawing the `Polygon` outline.

**7.4** The *TextureTest* applet rotates the entire scene—both the geometry as well as the texture. Rewrite the *TextureTest* applet so that the texture remains orthogonal (at a right angle) to the applet's frame.

**7.5** Modify the *CompositeTest* applet to allow the user to specify the number of boxes to create as an applet parameter. Also, randomly generate each box's transparency level using the `nextFloat` method from the `Random` class.

**7.6** Write code that checks whether a given font is available on your system. Why might it be good to first check for available fonts rather than just using them?

**7.7** Write code that centers text within an applet window. While you're at it, texture the text using a `TexturePaint` object.

# CHAPTER 8

# Rendering Shapes, Text, and Images with Java 2-D, Part II

In Chapter 7 you learned how to use Java 2-D to render shapes, images, and text. You also learned how to use some really fun features of the Java 2-D API, such as alpha blending and gradient paints. As promised, Chapter 8 will continue where Chapter 7 left off. So without further ado, let's start having some fun with geometry and see how to test multiple objects for collisions.

# Having Fun with Geometry

Unlike in your typical tenth grade geometry class, we will now look at some *fun* things you can do with two-dimensional geometry. In this section, we'll look at simple collision testing, creating complex shapes with additive geometry, and defining rendering regions with area clipping.

## Collision Testing

*Collision testing* is undoubtedly an essential part of most games available today. Whether players are shooting down ships with lasers and missiles, climbing ladders, or assembling puzzle pieces, the ability to detect collisions among objects is always needed. We'll begin our discussion with how to use bounding boxes to quickly and easily determine if any two given objects have collided.

### Bounding Boxes

You can test to see if objects moving about within a scene collide with one another, and you can usually use common sense to tell whether you need to do so. For example, in the real world, we all know that two things cannot exist in the same place at the same time (unless of course they have different quantum numbers!). So, if you have objects moving throughout your scene, you should test your objects for collision against any other object that would violate this rule. When collisions are detected, you can then take appropriate actions. For example, if an object runs into a wall, you might want to stop the moving object or have it rebound. A collision with a missile and an alien ship might cause the missile to explode and the ship to take damage. It all depends on the situation.

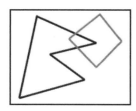

**Figure 8.1**

*That's gotta hurt.*

So how do you detect collisions between objects? Collision testing can be rather straightforward, if you're willing to weigh the pluses and minuses. Figure 8.1 shows two objects colliding. As you look at it, think about the ways in which the collision can be detected.

If the objects in Figure 8.1 were two images with transparent sections, you could test the actual pixel data and try to find two nontransparent pixels that occupy the same location. However, this is an extremely costly operation and is completely impractical for use in most games. Similarly, if the two objects were *Shape* objects, you could test for line intersections possibly using a `PathIterator` object. This, too, would be very costly and unusable in typical game code.

The technique I prefer, at least for two-dimensional space, is to use *bounding boxes* to check for collisions among objects. A bounding box is simply a tight rectangle that fits around a shape or image. Using them vastly simplifies the calculations involved in collision testing. Given the x, y coordinates of a rectangle and its width and height, you can determine if it collides with another rectangle in only a few steps. Better yet, the *Shape* interface already defines an `intersects` method for determining if one rectangle intersects another. Figure 8.2 shows the same objects as in Figure 8.1 along with their bounding boxes. Check out the area where the two rectangles overlap.

The following applet, *CollisionTest*, uses the `intersects` method to detect collisions among *Shape* objects. The applet also contains a reference to a selected shape, known as a *pick*, which can be picked up and dragged by the mouse to cause collisions with other objects. Objects that collide with the pick will be highlighted in red to show collision. For simplicity, the *CollisionTest* applet uses hard-coded position values and sizes rather than instance modeling.

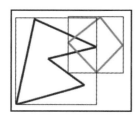

**Figure 8.2**

*That's gotta hurt, Part II.*

```java
import java.applet.*;
import java.awt.*;
import java.awt.geom.*;
import java.awt.event.*;
import java.util.*;

public class CollisionTest extends Applet implements MouseListener,
                                                     MouseMotionListener
{
    // the number of rectangles contained in our scene
    private final int NUM_RECTS = 10;

    // a list of rectangles
    private LinkedList rectangles;

    // an AlphaComposite to show semi-transparent rectangles
    private AlphaComposite alpha;

    // the rectangle that is currently selected
    private Rectangle2D pick;

    public void init()
    {
        rectangles = new LinkedList();
        pick = null;

        // create an AlphaComposite with 50% transparency
        alpha = AlphaComposite.getInstance(AlphaComposite.SRC_OVER, 0.5f);

        // create NUM_RECTS rectangles at random positions and add them
        // to the list
        Random r = new Random();
        int width = (int)getSize().getWidth();
        int height = (int)getSize().getHeight();

        for(int i = 0; i < NUM_RECTS; i++)
        {
            rectangles.add(new Rectangle2D.Double(
```

```
                    (double)(    Math.abs(r.nextInt())%width),
                    (double)(    Math.abs(r.nextInt())%height),
                    (double)(20+Math.abs(r.nextInt())%50),
                    (double)(20+Math.abs(r.nextInt())%50)));
    }

    // don't forget to register the applet to listen for mouse events
    addMouseListener(this);
    addMouseMotionListener(this);
}


public void paint(Graphics g)
{
    Graphics2D g2d = (Graphics2D)g;

    // tell our Graphics2D context to use transparency
    g2d.setComposite(alpha);

    // draw the rectangles
    g2d.setPaint(Color.BLACK);
    for(int i = 0; i < NUM_RECTS; i++)
    {
        g2d.draw((Rectangle2D.Double)rectangles.get(i));
    }

    // if pick refers to a valid rectangle, test it for collisions
    if(pick != null)
    {
        Rectangle2D rect;
        g2d.setPaint(Color.RED.darker());
        for(int i = 0; i < NUM_RECTS; i++)
        {
            // get the ith rectangle in the list
            rect = (Rectangle2D)rectangles.get(i);

            // test for intersection--note we shouldn't test
            // pick against itself
            if(pick != rect && pick.intersects(rect))
```

```
                    {
                        // fill collisions
                        g2d.fill(rect);
                    }
                }

                // fill the pick rectangle
                g2d.setPaint(Color.BLUE.brighter());
                g2d.fill(pick);
            }
        }

        // methods inherited from the MouseListener interface

        public void mouseClicked(MouseEvent e) { }

        public void mouseEntered(MouseEvent e) { }

        public void mouseExited(MouseEvent e)  { }

        public void mousePressed(MouseEvent e)
        {
            // attempt to pick up a rectangle
            if(pick == null)
            {
                Rectangle2D rect;
                for(int i = 0; i < NUM_RECTS; i++)
                {
                    rect = (Rectangle2D)rectangles.get(i);

                    // if the rectangle contains the mouse position,
                    // 'pick' it up
                    if(rect.contains(e.getPoint()))
                    {
                        pick = rect;
                        return;
                    }
                }
```

```
        }
    }

    public void mouseReleased(MouseEvent e)
    {
        // release the pick rectangle and repaint the scene
        pick = null;
        repaint();
    }


    // methods inherited from the MouseMotionListener interface

    public void mouseDragged(MouseEvent e)
    {
        // if we have a picked rectangle, set its position to the
        // current mouse position and repaint
        if(pick != null)
        {
            pick.setRect(e.getX(), e.getY(),
                        pick.getWidth(), pick.getHeight());
            repaint();
        }
    }

    public void mouseMoved(MouseEvent e)  { }

}    // CollisionTest
```

Figure 8.3 illustrates collision with the pick rectangle and two other rectangle objects.

To use the CollisionTest applet, simply hold the mouse button down over any rectangle and drag it around the scene. Be sure to note how the intersects and contains methods are used to detect collisions and inclusions.

For purposes of demonstration, the *CollisionTest* applet only used rectangles for collision testing. For nonrectangular shapes, you can call the getBounds2D method to generate a Rectangle2D object that completely encloses the shape. For complex shapes, bounding rectangles can cause some problems. For instance, look back at Figure 8.2 and imagine a fleeting collision with the lower-left corner of the diamond

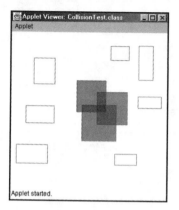

**Figure 8.3**

*The* CollisionTest *applet*

shape's bounding box with the upper-right corner of the other shape's bounding box. The actual geometric shapes would be nowhere near each other, but this situation would nonetheless report a collision! There must be a way to refine the bounding box technique to "tighten" collision testing.

## Improving Collision Detection

A simple solution to the above scenario involves shrinking your bounding boxes. It might be a good idea to center your bounding box on the center of mass of your shapes. The size of the box should be large enough to enclose the important areas of the shape, but not too large so that erroneous collisions are detected.

The following code snippet shrinks a bounding rectangle to 75 percent of its original size. You will be asked to methodize the following code in one of this chapter's exercises.

```
// assume poly refers to a valid Polygon or Shape object
Rectangle2D bounds = poly.getBounds2D();

// shrink the bounding rectangle by 75%
bounds.setRect(bounds.getX() + 0.125*bounds.getWidth(),
               bounds.getY() + 0.125*bounds.getHeight(),
               0.75*bounds.getWidth(),
               0.75*bounds.getHeight());
```

Bounding boxes generated by the above code may look similar to Figure 8.4.

Note that even though we've solved one problem, we've created another. Although tighter bounding boxes solve the "noncollision" problem, our geometry may now

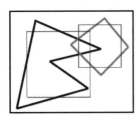

**Figure 8.4**

*(Somewhat) accurate collision detection using shrunken bounding boxes*

logically collide but the bounding boxes do not yet overlap. So like with most things, there is a trade-off. Here, the trade-off comes between detecting collisions too soon or too late. The effects of velocity on your objects will often cause the eye not to notice this side effect, so I suggest shrinking bounding rectangles whenever possible.

## Bounded Images

Undoubtedly, the use of images will dominate most of the graphic content in your games. Therefore, it is worthwhile to discuss some of the differences between testing for collision between images and shapes. In this section, we'll look at how to encapsulate image and bounding box information into a single class and test for collisions among images within a scene.

Graphically, the differences between an Image and a *Shape* may not be immediately apparent. But after looking at both more closely, we can make some generalizations.

- While *Shape* objects can contain information regarding screen position, Image objects cannot.
- Images are always rectangular in nature; shapes can be of any shape (including rectangular).
- Image objects know their own width and height; *Shape* objects must access them through the getBounds2D method (unless, of course, the shape *is* a Rectangle2D object).
- Images can contain transparent regions that might require their bounding boxes to be resized.

With those generalizations in mind, you can see some of the similarities and differences between images and shapes. One of the most important properties of an Image is that it only contains its own width and height information, but not information about its relative screen position. Remember that image screen positioning is always dictated by an AffineTransform object passed to a Graphics2D context. Therefore, you need to provide a way to associate an Image with a Rectangle2D bounding box.

One solution might be to create a container class that contains both an Image as well as its associated Rectangle2D bounding box. Using the bounding box, you can define the logical position of an image within your scene. The x- and y-components of the bounding box can then be used to create an AffineTransform object for rendering within a Graphics2D context. The code for a simple BoundedImage class might look similar to the following:

```java
import java.applet.*;
import java.awt.*;
import java.awt.image.*;
import java.awt.geom.*;
import java.util.*;

class BoundedImage extends Object
{
    // the Image and bounding data for this container
    private Image       image;
    private Rectangle2D bounds;

    public BoundedImage(Image img, ImageObserver obs)
    {
        image = img;

        // set the bounds to (0, 0) with the width and height of
        // the image data
        bounds = new Rectangle2D.Double(0, 0,
                                        image.getWidth(obs),
                                        image.getHeight(obs));
    }

    public Rectangle2D getBounds2D()
    {
        return bounds;
    }

    public Image getImage()
    {
        return image;
```

```
        }

        public AffineTransform getTransform()
        {
            return AffineTransform.getTranslateInstance(
                            bounds.getX(), bounds.getY());
        }

        public void moveTo(Point p)
        {
            bounds.setRect((double)p.x, (double)p.y,
                            bounds.getWidth(),
                            bounds.getHeight());
        }

    }   // BoundedImage
```

Note that the BoundedImage constructor takes both an Image as well as an *ImageObserver* object, which will typically be a reference to your main Applet class. The *ImageObserver* is needed to correctly report the width and height of the Image so the dimensions of your bounding rectangle can be properly set.

The next two methods are the basic access methods for getting the data and bounds of the image. The getTransform method generates an AffineTransform based on the position of the bounding rectangle. This transform can then be used by the Graphics2D context for rendering the image. The final method, moveTo, sets the bounding rectangle's position equal to a given Point object, while preserving its own width and height. You will use this method to use the mouse to move objects around your scene.

The following applet, *BoundedImageTest*, is similar to the *CollisionTest* applet, except that it uses the BoundedImage class rather than shapes. I designed it to be similar to the *CollisionTest* applet so that the differences when using images can be better highlighted. Look over the following listing, then try to modify the *CollisionTest* applet yourself to see if you can make the changes on your own.

```
    public class BoundedImageTest extends Applet implements MouseListener,
                                                            MouseMotionListener
    {
        // global reference to the image filename for easy editing
```

```java
private final String FILENAME = "simon.gif";

// the number of images contained in our scene
private final int NUM_IMAGES = 3;

// a list of BoundedImages
private LinkedList images;

// the BoundedImage that is currently selected
private BoundedImage pick;

// an AlphaComposite to highlight collisions
private AlphaComposite alpha;

public void init()
{
    images = new LinkedList();
    pick = null;

    // create NUM_IMAGES images at random positions and add them
    // to the list

    Random r = new Random();
    int width = (int)getSize().getWidth();
    int height = (int)getSize().getHeight();

    // create a MediaTracker object so our images are fully loaded
    // before being passed to the BoundedImage class
    MediaTracker mt = new MediaTracker(this);

    BoundedImage bi;      // BoundedImage to add to the list
    Image img;            // a single Image

    for(int i = 0; i < NUM_IMAGES; i++)
    {
        img = getImage(getCodeBase(), FILENAME);
        mt.addImage(img, i);
        try
        {    mt.waitForID(i);
```

```
            }
            catch(InterruptedException e) { /* do nothing */ }

            bi = new BoundedImage(img, this);
            bi.moveTo(new Point(Math.abs(r.nextInt())%width,
                                Math.abs(r.nextInt())%height));

            images.add(bi);
        }

        // create an AlphaComposite with 40% transparency
        alpha = AlphaComposite.getInstance(AlphaComposite.SRC_OVER, 0.4f);

        // don't forget to register the applet to listen for mouse events
        addMouseListener(this);
        addMouseMotionListener(this);
    }

    public void paint(Graphics g)
    {
        Graphics2D g2d = (Graphics2D)g;

        // draw the images
        BoundedImage bi;
        for(int i = 0; i < NUM_IMAGES; i++)
        {
            bi = (BoundedImage)images.get(i);
            g2d.drawImage(bi.getImage(), bi.getTransform(), this);
        }

        // if pick refers to a valid image, test it for collisions
        if(pick != null)
        {
            for(int i = 0; i < NUM_IMAGES; i++)
            {
                // get the ith image in the list
                bi = (BoundedImage)images.get(i);

                // test for intersection
```

```java
                if(imageCollision(pick, bi))
                {
                    // fill the bounding rectangle to highlight
                    // the collision
                    g2d.setComposite(alpha);
                    g2d.setPaint(Color.RED.darker());
                    g2d.fill(bi.getBounds2D());
                }
            }

            // draw and fill the pick rectangle
            g2d.setPaint(Color.BLUE.brighter());
            g2d.setComposite(alpha);
            g2d.drawImage(pick.getImage(), pick.getTransform(), this);
            g2d.fill(pick.getBounds2D());
        }
    }

    // determines if two BoundedImages intersect (collide). this method
    // will return false if i1 and i2 refer to the same object
    private boolean imageCollision(BoundedImage i1, BoundedImage i2)
    {
        return (i1 == i2) ? false :
                        i1.getBounds2D().intersects(i2.getBounds2D());
    }

    // methods inherited from the MouseListener interface

    public void mouseClicked(MouseEvent e) { }

    public void mouseEntered(MouseEvent e) { }

    public void mouseExited(MouseEvent e)  { }

    public void mousePressed(MouseEvent e)
    {
        // attempt to pick up an image
        if(pick == null)
        {
```

```
                BoundedImage bi;
                for(int i = 0; i < NUM_IMAGES; i++)
                {
                    bi = (BoundedImage)images.get(i);

                    // if the BoundedImage contains the mouse position,
                    // 'pick' it up
                    if(bi.getBounds2D().contains(e.getPoint()))
                    {
                        pick = bi;
                        return;
                    }
                }
            }
        }

        public void mouseReleased(MouseEvent e)
        {
            // release the pick image and repaint the scene
            pick = null;
            repaint();
        }

        // methods inherited from the MouseMotionListener interface

        public void mouseDragged(MouseEvent e)
        {
            // if we have a picked image, set its position to the
            // current mouse position and repaint
            if(pick != null)
            {
                pick.moveTo(e.getPoint());
                repaint();
            }
        }

        public void mouseMoved(MouseEvent e) { }

    }   // BoundedImageTest
```

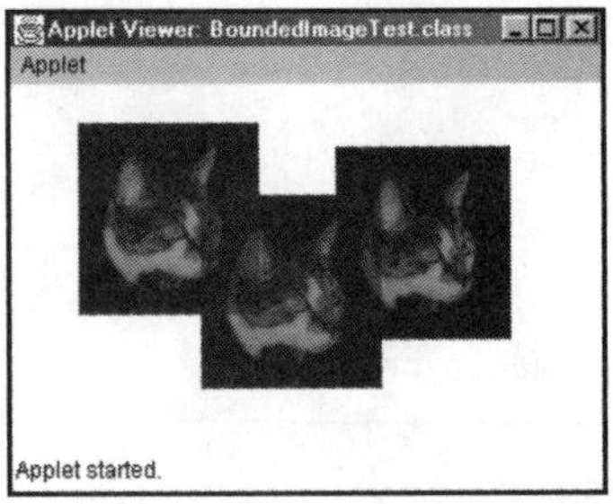

**Figure 8.5**

*The* BoundedImageTest *applet*

Figure 8.5 illustrates the BoundedImageTest applet with a photo of my fianceé's cat, Simon.

I hope you were able to make the changes to the *CollisionTest* applet with relative ease. If you are having trouble, try to focus on the broad concepts involved in the above program. If usage of the MediaTracker class seems confusing, you can either just copy it as it is or you can jump ahead to Chapter 9. Also, if you're not a cat lover, feel free to change the global FILENAME String object to whatever you like.

## Testing Large Lists of Objects

Thus far, you've looked at examples in which you're comparing a single entity from a list against the rest of the entities in the list. So for a list of length *n*, you would typically perform *n-1* collision tests per frame (*n-1* because you don't need to test the object against itself). If you're adept at algorithm complexity, you know this yields an algorithm of *order n* ($O(n)$).

The linear model stated above is great for games where you have one active (i.e., moving) object that can collide against one or more other static (i.e., nonmoving) objects. However, what if all of your objects are in motion, such as in an asteroid field? Here, any object can logically collide into any other object. Refer to Figure 8.6 for a visual representation of a group of mutually collide-able objects.

Since every asteroid can potentially collide with every other asteroid, the following algorithm can be used for the comparisons:

```
// assume list refers to a valid array of collide-able objects
for(int i = 0; i < list.length; i++)
{
    for(int j = 0; j < list.length; j++)
```

```
{
        // test for collision; don't test objects against themselves
        if(i != j && list[i].collidesWith(list[j]))
        {
                // handle collision
        }
    }   // j
}   // i
```

I hope you'll agree that the complexity of the above algorithm is $O(n^2)$. The above code will not only generate all of the collisions, but it will generate them *twice*. If element *n* collides with element *m*, then element *m* will collide with element *n*. This has two drawbacks.

- It wastes processor time.
- Subsequent collision code will be called twice.

Therefore, if the collision code for asteroids reduces an asteroid's hit points by five, then calling the code twice will, in essence, reduce the asteroid's hit points by ten! Soon you'll be wondering why your asteroids are exploding twice as fast as you had expected. There must be a better way.

An easy and efficient way to avoid the above problems would be to write an algorithm that ensures that any two objects are tested for collision *only once*. Furthermore, such an algorithm must follow this contract.

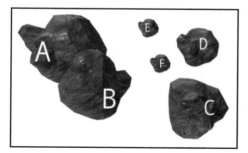

**Figure 8.6**

*A group of asteroids*

With this in mind, let's look at the actual code that reduces the number of collision tests:

```
// assume list refers to a valid array of collide-able objects
for(int i = 0; i < list.length - 1; i++)
{
    for(int j = i + 1; j < list.length; j++)
    {
        // test for collision
        if(list[i].collidesWith(list[j]))
        {
            // handle collision
        }
    }   // j
}   // i
```

With just a few simple code changes, we have actually solved the problem of double collisions, as well as reduced the amount of processing required by more than half. I'll let you numerologists (I'm sorry, *mathematicians*) out there figure out the actual speed gain. Also, since we are guaranteed that an object will not be tested against itself, we do not have to check the two index values for equality.

In the following chapters, we'll look at ways to reduce the number of collisions we need to test for even more. We'll also look at how to perform more complex actions when two objects collide.

> **NOTE**
>
> If you compiled and ran the examples from this section, you'll probably have noticed that much of the motion is not smooth and will often flicker. This is because you did not implement an off-screen, or back, rendering buffer. For more on implementing an off-screen buffer, see Chapter 9.

## Additive Geometry

One of the areas of Java 2-D that I think is rather fun is additive geometry, also known as *constructive area geometry*. Additive geometry allows you to use Boolean operations to combine multiple shapes into a single, more complex shape.

Take a quick look at Figure 8.7 and think about how many different shapes you can see.

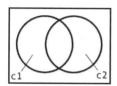

**Figure 8.7**

*Two overlapping circles*

You're probably able to see at least three or four different shapes that can be generated by the two overlapping circles in Figure 8.7. So how do you combine them? Java 2-D provides an `Area` class that implements the *Shape* interface. An `Area` defines an arbitrarily shaped object much like a polygon.

In addition to the common methods associated with the *Shape* interface, the `Area` class also defines four operations for combining shapes. These operations are

- Union
- Subtraction
- Intersection
- Exclusive *or* (*xor*)

The effects of these operations will become more apparent when we look at a solid code example. For now, think of them in terms of bitwise operations. Each `Area` operation works on the principle that each section of two shapes either overlaps or does not overlap. The comparisons made are purely binary.

In general, the steps needed to create an additive shape are as follows:

1. Create two or more *Shape* objects.
2. Create an Area object, specifying one of the shapes at the time of construction.
3. Apply one or more of the four Area operations to constructively create a new shape.

Let's apply these steps toward a complete code example, then we'll discuss each operation in more detail. The following applet, *AreaTest*, creates two circles, much like those in Figure 8.7, and applies each `Area` operation to them to create new shapes. These newly created shapes are drawn to the screen, along with the name of each operation used.

```java
import java.applet.*;
import java.awt.*;
import java.awt.event.*;
```

```java
import java.awt.geom.*;
import java.util.*;

public class AreaTest extends Applet
{
    // an array of Area objects and an associated array of String
    // geometry descriptions
    private Area[] shapes;
    private String[] ops;

    public void init()
    {
        // create 4 Areas and Strings
        shapes = new Area[4];
        ops = new String[4];

        // create two circles that overlap about the origin
        Ellipse2D e1 = new Ellipse2D.Double(-0.125, 0.0, 0.5, 0.5);
        Ellipse2D e2 = new Ellipse2D.Double(+0.125, 0.0, 0.5, 0.5);

        // create a Union between the shapes
        shapes[0] = new Area(e1);
        shapes[0].add(new Area(e2));
        ops[0] = "Union";

        // subtract e2 from e1
        shapes[1] = new Area(e1);
        shapes[1].subtract(new Area(e2));
        ops[1] = "Subtraction";

        // create an Intersection between the shapes
        shapes[2] = new Area(e1);
        shapes[2].intersect(new Area(e2));
        ops[2] = "Intersection";

        // use the Exclusive OR operation between the shapes
        shapes[3] = new Area(e1);
        shapes[3].exclusiveOr(new Area(e2));
        ops[3] = "XOR";
```

```
        }

        public void paint(Graphics g)
        {
            // cast the sent Graphics context to get a usable Graphics2D object
            Graphics2D g2d = (Graphics2D)g;

            // create a stroke to outline the shapes
            g2d.setStroke(new BasicStroke(2.0f/100.0f));

            // create a Random object for creating random colors
            Random r = new Random();

            // render the shapes and the operation descriptions
            for(int i = 0; i < 4; i++)
            {
                g2d.setTransform(new AffineTransform());
                g2d.translate(50+(i*100), 40);

                g2d.drawString(ops[i], 0, 70);

                g2d.scale(100, 100);

                // fill then outline the shape in black
                g2d.setPaint(new Color(r.nextInt()));
                g2d.fill(shapes[i]);
                g2d.setPaint(Color.BLACK);
                g2d.draw(shapes[i]);
            }
        }

    }    // AreaTest
```

Figure 8.8 shows the AreaTest applet in action. It's amazing what the Java 2-D system can do!

Now that you've had a chance to review the code and its output, let's note the similarities to Area operations and their equivalent bitwise Boolean operations.

- The *union* operation is similar to the bitwise *or* operation.
- The *subtract* operation is similar to the bitwise *not* operation.

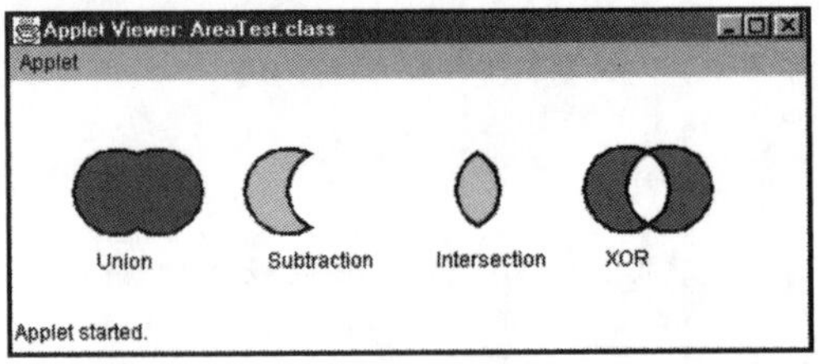

**Figure 8.8**

The AreaTest *applet*

- The *intersect* operation is similar to the bitwise *and* operation.
- The *xor* operation is similar to, well, the bitwise *or* operation.

What does this mean for you? Well, it gives you another way to look at Area operations. If you're having trouble deciding which operation will yield a specific shape, think about each operation in terms of binary operations. For example, a union simply encloses the area that is defined within one shape or the other (or even the area common to both shapes, since 1 *or* 1 equals 1). This will define a different shape than would the *xor* operation, which defines only the area that lies exclusively within one shape or within the other.

Remember, constructive area geometry works on more than just circles. You can combine a triangle with a circle, a circle with a polygon, or any other shapes you can imagine.

## Area Clipping

Another fun geometric operation found in the Java 2-D API is known as *area clipping*. Area clipping simply allows you to specify an arbitrary Shape object, called a *clip*, to restrict the area of the screen to be rendered. Area clipping is similar to constructive area geometry in that it allows you to use geometry to enhance or restrict how objects are rendered in your scenes.

To set a path to clip against, you must first create a Shape object. Then pass the Shape to your Graphics2D context using one of two methods, setClip or clip. If you send the Shape to the Graphics2D setClip method, the shape of the clip will directly define the clipping region. Note that the final screen coordinates for your clip are generated with respect to the Graphics2D context's current transform.

Alternatively, you could also call the Graphics2D clip method to set the clipping path. This method actually changes the clipping path by taking the intersection between the current clipping path and the sent Shape object. This method is useful when you want to narrow the clipping path to an area common to two different shapes.

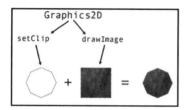

**Figure 8.9**

*Generating a clipped image*

Figure 8.9 illustrates how an image and a clipping region can be combined to create a clipped image.

To illustrate how shapes can be used to define clipping regions for your images, I whipped up the following applet, cleverly named *ClipTest*. It allows the user to select from three rendering examples using a Choice object. The first choice renders an image with no clipping. The second choice renders just the clipping area as a *Shape* object using the Graphics2D draw method. The third and final choice defines the *Shape* object as the clipping region and renders the image within it.

```java
import java.applet.*;
import java.awt.*;
import java.awt.geom.*;
import java.awt.event.*;

public class ClipTest extends Applet implements ItemListener
{
    // the Image and clip region to render
    private Image image;
    private Polygon clip;

    // a Choice to display the Image and clip region
    private Choice dropBox;

    // indices for our drop box
    private final int SHOW_IMAGE_ONLY    = 0;
    private final int SHOW_CLIP_ONLY     = 1;
    private final int SHOW_CLIPPED_IMAGE = 2;

    public void init()
    {
        // load an image from file
        MediaTracker mt = new MediaTracker(this);
```

```java
        image = getImage(getCodeBase(), "blabber.gif");
        mt.addImage(image, 0);
        try
        {
            mt.waitForID(0);
        }
        catch(InterruptedException e) { /* do nothing */ }

        // create an 8-sided clip region about an anchor point
        // the anchor point will be located at the center of our Image

        clip = new Polygon();
        int anchor = image.getWidth(this)/2;
        for(int i = 0; i < 8; i++)
        {
            clip.addPoint(anchor+(int)(anchor*Math.cos(Math.toRadians(i*45))),
                          anchor+(int)(anchor*Math.sin(Math.toRadians(i*45))));
        }

        // add the drop box to the bottom of the container, along with the
        // three render choices
        setLayout(new BorderLayout());
        dropBox = new Choice();
        dropBox.add("Show Image");
        dropBox.add("Show Clip Region");
        dropBox.add("Show Clipped Image");
        dropBox.addItemListener(this);
        add(dropBox, BorderLayout.SOUTH);
    }

    public void paint(Graphics g)
    {
        // cast the sent Graphics context to get a usable Graphics2D object
        Graphics2D g2d = (Graphics2D)g;

        // set the transform to the identity transform
        final AffineTransform at = new AffineTransform();

        // render based on the current selection
```

```java
        switch(dropBox.getSelectedIndex())
        {
            case SHOW_IMAGE_ONLY:
            {
                // just draw the Image
                g2d.drawImage(image, at, this);
                break;
            }

            case SHOW_CLIP_ONLY:
            {
                // just draw the clipping region
                g2d.setTransform(at);
                g2d.draw(clip);
                break;
            }

            case SHOW_CLIPPED_IMAGE:
            {
                // draw the Image with respect to the clipping region
                g2d.setClip(clip);
                g2d.drawImage(image, at, this);
                break;
            }

            default:
            {
                // invalid index
                System.out.println("Invalid Choice: " +
                    dropBox.getSelectedIndex());
                break;
            }
        }
    }

    public void itemStateChanged(ItemEvent e)
    {
        // our drop box has changed--redraw the scene
        repaint();
```

```
        }


    }    // ClipTest
```

Try running the *ClipTest* applet for yourself to see the three different image states: the image by itself, the clipping region by itself, and the clipping region combined with the image.  Figure 8.10 shows you the image combined with the clipping region.

Notice that when you run the *ClipTest* applet, the clipped image is not transformed or otherwise manipulated to fit within the clipping region. The clipping region merely defines the valid area you can render to. To disable a clipping region defined by setClip, just call the method again and send the null value to it.

```
// assume g2d refers to a valid Graphics2D object
g2d.setClip(null);     // remove any set clipping regions
```

If that's not exciting enough, you'll be pleased to know that you can extend the concept of clipping regions into text rendering. If you'll recall, you can use the FontRenderContext and TextLayout classes to extract the metrics of a given font and text string. You can also use these classes to generate a *Shape* object that represents the outline of a string of text. This *Shape* object can then be used as your clipping region. The following code snippet demonstrates the basic steps required to render an image within the bounds of a text string:

```
// set up our Font, text String, FontRenderContext, and TextLayout here...

// assume layout refers to a valid TextLayout object
Shape outline = layout.getOutline(null);

// set paint, transformation, and other Graphics2D attributes here...
...

// set the clipping region and draw an Image
```

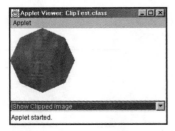

**Figure 8.10**

*The* ClipTest *applet*

```
g2d.setClip(outline);
g2d.drawImage(myImage, new AffineTransform(), this);
```

You should be able to fill in the code I left out. If you need a refresher on setting up the `Font`, `FontRenderContext`, or `TextLayout` objects, refer to the section entitled "Retrieving Font Metrics" in Chapter 7.

You should also recall that transformations for `Image` objects start from the upper-left of the image; text is transformed with respect to the lower-left (the baseline) of the text string.

Finally, I'd like to point out that the `getOutline` method in the `TextLayout` class takes one parameter: an `AffineTransform` that can optionally be applied to the resulting `Shape` object. If you do not wish to apply a transformation to your `Shape`, simply pass `null` to the method.

> **NOTE**
>
> Remember, if you decide to create your clip shapes using instance modeling, the screen coordinate (0, 0) will define the dead center of your geometry before transformation. However, (0, 0) will refer to the *upper-left* corner of an untransformed image, not the center of the image. So if, for example, you scale the shape by (50, 50) and translate the shape and the image by (100, 200), they probably won't be lined up the way you would want. You will most likely need to formulate an equation for anchoring both the shape and the image about the same point. You'll find that one of the chapter exercises will ask you to do just that.

# Setting Rendering Hints

In this section, we'll look at how to control the quality of the objects you render. Java 2-D provides us with a `RenderingHints` class, which contains all of the possible values for setting and controlling rendering quality.

In order to register control values with specific rendering metrics, the `RenderingHints` class implements the *Map* interface. The *Map* interface allows you to map `Object` values along with an associated key value. Key values can map to, at most, one `Object` value. Therefore, all key mapping values are guaranteed to be unique.

You're probably wondering by now just which rendering hints are supported by Java. Table 8.1 contains all of the key, value pairs available in the `RenderingHints` class.

## Table 8.1    *Key, Value* Pairs Contained in the RenderingHints Class

| Key | Values |
| --- | --- |
| KEY_ALPHA_INTERPOLATION | VALUE_ALPHA_INTERPOLATION_DEFAULT<br>VALUE_ALPHA_INTERPOLATION_QUALITY<br>VALUE_ALPHA_INTERPOLATION_SPEED |
| KEY_ANTIALIASING | VALUE_ANTIALIAS_DEFAULT<br>VALUE_ANTIALIAS_OFF<br>VALUE_ANTIALIAS_ON |
| KEY_COLOR_RENDERING | VALUE_COLOR_RENDER_DEFAULT<br>VALUE_COLOR_RENDER_QUALITY<br>VALUE_COLOR_RENDER_SPEED |
| KEY_DITHERING | VALUE_DITHER_DEFAULT<br>VALUE_DITHER_DISABLE<br>VALUE_DITHER_ENABLE |
| KEY_FRACTIONALMETRICS | VALUE_FRACTIONALMETRICS_DEFAULT<br>VALUE_FRACTIONALMETRICS_OFF<br>VALUE_FRACTIONALMETRICS_ON |
| KEY_INTERPOLATION | VALUE_INTERPOLATION_BICUBIC<br>VALUE_INTERPOLATION_BILINEAR<br>VALUE_INTERPOLATION_NEAREST_NEIGHBOR |
| KEY_RENDERING | VALUE_RENDER_DEFAULT<br>VALUE_RENDER_QUALITY<br>VALUE_RENDER_SPEED |
| KEY_STROKE_CONTROL | VALUE_STROKE_DEFAULT<br>VALUE_STROKE_NORMALIZE<br>VALUE_STROKE_PURE |
| KEY_TEXT_ANTIALIASING | VALUE_TEXT_ANTIALIAS_DEFAULT<br>VALUE_TEXT_ANTIALIAS_OFF<br>VALUE_TEXT_ANTIALIAS_ON |

In Table 8.1, all *key* values are static class fields of type RenderingHints.Key. Their associated values are also static class fields but are of type Object. As you can see, you have a decent number of metrics at your disposal, from controlling general rendering quality (KEY_RENDERING) to specifically controlling text-rendering quality (KEY_TEXT_ANTIALIASING).

Now that you are more familiar with the rendering hints available for your applications, let's look at how to set these attributes in your applets. There are two ways to set rendering hints. If you only wish to set a single rendering hint, you can call the Graphics2D setRenderingHint method and provide a specific key and value. The following code snippet turns on text antialiasing and draws a text string at the current Graphics2D transform. Figure 8.11 shows the same text string with antialiasing turned both on and off.

```
// assume g2d refers to a valid Graphics2D context
g2d.setRenderingHint(RenderingHints.KEY_TEXT_ANTIALIASING,
                     RenderingHints.VALUE_TEXT_ANTIALIAS_ON);
g2d.drawString("Text Antialiasing On", 0, 0);
```

You can make several calls to setRenderingHint if you wish to set several rendering hints, or create an entire map of values and set it all at once using the Graphics2D setRenderingHints method. The following code creates a new RenderingHints object and defines several key, value pairs for hinting. The setRenderingHints method is then called to set the map all at once.

```
RenderingHints rh = new RenderingHints(RenderingHints.KEY_ANTIALIASING,
                                RenderingHints.VALUE_TEXT_ANTIALIAS_ON);
rh.put(RenderingHints.KEY_STROKE_CONTROL,
       RenderingHints.VALUE_STROKE_PURE);
rh.put(RenderingHints.KEY_ALPHA_INTERPOLATION,
       RenderingHints.VALUE_ALPHA_INTERPOLATION_QUALITY);
g2d.setRenderingHints(rh);
// render something nice here...
```

As you can see from the above code snippet, you can define one rendering hint within the RenderingHints constructor method. To add subsequent additions to the map, call the put method, and send a single key, value pair. For any hint values

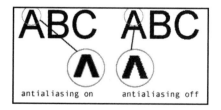

**Figure 8.11**

*Text antialiasing turned on and off*

ending with DEFAULT, the platform's default rendering operations will be used for the specified hint key.

Usage of rendering hints is a perfect example of the trade-off between speed and quality. If stringent rendering hints are given in regard to rendering quality, then there will be an obvious sacrifice in rendering speed. Just the opposite is true as well; low quality rendering hints will produce images faster, but rendering quality will be sacrificed. Therefore, it is often a good idea to write code that sets high-quality hints for "fast" machines and low or default quality hints for "slow" machines.

**NOTE**

There is no guarantee that any particular system will be capable of employing all of the rendering hints you set. If the particular rendering algorithm associated with the hints you set is not available on the system, it will resort to using the native default algorithms and settings. So don't get too upset if your applets look better on some systems and worse on others; it's just a side effect that platform independence gives us.

One way you can find out about the speed of a given system is to determine if special rendering hardware (such as AGP video acceleration) is available on the system. Let's assume you have a fictitious isAccelerated method that tells you if the system can (or is) using some type of graphics acceleration. The following code allows you to set hints based on the results of the isAccelerated method:

```
// assume renderQuality is a private class field of type RenderingHints
if(isAccelerated())
{
        renderQuality = new RenderingHints(RenderingHints.KEY_RENDERING,
                                           RenderingHints.VALUE_RENDER_QUALITY);
}
else
{
        renderQuality = new RenderingHints(RenderingHints.KEY_RENDERING,
                                           RenderingHints.VALUE_RENDER_SPEED);
}
```

You only need to call the above code once. Therefore, it will probably reside in the init method or in an associated method. Now to set your hints, all you have to do is call the setRenderingHints method in the paint method:

```
g2d.setRenderingHints(renderQuality);
// render something here...
```

We'll delve a bit deeper into the world of graphics acceleration and how to detect its presence in the next chapter.

# Image Manipulation

Thus far, our discussion on imaging in Java 2-D has been restricted to what we can consider static image data. By *static* I mean image data that can be created (such as from a file) but whose data cannot be directly accessed or modified. Although the Image class allows you to create a scaled instance of an image, there are no other methods for directly manipulating the image data itself.

In the following sections, we'll examine classes that do allow us to directly modify the contents of an image. We'll start by looking at the BufferedImage class.

## The BufferedImage Class

The BufferedImage class can be a very handy class for generating custom images on the fly. It extends the Image class but also provides methods for writing directly to the 2-D raster of data associated with it.

The magic of the BufferedImage class lies within its native Graphics2D context. Each instance of the BufferedImage class is capable of creating its own Graphics2D object by calling the createGraphics method. The Graphics2D context from a buffered image can then be used just like the one attained from the Applet class.

To create a BufferedImage object, you can use the constructor that takes three integer values: the *width, height,* and *image type* properties of the image. Since the width and height parameters represent length measurements, they must be greater than or equal to zero. Negative arguments will generate an IllegalArgumentException. The image type parameter refers to the method for storing pixel data within the image. For example, BufferedImage.TYPE_USHORT_555_RGB refers to pixel data stored as an RGB triple with five bits for red, five bits for green, and five bits for blue, with no alpha (transparency) channel. Some common image formats are TYPE_BYTE_GRAY, TYPE_INT_RGB, and TYPE_INT_ARGB. A complete list of these values can be found in the Java 2 documentation.

Figure 8.12 demonstrates the steps involved in using the BufferedImage class. You are able to copy data (such as shapes) to a buffered image and then render that image to your applet window.

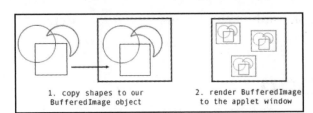

**Figure 8.12**

*Creating and rendering a*
*BufferedImage object*

Now let's get down to writing some code. The following applet, *BufferedImageTest*,
copies geometry to a BufferedImage object and then renders that image in random
locations to the applet window using its Graphics2D context. Try it out:

```
import java.applet.*;
import java.awt.*;
import java.awt.image.*;
import java.awt.geom.*;


public class BufferedImageTest extends Applet
{
    // a BufferedImage, along with its creation width and height
    private BufferedImage image;
    private final int BI_WIDTH  = 100;
    private final int BI_HEIGHT = 100;

    // for generating random colors and screen positions
    private java.util.Random random;

    public void init()
    {
        random = new java.util.Random();

        // create a (BI_WIDTH x BI_HEIGHT) buffered image
        image = new BufferedImage(BI_WIDTH, BI_HEIGHT,
                                BufferedImage.TYPE_INT_RGB);

        // create a Graphics2D context for our BufferedImage.  Remember this
        // has nothing to do with our Applet's Graphics2D context
        Graphics2D g2d = image.createGraphics();

        // we will render some stripes to the BufferedImage
```

```
        // the width and height of our stripes will be one-tenth the total
        // width and height of the image
        final int stripWidth  = BI_WIDTH  / 10;
        final int stripHeight = BI_HEIGHT / 10;

        // fill the image with a random color
        g2d.setPaint(new Color(random.nextInt()));
        g2d.fill(new Rectangle(0, 0, BI_WIDTH, BI_HEIGHT));

        // render the vertical stripes using a random color
        g2d.setPaint(new Color(random.nextInt()));
        int x = stripWidth / 2;
        while(x < BI_WIDTH)
        {
            g2d.fill(new Rectangle(x, 0, stripWidth, BI_HEIGHT));
            x += 2 * stripWidth;
        }

        // set a transparency channel for our stripes
        g2d.setComposite(AlphaComposite.getInstance(AlphaComposite.SRC_OVER,
                                                    0.5f));

        // render the horizontal stripes using a random color
        g2d.setPaint(new Color(random.nextInt()));
        int y = stripHeight / 2;
        while(y < BI_HEIGHT)
        {
            g2d.fill(new Rectangle(0, y, BI_WIDTH, stripHeight));
            y += 2 * stripHeight;
        }

        // render a dark opaque outline around the perimeter of the image
        g2d.setStroke(new BasicStroke(2.0f));
        g2d.setComposite(AlphaComposite.getInstance(AlphaComposite.SRC_OVER));
        g2d.setPaint(Color.BLACK);
        g2d.draw(new Rectangle(0, 0, BI_WIDTH, BI_HEIGHT));
    }

public void paint(Graphics g)
{
```

```
// cast the sent Graphics context to get a usable Graphics2D object
Graphics2D g2d = (Graphics2D)g;

// draw a bunch of images at random locations
for(int i = 0; i < 20; i++)
{
    g2d.drawImage(image,
                AffineTransform.getTranslateInstance(
                    random.nextInt()%getSize().getWidth(),
                    random.nextInt()%getSize().getHeight()),
                this);

}

}    // BufferedImageTest
```

With just a few lines of code, you can easily create patterns and textures where even the most powerful paint programs fail. I often find it difficult to make very precise textures (like the one shown in Figure 8.13) with a paint program, but using Java 2-D allows me to create very exact textures with minimal effort. Speaking of textures, why not use a `BufferedImage` as a `TexturePaint` object? Actually, we already did that in the *TextureTest* applet presented earlier in Chapter 7. Nonetheless, let's look at another example, just in case you need a refresher.

As you've seen, you can create a `BufferedImage` much like the following:

```
private BufferedImage image;

public void init()
```

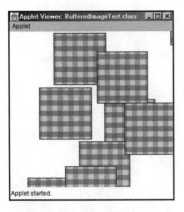

**Figure 8.13**

*The* BufferedImageTest *applet*

```
{
    image = new BufferedImage(50, 50, BufferedImage.TYPE_INT_RGB);
    Graphics2D g2d = image.createGraphics();

    g2d.setPaint(Color.RED);
    g2d.fill(new Rectangle(0, 0, 25, 25));

    g2d.setColor(Color.GREEN);
    g2d.fill(new Rectangle(25, 0, 25, 25));

    g2d.setColor(Color.BLUE);
    g2d.fill(new Rectangle(0, 25, 25, 25));

    g2d.setColor(Color.GRAY);
    g2d.fill(new Rectangle(25, 25, 25, 25));
}
```

You can then set the BufferedImage as your paint and render a shape:

```
public void paint(Graphics g)
{
    // cast the sent Graphics context to get a usable Graphics2D object
    Graphics2D g2d = (Graphics2D)g;

    // create and add a texture paint to the graphics context.
    g2d.setPaint(new TexturePaint(image, new Rectangle(0, 0, 25, 25)));

    // create and render an oval filled with the texture.
    g2d.translate(50, 25);
    g2d.fill(new Ellipse2D.Double(0, 0, 200, 100));
}
```

Figure 8.14 shows how a 50 x 50 texture can be applied to an arbitrary shape.

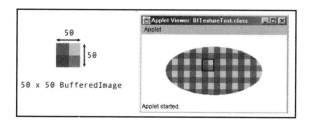

**Figure 8.14**

*Using a BufferedImage as a TexturePaint*

Notice in the above code that you can arbitrarily set the repetition frequency of your paint with respect to the actual image size. Here, the BufferedImage contains 50 rows and 50 columns of pixel data. However, your repetition rectangle is half that size. Your Graphics2D context will automatically resize your TexturePaint to fit the repetition area.

In Chapter 9 we'll revisit the BufferedImage class when we discuss creation of off-screen rendering buffers. We'll also look further into using BufferedImage objects to store complex *Shape* operations for faster rendering.

## Using Image Enhancement Operations

In addition to rendering basic shapes to a BufferedImage object, you can also per-form complex image enhancements. The java.awt.image package provides you with the *BufferedImageOp* interface, which is used to describe a single input-output opera-tion on your images. Therefore, you are able to apply an image operation to your source image and have the results stored in an output, or destination, image.

There are currently five classes that implement the *BufferedImageOp* interface: AffineTransformOp, ColorConvertOp, ConvolveOp, LookupOp, and RescaleOp. These classes implement the operations needed to geometrically transform, blur, sharpen, and color correct images.

As Figure 8.15 suggests, input image data is sent to one of your operation classes; the results are then sent to your output image. Here, we are using a blur operation to create a blurry image of an asteroid.

The general steps needed to enhance an image are as follows:

1. Create the original Image data.
2. Create a new BufferedImage object containing the characteristics you want for your output (including the dimensions and image type of your image).
3. Create your *BufferedImageOp* object, along with any associated data you might need.

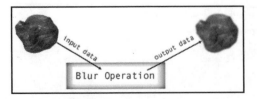

**Figure 8.15**

*Using a blur operation to enhance an image*

4. Filter the original Image using your *BufferedImageOp*, then storing the results in your destination BufferedImage object (which can sometimes be the same as your source image).

The next applet, *BlurTest*, follows the above steps to create a blurred image. It allows the user to enter a file name into a TextField. If the file exists, it will be rendered in the applet window along with a blurred version of itself. Here's the code:

```
import java.applet.*;
import java.awt.*;
import java.awt.event.*;
import java.awt.image.*;
import java.awt.geom.*;

public class BlurTest extends Applet implements ActionListener
{
    // the original and blurred BufferedImages
    private BufferedImage sourceImage;
    private BufferedImage destImage;

    // field for accepting a filename
    private TextField input;

    public void init()
    {
        // create a layout and add the textfield and "Ok" button
        setLayout(new BorderLayout());
        Panel p = new Panel();
        input = new TextField("", 20);
        p.add(input);
        Button ok = new Button("Ok");
        ok.addActionListener(this);
        p.add(ok);
        add(p, BorderLayout.SOUTH);
    }

    public void paint(Graphics g)
    {
        // cast the sent Graphics context to get a usable Graphics2D object
```

```java
Graphics2D g2d = (Graphics2D)g;

// draw a friendly reminder to input a filename if the text
// field just contains white-space
if("".equals(input.getText().trim()))
{
    g2d.drawString("Enter a filename to blur", 10, 50);
    return;
}


// load the input image
MediaTracker mt = new MediaTracker(this);
Image img = getImage(getCodeBase(), input.getText());
mt.addImage(img, 0);
try
{
    // wait until the image has loaded completely before continuing
    mt.waitForID(0);
}
catch(InterruptedException e) { /* do nothing */ }


// our blur operation will require a BufferedImage object, so render
// the input image to a new BufferedImage object
sourceImage = new BufferedImage(img.getWidth(this),
                                img.getHeight(this),
                                BufferedImage.TYPE_INT_RGB);
sourceImage.createGraphics().drawImage(img, null, this);


// create the destination image
destImage = new BufferedImage(sourceImage.getWidth(this),
                              sourceImage.getHeight(this),
                              BufferedImage.TYPE_INT_RGB);


// blur the input image
blur(sourceImage, destImage, 0.1f, 3, 3);


// draw both the source and destination images
AffineTransform at = new AffineTransform();
int width = sourceImage.getWidth(this);
```

```
            g2d.drawImage(sourceImage, at, this);
            at.translate(width+20, 0);
            g2d.drawImage(destImage, at, this);
        }

        // blurs an image using a ConvolveOp operation
        public void blur(
            BufferedImage sourceImage,    // the input image data
            BufferedImage destImage,      // the output image data
            float weight,                 // weight of the Kernel data
            int width,                    // width of the Kernel
            int height                    // height of the Kernel
            )
        {
            // this will be the data array for our Kernel
            float[] elements = new float[width*height];

            // fill the array with the weight
            java.util.Arrays.fill(elements, weight);

            // use the array of elements and the width and height to create
            // a Kernel
            Kernel k = new Kernel(width, height, elements);
            ConvolveOp blurOp = new ConvolveOp(k);

            // blur the image
            blurOp.filter(sourceImage, destImage);
        }

        public void actionPerformed(ActionEvent e)
        {
            // the "Ok" was pressed; update the changes
            repaint();
        }

    }   // BlurTest
```

Figure 8.16 shows a trial run of the *BlurTest* applet. Here, a `ConvolveOp` object was used to filter the source image into the destination image. This convolution operation uses a `Kernel` object to calculate output pixel data. A `Kernel` consists of a matrix of weights that are multiplied by neighboring pixels to produce a single output pixel value. Using surrounding pixel data to calculate output pixels is how we get the "blurred" effect. Convolution operations can also be used to brighten or color-adjust the source image as well. Try playing around with the above code and see what other results you can get.

So why would you ever want to go through all this work to alter an image with today's powerful paint programs? First of all, good paint programs are expensive. Also, many of them require that you purchase additional components to get the really cool effects. So I figure, since you've got the programming skills, why not use them?

Memory considerations bring me to a second advantage to programmatically altering images. Remember that your games will be typically downloaded from the Internet; therefore, the fewer base images you provide, the faster your users will be able to play your games. With the amazing speed of today's processors, it will probably take less time to generate your images in code than to include them as dedicated files with your games. But remember that most people will still be logging in with standard modems for a few more years to come.

It's amazing the amount of things you can do with classes that implement the *BufferedImageOp* interface. Besides blurring images, you can create gray-scaled images, provide image "negatives," enhance or remove color, and so on. So the next time your game contains the same images with different color palettes, consider implementing a simple palette-swapping mechanism instead of relying on your favorite graphics program. I'll leave the details up to you.

As a final consideration, note that since classes that implement the *BufferedImageOp* interface permit only a single image operation, they cannot be used for instances where you have multiple image sources or when you wish to apply several operations with respect to the original image data. Therefore, in these cases you must perform multiple steps one at a time and provide temporary images when necessary.

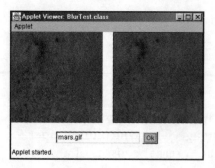

**Figure 8.16**

*Blurring images with the* BlurTest *applet*

# Conclusion

I believe that many graphics packages out there pale in comparison to Java 2-D in the basic two-dimensional services they provide. As seen in both Chapters 7 and 8, Java 2-D has tremendous capabilities as far as image, line, and text drawing are concerned. The use of shapes and basic fills should certainly come in handy and somewhat reduce the need for image files, thus greatly reducing download times. Constructive area geometry, built-in collision-testing methods, and area clipping are all great ways to take advantage of the geometric capabilities Java 2-D has to offer. Setting rendering hints is a good way to control the level of detail and rendering quality, leading to an overall control over game performance. Finally, image operations provide a very powerful way to enhance and alter images without the need to create additional memory-hogging image files.

If you're not convinced, try implementing the topics discussed in this chapter with one of those other graphics packages. I think you'll agree that Java 2-D is the clear choice for getting those games up and running with minimal effort and time.

# Exercises

**8.1** Write a method, named `createBounds`, that takes in an array of arbitrary `Point` objects and returns a `Rectangle2D` object that most tightly fits around the points. Figure 8.17 suggests how the `createBounds` method would provide such a tight-fitting `Rectangle2D` object.

Here's a hint: When looking for the extreme points to build your rectangle around, break each `Point` into its component x- and y-values. This way, you'll be able to calculate the minimum and maximum values with respect to the entire list of points and not to any particular point in the array.

**8.2** Write a general utility method, `adjustBounds`, that shrinks (or expands) a `Rectangle2D` object by a given `double` value. The method should retain the same midpoint of the `Rectangle2D` object after it is adjusted. You may want to sketch the problem on paper before writing the code. Test the method to make sure

**Figure 8.17**

*Creating a tight-fitting rectangle around a number of* Point *objects*

it properly preserves the midpoint of the rectangle and that it properly expands and contracts a given Rectangle2D object.

8.3  Add a method, moveBy, to the BoundedImage class. It should have the following prototype:

```
public void moveBy(double dx, double dy)
{
     // method body here
}
```

The method should translate the bounding rectangle by the given delta values. Test your code to make sure it works properly.

8.4  Write code that centers an image and shape about the same anchor point. Remember that you can directly access the centers of shapes, but images are referenced through their upper left-hand corner.

8.5  Write code that creates the "negative" of an image. For color-indexed images such as .gif images, this can mean replacing each pixel with one at the "opposite" end of the color lookup table. The following code should help you get started:

```
byte[] negatives = new byte[256];
for(int i = 0; i < 200; i++)
{
     negatives[i] = (byte)(256-i);
}

ByteLookupTable blut = new ByteLookupTable(0, negatives);
LookupOp lop = new LookupOp(blut, null);
lop.filter(sourceImage, destImage);
```

The ByteLookupTable class (found in the java.awt.image package) provides a way to resample color index data quickly and conveniently. Output for the above code might look like Figure 8.18.

**Figure 8.18**

*Negating an image using a* ByteLookupTable *and* LookupOp *filter*

There is another flavor of the `ByteLookupTable` constructor that takes a two-dimensional array (an array of arrays) of `byte` data as one of its parameters. This method is great for implementing the palette-swapping mechanism mentioned earlier in this chapter. Try it out. If you get stuck, wait until Chapter 14 to see how a single image can be used to generate a host of others.

8.6    By now, you should have a good handle on how a map is used to implement the Java `Hashtable` class. If you skipped the chapter exercise dealing with hash tables from Chapter 4, go back and try it again. You'll need to know how they're used in the next chapter when we talk about the custom font-rendering scheme.

# Where We Are and Where We're Going

Part Two presented the fundamentals necessary to successfully create attractive user interfaces. Java 2-D and the Abstract Window Toolkit come chock-full of goodies that will help make the graphical end of game programming as painless as possible. Now that you understand each component of the AWT, you'll be able to combine them to create some killer effects and user interfaces.

Believe it or not, we've covered a lot of ground as far as game programming in Java goes. If you've programmed games in C or C++, you can probably go ahead and combine what you already know with what you've learned and make some pretty cool stuff. Part Three will help you in this endeavor by bridging the gap between the visual aspect of games and behind-the-scenes game processing. Next, we'll look at topics such as buffered animation and framerate syncing, as well as creating your own custom menus and visual widgets and controls. You'll even learn how to create an actor class so you can give your objects something to think about. Before Part Three is over, you'll also learn how to create simple client-server connections over the Internet and create a basic 2-D game development engine. Finally, you'll be ready to dive in to a complete Java game example and see how to put everything together and create some games.

So once you feel comfortable with the material presented in both Parts One and Two, feel free to jump right into Part Three. The only thing keeping you from global domination is your imagination. So let's do as the natives do and take a look at the `MediaTracker` class and 2-D buffered animation.

# Part Three

# Java Gaming for the Masses

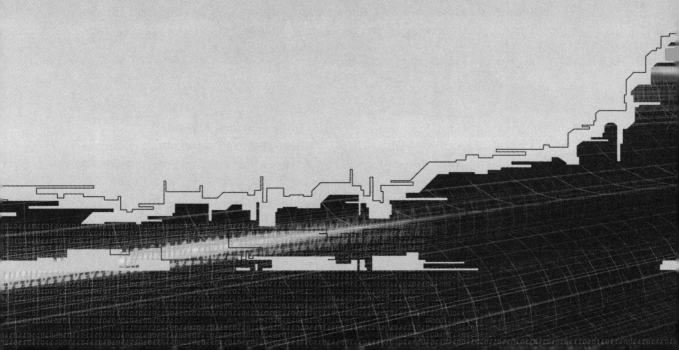

**"Is the Tao in a video game?" continued the novice.**
**"It is even in a video game," said the master.**
**-*From Geoffrey James'* The Tao of Programming**

In Part Two, you saw much of the power Java 2-D and the Java AWT have to offer. In Part Three you'll learn how to further apply these techniques to game programming. You'll also see how you can use the object-oriented paradigm to create reusable game objects for your games. In the following chapters, we'll focus on 2-D game development.

So, what exactly *is* a 2-D game, anyway? I define a 2-D game as a *game whose imaging does not preserve the true geometry of its objects.* Basically, 2-D is just a "flattening" of a realistic (or even unrealistic) universe onto a two dimensional plane. 2-D games can contain graphics that can be generated to "look" 3-D, but no operations exist that allow the images to be manipulated to show all sides.

Here's a quick roadmap of where you'll be headed in Part Three:

- **2-D Animation Techniques.** Includes a detailed look at the Java MediaTracker class, using image strips for animation, framerate synchronization, and using accelerated images for off-screen rendering.

- **Creating a Custom Actor Class.** A first-hand look at the custom `Actor2D` class, along with all of the utility classes that will enhance its functionality.

- **Implementing Custom Scene Management Classes.** A discussion on how to use custom scene managers in your games. You'll also see how to use quad trees for scene management, and learn how to move your games into the elusive full-screen exclusive mode.

- **Creating Visual Controls and Menus.** Since the basic AWT might be too "boring" for games, we'll examine how to implement a custom visual control system. We'll top it off with how to create a custom menuing system in your games.

- **Creating Client-Server Applications.** Games are often more fun to play over a network with two or more people. You'll see how to employ both connection-oriented as well as connection-less networking protocols in your games.

- **A Look at the Nodez! Game.** Here's where we'll top it all off by looking at a real, live Java-enabled game, *Nodez!* The *Nodez!* game will contain almost all of the major topics discussed in this book.

Before you can start making the *Nodez!* game you must start building the necessary tools for creating and managing game scenes. Let's begin in Chapter 9, by looking at how 2-D animation in Java takes place.

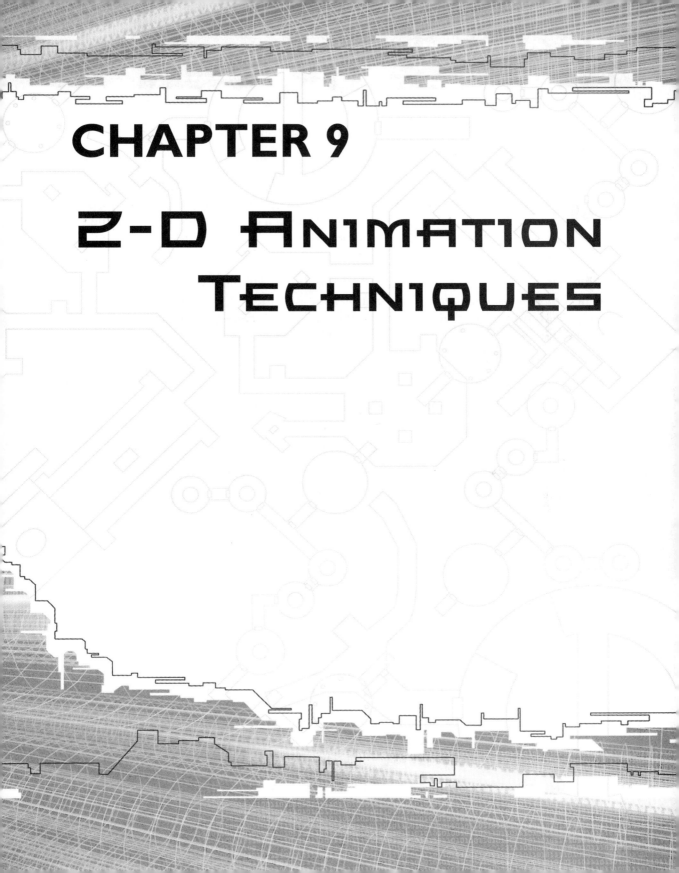

# CHAPTER 9

# 2-D Animation Techniques

**W** Without the ability to animate your scenes, games would not be capable of providing a whole lot of excitement. Video game animation gives you the ability to turn a collection of simple, static images and shapes into a dynamic, living environment.

There are many types of animation out there. In this chapter, we'll focus on what's called *frame-based animation,* or animation that is contained in a static rendering loop. With frame-based animation, objects within the scene are updated and rendered independently of the time elapsed. The code to update a scene is contained in a continuous event loop.

In this chapter, we'll examine the following topics:

- Remotely loading images with the MediaTracker class
- Creating an applet that uses threading to produce animation sequences
- Generating character animation and bitmapped fonts with image strips
- Implementing a double-buffered off-screen rendering mechanism
- Perfecting animation timing with framerate syncing

Armed and ready with the tools developed in Chapters 7 and 8, let's proceed with the MediaTracker class.

# Downloading Content with the MediaTracker Class

As promised, we will begin our quest to build an object-oriented actor class by optimizing the way in which images are downloaded from the network. When a request is made for a resource, such as calling the Applet getImage method for loading an image file, the called method returns immediately. In other words, methods such as getImage do not wait for the image to load completely before returning to the main program. Although this allows your programs to continue without waiting for the images to completely load, this can cause some problems.

Suppose you want to download a series of images and then perform a number of image enhancement operations on them. How can you be guaranteed that the image has finished loading before applying the image operations? Implementing a synthetic delay mechanism might work, but the value you use for your delay will most likely be longer or shorter than the actual time needed to completely load in the image data. You need a way to tell exactly when your images have completely loaded.

Luckily, your friends at Sun have provided an easy way to do this. With the MediaTracker class, located in the java.awt package, you can track the progress of the images you want to load. Currently, the MediaTracker class supports only the tracking of images, but later implementations of Java will probably include support for audio files as well. To create a MediaTracker object, simply pass a Component object to it in its constructor method (this will usually be a reference to your applet or frame window). The passed Component represents the object onto which the image will eventually be drawn.

You can attach as many images as you like to a MediaTracker object and then retrieve the loading status of a particular image or the status of all attached images collectively. You can also attach an ID number to distinguish image groups from one another. Lower numbered IDs have a greater priority than higher numbered IDs. So if you wish to load a group of images that you wish to enhance, you might assign a zero value to those images. Immediately after images with priority zero finish loading, you can perform your image enhancements while images with a lower priority continue to load.

Let's look at a full example so you can get a better feel for how the MediaTracker class works. The following applet, *TrackerTest*, loads in six different frames of animation from file. It then uses a Thread to handle animation updates (refer back to Chapter 4 if you need a refresher on using threads in Java). The paint method for the *TrackerTest* applet draws six instances of our animation sequence, each indexed to a different frame of animation.

```
import java.applet.*;
import java.awt.*;
import java.awt.geom.*;

public class TrackerTest extends Applet implements Runnable
{
    // a Thread for animation
    private Thread animation;

    // an array of Image objects, along with the animation index for the
    // first Image
    private Image images[];
```

```java
private int firstIndex;

// the number of images to load
private final int NUM_IMAGES = 6;

// the width and height of one Image frame
private int imageWidth;
private int imageHeight;

public void init()
{
    images = new Image[NUM_IMAGES];
    firstIndex = 0;

    // create a new MediaTracker object for this Component
    MediaTracker mt = new MediaTracker(this);
    java.net.URL baseURL = getDocumentBase();

    // load the image frames and add them to our MediaTracker with a
    // priority of 0
    for(int i = 0; i < NUM_IMAGES; i++)
    {
        images[i] = getImage(baseURL, "fire" + i + ".gif");
        mt.addImage(images[i], 0);
    }

    try
    {
        // wait until the images have loaded completely before continuing
        mt.waitForID(0);
    }
    catch(InterruptedException e) { /* do nothing */ }

    // now that we are guaranteed to have our images loaded, we can now
    // access their width and height
    imageWidth = images[0].getWidth(this);
    imageHeight = images[0].getHeight(this);

    setBackground(Color.BLACK);
```

```java
}    // init

public void start()
{
    // start the animation thread
    animation = new Thread(this);
    animation.start();
}

public void stop()
{
    animation = null;
}

public void run()
{
    Thread t = Thread.currentThread();
    while (t == animation)
    {
        try
        {
            Thread.sleep(100);
        }
        catch(InterruptedException e)
        {
            break;
        }

        // increment our animation index, looping if needed
        if(++firstIndex >= images.length)
        {    firstIndex = 0;
        }

        repaint();
    }
}    // run

public void paint(Graphics g)
{
```

```
            Graphics2D g2d = (Graphics2D)g;
            AffineTransform at = AffineTransform.getTranslateInstance(20, 20);

            // draw one frame of animation for each Image in the array
            int currFrame;      // the actual frame to draw
            for(int i = 0; i < images.length; i++)
            {
                currFrame = (firstIndex+i)%images.length;

                g2d.setTransform(at);
                g2d.drawImage(images[currFrame], null, this);

                g2d.setPaint(Color.WHITE);
                g2d.drawString("" + currFrame, imageWidth/2, imageHeight + 20);
                at.translate(100, 0);
            }
        }   // paint
    }
```

Of course, the fire images in Figure 9.1 are purple in ode to the folks at Sun Microsystems. Note the use of the try block when waiting for media to finish downloading. It is there to catch any interrupted exceptions that are caught while waiting for the media to download. If the graphical output of the applet appears to flicker somewhat, don't worry; I'll show you how to clear that up later in this chapter.

A few final features we'll discuss are the status-checking and error-checking capabilities of the MediaTracker class. Using the statusID and statusAll methods, you can check the status of the images associated with a MediaTracker object. The statusID method takes an integer ID for a specific priority you are interested in. Both the statusID and statusAll methods take a boolean value as well. If this value is set to true, then the

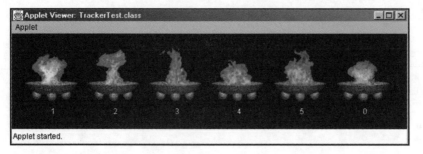

**Figure 9.1**

*The* TrackerTest *applet*

method will start to download any media that has not yet begun loading. These methods then return the bitwise inclusive OR of all media currently being tracked. If these methods return zero, then the associated media has not begun to load yet.

The code below shows how you can access the status of all the media being tracked by a MediaTracker object. Since your status contains a series of OR'ed attributes, taking the bitwise AND between the status and one of the four static int values contained in the MediaTracker class (ABORTED, COMPLETE, ERRORED, LOADING) will allow you to receive multiple status values. You can then write code to handle each possible status of your tracker.

```
int status = mt.statusAll(false);
if(status == 0)
{
    System.out.println("Media has not yet begun loading...");
    // wait code here...
}
else
{
    if((status & MediaTracker.ABORTED) != 0)
    {
        System.out.println("Media download aborted!");
        // abort code here...
    }
    if((status & MediaTracker.COMPLETE) != 0)
    {
        System.out.println("Media download complete!");
        // we're good to go...
    }
    if((status & MediaTracker.ERRORED) != 0)
    {
        System.out.println("Media download errored!");
        // error code here...
    }
    if((status & MediaTracker.LOADING) != 0)
    {
        System.out.println("Media still loading...");
        // wait code here...
    }
}
```

One way to make use of status checking is to only draw images that have been loaded completely. Suppose you have an array of images that represent a single animation that was loaded into a MediaTracker with a priority of zero. The following code will draw the current frame of animation only if *all* of the frames of animation have been completely loaded. This will prevent broken animations from being displayed.

```
if(mt.statusID(0, false) == MediaTracker.COMPLETE)
{
    g2d.drawImage(animation[currIndex], at, this);
}
```

This code will prevent broken animations, but at the cost of having to check the status of your MediaTracker object once per frame. I prefer to check the status of my images during the initialization phase of my programs, so that I am guaranteed to have complete images by the time the update and paint methods are called.

If your applications that use MediaTracker objects do encounter an error and it appears that all is lost, it might be a good idea to at least create *something* to render. A red square with the same dimensions as your image can be one alternative to the real image. Creating an alternative for images that have not properly loaded will provide a placeholder so your game is still at least playable. If you choose not to provide an alternative, nothing will be rendered, since the image will have a width and height of zero, or worse yet, the Image will reference the null value. So if certain images end up not being rendered at all, you might not notice anything is even wrong.

The following code snippet illustrates how you can provide placeholders for un-loaded images. If the MediaTracker reports an error, it will provide a BufferedImage filled with a random color for each Image that did not load.

```
// check for errors
if((mt.statusID(0, false) & MediaTracker.ERRORED) != 0)
{
    BufferedImage bi;      // our "alternative" image
    java.util.Random random = new java.util.Random();

    // the bounds of the BufferedImage
    Rectangle rect = new Rectangle(imageWidth, imageHeight);

    // we will check for "bad" images by checking for
    // widths that are less than or equal to 0
    for(int i = 0; i < NUM_IMAGES; i++)
```

```
        {
            if(images[i].getWidth(this) <= 0)
            {
                // create a (imageWidth x imageHeight) buffered image
                bi = new BufferedImage(imageWidth, imageHeight,
                                        BufferedImage.TYPE_INT_RGB);

                // fill the image with a random color
                Graphics2D g2d = bi.createGraphics();
                g2d.setPaint(new Color(random.nextInt()));
                g2d.fill(rect);

                // set the new image
                images[i] = bi;
            }
        }
    }
```

Figure 9.2 shows a sample applet much like the *TrackerTest* applet, except that it uses synthetic placeholder images in place of images that did not properly load.

Code to test this code has been provided in the *TrackerErrorTest* applet, but I will not provide the entire source listing here since it is similar to the *TrackerTest* applet. If you want to try the above code out, try modifying the *TrackerTest* applet yourself, or just pull the *TrackerErrorTest* applet down from the CD-ROM.

Also, feel free to make use of the MediaTracker methods isErrorAny, isErrorID, getErrorsAny, and getErrorsID in your media error-checking exploits. These methods can help you track down the actual images that have encountered an error while loading.

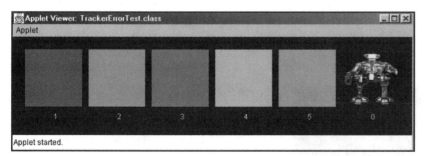

**Figure 9.2**

*Providing placeholders for unloaded images*

# Using Image Strips for Faster Download Time

If you're like me and just got finished fiddling around at an institute of higher learning, then chances are you lived in a dorm or similar complex equipped with high-speed Internet access. While you might think that high-speed Internet access would allow you to spend less time on the computer, just the opposite usually occurs. I mean, it's just too tempting to stay online all night when music and shareware games can be downloaded in seconds to minutes, not hours or days. Exam tomorrow? No problem. I can study during the 10-minute period when the network is put down for maintenance. Filling up my 96 gigabyte hard drive is just too important for matters such as "studying."

My point is, now that I'm done with school, I must toss my network card aside and reinstall my dinky 33.6 Kbps modem. Now I have to actually *wait* for programs and Web pages to download! Welcome to the world of standard access speed, a world inhabited by more than 85 percent of today's Internet users.

Download times can often make it or break it for games played on the Web. Most Internet users become impatient after only 2.5 seconds of waiting for a Web page to download! To avoid having your users hit the Back button on their Web browsers before your game has completely loaded, you need to find ways to offset the slow nature of the Net. Compacting your image content into *image strips* is just one way you can accomplish this.

The use of image strips is actually good for two reasons. First, it helps keep your files and projects organized. You can simply generate your entire image content in separate files, and then copy them into a single neat and tidy grid of cells. This allows you to organize entire animations in a single file, while keeping your directories as small as possible. Image strips are also good for decreasing download time. Since it takes time to send requests for remote files, implementing image strips will surely save you time. Requesting eight image files, each containing eight frames of animation each, will save you 56 retrieve requests over requesting each frame of animation as a dedicated file. Figure 9.3 shows a partial animation of a robot within a sample image strip.

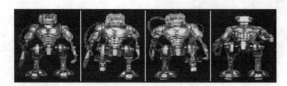

**Figure 9.3**

*Animation frames within an image strip*

You may have noticed in Figure 9.3 the gridlines surrounding each individual image frame. Collectively, these gridlines make up a series of *cells* to visually separate individual image frames. Your files can contain any number of rows and columns for your cell data. For example, you can load nine image frames within a 3 x 3 grid. Also, since you are transferring data over the Internet, try not to have any empty space or padding at the bottom of your image files. The more concise your files are, the better.

Taking the time to set up gridlines can help you determine exactly where to place frames within the parent image file. I suggest using a bright color that is not prominently used in your individual frames so they set themselves from the actual image data. Of course, you will need to find a way to avoid including gridlines when you parse the frame image data from the parent image. Figure 9.4 illustrates the component parts of an image strip.

Let's get down to the code needed to load an image strip from file. The code you'll develop can be placed directly into your applet class or can be added to a utility class. First, let's look at the header for the loadImageStrip method:

```
// loads an array of Images from the given filename
public Image[] loadImageStrip(
    String filename,    // file to load
    int numImages,      // number of images to load
    int cellWidth,      // the width and height of each cell
    int cellHeight,
    int cellBorder      // the width of the cell border
    ) {
```

The header is pretty self-explanatory. The goal is to produce an array of Image objects given a file name and count of images to load. You also provide the width and height of each individual cell, along with the width of the cell borders. If you choose not to use gridlines in your image, just send zero as the cellBorder parameter.

Next, you need to create an array of Image objects and load the parent image file. You will also need to calculate the number of cell columns contained in the image.

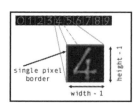

**Figure 9.4**

*The cell border and usable frame area of an image strip*

We already looked at how to use the `MediaTracker` class, but here's the complete code in case you need a refresher:

```
// an array of Images to act as our animation frames
Image[] images = new Image[numImages];

// create a new MediaTracker object for this Component
MediaTracker mt = new MediaTracker(this);

// load the main strip image
Image img = getImage(getDocumentBase(), filename);
mt.addImage(img, 0);
try
{
    // wait for our main image to load
    mt.waitForID(0);
}
catch(InterruptedException e) { /* do nothing */ }

// computing the number of columns will help us extract
// individual cells
int numCols = img.getWidth(this) / cellWidth;
```

According to the above code, if the parent image is 300 pixels wide and each cell is 25 pixels in width, then you will obviously have 12 cell columns. Easy. Now let's finish off the `loadImageStrip` method by actually loading the `Image` cells:

```
// get the ImageProducer source of our main image
ImageProducer sourceProducer = img.getSource();

// load the cells!
for(int i = 0; i < numImages; i++)
{
    images[i] = loadCell(sourceProducer,
                    ((i%numCols)*cellWidth)+cellBorder,
                    ((i/numCols)*cellHeight)+cellBorder,
                    cellWidth-cellBorder,
                    cellHeight-cellBorder);
}
```

```
        return images;
    }
```

This is definitely the most complex part of the loadImageStrip method. First, you
must attain an *ImageProducer* object from the source image. The *ImageProducer* interface contains the methods for reconstructing data from your images. Now that you
have your source *ImageProducer* object, you can load individual cells with the loadCell
method, which I'll define in just a moment. The second and third parameters for
the loadCell method are the x- and y-positions to begin copying image data. The
third and fourth parameters are the width and height of the cell you wish to extract.
It should be fairly clear why you need the cellBorder offsets—you don't want the
gridlines to appear in your final Image array. If it isn't obvious how I derived the
starting x- and y-positions, try drawing a grid with a 3 x 3 array of cells within it, and
fill in imaginary values for the width and height of the grid and the cells. Construct
a table with headers labeled *i*, *x*, and *y* and fill in the values for each value of *i*. By
playing around with the numbers a bit, you should be able to come up with the
same equations that I did.

Also, I prefer to orient my gridlines to the upper-left of each cell. However, if you
prefer orienting them from the lower-right of the cells, you would simply adjust
your call to loadCell as follows:

```
loadCell(sourceProducer,
        ((i%numCols)*cellWidth),
        ((i/numCols)*cellHeight),
        cellWidth-cellBorder,
        cellHeight-cellBorder);
```

With that taken care of, here's the code to load a single cell from your source image:

```
// loads a single cell from an ImageProducer given the area provided
public Image loadCell(
    ImageProducer ip,
    int x, int y,
    int width, int height
    )
{
    return createImage(new FilteredImageSource(ip,
                        new CropImageFilter(x, y, width, height)));
}
```

To create your cell, simply call the Component createImage method and provide another *ImageProducer* object. Here, the *ImageProducer* comes in the form of a FilteredImageSource object, which takes the source *ImageProducer* as well an ImageFilter, which implements how the source image should be filtered. So as long as you provide the proper filtering region for your image, you can just let these Java classes do the work for you.

The methods given above make a few assumptions as to how your images are laid out. First, they assume that the entire image is filled only with cells. That is, images containing empty space or padding may not load correctly. The

> **NOTE**
>
> Remember that although you are using .gif files for animation, you are not using files containing internal *gif animation*. You're probably familiar with .gif files that internally contain several frames of animation; your Web browser animates these files based on internal timer settings. These files will *not* animate when placed within the context of a Java applet. Therefore, make sure your .gif files contain only a single layer so that time is not wasted downloading files containing unusable data.

second assumption these methods make is that each cell is of the same uniform size. If you choose to create images that do not follow these rules, you can make individual calls to loadCell and load them manually, or possibly modify the loadImageStrip method to take arrays of point and size data so the image strip is read properly (looks like a chapter exercise to me!).

## Creating a Bitmapped Font Using Image Strips

To illustrate the use of image strips, let's create a bitmapped font class. A bitmapped font is similar to the native glyphic fonts found in the Font class, only bitmapped fonts are prerendered in the form of image files.

There are several reasons why you would want to implement your own font system. First, you get total control over the shape and style of your text. Therefore, you can prerender fancier fonts than the ones provided by the system. Also, since not all fonts are available on all systems, you can guarantee that all users will visualize text in the same way. Finally, since images are prerendered, you can avoid expensive computations associated with transforming a standard Font object.

I find that implementing bitmapped fonts in Java is much easier than with using C or C++ along with graphics packages such as the Windows GDI, OpenGL, or even

DirectX. This is not because these packages are any less powerful, but because Java comes with so many useful classes right out of the box.

For instance, suppose you wish to implement a bitmapped font scheme in C++. Your font will contain only capital and lowercase letters and will not include any punctuation marks or digits. You can create an array of images, one to represent each character found in your font. Your index for accessing the array can be the integer ASCII value for each character in a text string. If you use the index as a direct index to the array, then you will have a lot of wasted space to contend with. Since capital "A" has an ASCII code of 65, the first 64 entries of the array will just be wasted space. An alternative would be to compact the array and use an offset value to access the array. In this case, if the image representing the letter "A" were stored in array position zero, then your offset value for accessing capital letters would be -65. However, if you place lowercase "a" directly after "Z", then your offset value for lowercase letters would be different. In short, without some level of abstraction handy, implementing a bitmapped font scheme in C++ can be a royal pain.

To implement a bitmapped font scheme in Java, I like to use the Hashtable class (for a review of the Hashtable class, refer to Chapter 4). There are other data structures you could use for storing your font, but I feel this is a good way to illustrate the concept.

As you know, the Java Hashtable class stores entries as key, value pairs. Both the key and the value stored in the table are stored as type Object. Therefore, you cannot store primitive types without some sort of wrapper class to store them. Also, to properly insert and retrieve values from the table, the class used for your keys must implement the hashCode and equals methods.

For our font implementation, I chose to use the String class as the key, since you can create strings that textually represent your individual font images. For example, if a particular font image represents the letter "A", then the key for this image will be the String object "A". The String hashCode method will generate a distinct integer hash code for each letter of the alphabet, so you don't have to worry about table collisions.

Figure 9.5 shows how a hash table can be used to lookup character glyphs to be drawn to the screen.

Let's get down to the code. The following class, FontMap, encapsulates a collection of font images within a Hashtable object. It also provides the ability to set an alternative image just in case a requested image is not found in the table. It also allows us to make ad hoc additions to the table with the putImage method. Finally, it gives us a drawString method, which matches character strings to their mapped image values. But don't take my word for it—check out the code for yourself.

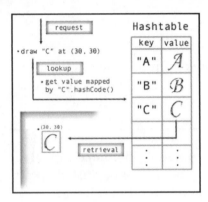

**Figure 9.5**

*Using a Hashtable to store font images*

```java
import java.awt.*;
import java.util.*;

public class FontMap extends Object
{
    // a Hashtable to store the Image data
    private Hashtable table;

    // the default image in case the table cannot find a match
    private Image defaultImage;

    // constructs a FontMap based on the given arrays of (key, value) pairs
    public FontMap(Object[] keys, Image[] images)
    {
        int numImages = images.length;

        // create a Hashtable with an initial capacity of numImages
        table = new Hashtable(numImages);

        // add each key and associated value to the table
        for(int i = 0; i < numImages; i++)
        {
            table.put(keys[i], images[i]);
        }

        setDefaultImage(null);
```

```
    }

    public boolean putImage(Object key, Image img)
    {
        if(table != null)
        {
            table.put(key, img);
            return true;
        }
        return false;
    }

    public void setDefaultImage(Image img)
    {
        defaultImage = img;
    }

    // draws the given string at position (x, y) given the sent
    // Graphics2D context
    public void drawString(String s, int x, int y, Graphics2D g2d)
    {
        int length = s.length();
        Image image;

        // draw the image equivalent to each character in the String
        for(int i = 0; i < length; i++)
        {
            // pull the Image from the table
            image = (Image)table.get(""+s.charAt(i));

            // use the default image if one was not found in our table
            if(image == null)
            {
                image = defaultImage;
            }

            // draw only a valid image
            if(image != null)
            {
```

```
                    g2d.drawImage(image, x, y, null);
                }

                // finally, increment our drawing location
                x += image.getWidth(null);
            }
        }    // drawString

    }    // FontMap
```

As you can see, the FontMap constructor takes in parallel arrays of keys and values and puts them into the table. Alternatively, you could provide a constructor that takes a *Map* object and sets it directly to your hash table. The constructor also provides the null value for the default image. Therefore, it is up to the encapsulating class to provide the keys, values, and alternative image. In return, the FontMap class is able to draw a string of bitmapped images based on a given String object.

Now that we have a basic FontMap class, let's look at a program that implements it. The following applet, *FontMapTest*, creates a FontMap object containing only digits. Each digit image is associated with its equivalent text representation. The applet then increments an int counter upward from -100, sending the String representation of the number to the FontMap drawString method. Since we're only implementing strings of numbers in this example, it should be fairly easy to follow along and try for yourself.

```
import java.applet.*;
import java.awt.*;
import java.awt.image.*;
import java.awt.geom.*;
import java.util.*;

public class FontMapTest extends Applet implements Runnable
{
```

```java
// a Thread for animation
private Thread animation;

// a FontMap for drawing text strings
private FontMap fontMap;

// just any old number to render
private int number = -100;

public void init()
{
    // the keys for our fontMap will be the String representation
    // of each digit
    Object[] keys = new Object[10];
    for(int i = 0; i < 10; i++)
    {
        keys[i] = String.valueOf(i);
    }

    // load 10 images into our image array; each cell is 20x20 pixels and
    // will have a 1 pixel border
    Image[] images = loadImageStrip("fontmap2.gif", 10, 20, 20, 1);

    // create our FontMap
    fontMap = new FontMap(keys, images);

    // create a BufferedImage for the FontMap's default Image
    // since image cells have a 1 pixel border, the actual images will be
    // 19x19 pixels in size
    BufferedImage bi = new BufferedImage(19, 19,
                                         BufferedImage.TYPE_INT_RGB);
    Graphics2D g2d   = bi.createGraphics();
    g2d.setPaint(Color.RED);
    g2d.fill(new Rectangle(19, 19));
    g2d.setPaint(Color.WHITE);
    g2d.draw(new Rectangle(1, 1, 17, 17));
    g2d.draw(new Line2D.Double(1,  1, 17, 17));
    g2d.draw(new Line2D.Double(17, 1,  1, 17));
```

```
                fontMap.setDefaultImage(bi);

                setBackground(Color.BLACK);

    }    // init

    // loads an array of Images from the given filename
    public Image[] loadImageStrip(
        String filename,    // file to load
        int numImages,      // number of images to load
        int cellWidth,      // the width and height of each cell
        int cellHeight,
        int cellBorder      // the width of the cell border
        )
    {

        // an array of Images to act as our animation frames
        Image[] images = new Image[numImages];

        // create a new MediaTracker object for this Component
        MediaTracker mt = new MediaTracker(this);

        // load the main strip image
        Image img = getImage(getDocumentBase(), filename);
        mt.addImage(img, 0);
        try
        {
            // wait for our main image to load
            mt.waitForID(0);
        }
        catch(InterruptedException e) { /* do nothing */ }

        // computing the number of columns will help us extract
        // individual cells
        int numCols = img.getWidth(this) / cellWidth;

        // get the ImageProducer source of our main image
        ImageProducer sourceProducer = img.getSource();

        // load the cells!
```

```java
        for(int i = 0; i < numImages; i++)
        {
            images[i] = loadCell(sourceProducer,
                                ((i%numCols)*cellWidth)+cellBorder,
                                ((i/numCols)*cellHeight)+cellBorder,
                                cellWidth-cellBorder,
                                cellHeight-cellBorder);
        }

        return images;
    }

    // loads a single cell from an ImageProducer given the area provided
    public Image loadCell(
        ImageProducer ip,
        int x, int y,
        int width, int height
        )
    {
        return createImage(new FilteredImageSource(ip,
                            new CropImageFilter(x, y, width, height)));
    }

    public void start()
    {
        // start the animation thread
        animation = new Thread(this);
        animation.start();
    }

    public void stop()
    {
        animation = null;
    }

    public void run()
    {
        Thread t = Thread.currentThread();
        while (t == animation)
```

```
      {
          try
          {
              Thread.sleep(100);
          }
          catch(InterruptedException e)
          {
              break;
          }
          repaint();
      }
  }    // run

  public void paint(Graphics g)
  {
      Graphics2D g2d = (Graphics2D)g;

      // draw the number at (30, 30)
      fontMap.drawString(String.valueOf(number++), 30, 30, g2d);
  }    // paint
}
```

Figure 9.6 illustrates a very large number drawn using the *FontMapTest* applet.

I purposely left in the loadImageStrip and loadCell methods here so you would have everything in one shot. By requiring the main application to create the image cells, the FontMap class is kept flexible so you can set as many or as few images as you like. For numbers less than zero, the use of an alternative image will immediately tell you that you forgot to include the image representing the negative sign.

Now let's fix the negative sign problem, as well as display numbers using American-style decimal formatting (where commas separate digits into groups of three from

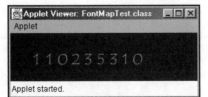

**Figure 9.6**

*The* FontMapTest *applet*

right to left). First, you can create a private `NumberFormat` object (we'll call it `formatter`) and initialize it as follows in your `init` method:

```
formatter = new java.text.DecimalFormat("###,###");
```

This will create a number formatter that uses the specified `String` pattern to separate digits into groups of three. You will also need to add minus and negative images to the `FontMap`, like the following:

```
fontMap.putImage(",", getImage(getDocumentBase(), "comma.gif"));
fontMap.putImage("-", getImage(getDocumentBase(), "minus.gif"));
```

This adds two additional images from file to the `FontMap`. For simplicity, I did not add these images to our `MediaTracker` object.

Finally, you must then adjust the `drawString` to pass in the correctly formatted `String` representation of our number:

```
fontMap.drawString(formatter.format(number++), 30, 30, g2d);
```

Figure 9.7 shows a large negative number correctly formatted using both a minus sign and commas.

Now the digit font will properly render negative numbers as well as positive numbers. The `DecimalFormat` class also allows you to format numbers as percentages, in scientific notation, and even in currency amounts. Refer to the Java documentation for more on the `DecimalFormat` class.

Just a few final comments on bitmapped fonts: First, I suggest using a monospaced font for your imaging. This allows you to more easily fill the area of each of your image cells, since lowercase "i" is just as wide graphically as capital "W" for any monospaced font. This way you'll be able to increment your horizontal drawing position by a constant value for each character in your strings. Another timesaving idea (as far as processing time is concerned) might be to pre-render static messages to a `BufferedImage` object. You can then simply render an individual image instead of using the `FontMap` `drawString` method. This saves your code from having to perform

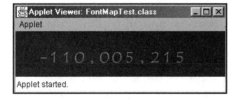

**Figure 9.7**

*Correctly displayed negative numbers in a decimal format*

redundant table retrievals. Static messages are those that seldom change over time, such as text labels, the player's name, or story line text.

There is much more you can do to enhance your bitmapped fonts. You can implement an entire alphabet (including digits and punctuation marks), allow for variable-width characters, and create fonts that can span across multiple lines. Take the time to consider all of the capabilities you want your bitmapped fonts to possess.

Now let's look at how to enhance your rendering by using off-screen rendering buffers.

# Creating an Off-Screen Rendering Buffer

Up until now, the examples shown have rendered objects directly to your window via the applet's `Graphics2D` context. Although this is fine for applications that are not visually updated often, this can present a problem for applications that support frame animation, such as games.

You've probably noticed "flickering" or "tearing" while running the animated programs presented thus far. This is, for the most part, because you are viewing the images as they are being drawn. Since you will most likely be drawing your objects out of sync with the monitor's electron gun, you will get a visual degradation. Even if it only takes a few milliseconds to render the entire scene, the flickering effect will persist over time.

The *CollisionTest* applet from Chapter 8 appeared (at least on my machine) to be the best (or is it the worst?) example of animation flickering presented in this book. The animation employed in the *CollisionTest* applet is sporadic since the scene is redrawn as often as the mouse cursor's position changes. The animation is also choppy because the rectangles are painted directly to the applet window. As mentioned earlier, regular updates made directly to the applet window will cause flickering. So how can this be fixed?

If you're a relative newcomer to game programming, welcome to the world of off-screen rendering. To put it simply, *off-screen rendering* (also called *double buffering*) involves rendering the entire scene to a "virtual window," or a window that exists only in memory. After all of the objects in the scene are rendered to the virtual window, its contents are rendered to the actual applet window all at once. The net effect is a single image being rendered to the applet window once per frame, therefore reducing flicker altogether. Figure 9.8 shows how the components of a scene can be assembled using an off-screen image.

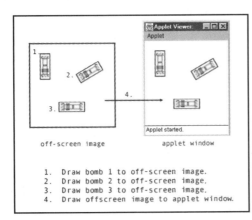

**Figure 9.8**

*Rendering objects to an off-screen image*

To actually implement a double-buffering scheme, just call the `Applet` `createImage` method in the body of your applet's `init` method. It will return an `Image` suitable for off-screen rendering. The `createImage` method takes two parameters describing both the width and height of the image to create. The following creates an off-screen image with the same width and height as the applet's window:

```
// assume offscreen references an instance of the Image class
offscreen = createImage(getSize().width, getSize().height);
```

Then you'll want to do your rendering to the off-screen image within the `Applet` `paint` method. After your scene is completely rendered to the off-screen image, you'll need to paint it to the main applet window so it will be visible. The following code snippet illustrates a skeleton double-buffered paint scheme:

```
public void paint(Graphics g)
{
    // get a valid Graphics2D rendering context from our off-screen image
    Graphics2D g2d = (Graphics2D) offscreen.getGraphics();

    // clear the contents of the offscreen image with the color of your choice
    g2d.setPaint(Color.WHITE);
    g2d.fillRect(0, 0, getSize().width, getSize().height);

    // *** do some wicked stuff using our newly created g2d object ***

    // dispose of the Graphics2D context when we're finished with it
```

```
        g2d.dispose();

        // draw the final off-screen image to the visible Graphics context
        g.drawImage(offscreen, 0, 0, this);
}
```

It's always a good idea to call the Graphics dispose method when employing a double-buffering mechanism. This releases all resources the Graphics context has allocated during rendering. Since continuous animation can cause a good number of Graphics objects to be created in a very short amount of time, cleaning it up manually will help keep memory free and alleviate the garbage collector from running frequently. Just keep in mind that you may not use a Graphics context for rendering after the dispose method has been called.

One final consideration I would recommend is to make sure that the off-screen image is valid before actually using it. One way to determine if an off-screen image is valid is to compare its size to the parent applet's size. If they don't match, it's probably a good idea to re-create the off-screen image.

I usually check my off-screen images at the end of the applet's update method. This is because validation of the off-screen image is not associated with the actual rendering of the scene, but rather the preparation for scene rendering. The following shows how to update an off-screen image:

```
public void update(Graphics g)
{
    // *** update scene objects here ***

    // make sure we have a valid offscreen image
    if(offscreen == null ||
       offscreen.getWidth(null)  != getSize().width ||
       offscreen.getHeight(null) != getSize().height)
    {
        offscreen = createImage(getSize().width, getSize().height);
    }

    // paint the scene
    paint(g);
}
```

I also like to check off-screen against the null reference, just in case I forgot to initialize it to begin with. Even if you prefer to validate the off-screen image elsewhere, it is still a good idea to override the Applet update method anyway. This is because the native update method conducts a screen clear on the applet window. This is a great waste of time because you will be drawing over it with your off-screen image anyway! So always try to define the update method, even if you decide to leave it empty.

There you have it. With only a few lines of code, you can completely vanquish flickering and tearing from your animations forever. Let's revisit the *CollisionTest* applet by looking at a similar example that employs double buffering. The following listing for the *OffscreenTest* applet automatically updates the position of a single rectangle and checks it for collision against nine other rectangles. You can also press the spacebar to change the active rectangle.

It's important to lock down off-screen rendering, especially if you haven't used it before, so try running this example on your own before continuing.

```
import java.applet.*;
import java.awt.*;
import java.awt.geom.*;
import java.awt.event.*;
import java.util.*;

public class OffscreenTest extends Applet implements KeyListener, Runnable
{
        // a thread for animation
        private Thread animation;

        // the number of rectangles contained in our scene
        private final int NUM_RECTS = 10;

        // a list of rectangles
        private LinkedList rectangles;
        private ListIterator iterator;

        // an AlphaComposite to show semi-transparent rectangles
        private AlphaComposite alpha;

        // index to the rectangle that is currently selected
        private int curr;

        // current position of the moving rectangle
        private double vx;
```

```java
private double vy;

// an offscreen image for offscreen rendering
Image offscreen;

public void init()
{
    animation = new Thread(this);

    rectangles = new LinkedList();

    // create our offscreen rendering Image
    offscreen = createImage(getSize().width, getSize().height);

    // create an AlphaComposite with 50% transparency
    alpha = AlphaComposite.getInstance(AlphaComposite.SRC_OVER, 0.5f);

    // create NUM_RECTS rectangles at random positions and add them
    // to the list
    Random r = new Random();
    int width  = (int)getSize().getWidth();
    int height = (int)getSize().getHeight();

    for(int i = 0; i < NUM_RECTS; i++)
    {
        rectangles.add(new Rectangle2D.Double(
                (double)(   Math.abs(r.nextInt())%width),
                (double)(   Math.abs(r.nextInt())%height),
                (double)(20+Math.abs(r.nextInt())%50),
                (double)(20+Math.abs(r.nextInt())%50)));
    }
    curr = 0;

    vx = vy = 6;

    // don't forget to register the applet to listen for key events
    addKeyListener(this);
```

```java
    }

    public void update(Graphics g)
    {
        // update the current rectangle
        double x, y, w, h;

        Rectangle2D active = (Rectangle2D)rectangles.get(curr);

        x = active.getX()+vx;
        y = active.getY()+vy;
        w = active.getWidth();
        h = active.getHeight();

        if(x < 0)
        {
            x = 0;
            vx = - vx;
        }
        else if(x + w > getSize().width)
        {
            x = getSize().width - w;
            vx = - vx;
        }

        if(y < 0)
        {
            y = 0;
            vy = - vy;
        }
        else if(y + h > getSize().height)
        {
            y = getSize().height - h;
            vy = - vy;
        }

        active.setRect(x, y, w, h);

        // make sure we have a valid offscreen image
```

```java
        if(offscreen == null ||
           offscreen.getWidth(null)  != getSize().width ||
           offscreen.getHeight(null) != getSize().height)
        {
            offscreen = createImage(getSize().width, getSize().height);
        }

        paint(g);
}

public void paint(Graphics g)
{
        Graphics2D g2d = (Graphics2D)offscreen.getGraphics();
        g2d.setPaint(Color.WHITE);
        g2d.fillRect(0, 0, getSize().width, getSize().height);

        // tell our Graphics2D context to use transparency
        g2d.setComposite(alpha);

        // draw the rectangles
        g2d.setPaint(Color.BLACK);
        for(int i = 0; i < NUM_RECTS; i++)
        {
            g2d.draw((Rectangle2D)rectangles.get(i));
        }

        Rectangle2D rect;
        Rectangle2D active = (Rectangle2D)rectangles.get(curr);
        g2d.setPaint(Color.RED.darker());
        for(iterator = rectangles.listIterator(0); iterator.hasNext(); )
        {
            // get the next rectangle in the list
            rect = (Rectangle2D)iterator.next();

            // test for intersection--note we shouldn't test
            // pick against itself
            if(active != rect && active.intersects(rect))
            {
                // fill collisions
```

```
                    g2d.fill(rect);
            }
        }

        // fill the pick rectangle
        g2d.setPaint(Color.BLUE.brighter());
        g2d.fill(active);

        // dispose of the Graphics2D context when we're finished with it
        g2d.dispose();

        // draw the final offscreen image to the visible Graphics context
        g.drawImage(offscreen, 0, 0, this);
    }

    public void start()
    {
        // start the animation thread
        animation = new Thread(this);
        animation.start();
    }

    public void stop()
    {
        animation = null;
    }

    public void run()
    {
        Thread t = Thread.currentThread();
        while (t == animation)
        {
            try
            {
                Thread.sleep(33);
            }
            catch(InterruptedException e)
            {
                break;
```

```
                    }

                repaint();
            }
    }    // run

    public void keyPressed(KeyEvent e)
    {
    }

    public void keyReleased(KeyEvent e)
    {
    }

    public void keyTyped(KeyEvent e)
    {
        // cycle through the rectangles when the space bar is pressed
        if(e.getKeyChar() == KeyEvent.VK_SPACE)
        {
            if(++curr >= rectangles.size())
            {
                curr = 0;
            }
        }
    }

}    // OffscreenTest
```

Figure 9.9 shows the *Offscreen Test* applet in action. It looks much like the *Collision Test* applet from Chapter 8, except that its animation is flicker-free.

I especially like this example for its use of alpha blending, but that's beside the point. Off-screen rendering is very easy to implement in Java, but it is also something that cannot be overlooked, especially when animation is continuous.

**NOTE**

If you choose to use Swing components for your games (although I would recommend against it), you will not need to implement an off-screen rendering scheme, because Swing components already implement their own double-buffering mechanism.

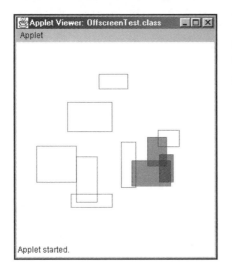

**Figure 9.9**

*Flicker-free animation with the OffscreenTest applet*

If you're a glutton for creating class like I am, check out the following sections on how to wrap an off-screen buffer within a class, as well as how to improve off-screen rendering by using hardware acceleration.

## Creating the BufferedGraphics Class

Although implementing an off-screen rendering system in Java is quite trivial and easy to do, it might be a good idea to wrap the components that make it up into a single class component. This will not only alleviate some overhead within your main applet class, but it will also allow you to extend its functionality through subclasses, which you'll see later.

Writing the code for the BufferedGraphics class should be a no-brainer. All it needs to do is maintain a reference to its Component owner (which will usually be the main applet) and the Image object that will act as the off-screen rendering image. To complete the BufferedGraphics class, you must implement methods for creating, validating, and returning the off-screen image as well as its Graphics context.

Let's get right to it—here's the code for my BufferedGraphics class:

```
import java.awt.*;

public class BufferedGraphics extends Object
{
    // the Component that will be drawing the offscreen image
```

```java
protected Component parent;

// the offscreen rendering Image
protected Image buffer;

// creates a new BufferedGraphics object
protected BufferedGraphics()
{
    parent = null;
    buffer = null;
}


// creates a new BufferedGraphics object with the sent parent Component
public BufferedGraphics(Component c)
{
    parent = c;

    createBuffer();
}


public final Image getBuffer()
{
    return buffer;
}


// returns the buffer's Graphics context after the buffer has been validated
public Graphics getValidGraphics()
{
    if(! isValid())
    {
        createBuffer();
    }
    return buffer.getGraphics();
}


// creates an offscreen rendering image matching the parent's width
// and height
protected void createBuffer()
{
```

```
        Dimension size = parent.getSize();
        buffer = parent.createImage(size.width, size.height);
    }

    // validates the offscreen image against several criteria, namely
    // against the null reference and the parent's width and height
    protected boolean isValid()
    {
        if(parent == null)
        {
            return false;
        }

        Dimension s = parent.getSize();

        if(buffer == null ||
           buffer.getWidth(null)  != s.width ||
           buffer.getHeight(null) != s.height)
        {
            return false;
        }

        return true;
    }

} // BufferedGraphics
```

If you don't feel like implementing the code for double buffering over and over, just create a BufferedGraphics object and let it do the work for you.

The following applet, *BufferedGraphicsTest*, creates an animation using a BufferedGraphics object. Note how the use of the BufferedGraphics class minimizes the code required to maintain an off-screen rendering image.

```
import java.applet.*;
import java.awt.*;
import java.awt.image.*;
import java.awt.geom.*;

public class BufferedGraphicsTest extends Applet implements Runnable
{
```

```
// a Thread for animation
private Thread animation;

// the offscreen rendering image
private BufferedGraphics offscreen;

// an Image to render
private Image pipe;

// the width and height of one Image frame
private int imageWidth;
private int imageHeight;

// the position, velocity, and rotation of the Image object
private int x;
private int y;

private int vx;
private int vy;

private double rot;

private AffineTransform at;
private final double ONE_RADIAN = Math.toRadians(10);

public void init()
{
    // create the image to render
    pipe = getImage(getDocumentBase(), "pipe.gif");
    while(pipe.getWidth(this) <= 0);

    // create the offscreen image
    offscreen = new BufferedGraphics(this);

    imageWidth = pipe.getWidth(this);
    imageHeight = pipe.getHeight(this);

    vx = 3+(int)(Math.random()*5);
```

```java
        vy = 3+(int)(Math.random()*5);

        x = getSize().width/2  - imageWidth/2;
        y = getSize().height/2 - imageHeight/2;
        rot = 0;
        at = AffineTransform.getTranslateInstance(x, y);

    }   // init

    public void start()
    {
        // start the animation thread
        animation = new Thread(this);
        animation.start();
    }

    public void stop()
    {
        animation = null;
    }

    public void run()
    {
        Thread t = Thread.currentThread();
        while (t == animation)
        {
            try
            {
                Thread.sleep(33);
            }
            catch(InterruptedException e)
            {
                break;
            }

            repaint();
        }
    }   // run

    public void update(Graphics g)
```

```java
{
    // update the object's position
    x += vx;
    y += vy;

    // keep the object within our window
    if(x < 0)
    {
        x = 0;
        vx = -vx;
    }
    else if(x > getSize().width - imageWidth)
    {
        x = getSize().width - imageWidth;
        vx = -vx;
    }

    if(y < 0)
    {
        y = 0;
        vy = -vy;
    }
    else if(y > getSize().height - imageHeight)
    {
        y = getSize().height - imageHeight;
        vy = -vy;
    }

    if(vx > 0)
        rot += ONE_RADIAN;
    else
        rot -= ONE_RADIAN;


    // set the transform for the image
    at.setToIdentity();
    at.translate(x + imageWidth/2, y + imageHeight/2);
    at.rotate(rot);
```

```
        at.translate(-imageWidth/2, -imageHeight/2);

        paint(g);
    }

    public void paint(Graphics g)
    {
        // validate and clear the offscreen image
        Graphics2D bg = (Graphics2D)offscreen.getValidGraphics();
        bg.setColor(Color.BLACK);
        bg.fill(new Rectangle(getSize().width, getSize().height));

        // draw the pipe to the offscreen image
        bg.drawImage(pipe, at, this);

        // draw the offscreen image to the applet window
        g.drawImage(offscreen.getBuffer(), 0, 0, this);

    }   // paint

}   // BufferedGraphicsTest
```

Figure 9.10 shows the *BufferedGraphicsTest* applet, which bounces a single pipe object around the screen.

**Figure 9.10**

*The* BufferedGraphicsTest *applet*

Next, we'll take a look at how to implement an off-screen rendering scheme that takes advantage of hardware acceleration.

## Using Hardware Acceleration with the VolatileImage Class

With the advent of Java 2-D, developers have been able to take greater advantage of the more advanced graphical features Java has to offer. With this increase in functionality has also come a decrease in performance: if developers are using more complex rendering algorithms in their applications, then this will obviously become a strain on the CPU.

The designers of the Java language have devised a way to make use of hardware acceleration as one way to combat this strain on the processor. Most PC gamers who use Windows are very familiar with video acceleration, in the form of AGP video accelerator cards. These cards contain memory along with processing units that work alongside the system processor and RAM. By taking on the workload of performing complex graphics computations, a video card can greatly enhance application performance.

To make a long story short, the architects of Java have developed the VolatileImage class in Java version 1.4 to take advantage of such acceleration. On Windows platforms, this means storing images directly in video RAM (VRAM) and allowing packages such as DirectDraw to provide access to this memory. On platforms that do not provide access to VRAM, such as Solaris, the VolatileImage class can access images through Pixmap objects on the X Server. In short, the VolatileImage class uses the fastest methods of accessing images that the current platform has to offer.

Although the use of DirectDraw along with VRAM can greatly enhance rendering speed, there can be a problem. The VolatileImage class is named as such because the contents of the image can be lost at any time; in other words, the image is *volatile*. The RAM in your system is another example of volatile memory; when you turn off your computer's power, the contents of RAM is lost forever. In Windows, enabling a screen saver, changing the screen resolution, or running another program in full-screen exclusive mode can all cause a VolatileImage object's contents to be lost.

Unfortunately, Windows does not transmit any messages when it clears the contents of a VolatileImage. Therefore, you must test the image to determine if its contents were lost. Once an image's contents are deleted, they cannot be regained. In such a case, the current scene must be redrawn to restore the image's contents.

The following applet, *VolatileImageTest*, allows the user to choose between standard and hardware-accelerated off-screen rendering images. The program reports the time taken to draw a simple scene 1,000 times.

```java
import java.applet.*;
import java.awt.*;
import java.awt.event.*;
import java.awt.image.*;
import java.awt.geom.*;

public class VolatileImageTest extends Applet implements ItemListener
{
    // a Thread for animation
    private Thread animation;

    // an offscreen rendering image
    private Image offscreen;

    // an Image to tile
    private Image tile;

    // the width and height of the tile
    private int tileWidth;
    private int tileHeight;

    // allows the user to decide between accelerated and non-accelerated
    // offscreen images
    private Checkbox accelerated;

    public void init()
    {
        // create the tile image
        tile = getImage(getDocumentBase(), "bevel.gif");
        while(tile.getWidth(this) <= 0);

        tileWidth = tile.getWidth(this);
        tileHeight = tile.getHeight(this);

        // create the radio button
```

```
        setLayout(new BorderLayout());
        accelerated = new Checkbox("use accelerated image", null, true);
        accelerated.addItemListener(this);
        Panel p = new Panel();
        p.add(accelerated);
        add(p, BorderLayout.SOUTH);

        // create the offscreen rendering image
        createOffscreenImage(accelerated.getState());

    }    // init

    // creates either a VolatileImage or a BufferedImage, based on the sent
    // parameter
    private void createOffscreenImage(boolean createAccelerated)
    {
        if(createAccelerated)
        {
            // create an accelerated image
            offscreen =
                getGraphicsConfiguration().createCompatibleVolatileImage(
                    getSize().width, getSize().height);
        }

        else
        {
            // otherwise, just create a plain-old BufferedImage
            offscreen =
                getGraphicsConfiguration().createCompatibleImage(
                    getSize().width, getSize().height);
        }
    }

    public void update(Graphics g)
    {
        // calculate the time it takes to render the scene 1000 times

        long time = System.currentTimeMillis();

        for(int i = 0; i < 1000; i++)
```

```
        {
            paint(g);
        }

        if(offscreen instanceof VolatileImage)
        {
            System.out.println("It took " + (System.currentTimeMillis() -
                    time) + " ms to render " +
                    " the scene 1000 times using an accelerated image.");
        }

        else
        {
            System.out.println("It took " + (System.currentTimeMillis() -
                    time) + " ms to render " +
                    "the scene 1000 times using a non-accelerated image.");
        }
    }

    public void paint(Graphics g)
    {
        // validates the offscreen image and paints the scene

        if(offscreen instanceof VolatileImage)
        {
            VolatileImage volatileImage = (VolatileImage) offscreen;

            do
            {
                // restore the offscreen image if it is invalid
                if(volatileImage.validate(getGraphicsConfiguration()) ==
                    VolatileImage.IMAGE_INCOMPATIBLE)
                {
                    createOffscreenImage(true);
                }

                // paint the scene
                paintScene(volatileImage.getGraphics());

                // loop if contents are lost
```

```
        }    while(volatileImage.contentsLost());

    }

    else
    {
        if(offscreen == null ||
          offscreen.getWidth(null)  != getSize().width ||
          offscreen.getHeight(null) != getSize().height
          )
        {
            createOffscreenImage(false);
        }

        paintScene(offscreen.getGraphics());
    }

    // draw the offscreen image to the applet window
    g.drawImage(offscreen, 0, 0, this);

}    // paint

private void paintScene(Graphics g)
{
    // tiles the image within the applet window

    Graphics2D g2d = (Graphics2D) g;

    int width  = getSize().width;
    int height = getSize().height;
    for(int y = 0; y < height; y += tileHeight)
    {
        for(int x = 0; x < width; x += tileWidth)
        {
            g2d.drawImage(tile, x, y, this);
        }
    }

    // dispose of any resources the Graphics object may be using
```

```
            g2d.dispose();
        }

        public void itemStateChanged(ItemEvent e)
        {
            if(accelerated == e.getSource())
            {
                createOffscreenImage(accelerated.getState());
                repaint();
            }
        }
    }

}   // VolatileImageTest
```

Figure 9.11 depicts the *VolatileImageTest* applet in action. It allows the user to switch between accelerated and non-accelerated drawing modes to draw a tiled scene.

The output of this applet can vary widely based on the system configuration and whether or not it contains accelerated capabilities. I have seen up to a two second difference on some systems. This can lead to a great performance boost over the entire life cycle of an applet.

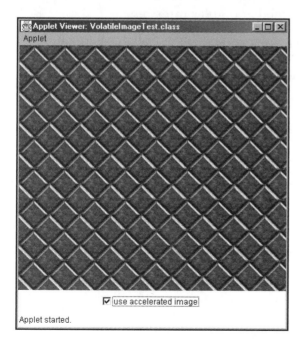

**Figure 9.11**

*The* VolatileImageTest *applet*

Also, notice how hardware-accelerated rendering is contained within a loop, as the contents of the off-screen image can be lost at any time. The loop also tests to make sure that the off-screen image is compatible with the current graphics configuration. For more on the methods contained within the `VolatileImage` class, see your Java documentation from version 1.4 or later.

To save space, I will not always carry out all the steps involved in correctly implementing an accelerated off-screen rendering image from here on. However, be sure to follow through and conduct all the necessary checks on volatile images in games that you wish to publish or otherwise distribute. We'll look at how to let your programs automatically choose whether to implement hardware-accelerated images in Chapter 11. For now, try using them in your programs if your system contains accelerated hardware. The increase in speed can be quite dramatic.

# Perfecting Your Animations Using Framerate Syncing

Thus far, we have talked about most of the concepts needed to create animations using Java. Threading, image arrays, and off-screen rendering images are all necessary components for animation. One topic we have yet to discuss is that of *timing*, or *synchronizing*, animation so that it is performed at regular intervals.

Animations that run within a continuous rendering loop should behave much like frames on a movie reel. A movie reel moves at a constant rate so frame animation will appear smooth and continuous. But with the varying hardware out there, it can sometimes be a challenge making everything look right on all systems.

For instance, suppose you just developed a Java puzzle game and are anxious to distribute it. Sure, it might run fine on your friend's clunky old 166 MHz Pentium I machine. However, you may then find that it runs way too fast to be playable on his brand-new 2 GHz bruiser. What happened? You neglected syncing the framerate to occur at a constant rate.

In the case of your puzzle game, it isn't a question of its minimum requirements but rather its *maximum* requirements. Fortunately, most games today implement some sort of animation synchronization to guarantee it works on systems across the board.

To maintain a constant framerate, all you need to do is make sure that each frame takes the same amount of time to fully execute. So if you can guarantee that each frame takes no less than 20 milliseconds to run, you can execute 50 such cycles every second. Thus, you would be maintaining a constant framerate of 50 frames per second (fps).

Once you decide upon a constant framerate you wish your game to have, calculating the minimum time per frame is as easy as follows:

```
one_frame_ms = 1000/target_framerate;
```

If you're already an experienced C or C++ game programmer, then you have probably already implemented a framerate sync mechanism in your games. In Java, a similar mechanism can be used within your main game loop, the `run` method. The algorithm I use to maintain a constant framerate is as follows:

1. Loop (forever).
2. Save the current time, *t0*.
3. Update/render the scene.
4. Save the current time, *t1*.
5. Calculate the elapsed time, *dt*, as (*t1* − *t0*).
6. If *dt* is less than *one_frame_ms*, call `Thread.sleep` for (*one_frame_ms* − *dt*).
7. Otherwise, sleep the currently executing thread for a few milliseconds.

For instance, if `one_frame_ms` is set to 25 milliseconds (giving you 40 frames of animation per second), but a given frame only takes 18 milliseconds to be updated and rendered, then you would need to sleep for an additional 7 milliseconds to make sure the framerate is constant.

One problem associated with framerate syncing occurs when it takes longer than the predetermined `one_frame_ms` time to update and render the frame. So if `one_frame_ms` is set to 15 milliseconds and it takes up to 25 milliseconds to update and render the frame on a slow machine, then the framerate is not guaranteed to be constant. Furthermore, the current thread will not be put to sleep and might thus starve the garbage collector. If the garbage collector is starved for very long, you may run out of available memory and lock up your system. That is why it is always a good idea to allow the current thread to sleep for at least a few milliseconds even if your frames are taking too long to be updated and rendered.

The following applet, *FramerateTest*, does nothing other than maintain a constant framerate of 60 fps. The bottom of the `run` loop counts the number of frames as well as the elapsed time so that the actual framerate can be reported once per second. Give it a try.

```
import java.applet.*;
import java.awt.*;

public class FramerateTest extends Applet implements Runnable
```

```
{
    // a Thread for animation
    private Thread animation;

    // the minimum number of milliseconds spent per frame
    private long framerate;

    public void init()
    {
        setBackground(Color.BLACK);
        animation = new Thread(this);

        // set the framerate to 60 frames per second (16.67 ms / frame)
        framerate = 1000/60;
    }

    public void start()
    {
        // start the animation thread
        animation.start();
    }

    public void stop()
    {
        animation = null;
    }

    public void run()
    {
        // time the frame began
        long frameStart;

        // number of frames counted this second
        long frameCount = 0;

        // time elapsed during one frame
        long elapsedTime;

        // accumulates elapsed time over multiple frames
```

```java
long totalElapsedTime = 0;

// the actual calculated framerate reported
long reportedFramerate;

Thread t = Thread.currentThread();
while (t == animation)
{
    // save the start time
    frameStart = System.currentTimeMillis();

    // paint the frame
    repaint();

    // calculate the time it took to render the frame
    elapsedTime = System.currentTimeMillis() - frameStart;

    // sync the framerate
    try
    {
        // make sure framerate milliseconds have passed this frame
        if(elapsedTime < framerate)
        {
            Thread.sleep(framerate - elapsedTime);
        }
        else
        {
            // don't starve the garbage collector
            Thread.sleep(5);
        }
    }

    catch(InterruptedException e)
    {
        break;
    }

    // update the actual reported framerate
    ++ frameCount;
```

```
                    totalElapsedTime += (System.currentTimeMillis() - frameStart);
                    if(totalElapsedTime > 1000)
                    {
                            reportedFramerate = (long)((double) frameCount /
                                                (double) totalElapsedTime * 1000.0);

                            // show the framerate in the applet status window
                            showStatus("fps: " + reportedFramerate);

                            frameCount = 0;
                            totalElapsedTime = 0;
                    }
                }
            }    // run

        }    // FramerateTest
```

Figure 9.12 shows a small window that will redraw itself at a rate of 60 fps. Note that because of number rounding and uncalculated clock cycles, the actual framerate performance will come *close* to the target framerate, but will usually fall just a bit short.

Note that the current framerate is displayed in the applet's status window via the showStatus method. You will be asked in the chapter exercises to modify the *FramerateTest* applet so that the user can change the framerate at any time.

> **NOTE**
>
> **Frame-based animation needs to run at about 20 fps to fool the human eye into believing that the animation is real and continuous. Furthermore, the slowest monitors have a built-in refresh rate of about 60 fps. Therefore, you will typically need to choose a framerate between these two values. If the framerate is set too low, the eye will tell that the animation is not authentic. On the other hand, if the framerate is set too high, frames will be sent to the raster faster than the monitor can draw them, resulting in missed frames.**

**Figure 9.12**

*Syncing the framerate to 60 fps*

# Conclusion

This chapter presented some fun ways to animate your Java scenes. The MediaTracker class provides a great way to remotely load in images and check any errors that may occur. The use of bitmapped fonts is a great way to test image strips as well as create a custom text-rendering system. Also, implementing a double-buffering system is essential for flicker-free animations. Finally, framerate syncing will inevitably perfect your animations by generating them at a constant rate. Try the following exercises and you too will soon be an animation master.

# Exercises

**9.1**  Suggest a way to test the status of a loading image without using a MediaTracker object. (Hint: Use a loop and one of the properties of an Image that is not set until the image has completely loaded.) What is the danger in doing this?

**9.2**  Modify the loadImageStrip method so that it will properly load "irregular" image files—that is, ones that contain cells of different sizes or ones that contain extra space or padding.

**9.3**  Change the key value in the FontMap class to be of type Character. Your code for retrieving values from the table will change only slightly. Which way to you prefer? Which way is more flexible?

**9.4**  Introduce a way to implement "padding" when formatting bitmapped numbers. For instance, padding the number 29 to five digits would be rendered as "00029." The prototype for a method that pads strings might look like

```
drawPaddedString(String s, int preferredLength, char padChar, Graphics2D g2d)
```

where s is the String to draw, preferredLength refers to the minimum number of characters to render, padChar represents the padding character to append to the front of short strings, and g2d references the current Graphics2D rendering context. You can also add additional parameters representing the x, y coordinates to draw at, additional transforms, and so on. Add the drawPaddedString method to the FontMap class as a utility for drawing padded strings.

**9.5**  You've already looked at how to render negative numbers using a bitmapped font. Extend this to implement a scheme for rendering a full alphabet, including commonly used characters such as "%", "$", and "*". Your final bitmapped font class should provide operations for rendering strings, integers, floats, and doubles as a bitmapped string.

**9.6** Investigate the `ImageCapabilities` class, namely the `isAccelerated` method. Edit the *VolatileImageTest* applet to test for video acceleration capabilities before choosing an off-screen rendering scheme. The image capabilities for the currently running operating system can be found by using the `Component` `getGraphicsConfiguration` method.

**9.7** Add a `TextField` component to the *FramerateTest* applet to allow the user to change the framerate at any time. Also, try allowing the user to add an applet parameter to specify an initial framerate to use at run time.

# CHAPTER 10

# CREATING THE CUSTOM GAME OBJECT CLASS, ACTOR2D

Invariably, the games you develop will contain dozens, hundreds, even thousands of entities that have the ability to move and interact with one another. Most game entities have similar properties, such as position, velocity, state, color, and so on. For example, your typical game of *Asteroids* pits you (usually in the form of a spaceship or plane) against a seemingly never-ending barrage of asteroids that are on a collision course with your home planet (Mars or Venus—whichever it might be). Although most game objects will exhibit their own unique state at any given time, they all contain similar attributes for animation. So is it possible then to create a single, generic game entity that can be molded to fit the needs of your games? You bet it is.

The nature of games presents the perfect opportunity to use the object-oriented capabilities of Java to create flexible, reusable game objects. For a checkers game, it would be foolish to write the code for each checker independently. Rather, it makes better sense to write code that describes a single checker, and then allow that single code base to control all of the checkers on the board. Obviously, this will make the game easier to code and maintain. This is what object-oriented programming is all about.

In this chapter, I'll discuss the following topics for creating reusable game objects:

- Defining generic attributes common to all game entities
- Developing code for the Actor2D class
- Creating helper classes to make our lives easier
- Putting the Actor2D class to work

Let's get started by examining some attributes common to most game entities.

# Prelude to the Actor2D Class

To prepare for coding a game entity object class, let's first consider what attributes are common to most game entities. From there, you can turn object requirements into code.

First of all, game objects are *visual*. Therefore, you're going to need to figure out a general structure for containing your objects' visuals. Should you only permit images to be loaded from file, or should you only support basic shape and line drawing? Or can you find a way to allow the use of both shape drawing and pre-rendered images loaded from disk? You will also need to specify a way for objects to animate themselves from one frame to the next.

Game objects are also *spatial.* They all contain a specific x, y position as well as a specific width and height. Many game objects also contain a given x- and y-velocity as well as a rotation about an anchor point. Most game objects will also need to observe some sort of scene bounds, whether it be the walls that border the applet window or the bounds of a virtual universe.

Game objects will also usually exhibit some sort of *state.* State attributes such as living, dead, and dying are commonly used to describe many game entity types. For example, if an asteroid object is *living,* then it is free to move about the scene and bounce off other objects. However, once an asteroid's state moves to *dying,* then the asteroid will not be free to move on its own or collide with other objects; it will merely cycle through its death animation sequences. Finally, once the asteroid is finished being in its dying state, it will move to the *dead* state. Here, the asteroid will no longer be valid and will probably not be updated or rendered at all.

Many game objects will also contain fields to track remaining health, shields, and ammunition. However, these fields are not common to most or all game entities. It would cloud the purpose of a flexible game class to force all game entities to exhibit these properties. Furthermore, it would waste valuable memory to have game entities bulked up with fields that they do not need to have.

With these things in mind, we can begin solidifying which attributes will make the cut to our final actor class. Figure 10.1 shows one possible group of associations to maintain.

Notice that I have labeled the game entity "Actor." I give that name to any visual object that plays some sort of role within the game. Just as the heroes and villains

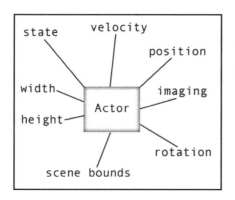

**Figure 10.1**

*Attributes common to most game entities*

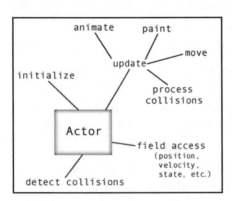

**Figure 10.2**

*Action capabilities of most game entities*

that define a game's action are "actors," so are walls, bullets, and scenery, because they too can play important roles in how a game is played.

Besides having a set of common properties, our actors also need ways to perform common tasks. For instance, given a brush to paint with, all actors should know how to draw themselves. They should also have a common interface for updating themselves. If an actor is in motion or is acted upon by an external stimulus, such as a mouse click, it should be able to update its position and bounds accordingly. Furthermore, actors should know how to animate themselves as well as detect a collision with another object when given another object's coordinates and size.

Much like Figure 10.1, Figure 10.2 illustrates actions that any game object should be able to perform.

This is not meant to be a complete or finalized list of what a game object should be, so once we write the code for the actor class feel free to make any additions or deletions as you see fit. With that out of the way, let's look at how you can implement the above requirements using Java code.

# Actor2D, Front and Center

You've already seen the components that make up a general actor object. Here is where I'll present my code for the Actor2D class. You know enough about Java by now to be able to read and understand the code. What I'd like to do is show you the code for the Actor2D class and its related classes, then tie up any loose points afterward. So without further ado, here's the code for the Actor2D class:

```
import java.awt.*;
import java.awt.geom.*;
```

```java
import java.util.*;

// contains general information for moving and rendering a 2-D game object
public abstract class Actor2D extends Object implements Moveable
{
    // some general states an actor might have
    public final int STATE_ALIVE = 1;
    public final int STATE_DYING = 2;
    public final int STATE_DEAD  = 4;

    // the state of this actor
    protected int state;

    // the actor group this actor belongs to
    protected ActorGroup2D group;

    // position, velocity, and rotation of the actor, along with cached
    // transformation
    protected Vector2D pos;
    protected Vector2D vel;
    protected double    rotation;
    protected AffineTransform xform;

    protected final double TWO_PI = 2*Math.PI;

    // a bounding rectangle for things such as collision testing
    protected Rectangle2D bounds;

    // a list of actors this actor has collided with during one frame
    protected LinkedList collisionList;

    // width and height of this actor
    protected int frameWidth;
    protected int frameHeight;

    // reference to this actor's current animation strip
    protected AnimationStrip currAnimation;

    // number of frames to wait before animating the next frame, plus a wait
```

```java
        // counter
        protected int animWait;
        protected int animCount;

        // creates a new Actor2D object belonging to the given ActorGroup
        public Actor2D(ActorGroup2D grp)
        {
            group = grp;

            bounds = new Rectangle2D.Double();
            collisionList = new LinkedList();

            state = 0;

            pos    = new Vector2D.Double();
            vel    = new Vector2D.Double();
            rotation = 0;
            xform = new AffineTransform();

            currAnimation = null;
            animWait  = 0;
            animCount = 0;

            frameWidth  = 0;
            frameHeight = 0;
        }

        // animates the actor every animWait frames
        public void animate()
        {
            if(currAnimation != null)
            {
                if(++animCount >= animWait)
                {
                    currAnimation.getNextFrame();
                    animCount = 0;
                }
            }
```

```java
    }

    // draws the actor using its native transformation
    public void paint(Graphics2D g2d)
    {
        if(currAnimation != null)
        {
            g2d.drawImage(currAnimation.getCurrFrame(), xform,
                        AnimationStrip.observer);
        }
    }

    // draws the actor at the sent x,y coordinates
    public void paint(Graphics2D g2d, double x, double y)
    {
        if(currAnimation != null)
        {
            g2d.drawImage(currAnimation.getCurrFrame(),
                        AffineTransform.getTranslateInstance(x, y),
                        AnimationStrip.observer
                        );
        }
    }

    // simple bounding-box determination of whether this actor has collided with
    // the sent actor
    public boolean intersects(Actor2D other)
    {
        return bounds.intersects(other.getBounds());
    }

    // updates the bounding rectangle of this actor to meet its current x and y
    // positions
    public void updateBounds()
    {
        // make sure we know the correct width and height of the actor
        if(frameWidth <= 0 && currAnimation != null)
        {
            frameWidth = currAnimation.getFrameWidth();
```

```
            }

            if(frameHeight <= 0 && currAnimation != null)
            {
                  frameHeight = currAnimation.getFrameHeight();
            }

            bounds.setRect(pos.getX(), pos.getY(), frameWidth, frameHeight);
      }

      // makes sure the actor's bounds have'nt exceeded the bounds specified
      // by its actor group
      public void checkBounds()
      {
            if(group == null) return;

            if(bounds.getX() < group.MIN_X_POS)
            {
                  pos.setX(group.MIN_X_POS);
            }

            else if(bounds.getX() + frameWidth > group.MAX_X_POS)
            {
                  pos.setX(group.MAX_X_POS - frameWidth);
            }

            if(bounds.getY() < group.MIN_Y_POS)
            {
                  pos.setY(group.MIN_Y_POS);
            }

            else if(bounds.getY() + frameHeight > group.MAX_Y_POS)
            {
                  pos.setY(group.MAX_Y_POS - frameHeight);
            }
      }

      // returns a String representation of this actor
      public String toString()
```

```
{
    return super.toString();
}


// bitwise OR's the sent attribute state with the current attribute state
public final void setState(int attr)
{
    state |= attr;
}


// resets an attribute using the bitwise AND and NOT operators
public final void resetState(int attr)
{
    state &= ~attr;
}


public final int getState()
{
    return state;
}


public final void clearState()
{
    state = 0;
}


// determines if the sent state attribute is contained in this actor's state
// attribute
public final boolean hasState(int attr)
{
    return ((state & attr) != 0);
}


// access methods for the velocity, position, and rotation of the actor

public final void setX(double px)
{
    pos.setX(px);
```

```
        }

        public final void setY(double py)
        {
            pos.setY(py);
        }

        public final double getX()
        {
            return pos.getX();
        }

        public final double getY()
        {
            return pos.getY();
        }

        public final void setPos(int x, int y)
        {
            pos.setX(x);
            pos.setY(y);
        }

        public final void setPos(double x, double y)
        {
            pos.setX(x);
            pos.setY(y);
        }

        public final void setPos(Vector2D v)
        {
            pos.setX(v.getX());
            pos.setY(v.getY());
        }

        public final Vector2D getPos()
        {
            return pos;
```

```
    }

    public final void setRot(double theta)
    {
        rotation = theta;
    }

    public final double getRot()
    {
        return rotation;
    }

    public final void rotate(double theta)
    {
        rotation += theta;

        while(rotation > TWO_PI)
        {
            rotation -= TWO_PI;
        }
        while(rotation < -TWO_PI)
        {
            rotation += TWO_PI;
        }
    }

    public final void setVel(int x, int y)
    {
        vel.setX(x);
        vel.setY(y);
    }

    public final void setVel(Vector2D v)
    {
        vel.setX(v.getX());
        vel.setY(v.getY());
    }

    public final Vector2D getVel()
```

```java
    {
        return vel;
    }

    public final void moveBy(double x, double y)
    {
        pos.translate(x, y);
    }

    public final void moveBy(int x, int y)
    {
        pos.translate(x, y);
    }

    public final void moveBy(Vector2D v)
    {
        pos.translate(v);
    }

    public final void accelerate(double ax, double ay)
    {
        vel.setX(vel.getX() + ax);
        vel.setY(vel.getY() + ay);
    }

    public int getWidth()
    {
        return frameWidth;
    }

    public int getHeight()
    {
        return frameHeight;
    }

    // methods inherited from the Moveable interface

    public Rectangle2D getBounds()
    {
        return bounds;
```

```java
    }

    // determines if a Moveable object has collided with this object
    public boolean collidesWith(Moveable other)
    {
        return (bounds.contains(other.getBounds()) ||
                other.getBounds().contains(bounds) ||
                bounds.intersects(other.getBounds()));
    }

    // adds a collision object to this collision list
    public void addCollision(Moveable other)
    {
        if(collisionList == null)
        {
            collisionList = new LinkedList();
            collisionList.add(other);
            return;
        }

        if(! collisionList.contains(other))
        {
            collisionList.add(other);
        }
    }

    // stub method for processing collisions with those actors contained within
    // the collisionsList. this method is left empty, but not abstract
    public void processCollisions()
    {

    }

    // updates the object's position and bounding box, animates it, then updates
    // the transformation
    public void update()
    {
        pos.translate(vel);

        updateBounds();
```

```
        checkBounds();

        animate();

        // subclasses that require the transformation to be centered about an
        // anchor point other than the position will need to override this
        // method
        if(rotation != 0)
        {
            xform.setToIdentity();
            xform.translate(pos.getX()+frameWidth/2,
                            pos.getY()+frameHeight/2);
            xform.rotate(rotation);
            xform.translate(-frameWidth/2, -frameHeight/2);
        }
        else
        {
            xform.setToTranslation(pos.getX(), pos.getY());
        }
    }

}    // Actor2D
```

First of all, you'll note that the Actor2D class implements the *Moveable* interface. The *Moveable* interface provides methods for implementing classes to move and update themselves. It also provides methods for detecting collisions with other objects and processing collision code. Here's the code for the *Moveable* interface:

```
import java.awt.geom.*;

public interface Moveable
{
    public Rectangle2D getBounds();
    public boolean collidesWith(Moveable other);
    public void addCollision(Moveable other);
    public void processCollisions();
    public void update();

}    // Moveable
```

I wrote the *Moveable* interface in anticipation of times when I'd want to define nonactor classes that still want to update and move themselves. This will come in handy when we look at scene management in Chapter 11.

You should also notice that the Actor2D class is declared as abstract. This means that you will not be instantiating this class as it is, but rather you will need to subclass it to make it usable. We'll look at an example of creating a usable Actor2D class at the end of this chapter. As for the other strange things going on with the Actor2D class, keep reading. After looking at the support classes for the Actor2D class, everything should fall into place and make sense.

# Support for the Actor2D Class

Creating support classes allows you to offload some of the burden within your main classes. For the Actor2D class, support classes allow you to store data such as position and orientation information, as well as static data related to Actor2D classes as a whole, such as image data.

Let's begin our look into the Actor2D support classes with the Vector2D class.

## The Vector2D Class

You may have noticed that some Actor2D fields, such as its velocity, are defined as Vector2D objects. Thinking back to physics class, you probably know a *vector* as anything with magnitude *and* direction. The velocity of an object is a vector property because it describes both the magnitude and direction of travel. For instance, a car might be traveling with a velocity of 60 miles per hour northeast; both magnitude (60 mph) and direction (northeast) describe the way the car is traveling.

Although Java provides classes that contain the x, y coordinates of the object, such as the Point2D class, these classes don't organically describe these coordinates in the way we need them to. For instance, the velocity of an object isn't a point in space—it's a true vector. The same operations can be applied to the velocity of an object as can be applied to vectors in general. That's why I came up with the Vector2D class (which shouldn't be confused with the native java.util.Vector class). The Vector2D class provides the normal access methods for setting and retrieving the x- and y-components of the vector, plus the following operations:

- Vector2D plus(Vector2D v): adds two vectors
- Vector2D minus(Vector2D v): subtracts two vectors
- boolean equals(Vector2D other): determines if two vectors are equal

- **void**     `normalize()`: normalizes this vector to unit length
- **void**     `scale(double k)`: scales the vector by the given multiplier
- **void**     `translate(double dx, double dy)`: translates the vector by the sent values
- **double**   `dot(Vector2D v)`: calculates the dot product of this and the sent vector
- **double**   `length()`: returns the length of this vector

If you've worked with vector arithmetic before, then you should be familiar with what the above operations mean and how they can be implemented. If you're not so sure how they work, check out Figure 10.3 to see how some basic vector operations are graphically represented.

Here's the code for the `Vector2D` class. Pay attention to how the more advanced methods are implemented and how this class can help you describe spatial properties of the `Actor2D` class.

```
// defines a vector in two dimensions
public abstract class Vector2D extends Object
{
    // static reference to the zero vector
    public static final Vector2D.Double ZERO_VECTOR = new Vector2D.Double(0, 0);

    public static class Double extends Vector2D
    {
        // the x and y components of this Vector2D.Double object
```

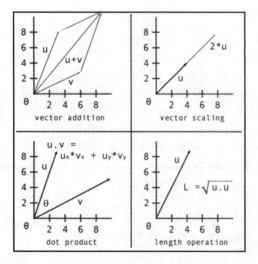

**Figure 10.3**

*Some 2-D vector operations*

```java
public double x;
public double y;

// creates a default Vector2D with a value of (0, 0)
public Double()
{
    this(0.0, 0.0);
}

// creates a Vector2D.Double object with the sent values
public Double(double m, double n)
{   setX(m);
    setY(n);
}

private Double(int m, int n)
{   setX((double) m);
    setY((double) n);
}

// get/set access methods for the x and y components

public final void setX(double n)
{   x = n;
}

public final void setY(double n)
{   y = n;
}

public final double getX()
{   return x;
}

public final double getY()
{   return y;
}

// adds this vector to the sent vector
```

```java
public Vector2D plus(Vector2D v)
{
    return new Double(getX() + v.getX(), getY() + v.getY());
}

// subtracts the sent vector from this vector
public Vector2D minus(Vector2D v)
{
    return new Double(getX() - v.getX(), getY() - v.getY());
}

}    // Double

public static class Integer extends Vector2D
{
    // the x and y components of this Vector2D.Integer object
    public int x;
    public int y;

    // creates a default Vector2D with a value of (0, 0)
    public Integer()
    {
        this(0, 0);
    }

    // creates a Vector2D.Integer object with the sent values
    public Integer(int m, int n)
    {   setX(m);
        setY(n);
    }

    private Integer(double m, double n)
    {   setX((int) m);
        setY((int) n);
    }

    // get/set access methods for the x and y components

    public final void setX(double n)
```

```java
        {    x = (int) n;
        }

        public final void setY(double n)
        {    y = (int) n;
        }

        public final double getX()
        {    return (double) x;
        }

        public final double getY()
        {    return (double) y;
        }

        // adds this vector to the sent vector
        public Vector2D plus(Vector2D v)
        {
            return new Integer(getX() + v.getX(), getY() + v.getY());
        }

        // subtracts the sent vector from this vector
        public Vector2D minus(Vector2D v)
        {
            return new Integer(getX() - v.getX(), getY() - v.getY());
        }

    }    // Integer

protected Vector2D()  {   }

public abstract void setX(double n);

public abstract void setY(double n);

public abstract double getX();

public abstract double getY();

// adds this vector to the sent vector
```

```java
public abstract Vector2D plus(Vector2D v);

// subtracts the sent vector from this vector
public abstract Vector2D minus(Vector2D v);

// determines if two vectors are equal
public boolean equals(Vector2D other)
{
    return (getX() == other.getX() && getY() == other.getY());
}

// normalizes this vector to unit length
public void normalize()
{
    double len = length();
    setX(getX() / len);
    setY(getY() / len);
}

public void scale(double k)
{
    setX(k * getX());
    setY(k * getY());
}

// translates the Vector2D by the sent value
public void translate(double dx, double dy)
{
    setX(getX() + dx);
    setY(getY() + dy);
}

// translates the Vector2D by the sent vector
public void translate(Vector2D v)
{
    setX(getX() + v.getX());
    setY(getY() + v.getY());
}

// calculates the dot (or inner) product of this and the sent vector
```

```
public double dot(Vector2D v)
{
     return getX()*v.getX() + getY()*v.getY();
}


// returns the length of this vector
public double length()
{
     return Math.sqrt(this.dot(this));
}


// returns the String representation of this Vector2D
public String toString()
{
     return getClass().getName() + " [x=" + getX() + ",y=" + getY() + "]";
}


}    // Vector2D
```

Notice right away one of the major pitfalls associated with the normalization of a vector. If you normalize the zero vector (which always has a length of zero), you will be violating one of the ten commandments of floating-point arithmetic: Thou shalt not divide by zero. You might want to wrap the code around a try block, or even better yet, just do an explicit check for zero in your code.

Also note that the Vector2D class is declared as abstract. Furthermore, the Vector2D class does not define any fields to describe its x- and y-components. That's where the use of static inner classes comes in. I defined both an Integer as well as a Double class to define two-dimensional vectors in both int and double precision, respectively. We can therefore define a Vector2D object in several ways:

```
Vector2D v;
v = new Vector2D.Double(40.9, 33.445);
v = new Vector2D.Integer(3, 55);
v = new Vector2D.Double();
v = Vector2D.ZERO_VECTOR;
```

You'll see in the upcoming examples, as well as in the *Nodez!* game presented in Chapter 14, how the methods contained in the Vector2D class can save you valuable time when working with Actor2D objects. For now, check out the *VectorTest* applet, which illustrates some basic vector graphics. It creates an array of Vector2D objects and bounces them around the window, drawing lines connecting each node with the next.

```java
import java.applet.*;
import java.awt.*;
import java.util.*;

public class VectorTest extends Applet implements Runnable
{
    // an array of vector positions
    private Vector2D[] vects;

    // an array of velocity values for the above array
    private Vector2D[] vels;

    // colors used to draw lines
    private final Color[] COLORS = {
        Color.BLUE,  Color.RED,    Color.GREEN, Color.DARK_GRAY,
        Color.BLACK, Color.ORANGE, Color.PINK, Color.CYAN
        };

    // a thread for animation
    private Thread animation;

    // an offscreen rendering image
    private Image offscreen;

    public void init()
    {
        int len = COLORS.length;

        vects = new Vector2D[len];
        vels  = new Vector2D[len];

        Random r = new Random();

        for(int i = 0; i < len; i++)
        {
            // create points that make up a circle
            vects[i] = new
                Vector2D.Double(50*(Math.cos(Math.toRadians(i*(360/len))))),
```

```java
                            50*(Math.sin(Math.toRadians(i*(360/len))))));

            // translate the point to the center of the screen
            vects[i].translate(getSize().width/2, getSize().height/2);

            vels[i] = new Vector2D.Integer(1 + r.nextInt()%5,
                                           1 + r.nextInt()%5);
        }

        offscreen = createImage(getSize().width, getSize().height);

        animation = new Thread(this);
    }

    public void start()
    {
        animation.start();
    }

    public void stop()
    {
        animation = null;
    }

    public void run()
    {
        Thread t = Thread.currentThread();
        while(t == animation)
        {
            repaint();
            try
            {
                t.sleep(20);
            }
            catch(InterruptedException e)
            {
            }
        }
```

```java
        }

    public void update(Graphics g)
    {
        // save the width and height of the applet window
        double width  = (double) getSize().width;
        double height = (double) getSize().height;

        for(int i = 0; i < COLORS.length; i++)
        {
            vects[i].translate(vels[i].getX(), vels[i].getY());

            if(vects[i].getX() > width)
            {
                vects[i].setX(width);
                vels[i].setX(-vels[i].getX());
            }
            else if(vects[i].getX() < 0)
            {
                vects[i].setX(0);
                vels[i].setX(-vels[i].getX());
            }

            if(vects[i].getY() > height)
            {
                vects[i].setY(height);
                vels[i].setY(-vels[i].getY());
            }
            else if(vects[i].getY() < 0)
            {
                vects[i].setY(0);
                vels[i].setY(-vels[i].getY());
            }
        }

        if(offscreen == null ||
           offscreen.getWidth(null)  != getSize().width ||
           offscreen.getHeight(null) != getSize().height)
        {
```

```
                offscreen = createImage(getSize().width, getSize().height);
            }

            paint(g);
        }

    public void paint(Graphics g)
    {
        // cast the sent Graphics context to get a usable Graphics2D object
        Graphics2D g2d = (Graphics2D)offscreen.getGraphics();
        g2d.setPaint(Color.WHITE);
        g2d.fillRect(0, 0, getSize().width, getSize().height);

        g2d.setStroke(new BasicStroke(3.0f));

        // connect all of the lines together
        Vector2D prev = vects[COLORS.length-1];
        for(int i = 0; i < COLORS.length; i++)
        {
            g2d.setPaint(COLORS[i]);

            g2d.drawLine((int) prev.getX(),     (int) prev.getY(),
                            (int) vects[i].getX(), (int) vects[i].getY());

            prev = vects[i];
        }

        g.drawImage(offscreen, 0, 0, this);
    }

}    // VectorTest
```

Figure 10.4 shows the *VectorTest* applet in action, animating a series of connected line segments reprsented by Vector2D objects. Try it out to see the animation for yourself.

To add more points to the scene, just add more colors to the Color array and the applet will do everything else for you. Also try implementing some of the other operations provided in the Vector2D class, such as vector addition, scaling, and normalization to make some really cool scenes.

Now let's switch gears a bit and look at the custom ImageLoader class.

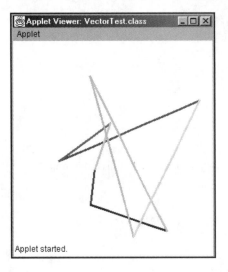

**Figure 10.4**

*Creating vector graphics with the Vector2D class*

## The ImageLoader Class

I have provided the ImageLoader class as a convenience class for loading images from within a Java applet. You've seen the loadImageStrip and loadCell methods as presented in Chapter 9. These methods are basically wrapped within a class that saves a copy of the original image so that as many cells can be loaded as needed without having to reconstruct the parent image. I wrote this class so that the work of loading image strips and image cells can be offset from your applet class and delegated elsewhere. All the ImageLoader class needs is the name of the image to load from file and a reference to the applet that is capable of loading the images. The ImageLoader class will then do all of the maintenance work for you.

Here's the code for the ImageLoader class. Remember, if you have any trouble with the code, just think of it as the loadImageStrip and loadCell methods wrapped into a formal class structure.

```
import java.applet.*;
import java.awt.*;
import java.awt.image.*;
import java.util.*;

public class ImageLoader extends Object
{
    // an Applet to load and observe loading images
```

```java
protected Applet applet;

// an Image, along with its width and height
protected Image   image;
protected int     imageWidth;
protected int     imageHeight;

// a buffer to render images to immediately after they are loaded
protected static BufferedImage buffer = new BufferedImage(200, 200,
                                            BufferedImage.TYPE_INT_RGB);

public ImageLoader(
    Applet a,           // creates and observes loading images
    String filename,    // name of image to load on disk
    boolean wait        // if true, add to a MediaTracker object and wait to
                        // finish loading
    )
{
    applet = a;

    image = applet.getImage(applet.getDocumentBase(), filename);

    if(wait)
    {
        // create a new MediaTracker object for this image
        MediaTracker mt = new MediaTracker(applet);

        // load the strip image
        mt.addImage(image, 0);
        try
        {
            // wait for our main image to load
            mt.waitForID(0);
        }
        catch(InterruptedException e) { /* do nothing */ }
    }

    // get the width and height of the image
    imageWidth = image.getWidth(applet);
```

```java
        imageHeight = image.getHeight(applet);
}

public int getImageWidth()
{
    return imageWidth;
}

public int getImageHeight()
{
    return imageHeight;
}

public Image getImage()
{
    return image;
}

// extracts a cell from the image using an image filter
public Image extractCell(int x, int y, int width, int height)
{
    // get the ImageProducer source of our main image
    ImageProducer sourceProducer = image.getSource();

    Image cell = applet.createImage(new FilteredImageSource(sourceProducer,
                            new CropImageFilter(x, y, width, height)));

    // draw the cell to the off-screen buffer
    buffer.getGraphics().drawImage(cell, 0, 0, applet);

    return cell;
}

// extracts a cell from the image and scales it to the sent width and height
public Image extractCellScaled(int x, int y, int width, int height,
                            int sw, int sh)
{
    // get the ImageProducer source of our main image
```

```
ImageProducer sourceProducer = image.getSource();

Image cell = applet.createImage(new FilteredImageSource(sourceProducer,
                               new CropImageFilter(x, y, width, height)));

// draw the cell to the off-screen buffer
buffer.getGraphics().drawImage(cell, 0, 0, applet);

return cell.getScaledInstance(sw, sh, Image.SCALE_SMOOTH);
      }


   }    // ImageLoader
```

The above code is relatively straightforward. If you haven't already looked at the
theory behind these methods in Chapter
9, now might be a good time to look.

In the next section, you'll see how to put
the ImageLoader class to work when we
create ImageGroup and, ultimately,
ActorGroup2D objects.

## Creating an Image Group

Although the ImageLoader class is a great
utility for loading in image strips with
little fuss, it would be nice if there were
also a handy way to store loaded images.
Fortunately, the ImageGroup class has
come to the rescue.

In the discussion on basic components
that will make up the Actor2D class, I
talked about how several objects could share a single set of imagery. For instance,
suppose you have a class named Asteroid that holds information about simple space
debris. If each Asteroid object contains similar looking images that were loaded
from the same file, it would be foolish to load the file more than once. So if these
asteroids share the same images, then why not load all of the images only once,
then have each Asteroid paint the current frame of animation from the pool of

> **TIP**
>
> I threw in the extractCellScaled
> method just for fun. You might have
> also noticed the use of a
> BufferedImage object that all images
> are rendered to just after creation. I
> did this because I noticed that most
> images do not render properly the
> first time they are used in my
> applets, causing a great deal of
> flicker for the first few seconds the
> applet is run. But by pre-rendering
> images to this off-screen image, you
> are making sure that all images have
> completely loaded and are ready to
> go. This eliminates the flickering
> problem from programs.

asteroid images? That way, if a scene is currently maintaining 200 Asteroid objects, only one instance if its imagery will be loaded into memory, rather than 200. This will obviously save loading time when the applet initializes as well as the memory it would take to hold the extra 199 instances of the image.

So how do you group the images so that they can be pooled from a common source? Well, I started by creating a generic way to store image pools. The custom ImageGroup class groups related image frames together into a cohesive animation structure. The ImageGroup class is an abstract class that encourages subclasses to load specific images on its own. Generally, this can be done through an ImageLoader object. All you need to do is create an ImageLoader object and give it commands to start pumping out image cells for your animations.

Anyway, here's the source for the ImageGroup class. I'd like to get all of these classes out of the way first, and then I promise we'll get to an example!

```java
import java.applet.*;

// provides methods for creating and accessing AnimationStrip objects
public abstract class ImageGroup
{
    // an array of AnimationStrip objects that create our animation sequences as
    // a whole
    protected AnimationStrip[] animations;

    // the width and height of an individual image frame
    protected int frameWidth;
    protected int frameHeight;

    // creates a new ImageGroup object
    protected ImageGroup()
    {
        animations = null;
    }

    // initializes the ImageGroup using the sent Applet reference object
    public abstract void init(Applet a);

    public final int getFrameWidth()
    {
        return frameWidth;
```

```
        }

        public final int getFrameHeight()
        {
            return frameHeight;
        }

        // accesses the AnimationStrip at the given index
        public final AnimationStrip getAnimationStrip(int index)
        {
            if(animations != null)
            {
                try
                {
                    return animations[index];
                }
                catch(ArrayIndexOutOfBoundsException e)
                {
                    // send error to debugger or standard err output...
                }
            }

            return null;
        }

    }    // ImageGroup
```

So, you ask, what's the AnimationStrip class all about? For now, just think of it as a container for Image objects. We'll get to the specifics of that class in the next section. First, I want to look at an important subclass of the ImageGroup class, the ActorGroup2D class.

## The ActorGroup2D Class

You know by now that it's okay for several instances of a single Actor2D class to share images for animation—it just makes sense. I see two basic ways to allow class instances to share the same data.

1. Include static class fields inside of the parent Actor2D class.
2. Pass an instance of a class that contains the single set of data to each Actor2D instance.

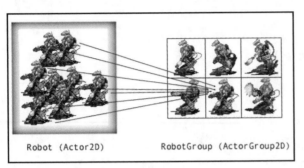

**Figure 10.5**

*Allowing several actors to read from a single actor group*

Robot (Actor2D)          RobotGroup (ActorGroup2D)

Static class fields might be all right for some instances, but for something like animation that is inherently complex and requires a lot of code, it would only cause confusion. Your Actor2D class would become bulky quite quickly, making it difficult to see through the clutter. Instead, I prefer passing an object (whoopee!) to each Actor2D instance and provide the appropriate methods for these two objects to communicate. Figure 10.5 shows this in action.

Now although Figure 10.5 shows several actors each displaying the same animation frame, you could just as easily show each actor displaying a different frame of animation. The indexing involved is unique to each actor instance, but the collection of image frames available is global to all actors belonging to the same actor group.

This is where the ActorGroup2D class comes in. You might remember seeing this class within the implementation of the Actor2D class. This class extends upon the ImageGroup class so that it can provide access to animation frames to Actor2D objects. This class adds additional fields for setting the maximum and minimum bounds and object velocity. I also used minimum and maximum tolerance values for both int and double types to serve as default values. All Actor2D objects must do is request these extreme values from their respective actor groups and compare them against their own position and velocity. ActorGroup2D subclasses are welcome to impose more minimum and maximum values—I just provided these to get you started.

We're almost there! Just take a quick glance at the ActorGroup2D class and note the extensions it makes over the ImageGroup class.

```
import java.applet.*;


// defines related attributes common to Actor2D objects
public abstract class ActorGroup2D extends ImageGroup
```

```
    {
        // default min/max values for int's and float's

        protected static final int MAX_INT_UNBOUND = Integer.MAX_VALUE;
        protected static final int MIN_INT_UNBOUND = Integer.MIN_VALUE;

        protected static final double MAX_DBL_UNBOUND = Double.MAX_VALUE;
        protected static final double MIN_DBL_UNBOUND = Double.MIN_VALUE;

        // the maximum and minimum position and velocity an Actor2D can have
        // overriding classes can change these values at construction time or within
        // the init method

        public int MAX_X_POS = MAX_INT_UNBOUND;
        public int MAX_Y_POS = MAX_INT_UNBOUND;

        public int MIN_X_POS = MIN_INT_UNBOUND;
        public int MIN_Y_POS = MIN_INT_UNBOUND;

        public int MAX_X_VEL = MAX_INT_UNBOUND;
        public int MAX_Y_VEL = MAX_INT_UNBOUND;

        public int MIN_X_VEL = MIN_INT_UNBOUND;
        public int MIN_Y_VEL = MIN_INT_UNBOUND;

        // constructs a new ActorGroup2D object
        protected ActorGroup2D()
        {
            super();
        }

        // initializes shared Actor2D attributes
        public abstract void init(Applet a);

    }   // ActorGroup2D
```

Indeed, the ActorGroup2D class is declared as abstract as well, so you'll have to sub-class it too. Fortunately, subclassing should be quick and painless, since the only required method to override is the init method.

Next, we'll look at the guts of the animation support classes for the Actor2D class. After that, we'll get to an example that ties everything together. Hang in there; we're almost finished!

## Animating Actor2D Objects

The final phase to implementing the Actor2D class is to define the classes that actually animate the images contained within the image strips. You've seen how the ImageGroup class defines an array of AnimationStrip objects. Each AnimationStrip holds a linked list of image frames that can be filled using an ImageLoader object. The only step now is to define the various ways to actually generate the order in which animation frames are presented. Before doing so, check out the code listing below for the custom AnimationStrip class.

```java
import java.awt.*;
import java.awt.image.*;
import java.util.*;

// defines a dynamic list of Image frames that can be animated using a given
// Animator object
public class AnimationStrip extends Object
{
    // observes drawing for external objects
    public static ImageObserver observer;

    // a linked list of Image frames, along with the size of the list
    protected LinkedList frames;
    protected int        numFrames;

    // the Animator responsible for animating frames
    protected Animator animator;

    // creates a new AnimationStrip object
    public AnimationStrip()
    {
        frames    = null;
        numFrames = 0;
```

```
        animator  = null;
    }

    public final void setAnimator(Animator anim)
    {
        animator = anim;
        animator.setFrames(frames);
    }

    // adds an Image frame to the list
    public void addFrame(Image i)
    {
        if(frames == null)
        {
            frames = new LinkedList();
            numFrames = 0;
        }

        frames.add(i);
        numFrames++;
    }

    // returns the Animator's current frame
    public Image getCurrFrame()
    {
        if(frames != null)
        {
            return animator.getCurrFrame();
        }
        return null;
    }

    // allows the Animator to generate the next frame of animation
    public void animate()
    {
        if(animator != null)
```

```java
    {
        animator.nextFrame();
    }
}


// returns the Animator's next frame of animation
public Image getNextFrame()
{
    if(animator != null)
    {
        animator.nextFrame();
        return animator.getCurrFrame();
    }

    return null;
}


// returns the first frame of animation
public Image getFirstFrame()
{
    if(frames != null)
    {
        return (Image)frames.getFirst();
    }

    return null;
}


// returns the last frame of animation
public Image getLastFrame()
{
    if(frames != null)
    {
        return (Image)frames.getLast();
```

```java
        }

        return null;
    }

    // resets the Animator's internal animation sequence
    public void reset()
    {
        if(animator != null)
        {
            animator.reset();
        }
    }

    // returns an animation frame's width
    public int getFrameWidth()
    {
        if(frames != null && !frames.isEmpty())
        {
            return getFirstFrame().getWidth(observer);
        }
        return 0;
    }

    // returns an animation frame's height
    public int getFrameHeight()
    {
        if(frames != null && !frames.isEmpty())
        {
            return getFirstFrame().getHeight(observer);
        }
        return 0;
    }

}    // AnimationStrip
```

As you can see, all the AnimationStrip provides is a container for holding images. The method that animates the object delegates the task to an Animator object. So let's cut to the chase and check out my take on the custom Animator class, Java style:

```java
import java.awt.*;
import java.util.*;

// defines a custom way of animating a list of Image frames
public abstract class Animator extends Object
{
    // references a linked list of Image frames
    protected LinkedList frames;

    // the current index of animation
    protected int currIndex;

    // creates a new Animator object with a null-referenced set of frames
    protected Animator()
    {
        frames = null;
        currIndex = 0;
    }

    public final void setFrames(LinkedList list)
    {
        frames = list;
    }

    // resets this animation
    public void reset()
    {
        currIndex = 0;
    }

    // returns the current frame of animation
    public Image getCurrFrame()
    {
        if(frames != null)
        {
```

```java
                return (Image)frames.get(currIndex);
        }
        return null;
    }


    // this method defines how frames are animated
    public abstract void nextFrame();


    // animates frames based on a sent array of indices
    public static class Indexed extends Animator
    {
        protected int[] indices;
        protected int   arrayIndex;

        public Indexed()
        {
            super();
            arrayIndex = 0;
        }


        public Indexed(int[] idx)
        {
            indices = new int[idx.length];

            System.arraycopy(idx, 0, indices, 0, idx.length);
            arrayIndex = 0;
        }


        public void nextFrame()
        {
            if(frames != null)
            {
                // increments the index counter
                if(++arrayIndex >= indices.length)
                {
                    arrayIndex = 0;
                }
                currIndex = indices[arrayIndex];
            }
```

```
            }

      }     // Animator.Indexed

// iterates through the animation frames, looping back to the start when
// we've reached the last frame
public static class Looped extends Animator
{
      public Looped()
      {
            super();
      }

      public void nextFrame()
      {
            if(frames != null)
            {
                  if(++currIndex >= frames.size())
                  {
                        reset();
                  }
            }
      }

}     // Animator.Looped

// iterates through the animation frames, but stops once it reaches the
// last frame
public static class OneShot extends Animator
{
      public OneShot()
      {
            super();
      }

      public void nextFrame()
      {
            if(frames != null)
            {
                  if(++currIndex >= frames.size());
```

```
                    {
                            currIndex = frames.size()-1;
                    }
                }
        }

}    // Animator.OneShot

// generates a random animation frame during each call to nextFrame
public static class Random extends Animator
{
    private java.util.Random random;

    public Random()
    {
        super();

        random = new java.util.Random();
    }

    public void nextFrame()
    {
        if(frames != null)
        {
            currIndex = random.nextInt() % frames.size();
        }
    }

}    // Animator.Random

// represents an animation containing only one frame--this class saves time
// since it does no processing
public static class Single extends Animator
{
    public Single()
    {
        super();
    }

    public void nextFrame()
```

```
            {
                // do nothing...
            }

        }   // Animator.Single

    }   // Animator
```

And of course the Animator class is abstract—all these levels of abstraction will lead to a flexible development system. The Animator class holds a reference to the image list maintained by the parent AnimationStrip. It also tags an incomplete method for generating the next frame, a method that needs to be implemented by all of its subclasses.

The beauty of the Animator class lies in its completed inner classes. Each inner class defines a specific way of animating frames. In the previous listing I defined five such inner classes: Indexed, Looped, OneShot, Random, and Single. Of course, this is just a starter set that covers the major animation styles; feel free to add your own as the need arises.

*Indexed animation* allows you to provide an array of integer indices. Each array member indexes an image found in the master image list. So for example, an array defined as

```
    { 1, 2, 3, 7, 6, 5, 4, 4, 3 }
```

would display frames 1, 2, 3, 7, 6, 5, 4, 4, and 3 in that specific order. This is great when your animation frames are contained in a single file but are in no specific order. It also allows you to skip around and even repeat frames sequentially. This gives you an unlimited number of animation sequences from a single list of image frames.

- **Looped animation** does as its name implies: it iterates through the image list and then wraps back to the beginning once the last frame is displayed. This works well with animations such as walking, where the first frame of animation appears as a smooth transition from the last frame of animation.

- **One-shot animation** is another straightforward animation style. Unlike looped animation, one-shot animation halts once it reaches the last animation frame. After the animation has terminated, the nextFrame method continues to return the last animation frame until the reset method is called. This style works well with "death" sequences, such as blowing up an asteroid, where the final frame of animation represents the final visual state of the object.

- **Random animation** provides you with a way to generate animations with no set beginning or ending frame. It uses a Random object to generate list indices. This style might come in handy when special events, such as picking up an invincibility power-up, occur. In this case, the invincibility power-up might cause your character to flash using different colors. It doesn't matter the order in which animation frames are selected; in fact, the more random, the better.

- **Single animations** are similar to one-shot animations, except that it is assumed that the image list contains a single entry. This is handy for objects that don't really animate their frames, such as a wall or other static scenery. The nextFrame method is left empty so that no unneeded processing is carried out when the object is to be animated.

Figure 10.6 illustrates an overall look at what an applet that uses Actor2D objects looks like. It links each component with either a "has-a" or an "is-a" relationship. Take a quick look at it before going to the final section of this chapter.

Phew! We've finally finished creating the Actor2D class! I hope you're as eager as I am to see it in action, because next up is a real (yet simple) example of how you can put the Actor2D class to good use.

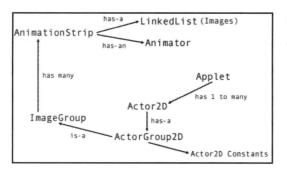

**Figure 10.6**

*An overall look at an applet using Actor2D objects*

# Extending the Actor2D Class

Okay, you've waited this long; I applaud you for drudging though the source code required to set up the Actor2D class structure. Now let's look at that example I've been promising.

In order to create a living, breathing Actor2D demo, you'll need to create three classes: an Actor2D subclass that defines the behavior of your actor, an ActorGroup2D object that loads in image frames and defines animation styles, and finally an Applet class that pulls everything together and drives the main event loop. So without further delay, let's get a user-controlled robot animation up and running.

## The Robot Class

The Robot class extends the Actor2D class. It defines a robot that is capable of walking in any one of the four ordinal directions: north, south, east, or west. It can also fire its weapon while facing these directions. You'll leave it up to the main Applet class to define and handle the control mechanism. Here is where you just define the acceptable behaviors your robot can exhibit.

I'll let you examine the code for the Robot class here. If you get stuck along the way just refer back to its parent's source code to get back on track.

```java
import java.awt.*;

// creates a simple robot that can move in the ordinal directions as well as
// fire its weapon
public class Robot extends Actor2D
{
    // index correlating to the current animation
    protected int currAnimIndex;

    // saves the previous animation for shooting animations
    protected int prevAnimIndex;

    // the Robot state SHOOTING
    public final static int SHOOTING = 8;

    // used to tell the robot which direction to move in
    public final static int DIR_NORTH = 0;
    public final static int DIR_SOUTH = 1;
    public final static int DIR_EAST  = 2;
    public final static int DIR_WEST  = 3;

    // creates a new Robot with the given actor group
    public Robot(ActorGroup2D grp)
    {
        super(grp);

        vel.setX(5);
```

```
        vel.setY(5);

        animWait = 3;

        currAnimIndex = 0;
        prevAnimIndex = 0;

        currAnimation = group.getAnimationStrip(RobotGroup.WALKING_SOUTH);

        frameWidth  = currAnimation.getFrameWidth();
        frameHeight = currAnimation.getFrameHeight();
    }

    // updates the position of the robot, and animates it if it is shooting
    public void update()
    {
        if(hasState(SHOOTING))
        {
            animate();
        }

        xform.setToTranslation(pos.getX(), pos.getY());

        updateBounds();
        checkBounds();
    }

    // flags the robot to shoot until stopShooting is called
    public void startShooting()
    {
        prevAnimIndex = currAnimIndex;
        if((currAnimIndex % 2) == 0)
        {
            currAnimIndex++;
        }
        currAnimation = group.getAnimationStrip(currAnimIndex);
        currAnimation.reset();
        setState(SHOOTING);
```

```
        }

        // stops shooting and restores the previous animation
        public void stopShooting()
        {
            currAnimIndex = prevAnimIndex;
            currAnimation = group.getAnimationStrip(currAnimIndex);
            currAnimation.reset();
            resetState(SHOOTING);
        }

        // moves and animates the robot based on the sent ordinal direction
        public void move(int dir)
        {
            // prevent further shooting
            resetState(SHOOTING);

            switch(dir)
            {
                case DIR_NORTH:
                    if(currAnimIndex != RobotGroup.WALKING_NORTH)
                    {
                        prevAnimIndex = currAnimIndex;
                        currAnimation =
                            group.getAnimationStrip(RobotGroup.WALKING_NORTH);
                        currAnimIndex = RobotGroup.WALKING_NORTH;
                        currAnimation.reset();
                    }
                    else
                    {
                        animate();
                        pos.translate(0, -vel.getY());
                    }
                    break;

                case DIR_SOUTH:
                    if(currAnimIndex != RobotGroup.WALKING_SOUTH)
                    {
                        prevAnimIndex = currAnimIndex;
```

```
                    currAnimation =
                        group.getAnimationStrip(RobotGroup.WALKING_SOUTH);
                    currAnimIndex = RobotGroup.WALKING_SOUTH;
                    currAnimation.reset();
                }
                else
                {
                    animate();
                    pos.translate(0, vel.getY());
                }
                break;

            case DIR_WEST:
                if(currAnimIndex != RobotGroup.WALKING_WEST)
                {
                    prevAnimIndex = currAnimIndex;
                    currAnimation =
                        group.getAnimationStrip(RobotGroup.WALKING_WEST);
                    currAnimIndex = RobotGroup.WALKING_WEST;
                    currAnimation.reset();
                }
                else
                {
                    animate();
                    pos.translate(-vel.getX(), 0);
                }
                break;

            case DIR_EAST:
                if(currAnimIndex != RobotGroup.WALKING_EAST)
                {
                    prevAnimIndex = currAnimIndex;
                    currAnimation =
                        group.getAnimationStrip(RobotGroup.WALKING_EAST);
                    currAnimIndex = RobotGroup.WALKING_EAST;
                    currAnimation.reset();
                }
                else
                {
```

```
                            animate();
                            pos.translate(vel.getX(), 0);
                    }
                    break;

                default:
                    break;
            }
        }

    }   // Robot
```

You get some rather decent capabilities for the `Robot` class in just about 150 lines of code. Notice the use of the `static final SHOOTING` field. I gave it a value of eight (a power of two), so that it won't override or interfere with the state variables given in the `Actor2D` class. Refer all the way back to Chapter 2 if you need a refresher on how bitwise operators work.

Now you can get on to the second step: creating the `RobotGroup` class. This class loads in eight animation sequences; one for walking in each ordinal direction, and one for firing the weapon in each direction. The `Robot` class will then be able to select its current animation strip based on the direction it is facing. If you're building this demo as you go along, feel free to pull it from the CD-ROM so that you don't have to type it all in. If you're feeling ambitious, try typing it in after looking at the chapter exercise that asks you to load in all four animations in a single loop. I left the loop unrolled here merely for demonstration purposes.

```java
import java.applet.*;

public class RobotGroup extends ActorGroup2D
{
    // indices to pre-defined animation sequences
    public static final int WALKING_NORTH  = 0;
    public static final int SHOOTING_NORTH = 1;

    public static final int WALKING_SOUTH  = 2;
    public static final int SHOOTING_SOUTH = 3;

    public static final int WALKING_EAST   = 4;
    public static final int SHOOTING_EAST  = 5;
```

```java
public static final int WALKING_WEST   = 6;
public static final int SHOOTING_WEST  = 7;

// creates a new RobotGroup object
public RobotGroup()
{
    super();

    animations = new AnimationStrip[8];
}

// initializes the eight animation sequences
public void init(Applet a)
{
    ImageLoader loader;
    int i;

    // NORTH
    loader = new ImageLoader(a, "robot_north.gif", true);
    animations[WALKING_NORTH] = new AnimationStrip();
    for(i = 0; i < 4; i++)
    {
        animations[WALKING_NORTH].addFrame(
                loader.extractCell((i*72)+(i+1), 1, 72, 80));
    }
    animations[WALKING_NORTH].setAnimator(new Animator.Looped());

    animations[SHOOTING_NORTH] = new AnimationStrip();
    for(i = 0; i < 2; i++)
    {
        animations[SHOOTING_NORTH].addFrame(
                loader.extractCell((i*72)+(i+1), 82, 72, 80));
    }
    animations[SHOOTING_NORTH].setAnimator(new Animator.Looped());


    // SOUTH
    loader = new ImageLoader(a, "robot_south.gif", true);
    animations[WALKING_SOUTH] = new AnimationStrip();
```

```
for(i = 0; i < 4; i++)
{
     animations[WALKING_SOUTH].addFrame(
             loader.extractCell((i*72)+(i+1), 1, 72, 80));
}
animations[WALKING_SOUTH].setAnimator(new Animator.Looped());

animations[SHOOTING_SOUTH] = new AnimationStrip();
for(i = 0; i < 2; i++)
{
     animations[SHOOTING_SOUTH].addFrame(
             loader.extractCell((i*72)+(i+1), 82, 72, 80));
}
animations[SHOOTING_SOUTH].setAnimator(new Animator.Looped());


// EAST
loader = new ImageLoader(a, "robot_east.gif", true);
animations[WALKING_EAST] = new AnimationStrip();
for(i = 0; i < 4; i++)
{
     animations[WALKING_EAST].addFrame(
             loader.extractCell((i*72)+(i+1), 1, 72, 80));
}
animations[WALKING_EAST].setAnimator(new Animator.Looped());

animations[SHOOTING_EAST] = new AnimationStrip();
for(i = 0; i < 2; i++)
{
     animations[SHOOTING_EAST].addFrame(
             loader.extractCell((i*72)+(i+1), 82, 72, 80));
}
animations[SHOOTING_EAST].setAnimator(new Animator.Looped());


// WEST
loader = new ImageLoader(a, "robot_west.gif", true);
animations[WALKING_WEST] = new AnimationStrip();
for(i = 0; i < 4; i++)
```

```
        {
            animations[WALKING_WEST].addFrame(
                    loader.extractCell((i*72)+(i+1), 1, 72, 80));
        }
        animations[WALKING_WEST].setAnimator(new Animator.Looped());

        animations[SHOOTING_WEST] = new AnimationStrip();
        for(i = 0; i < 2; i++)
        {
            animations[SHOOTING_WEST].addFrame(
                    loader.extractCell((i*72)+(i+1), 82, 72, 80));
        }
        animations[SHOOTING_WEST].setAnimator(new Animator.Looped());
    }


}    // RobotGroup2D
```

The final task is to set up an Applet to hold the robot and run the event loop. The ActorTest class is preceded by the RobotAdapter class, which will sit and listen to keystrokes being pressed and released. I thought this was a good way to provide an out-of-the-way class that handles robot movement all in one place. The applet will then register the adapter class to pick up keystrokes and move the robot accordingly. I have also included code to create a tiled paint to fill in the background.

What are you waiting for? Compile this baby and try it out!

```java
import java.applet.*;
import java.awt.*;
import java.awt.event.*;
import java.awt.image.*;
import java.awt.geom.*;
import java.util.*;

// adapter class for controlling a Robot object
class RobotAdapter extends KeyAdapter
{
    private Robot robot;

    public RobotAdapter(Robot r)
    {
        robot = r;
```

```
        }

        // fires the robot gun or moves the robot
        public void keyPressed(KeyEvent e)
        {
            robot.resetState(Robot.SHOOTING);

            switch(e.getKeyCode())
            {
                case KeyEvent.VK_SPACE:
                    robot.startShooting();
                    break;

                case KeyEvent.VK_UP:
                    robot.move(Robot.DIR_NORTH);
                    break;

                case KeyEvent.VK_DOWN:
                    robot.move(Robot.DIR_SOUTH);
                    break;

                case KeyEvent.VK_LEFT:
                    robot.move(Robot.DIR_WEST);
                    break;

                case KeyEvent.VK_RIGHT:
                    robot.move(Robot.DIR_EAST);
                    break;

                default:
                    break;
            }
        }

        // if the space bar is released, stop the robot from shooting
        public void keyReleased(KeyEvent e)
        {
            if(e.getKeyCode() == KeyEvent.VK_SPACE)
            {
```

```java
            robot.stopShooting();
        }
    }
}    // RobotAdapter


public class ActorTest extends Applet implements Runnable
{
    // a thread for animation
    private Thread animation;

    // an offscreen rendering buffer
    private BufferedGraphics offscreen;

    // a Paint for drawing a tiled background
    Paint paint;

    // geometry for filling the background
    private Rectangle2D floor;

    // our moveable robot
    private Robot robot;

    public void init()
    {
        // create the RobotGroup
        RobotGroup group = new RobotGroup();
        group.init(this);

        // set the Robot bounds equal to the window size
        group.MIN_X_POS = 0;
        group.MIN_Y_POS = 0;

        group.MAX_X_POS = getSize().width;
        group.MAX_Y_POS = getSize().height;

        // create our robot in the center of the screen
        robot = new Robot(group);

        robot.setPos((getSize().width  - robot.getWidth()) /2,
```

```java
                        (getSize().height - robot.getHeight())/2);

    // register a new RobotAdapter to receive Robot movement commands
    addKeyListener(new RobotAdapter(robot));

    // create the background paint
    createPaint();

    offscreen = new BufferedGraphics(this);

    AnimationStrip.observer = this;

    animation = new Thread(this);
}   // init

// create a tiled background paint
private void createPaint()
{
    Image image = getImage(getDocumentBase(), "stile.gif");
    while(image.getWidth(this) <= 0);

    // create a new BufferedImage with the image's width and height
    BufferedImage bi = new BufferedImage(
            image.getWidth(this), image.getHeight(this),
            BufferedImage.TYPE_INT_RGB);

    // get the Graphics2D context of the BufferedImage and render the
    // original image onto it
    ((Graphics2D)bi.getGraphics()).drawImage(
                                    image, new AffineTransform(), this);

    // create the anchoring rectangle for the paint's image equal in size
    // to the image's size
    floor = new Rectangle2D.Double(0, 0,
                            getSize().width, getSize().height);

    // set the paint
    paint = new TexturePaint(bi, new Rectangle(0, 0,
                            image.getWidth(this),
```

```
image.getHeight(this)));

    }

    public void start()
    {
        // start the animation thread
        animation.start();
    }

    public void stop()
    {
        animation = null;
    }

    public void run()
    {
        Thread t = Thread.currentThread();
        while (t == animation)
        {
            try
            {
                Thread.sleep(10);
            }
            catch(InterruptedException e)
            {
                break;
            }
            repaint();
        }
    }   // run

    public void update(Graphics g)
    {
        robot.update();

        paint(g);
    }

    public void paint(Graphics g)
```

```
        {
            Graphics2D bg = (Graphics2D)offscreen.getValidGraphics();

            // set the paint and fill the background
            bg.setPaint(paint);
            bg.fill(floor);

            // paint the robot
            robot.paint(bg);

            // draw the offscreen image to the window
            g.drawImage(offscreen.getBuffer(), 0, 0, this);
        }    // paint

    }    // ActorTest
```

Figure 10.7 shows an Actor2D object in action. Run the *ActorTest* applet for yourself to see all the Robot class can do.

If you've worked through any of André LaMothe's game programming books, then the robot shown in the *ActorTest* applet should look familiar. The exercises at the end of this chapter will give you a lot of flexibility in modifying the applet. Load in your own graphics, design more Actor2D classes—go wild!

Before wrapping this chapter up, I'd like to go over one more quick extension of the Actor2D class: the StaticActor class.

**Figure 10.7**

*Output from the*
*ActorTest applet*

## The StaticActor Class

You may already be thinking about implementing scenery or other unmoveable objects in your games. So you don't waste time implementing the same code for a static object over and over, consider extending the Actor2D class to a StaticActor class.

The StaticActor class, when combined with the StaticActorGroup class, will provide you with a quick container class for objects that contain a single animation frame. I'll present you with the code and then allow you to write up the test programs.

```java
import java.awt.*;

public class StaticActor extends Actor2D
{
    public StaticActor(ActorGroup2D grp)
    {
        super(grp);

        // just reference the 0th (and only) animation strip
        currAnimation = group.getAnimationStrip(0);

        frameWidth = currAnimation.getFrameWidth();
        frameHeight = currAnimation.getFrameHeight();
    }

} // StaticActor
```

And here's the code for the StaticActorGroup class:

```java
import java.applet.*;

public class StaticActorGroup extends ActorGroup2D
{
    private String filename;

    protected StaticActorGroup()
    {
        filename = null;
    }

    public StaticActorGroup(String fn)
    {
```

```
            filename = fn;
            animations = new AnimationStrip[1];
        }

        public void init(Applet a)
        {
            animations[0] = new AnimationStrip();
            animations[0].addFrame(a.getImage(a.getCodeBase(), filename));
            animations[0].setAnimator(new Animator.Single());
        }

    }    // StaticActorGroup
```

These two classes are *very* simple; they represent objects with one-frame animations that still have the ability to move and rotate within the scene. These classes can come in handy when adding static scenery to your games, a topic you can look into further in Chapter 11.

Note that you don't need to subclass the `StaticActor` or `StaticActorGroup` classes—you just need to provide instances to them with the correct parameters. Subclass the `StaticActor` class if you need it to perform any specific transformations or other updates, or just allow your applet class to make the method calls for it.

# Conclusion

*Please* don't take this as a final treatise on creating game entities in Java. This is just one way I have used to create games quickly and easily. I left some of the code unoptimized because the ideas come through more clearly that way. Feel free to make any changes, insertions, or deletions as you see necessary. One of the great challenges of game programming is evolving your existing code into faster, cleaner, and better code.

It took me only a few minutes to get a working version of the *ActorTest* applet up and running. Since all of the major groundwork is covered by the `Actor2D` and supporting classes, defining specific behaviors for custom objects really becomes a trivial task. This chapter presented a lot of material that built up upon itself, so you may need to read it over again to make sure everything solidifies in your mind. Once you're sure you feel comfortable with what's going on, try the following exercises or start creating your own games using the custom `Actor2D` class.

# Exercises

**10.1** Change the Animator class to use a ListIterator object rather than the get method. Is a ListIterator better than the get method for all of the known Animator subclasses? How much processing time would a ListIterator save over using get for lists that contain a very large number of animation frames?

**10.2** Rewrite the RobotGroup init method so that it loads all four sets of ordinal animations within a single loop. You'll probably want to save the file name String objects as an array so everything works algorithmically.

**10.3** Create a pair of synchronized Robot objects, each at a different starting screen position. Each Robot should have its own RobotAdapter object listening for keystrokes. Both robots should react to your keystrokes and move in a synchronized manner, only at different screen positions.

**10.4** Better yet, create an applet that contains one Robot that is controlled by a human-controlled RobotAdapter and a second Robot that is controlled by a separate computer-controlled mechanism. Add in bullets and a touch of artificial intelligence, and you have a one-on-one robot fighting game! Let loose with this one and see what you can come up with.

# CHAPTER 11

# Implementing a Scene Management System

In Chapter 10 you learned how to code a flexible, reusable game entity class, Actor2D. Although it takes some work getting the Actor2D system up and running, you now have a quick and easy way to create custom game components.

In this chapter, you'll learn some of the ways in which a custom scene manager can be deployed to automatically update and render your game scenes. By the end of this chapter, you'll become familiar with the following topics:

- Creating a skeleton Scene class for holding the contents of your game scenes
- Using the QuadTree class to divide and conquer complex scenes
- Rendering scenes in full-screen exclusive mode
- Creating custom scenes, such as scrollable scenes, isometric tiled scenes, and wrapped scenes

Before we look at the skeleton Scene class, let's discuss some of the benefits of using a scene management system.

# Why Implement a Scene Manager?

Thus far, the example programs presented in this book implemented scene management all in one place—all of the game entities, update procedures, and rendering were carried out within an Applet class. The Applet class also provides the methods for carrying out these processes. So why, then, would you need to implement a scene manager?

The main reason for implementing a scene manager would be that it offsets much of the processing and overhead previously handled by the Applet class. Just like methods, it is always a good idea to have your classes perform a single task. With this in mind, the Applet class should only handle initialization for the application, as well as drive the main event loop. The update and paint methods should not perform game processing, but should delegate these responsibilities to other objects. This allows you to program modularly, which keeps your projects organized and makes it easier to modify and fix your programs.

We'll now look at the abstract Scene class and how you can extend it to provide custom game scenes.

# The Scene Class

In the never-ending quest for flexibility in program code, I'd like to present the Scene class. The Scene class is nothing other than a skeleton class with a few abstract methods for updating and painting the scene. I defined the Scene class as the following:

```java
import java.awt.*;
import java.awt.geom.*;

// skeleton class for providing scene management
public abstract class Scene
{
    // the overall bounds of the scene
    protected Rectangle2D bounds;

    // the part of the scene that is viewable; usually this is the size of the
    // Applet window
    protected Rectangle2D viewable;

    // creates a new Scene object with the sent bounds and viewable area
    public Scene(Rectangle2D v, Rectangle2D b)
    {
        setViewable(v);
        setBounds(b);
    }

    // adds an Actor to the scene, subclasses that use Actor2D objects should
    // override this method
    public void add(Actor2D a)
    {

    }

    public final void setViewable(Rectangle2D r)
    {
        viewable = new Rectangle2D.Double(r.getX(), r.getY(),
                                          r.getWidth(), r.getHeight());
    }

    public final Rectangle2D getViewable()
```

```
        {
                return viewable;
        }

        public final void setBounds(Rectangle2D r)
        {
                bounds   = new Rectangle2D.Double(r.getX(), r.getY(),
                                                r.getWidth(), r.getHeight());
        }

        public final Rectangle2D getBounds()
        {
                return bounds;
        }

        // updates the scene
        public abstract void update();

        // paints the scene to the sent Graphics2D context
        public abstract void paint(Graphics2D g2d);

    }    // Scene
```

Note that Scene is declared as a class rather than as an interface. I did this for several reasons. First, I wanted it to contain two Rectangle2D objects to hold the size of the scene and the size of the viewable window (remember, an interface cannot hold fields other than class constants). Another reason for not declaring the Scene class as an interface is because I don't want *all* of the methods to be incomplete. For instance, the add method allows an Actor2D object to be added to the scene. Although this method has been left empty at this level, I did not want to force subclasses to implement it by declaring it as abstract. If a subclass of Scene does not use Actor2D objects, then it does not have to worry about implementing this method.

Next, we'll dig right in and look at a few examples of extending the Scene class to some usable management classes.

## Extending the Scene Class

Extending the Scene class is actually quite easy, since there are not many methods that you are required to override. Once you determine the nature of the scene you wish to create, you're only obligated to override the update and paint methods, since they are declared as abstract. You will usually want to create other methods, such as the add method or any other helper methods, for carrying out scene management.

For complex scenes—scenes that contain many objects—processes such as collision testing and rendering can bog down the processor. In the next section, we'll look at a data structure that you can use to make these complex scenes more manageable.

## Using the QuadTree Class for Scene Management

As I just mentioned, operations such as collision testing can be quite labor intensive and can bog down the processor quite quickly. For instance, if all objects within a scene are compared against every other object for collision, then the complexity of the collision testing for the scene would be $O(n^2)$. So if you have a scene containing only seven objects, that would be 49 collision tests! If your scene requires collision testing once per frame, then that will cause bottlenecks in your processing loop. Such bottlenecks are usually not worth the time, especially if the objects aren't even within proximity of one other. Figure 11.1 depicts a sparsely populated scene; out of the 49 possible collisions that can be made, only two hits will be made (assuming collision checks are made both ways).

What if you could design a mechanism that lets you perform collisions only between objects you are sure will register a positive hit for collision? Actually, it would be rather paradoxical to make collision testing *that* exact, since how could you know that two objects will test positive for collision if you haven't yet performed the collision test? But you can design a way to take some of the burn out of procedure such as collision testing. One such way involves the use of what's known as a *quad tree*.

**Figure 11.1**

*Most collision checks are just a waste of time*

Quad tree implementation involves partitioning a large scene into smaller component parts. Although there are numerous data structures for partitioning scenes, I feel that quad trees are one of the best for both illustrative and practical purposes.

Like most tree structures, a quad tree contains a single root node, branches connecting child nodes, and, finally, leaf nodes at the tips of the tree branches. A quad tree works by dividing the scene into *quadrants;* each quadrant is capable of dividing itself into four smaller quadrants. The number of times each group of quadrants is divided into smaller quadrants is known as the *depth* of the tree. This recursive mechanism can continue as far as you need it to.

Perhaps the best way to illustrate quad trees is with a visual. Figure 11.2 shows a quad tree with a depth of four.

Nodes are numbered starting from zero and going counterclockwise, starting at the lower-left corner of the quadrant group. The *main node* (or *root node*) represents the full extent of the scene and is represented as node 0. Nodes numbered 1, 2, 3, and 4 are direct descendents of the root node. I assigned nodes 5, 6, 7, and 8 as the descendants of node 3, and so on.

Now that you have the numbering scheme down, how do you actually place the scene objects? In Figure 11.2, nodes 9 through 24 are all *leaf nodes;* that is, they contain no descendents. It will be these nodes that contain the actual scene objects. Each leaf node will contain a list of objects that either intersect or are completely contained within its bounds. Now, when you perform collision testing for the scene, only those objects contained within the same node need be tested for collision.

The principles behind the quad tree mechanism seem fine at first glance, but there are several fine points that can cause trouble. For instance, what if an object is contained within more than one quad node, such as shown in Figure 11.3?

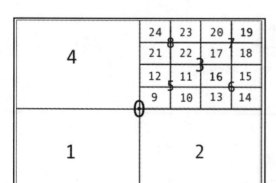

**Figure 11.2**

*Partitioning a scene with a quad tree*

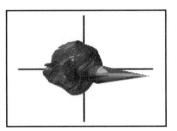

**Figure 11.3**

*Objects residing in multiple nodes*

If you insert the asteroid depicted in Figure 11.3 only into the first leaf node you find that it fits within, then you'll be neglecting collision testing with the other three nodes in which the asteroid resides. Instead, you must insert your object into *each* node that it fits within. This is an important fact to remember when it comes time to implement your code.

This brings us to another fine point concerning quad tree implementation. Say that the ship depicted in Figure 11.3 will detect a collision with the asteroid in both nodes that contain them. To combat this effect, it might be a good idea to give each object its own list of objects that it has collided with during the collision testing process. You might recall the addCollision method from the Actor2D class. Here's the code, if you need a refresher:

```
// adds a collision object to this collision list
public void addCollision(Moveable other)
{
    if(collisionList == null)
    {
        collisionList = new LinkedList();
        collisionList.add(other);
        return;
    }

    if(! collisionList.contains(other))
    {
        collisionList.add(other);
    }
}    // addCollision
```

The above method inserts a *Moveable* object into the collision list, only if the list does not already contain the object. After collision testing for the entire scene has completed, objects that have detected at least one collision can then process collision code. This will prevent objects from performing collision code more than it is needed.

Let's get down to the actual code for the QuadNode class. Some of the methods are recursive in nature, so refer to Chapter 2, Exercise 12, if you need a refresher on how recursion works.

```java
import java.awt.*;
import java.awt.geom.*;
import java.util.*;

// represents a single node within a QuadTree structure
public class QuadNode extends Object
{
    // the next unique id to assign a node
    protected static int UNIQUE_ID = 0;

    // a unique integer to identify this node
    protected int id;

    // the parent that contains this node
    protected QuadNode parent;

    // an array of child nodes for this QuadNode
    protected QuadNode[] nodes;

    // true if this node is a leaf node (has no children)
    protected boolean leaf;

    // a linked-list of objects this node contains
    protected LinkedList objects;

    // the bounds of the node
    protected Rectangle2D bounds;

    // default constructor
    private QuadNode()
    {
        id = -1;
        parent  = null;
        nodes   = null;
        leaf    = true;
        objects = null;
```

```
        bounds  = null;
    }


    // constructs a QuadNode with the given parent, depth, and bounds
    public QuadNode(QuadNode p, int depth, Rectangle2D r)
    {
        parent = p;
        bounds = r;

        id = UNIQUE_ID++;

        // this node is a leaf if the remaining depth is zero
        if(depth == 0)
        {
            leaf = true;
            objects = new LinkedList();
            nodes = null;

            QuadTree.addLeaf(this);
        }

        // otherwise, this node contains 4 child nodes
        else
        {
            leaf = false;
            objects = null;

            nodes = new QuadNode[4];
            double x = bounds.getX();
            double y = bounds.getY();
            double w = bounds.getWidth();
            double h = bounds.getHeight();

            // create the children
            nodes[0] = new QuadNode(this, depth - 1, new Rectangle2D.Double(
                                x, y + h/2, w/2, h/2));
            nodes[1] = new QuadNode(this, depth - 1, new Rectangle2D.Double(
                                x + w/2, y + h/2, w/2, h/2));
            nodes[2] = new QuadNode(this, depth - 1, new Rectangle2D.Double(
```

```java
                                        x + w/2, y, w/2, h/2));
                nodes[3] = new QuadNode(this, depth - 1, new Rectangle2D.Double(
                                        x,   y, w/2, h/2));
        }
    }


    // returns true if this node is a leaf node
    public final boolean isLeaf()
    {
        return leaf;
    }


    // attempts to insert the sent object into this node
    public void insert(
        Moveable c,       // the Moveable object to insert
        boolean propagate // if true, propagate upward if c does
                          // not fit within this node's bounds
        )
    {
        // try to insert the node
        if(bounds.contains(c.getBounds()) || bounds.intersects(c.getBounds()))
        {
            // if this node is a leaf node, insert the object into the list
            if(isLeaf())
            {
                if(objects == null)
                {
                    objects = new LinkedList();
                }
                if(! objects.contains(c))
                {
                    objects.add(c);
                }
            }

            // if this node is not a leaf, try to insert downward
            else
            {
                for(int i = 0; i < 4; i++)
```

```
                              {
                                  if(nodes[i] != null)
                                  {
                                      nodes[i].insert(c, false);
                                  }
                              }
                          }
                  }

              // otherwise, insert the object upward if propagation is allowed
              else
              {
                  if(propagate)
                  {
                      if(parent != null)
                      {
                          parent.insert(c, true);
                      }
                  }
              }
      }

      // translates all of the objects this node contains by x, y
      public void moveAll(double x, double y)
      {
          if(objects == null || objects.isEmpty()) return;

          Actor2D a;
          for(int i = 0; i < objects.size(); i++)
          {
              a = (Actor2D) objects.get(i);
              a.moveBy(x, y);
          }
      }


      public void update()
      {
          if(objects == null || objects.isEmpty()) return;

          // update the list, then remove objects that are no longer in this node
```

```java
Moveable m;
for(int i = 0; i < objects.size(); i++)
{
    m = (Moveable)objects.get(i);
    m.update();

    // test if the object left the node; if so, insert upward
    if(!bounds.contains(m.getBounds()) &&
       !bounds.intersects(m.getBounds())) // might propagate upward
    {
        insert((Moveable)objects.remove(i), true);
    }
}

// get the updated size since some objects may have been removed
int size = objects.size();

// test each object for collision against each other object
// in this node
for(int i = 0; i < size-1; i++)
{
    Moveable a = (Moveable)objects.get(i);

    for(int j = i+1; j < size; j++)
    {
        Moveable b = (Moveable)objects.get(j);

        if(a.collidesWith(b))
        {
            a.addCollision(b);
            b.addCollision(a);
        }
    }
}
}

public void paintBounds(Graphics2D g2d, Color c)
{
    if(c == null) c = Color.RED;
```

```
            g2d.setPaint(c);
            g2d.draw(bounds);
        }

    }    // QuadNode
```

The `QuadNode` class contains the components we discussed earlier. Each node contains a `Rectangle2D` object representing the area that the node controls. A node also contains a reference to its parent node as well as its four child nodes. If the node is a leaf node, its children will all reference the `null` value and `objects` will reference a valid `LinkedList` object. Otherwise, it will be `objects` that will reference `null` and the children that will reference valid `QuadNode` objects. Note that it is at construction time that the nature of the node is established. If the `depth` parameter is zero, then the node will be a leaf node. Nonleaf nodes will pass a value of `depth-1` to each of its descendant nodes.

One final aspect of the `QuadNode` class I'll mention is within the `insert` method, namely its `propagate` parameter. If `propagate` is set to `false`, then the method will only attempt to insert the sent object "downward." So if the object fits within the node's bounds, it will either be inserted into the objects list (if the node is a leaf) or it will be sent to the four child nodes. The insertion will cease if the object does not fit within the node's bounds. On the other hand, if `propagate` is `true`, then the method will delegate insertion to its parent if it does not fit within the node's bounds. Generally, you'll want to set `propagate` to `false` if the object is being inserted into the tree for the first time. The `propagate` parameter should be set to `true` if the node determines that the object has left the node and needs to be reinserted. In this case, the node may need to be inserted into a neighboring node owned by the parent. Figure 11.4 illustrates why you would want to insert an object upward so that it will be properly reinserted into the tree.

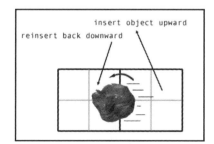

**Figure 11.4**

*Propagating the insert operation upward*

Now that we have established how to create a single quad tree node we need an "entry point" for scene operations such as inserting, updating, and painting. Recall that we assigned a value of zero to the main root node of the overall tree. We'll use this node as the entry point for creating and maintaining the scene.

To implement the quad tree entry point, I've created the QuadTree class. Since the QuadTree class still represents a quad tree node, it will extend the QuadNode class. This class will provide methods for inserting objects into the scene, as well as methods for updating and painting exiting scenes. To help speed things up, I have also provided a few shortcuts for accessing leaf nodes as well as paintable objects.

Here's the code for the QuadTree class. As you go through it, note both the similarities as well as the extensions it makes from the QuadNode class.

```java
import java.awt.*;
import java.awt.geom.*;
import java.util.*;


// the root node for QuadTree management
public class QuadTree extends QuadNode
{
    // the overall depth of the tree
    protected int globalDepth;

    // a global linked list of leaf nodes
    public static LinkedList leaves = new LinkedList();

    // global linked list of objects that will be painted
    public static LinkedList paintList = new LinkedList();

    // creates a QuadTree with the sent depth, overall bounds, and viewable
    // screen bounds
    public QuadTree(int depth, Rectangle2D r)
    {
        super(null, depth, r);

        // global depth must be greater than zero
        if(depth <= 0)
        {
            throw new IllegalArgumentException(
                    "depth must be greater than zero");
```

```java
        }

        globalDepth = depth;

        // initialize the overflow list
        objects = new LinkedList();
    }


    // adds a leaf node to the global leaf list
    public static void addLeaf(QuadNode node)
    {
        if(! leaves.contains(node))
        {
            leaves.add(node);
        }
    }


    // adds a Moveable object to the global paint list
    public static void addToPaintList(Moveable m)
    {
        if(! paintList.contains(m))
        {
            paintList.add(m);
        }
    }


    // QuadTree must override insert method to deal with objects that are not
    // within scene bounds
    public void insert(Moveable c)
    {
        // if the object is not within scene bounds, add it to the heap
        if(! bounds.contains(c.getBounds()) &&
           ! bounds.intersects(c.getBounds()))
        {
            if(! objects.contains(c))
            {
                objects.add(c);
            }
            return;
```

```java
        }

        // add the object to the global paint list
        addToPaintList(c);

        // try adding the object to all child nodes
        for(int i = 0; i < 4; i++)
        {
            if(nodes[i] != null)
            {
                nodes[i].insert(c, false);
            }
        }
    }


    public void update()
    {
        // update the heap list
        if(objects != null && !objects.isEmpty())
        {
            for(int i = 0; i < objects.size(); i++)
            {
                Moveable a = (Moveable) objects.get(i);
                a.update();

                // test if the object entered the tree; if so, insert it and
                // remove it from the heap
                if(bounds.contains(a.getBounds()) ||
                   bounds.intersects(a.getBounds()))
                {
                    insert((Moveable) objects.remove(i), false);
                }
            }
        }

        //  update all leaf nodes for collisions and frame movement
        for(int i = 0; i < leaves.size(); i++)
        {
            ((QuadNode) leaves.get(i)).update();
```

```
            }
        }

        // paints all objects in the global paint list
        public void paint(Graphics2D g2d)
        {
            Actor2D a;
            for(int i = 0; i < paintList.size(); i++)
            {
                a = (Actor2D) paintList.get(i);
                // only paint the object if it is in bounds
                if(bounds.contains(a.getBounds()) ||
                   bounds.intersects(a.getBounds()))
                {
                    a.paint(g2d);
                }
            }
        }

        // paints gridlines showing the bounds of each leaf node
        public void paintBounds(Graphics2D g2d, Color color)
        {
            // paint all leaf nodes
            for(int i = 0; i < leaves.size(); i++)
            {
                ((QuadNode)leaves.get(i)).paintBounds(g2d, color);
            }
        }

    }    // QuadTree
```

The QuadTree class constructs itself much like the QuadNode class, but it uses its objects list as an overflow list for objects that do not fit within scene bounds. The QuadTree class will then monitor these objects for them to enter the scene. Once they enter the scene, they will be removed from the overflow list and added to one or more leaf nodes. The opposite also holds true; once an object leaves the scene, it will be removed from the leaf nodes and added to the overflow list.

Other additions worth noting are the paintList and leafList LinkedList objects. These lists merely serve as shortcuts to leaf nodes and objects that should be painted. As nodes discover at construction time that they are leaf nodes, they can call the static addLeaf method, which adds them to the leaf node list. That way, when the tree calls methods such as the update method, it will have a predetermined list for quick access to all leaf nodes objects. The same thing holds true for the paintList list. When the scene requires painting, the tree can traverse through the list of paintable objects and allow each object to paint itself. Both the leafList and paintList fields save you from having to repeatedly search for the same objects every time they are needed.

Getting back to our discussion of scene management, let's look at a simple scene that implements a quad tree to hold scene objects. The following TreeScene class simply holds a QuadTree object and provides wrapper methods for adding objects and maintaining scene objects:

```java
import java.awt.*;
import java.awt.geom.*;
import java.util.*;

public class TreeScene extends Scene
{
    // a QuadTree to contain scene objects
    private QuadTree tree;

    // constructs a TreeScene with the given bounds
    public TreeScene(Rectangle2D bounds)
    {
        super(bounds, bounds);

        tree = new QuadTree(3, bounds);

    }    // init

    // adds the sent Actor2D to the QuadTree
    public void add(Actor2D a)
    {
        tree.insert(a);
    }

    // delegates updating to the QuadTree
    public void update()
```

```
        {
             tree.update();
        }

        // paints the QuadTree and outlines of its leaf nodes
        public void paint(Graphics2D g2d)
        {
             tree.paint(g2d);
             tree.paintBounds(g2d, Color.BLACK);

        }    // paint

    }    // TreeScene
```

Of course, you'll most likely need to make additions, such as character control, to the TreeScene class. Feel free to do so.

Although the quad tree structure can be quite delicate to implement, it gives you a pretty slick way to control your scene and quickly determine things such as object collisions. Be sure to choose a global depth that will speed up your scene the most. A global depth that is too small will cause too many erroneous collision tests, while a global depth that is too high can force individual objects to be contained in 8, 16, or even more leaf nodes, which will equally cause problems such as an increased number of required reinsertions. Consider the number and sizes of average scene objects and try different global depths to get the most efficiency out of your quad tree-powered scenes.

There are many optimizations that can be made to both the QuadNode and QuadTree classes. A few of the exercises at the end of this chapter will ask you to improve the overall efficiency of these classes.

Now let's take a look at the elusive full-screen exclusive mode, a newly added feature to Java as of version 1.4.

## Venturing into Full-Screen Exclusive Mode

Almost none of the big-name commercial games out there perform rendering within a window or a frame. Rather, they enter full-screen mode and use the entire renderable screen. If you're a DirectX aficionado, you are most likely familiar with the concept of *full-screen exclusive mode*. In short, full-screen exclusive mode forces the operating system to suspend its windowing environment and allow the full-screen application exclusive, or direct, access to the screen. Entering full-screen mode can add immersiveness to your games by allowing them to bypass the look and feel of the current desktop environment and use the full bounds of the monitor.

Full-screen exclusive mode also gives you additional control over the way your games are presented. When you load a program into an applet context, whether through a Web browser or the `appletviewer` utility, you're subject to rendering in the user's current desktop screen resolution's size and image depth. In full-screen mode, however, you get to choose the resolution and bit depth, assuming the system is capable of displaying it. This gives you absolute control over how your game objects are presented.

Rendering in full-screen mode differs slightly from the style you're currently used to. Rather than controlling rendering directly through the `Graphics` context specified by a `Component` object such as an `Applet`, rendering in full-screen mode is accomplished through `GraphicsDevice` contained by a `Frame` object.

One good reason for using full-screen mode is that doing so allows you to perform more advanced rendering techniques, such as page flipping and chain flipping. *Page flipping* involves moving a video pointer among various rendering buffers. The active pointer refers to the currently visible video buffer. The active pointer can simply point to the next page while pending pages can do their rendering. *Chain flipping,* such as double and triple buffering, occurs when a frame is rendered to a back buffer, and then its content is passed, or blitted, to the next frame in the chain. As the buffer is passed, the back buffer is then free to begin rendering the next frame.

Figure 11.5 illustrates both chain (shown at the top of the figure) and page (shown at the bottom) flipping. Both rendering techniques are implemented through the `BufferStrategy` class, found under the `java.awt.image` package. A `BufferStrategy` can be created via the `createBufferStrategy` method found in the `Window` and `Frame` classes. This method allows you to specify the number of buffers you would like to use. Based on the current graphics configuration and the number of buffers desired, the system will attempt to use the best available rendering method available. Page flipping is the preferred rendering method for a `BufferStrategy` to use. If page flipping is not available, then a chain-flipping mechanism using accelerated images is attempted. If all else fails, a chain-flipping strategy using unaccelerated images is used.

Let's get right down to an example that looks at all of the rendering techniques you've seen thus far. The following applet, *FullscreenTest,* starts out within a window, giving a choice between two buttons. One button opens a new frame in windowed

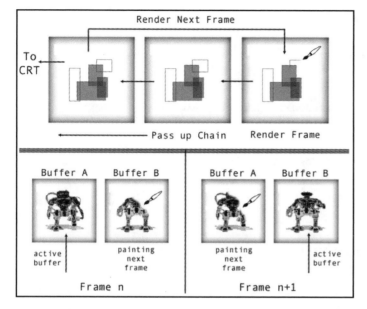

**Figure 11.5**

*Page versus chain flipping*

mode; the other opens a frame in full-screen exclusive mode. Much of the applet uses concepts we've already talked about, so I'll leave the rest for you to mull over yourself.

```java
import java.awt.*;
import java.awt.image.BufferStrategy;
import java.applet.*;
import java.awt.event.*;
import java.util.*;


public class FullscreenTest extends Applet implements Runnable,
                                                      ActionListener,
                                                      MouseMotionListener
{

    // the windowed or fullscreen frame to render on
    protected Frame  frame;

    // the graphics device available to the graphics environment
    protected GraphicsDevice device;

    // flags windowed or fullscreen mode
```

```java
protected boolean frameWindowed;

// the size of the frame
protected Rectangle bounds;

// an offscreen image for windowed rendering
protected Image offscreen;

// buttons for selecting windowed or fullscreen modes
protected Button windowed;
protected Button fullscreen;
protected Label  desc;

// just your average array of Actor2D objects
protected Actor2D[] actors;

// a thread for animation
protected Thread animation;

public void init()
{
    // set up the applet's visual components
    Panel p;

    setLayout(new BorderLayout());

    p = new Panel();
    p.add(new Label("Choose your destiny!"));
    add(p, BorderLayout.NORTH);

    p = new Panel();
    windowed = new Button("Give me the Blue pill!");
    windowed.addActionListener(this);
    windowed.addMouseMotionListener(this);
    p.add(windowed);

    fullscreen = new Button("I want the Red pill!");
    fullscreen.addActionListener(this);
```

```java
        fullscreen.addMouseMotionListener(this);
        p.add(fullscreen);

        add(p, BorderLayout.CENTER);

        p = new Panel();
        desc = new Label("                       ");
        p.add(desc);
        add(p, BorderLayout.SOUTH);

        // set up the frame's visual components

        ActorGroup2D group = new AsteroidGroup();
        group.init(this);

        group.MIN_X_POS = 0;
        group.MIN_Y_POS = 0;

        group.MAX_X_POS = 800;
        group.MAX_Y_POS = 600;

        Random random = new Random();
        actors = new Asteroid[10];
        for(int i = 0; i < 10; i++)
        {
            actors[i] = new Asteroid(group);
            actors[i].setPos(Math.abs(random.nextInt(800)),
                            Math.abs(random.nextInt(600)));
        }

        bounds = null;

        // create a new Thread for animation
        animation = new Thread(this);
    }

    public void stop()
    {
```

```java
            animation = null;
    }

    public void run()
    {
        // the code for fullscreen mode
        if(! frameWindowed)
        {
            // create a chain-flipped buffer strategy
            frame.createBufferStrategy(3);

            Thread x = Thread.currentThread();
            while(x == animation && frame.isShowing())
            {
                BufferStrategy bufferStrategy = frame.getBufferStrategy();

                // update and draw the frame
                do
                {
                    Graphics2D g2d = (Graphics2D)
                                        bufferStrategy.getDrawGraphics();

                    for(int i = 0; i < 10; i++)
                    {
                        actors[i].update();
                    }

                    paintFrame(g2d);
                    bufferStrategy.show();
                    g2d.dispose();

                } while(bufferStrategy.contentsLost());

                try
                {
                    Thread.sleep(10);
                }
                catch (InterruptedException e) { break; }
            }
        }
```

```java
        // the code for windowed mode
        else
        {
            Graphics2D g2d;

            Thread x = Thread.currentThread();
            frame.show();
            while(x == animation && frame.isVisible())
            {
                // update and draw the frame
                g2d = (Graphics2D) offscreen.getGraphics();

                for(int i = 0; i < 10; i++)
                {
                    actors[i].update();
                }

                paintFrame(g2d);
                g2d.dispose();
                frame.getGraphics().drawImage(offscreen, 0, 0, this);

                try
                {
                    Thread.sleep(10);
                }
                catch (InterruptedException e) { break; }
            }
        }
    }

    // draws one frame of animation--the sent Graphics2D context can refer to
    // either windowed or fullscreen drawing
    protected void paintFrame(Graphics2D g2d)
    {
        g2d.setPaint(Color.BLACK);
        g2d.fillRect(0, 0, bounds.width, bounds.height);

        for(int i = 0; i < 10; i++)
        {
```

```
                    actors[i].paint(g2d);
            }
        }


        // opens the frame either in windowed or fullscreen mode
        protected void openFrame()
        {
            // code for opening the window in fullscreen mode
            if(! frameWindowed)
            {
                try
                {
                    // get the default graphics device from the graphics
                    // environment
                    device =
GraphicsEnvironment.getLocalGraphicsEnvironment().getDefaultScreenDevice();

                    // create a Frame with using our graphics device
                    frame = new Frame(device.getDefaultConfiguration());

                    // don't paint the frame's decorations
                    frame.setUndecorated(true);

                    // since drawing will be done actively, ignore paint requests
                    // from the operating system
                    frame.setIgnoreRepaint(true);

                    // create the fullscreen window
                    device.setFullScreenWindow(frame);

                    // resize the window if it is supported
                    if (device.isDisplayChangeSupported())
                    {
                        // try several display modes before resorting back to
                        // windowed mode

                        if(displayModeSupported(800, 600, 32))
                        {
                            device.setDisplayMode(
```

```
                        new DisplayMode(800, 600, 32, 0));
            }
            else if(displayModeSupported(800, 600, 16))
            {
                device.setDisplayMode(
                    new DisplayMode(800, 600, 16, 0));
            }
            else if(displayModeSupported(640, 480, 16))
            {
                device.setDisplayMode(
                    new DisplayMode(640, 480, 16, 0));
            }
        }

        bounds = frame.getBounds();

        // start the animation
        animation.start();
    }
    catch (Exception e)
    {
        e.printStackTrace();
    }
}

else // windowed mode
{
    // create a standard Frame 800 by 600 pixels in size

    offscreen = createImage(800, 600);

    frame = new Frame();
    frame.setSize(800, 600);
    frame.addWindowListener(new WindowAdapter()
        {
            public void windowClosing(WindowEvent e)
            {
                frame.hide();
                frame.setVisible(false);
```

```java
                                            frame.dispose();
                                    }
                            } );

                    bounds = frame.getBounds();

                    animation.start();
            }
    }


    // determines if the current graphics device supports the sent display mode
    private boolean displayModeSupported(int width, int height, int bitDepth)
    {
            DisplayMode[] modes = device.getDisplayModes();
            for(int i = 0; i < modes.length; i++)
            {
                    if(width    == modes[i].getWidth()  &&
                       height   == modes[i].getHeight() &&
                       bitDepth == modes[i].getBitDepth())
                    {
                            return true;
                    }
            }

            // no compatible display modes found!
            return false;
    }


    // opens the frame in either fullscreen or windowed mode
    public void actionPerformed(ActionEvent e)
    {
            if(windowed == e.getSource())
            {
                    frameWindowed = true;
                    windowed.setEnabled(false);
                    fullscreen.setEnabled(false);
                    openFrame();
            }

            else if(fullscreen == e.getSource())
```

```
        {
            frameWindowed = false;
            windowed.setEnabled(false);
            fullscreen.setEnabled(false);
            openFrame();
        }
    }

    // updates the description of the hovered button
    public void mouseMoved(MouseEvent e)
    {
        if(windowed == e.getSource())
        {
            desc.setText(" Enter windowed mode ");
        }

        else if(fullscreen == e.getSource())
        {
            desc.setText("Enter fullscreen mode");
        }
    }

    public void mouseDragged(MouseEvent e)  {  }

}   // FullscreenTest
```

Figure 11.6 shows the *FullscreenTest* selection screen for entering either full-screen or windowed mode.

If your machine contains accelerated hardware, then the rendering performance exhibited by the full-screen exclusive window contained in the *FullscreenTest* applet is as good as (or possibly even better than) an applet window that uses a VolatileImage for its rendering. I decided to use a BufferStrategy that makes use of three buffers

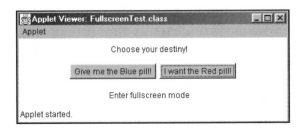

Applet started.

**Figure 11.6**

*The* FullscreenTest *applet*

for drawing. Also notice that a Graphics2D rendering context can be obtained through the BufferStrategy getDrawGraphics method. After the scene has been drawn the show method will display the currently active frame. Rendering should be attempted again each time the BufferStrategy experiences a loss in its contents.

As mentioned earlier, not only does full-screen mode use the entire rendering area of the monitor, but it also allows you to choose a specific resolution at which to display. The GraphicsDevice setFullScreenWindow method takes a Frame object in which to display in full-screen mode. Once you're finished being in full-screen mode, just call the setFullScreenWindow method again and send null as its parameter; this will restore the desktop to its original resolution and state. Once a full-screen window is established, you can then change the resolution (if the current device supports display changes). I wrote the displayModeSupported utility that checks the sent screen width, height, and bit depth against all those supported by the system. By comparing several display modes, in order of preference, you're sure to eventually come across a supported mode for any system. Exercise 5 will ask you to write a program that allows the user to select from a number of different display modes before going into full-screen mode.

There are a few final notes on full-screen rendering I'd like to briefly mention. First, remember that full-screen rendering is done actively; that is, it is not dependent on messages sent by the operating system. Therefore, it is a good idea to have your frame call the Component setIgnoreRepaint method to make sure that all operating-system level repaint messages are immediately ignored by your program. This should improve overall performance. Secondly, be sure to turn off decorations, such as the frame borders, by calling the Frame setUndecorated before you display the frame.

Finally, note that games presented in full-screen exclusive mode may be difficult to deploy since the user must explicitly set permissions to allow programs to enter full-screen exclusive mode. This security permission must be set because those with questionable moral codes can do some considerable damage after first taking the program into full-screen mode. Setting these permissions can also be a pain in the neck for your users to do manually.

## Creating a Scrollable Scene

Next, we'll look at another way to manage dynamic Java scenes. In this section, you'll learn how to create scrollable scenes using a scene manager. A *scrollable scene* refers to a scene where the same scenery or decorations are recycled over and over as they move across the screen. This allows you to give the illusion that a game level is massive when in fact the same few images are being used over and over again.

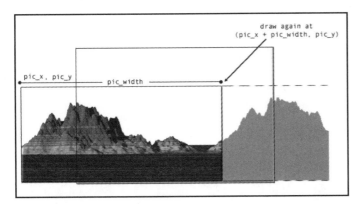

**Figure 11.7**

*Tiling components within a scrollable scene*

Cartoon animators have been using this technique forever, doing so saves both time and resources.

You may have already implemented a scrollable or tiled scene before, so I'll get right to the point. When implementing scrollable scenes, it is often convenient to separate the work into two areas: physically wrapping objects around once they leave the scene, and repainting objects so they look continuous. The first area is fairly self-explanatory. Once a scrollable object leaves the scene, it should seamlessly be replaced back within scene bounds. The second area is just as simple. Once a scrollable object begins to leave the scene bounds, it will most likely begin to leave a gap at the opposite end of the window. This can be fixed by tiling the image over and over until the gap is filled. Figure 11.7 illustrates how images can be painted to fill the entire scene so that it looks whole.

Now let's jump right into some more code. The following SpaceScene class represents one way in which a scrolling scene manager can be used.

```java
import java.awt.*;
import java.awt.geom.*;
import java.util.*;

// represents a basic scrolling scene
public class SpaceScene extends Scene
{
    // items in our scene
    protected StaticActor[] scenery;

    public SpaceScene(Rectangle2D view)
```

```java
    {
        super(view, view);

        scenery = null;
    }

    public void setScenery(StaticActor[] v)
    {
        scenery = v;
    }

    // moves the items in the scene
    public void update()
    {
        if(scenery == null) return;

        for(int i = 0; i < scenery.length; i++)
        {
            if(scenery[i] != null)
            {
                // wrap the object back around once it completely
                // leaves the scene
                if(scenery[i].getX() <= -scenery[i].getWidth())
                {
                    // prepare the scenery for the next frame
                    scenery[i].setX(scenery[i].getX() +
                                    scenery[i].getWidth());
                }
                scenery[i].update();
            }
        }
    }


    public void paint(Graphics2D g2d)
    {
        if(scenery == null) return;

        // set the clipping region to the window bounds
```

```
g2d.setClip(getBounds());

for(int i = 0; i < scenery.length; i++)
{
    if(scenery[i] != null)
    {
        scenery[i].paint(g2d);

        // append the object to itself if it does not completely
        // fill the bounds
        if(scenery[i].getX() + scenery[i].getWidth() <
            bounds.getWidth())
        {
            scenery[i].paint(g2d,
                        scenery[i].getX() + scenery[i].getWidth(),
                        scenery[i].getY());
        }
    }
}
}

}   // SpaceScene
```

Note that this class is not very reusable, since objects within a scene can scroll in many different ways. They can scroll in practically any direction, and the rules on how objects should be wrapped can vary. Try writing your own reusable scrolling scene manager if you're interested in creating more complex scrolling scenes of your own.

As a general rule, the above code works well with objects that are as wide as, or wider than, the anticipated applet window size. Objects that are not as wide as the window may need more than one repaint to fill in all of the gaps.

Also note that real applications may require separate lists to differentiate between objects that are meant to be scrolled and those that aren't. The ScrollableScene class can be adjusted to also maintain nonscrollable objects, such as ships, missiles, and asteroids. Games objects can also be tweaked to do their own tiling and scrolling, or this task can be delegated to their own actor group objects. Try different ways to organize your scenes to see which ways work best for you.

I'll wrap up this section with a quick example. The following applet, *SceneScrollTest*, creates two background images, each with a different velocity. These objects are sent to the scene manager, and all updates and paints are delegated through the scene manager.

```java
import java.applet.*;
import java.awt.*;
import java.awt.image.*;
import java.awt.geom.*;
import java.util.*;

public class SceneScrollTest extends Applet implements Runnable
{
    // a Thread for animation
    private Thread animation;

    // an offscreen rendering image
    private VolatileGraphics offscreen;

    // a scene to place scrollable objects
    private SpaceScene scene;

    public void init()
    {
        // create the scene with the full applet window size
        scene = new SpaceScene(getBounds());

        // "background" and "foreground" scene images
        StaticActor[] actors = new StaticActor[2];
        StaticActorGroup group;

        // create the foreground
        group = new StaticActorGroup("mountain.gif");
        group.init(this);

        actors[1] = new StaticActor(group);
        actors[1].setPos(0.0,
                        (double) getSize().height - actors[1].getHeight());
        actors[1].setVel(-3, 0);

        // create the background
        group = new StaticActorGroup("haze.gif");
```

```java
        group.init(this);

        actors[0] = new StaticActor(group);
        actors[0].setPos(0.0,
                        (double) getSize().height - actors[1].getHeight());
        actors[0].setVel(-1, 0);

        // set the scenery
        scene.setScenery(actors);


        offscreen = new VolatileGraphics(this);

        animation = new Thread(this);

        AnimationStrip.observer = this;

    }    // init


public void start()
{
    // start the animation thread
    animation.start();
}

public void stop()
{
    animation = null;
}

// performs a standard rendering loop
public void run()
{
    Thread t = Thread.currentThread();
    while (t == animation)
    {
        try
        {
```

```
                    Thread.sleep(10);
            }
            catch(InterruptedException e)
            {
                    break;
            }
            repaint();
        }
    }   // run


    // allows the scene to perform its update
    public void update(Graphics g)
    {
        scene.update();

        paint(g);
    }


    // paints the scene
    public void paint(Graphics g)
    {
        Graphics2D bg = (Graphics2D)offscreen.getValidGraphics();
        bg.setPaint(Color.BLACK);
        bg.fill(getBounds());

        scene.paint(bg);

        g.drawImage(offscreen.getBuffer(), 0, 0, this);
    }


}       // SceneScrollTest
```

Figure 11.8 shows a snapshot of the *SceneScrollTest* applet. Go ahead and try it for yourself.

When you run the *SceneScrollTest* applet, try to see where one image ends and the other begins. I can't, and I bet you won't be able to, either. The key to making scrolling scenery work is to make your images seamless on all sides that you anticipate wrapping. Shear filters contained in many graphics programs will let you do this quickly and painlessly. Tiled images are also great for use with TexturePaint objects or any other time you wish to create image patterns, such as the one shown in Figure 11.9.

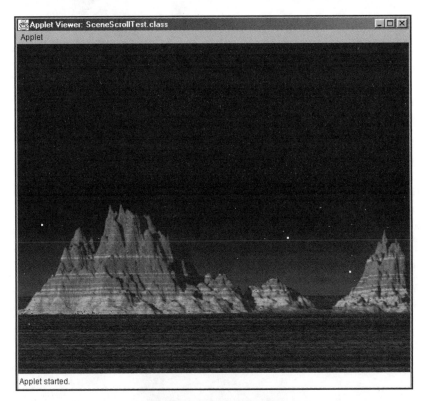

**Figure 11.8**

*The* SceneScrollTest *applet*

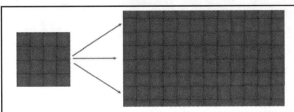

**Figure 11.9**

*Seamless images make tiling fun and easy*

Next, we'll look at another quick example that uses isometric images to create a simple isometric tile walker.

## Creating an Isometric Tile Walker

If you're a fan of games based on the use of isometric tiles, such as Blizzard's ever-popular *Starcraft,* you might be interested in implementing isometric tile-based scenes in your games. Isometric scenes are easy to implement in Java, especially when you use a scene management system. In this section, we'll create a real simple isometric tile walker to illustrate just how easy isometric scenes are to set up.

The simplest example of an isometric scene that I can think of would contain a character capable of traversing a plane of tiles. Figure 11.10 depicts such a scene.

Obviously, the rendering mechanism used to illustrate Figure 11.10 was done in 2-D, but isometric rendering is a good way to look almost 3-D. In my simple isometric scene, I chose to use the character as an anchor point with respect to the rest of the scene. Since your windowing system is fixed, it would be difficult to allow your character to actually move from tile to tile. Therefore, you have to find a way to make it look like the character is moving when it is actually not. The magic behind your tile walker lies in moving the scene objects with respect to the anchor point, rather than moving the character about the scene. Although it defies the logics of how objects move in the real world, you must remember that you are not dealing with the real world. As long as it gets the job done and is still somewhat "organic," using tricks such as this is all right with me. Figure 11.11 shows a graphical representation of how scene traversal can be done.

Let's get down to writing the isometric scene. The following class, IsoScene, extends the Scene class and provides a Vector object to hold scrolling objects, as well as a separate reference to the anchor character. It will also be responsible for receiving keyboard strokes and updating the scene appropriately.

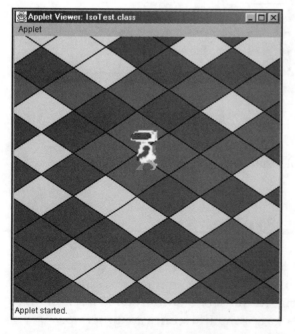

**Figure 11.10**

*A simple isometric tile scene*

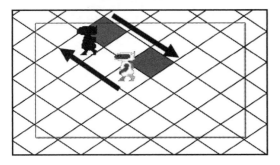

**Figure 11.11**

*Logically moving the anchor character physically moves the scene.*

```java
import java.awt.*;
import java.awt.geom.*;
import java.util.*;
import java.awt.event.*;

public class IsoScene extends Scene implements KeyListener
{
    // a vector of background Actor2D objects
    protected Vector actors;

    // the "anchor" character for the scene to revolve about
    protected Actor2D anchor;

    // references the anchor's current position
    protected Vector2D anchorPos;

    public IsoScene(Rectangle2D v, Rectangle2D b, int qt_depth)
    {
        super(v, b);

        actors = new Vector();

        anchor    = null;
        anchorPos = null;
    }

    public void add(Actor2D a, boolean isAnchor)
    {
        // only add the Actor to the vector if it is not the anchor; the anchor
```

```java
          // character will be handled differently
          if(! isAnchor)
          {
                    actors.add(a);
          }

          else
          {
              // set the anchor and anchor position
              anchor    = a;
              anchorPos = new Vector2D.Double(anchor.getX(), anchor.getY());
          }
    }

    public void update()
    {
          // update the anchor character
          anchor.update();

          // update the rest of the scene with respect to the position of the
          // anchor character
          // updates only need to be made if the anchor is moving
          if(! anchor.getVel().equals(Vector2D.ZERO_VECTOR))
          {
              double x = 0.0;
              double y = 0.0;

              x = -anchor.getVel().getX();
              y = -anchor.getVel().getY();

              for (Enumeration e = actors.elements() ; e.hasMoreElements() ;)
              {
                  ((Actor2D) e.nextElement()).moveBy(x, y);
                  ((Actor2D) e.nextElement()).update();
              }
          }
    }

    public void paint(Graphics2D g2d)
    {
```

```java
            // paint the non-anchor components
            for (Enumeration e = actors.elements(); e.hasMoreElements() ;)
            {
                ((Actor2D) e.nextElement()).paint(g2d);
            }

            // paint the anchor character
            anchor.paint(g2d);
    }


    public void keyTyped(KeyEvent e)
    {

    }


    public void keyPressed(KeyEvent e)
    {
        if(anchor == null) return;

        // give the anchor a constant velocity with a magnitude of 1/4 of the
        // tile size
        switch(e.getKeyCode())
        {
            case KeyEvent.VK_UP:
                anchor.setVel(-IsoTileGroup.TILE_WIDTH/4,
                              -IsoTileGroup.TILE_HEIGHT/4);
                break;

            case KeyEvent.VK_DOWN:
                anchor.setVel(+IsoTileGroup.TILE_WIDTH/4,
                              +IsoTileGroup.TILE_HEIGHT/4);
                break;

            case KeyEvent.VK_LEFT:
                anchor.setVel(-IsoTileGroup.TILE_WIDTH/4,
                              +IsoTileGroup.TILE_HEIGHT/4);
                break;

            case KeyEvent.VK_RIGHT:
                anchor.setVel(+IsoTileGroup.TILE_WIDTH/4,
```

```
                                         -IsoTileGroup.TILE_HEIGHT/4);
                    break;

                default: break;
            }
        }


        public void keyReleased(KeyEvent e)
        {
            if(anchor == null) return;

            // once a key is released, stop the anchor character
            switch(e.getKeyCode())
            {
                case KeyEvent.VK_UP:
                case KeyEvent.VK_DOWN:
                case KeyEvent.VK_LEFT:
                case KeyEvent.VK_RIGHT:
                    anchor.setVel(0, 0);
                    break;

                default: break;
            }
        }


}    // IsoScene
```

As long as one of the directional arrow keys is held down, the anchor character will
be given a constant velocity. Although the anchor character doesn't actually move,
its velocity flags the scene to move the tiles. The scene will move the tiles at a rate
equal and opposite to the velocity of the anchor character. The scene also moves in
increments equal to one-quarter of the tiles' width and height, thus keeping the
character somewhat flush with the tiles.

Now that you have a mechanism for controlling your isometric scene, let's create a
quick applet that uses it. The following applet, *IsoTest*, creates a bunch of isometric
tiles as well as an isometric anchor character and loads them all to a single IsoScene
object. As you've seen in earlier examples, the scene will be responsible for updating and painting the scene objects; the applet class is there merely to direct traffic.
Although you would usually have the applet itself catch keyboard strokes, I decided
to let the scene do it just to mix things up a bit.

```java
import java.applet.*;
import java.awt.*;

public class IsoTest extends Applet implements Runnable
{
    // a Thread for animation
    private Thread animation;

    private VolatileGraphics offscreen;

    // an isometric scene
    private IsoScene scene;

    public void init()
    {
        // initialize the scene
        scene = new IsoScene(getBounds());

        // create the iso tile group
        IsoTileGroup tileGroup = new IsoTileGroup();
        tileGroup.init(this);

        int x = -getSize().width *2 - (IsoTileGroup.TILE_WIDTH /2);
        int y = -getSize().height*2 - (IsoTileGroup.TILE_HEIGHT/2);

        int width  = getSize().width *4;
        int height = getSize().height*4;

        // fill the scene with iso tiles--note how the offset flag offsets
        // every other row of tiles so that they interlock
        IsoTile tile;
        boolean offset = false;
        while(y < height)
        {
            while(x < width)
            {
                tile = new IsoTile(tileGroup);
                tile.setPos(x, y);

                // add the tile as a non-anchor object
```

```
                    scene.add(tile, false);
                    x += IsoTileGroup.TILE_WIDTH;
            }

            offset = !offset;
            if(offset) x = -getSize().width*2;
            else       x = -getSize().width*2 - (IsoTileGroup.TILE_WIDTH /2);

            y += IsoTileGroup.TILE_HEIGHT/2;
        }

        // create the isoman group and a single isoman character
        IsoManGroup group = new IsoManGroup();
        group.init(this);

        IsoMan isoMan = new IsoMan(group);
        isoMan.setPos(getSize().width/2, getSize().height/2);

        // add the isoman to the scene as the anchor
        scene.add(isoMan, true);

        // register the scene to receive keyboard events
        addKeyListener(scene);

        offscreen = new VolatileGraphics(this);

        animation = new Thread(this);

        AnimationStrip.observer = this;

    }   // init

    public void start()
    {
        // start the animation thread
        animation.start();
```

```
    }

    public void stop()
    {
        animation = null;
    }

    public void run()
    {
        Thread t = Thread.currentThread();
        while (t == animation)
        {
            repaint();

            try
            {
                Thread.sleep(10);
            }
            catch(InterruptedException e)
            {
                break;
            }
        }

    }  // run

    public void update(Graphics g)
    {
        // update the scene
        scene.update();

        paint(g);
    }

    public void paint(Graphics g)
    {
        Graphics2D bg = (Graphics2D)offscreen.getValidGraphics();
```

```
            bg.setPaint(Color.WHITE);
            bg.clearRect(0, 0, getSize().width, getSize().height);

            // paint the scene
            scene.paint(bg);

            g.drawImage(offscreen.getBuffer(), 0, 0, this);

        }    // paint

    }    // IsoTest
```

Note how the tiles are set up; you need an offset mechanism that will place all of the tiles flush up against one another. Also note that the tile images are loaded from file, so if you were working with a graphics package that didn't make use of image transparency, you would need a rendering mechanism that makes sure that the tiles are drawn to properly overlap each other. But since we have the luxury of using images that contain native transparency, our tiles can be rendered in any order, since transparent regions won't be drawn.

The output of the *IsoTest* applet was shown in Figure 11.10, but the best way to see it is to run it for yourself. This applet really cooks, so it's worth trying out. I left the specifics of the IsoMan and IsoManGroup classes out of this discussion for now, but their full implementation can be found on the CD-ROM. Also, if you're interested in learning more about Isometric 3D Game Programming then check out *Isometric Game Programming with DirectX 7.0* by Ernest Pazera, also published by Premier Press.

Next, let's look at one final example of scene management; namely, the ever-present wrapped scene.

## Creating a Wrapped Scene

The final scene management system we'll look at in this chapter is what I call a *wrapped scene.* A wrapped scene simply tracks objects that leave one end of the scene and wrap them back to the other side. Think of it like a globe converted to a map. A map is merely a flat projection of the spherical earth. Although a map has distinct bounds, objects should logically still be able to fall off one end and "wrap" back around to the other.

Wrapped scenes have been around for a long time, ever since the times when games that used vector graphics were popular. Classics such as *Asteroids* and *Pac-Man* make use of wrapping. You may have even written several games that use wrapping yourself.

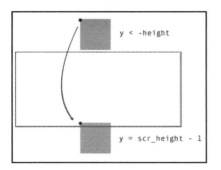

**Figure 11.12**

*Reentering a scene by intersecting its bounds*

Implementing a wrapped scene should be fairly straightforward. However, I will point out one slight oversight that can give people problems. When the scene is updated, objects are checked as to whether they have completely left the scene. Those objects that have left the scene should be translated to reenter the scene. If the object is not translated so that at least one pixel intersects the bounds of the scene, the scene manager will probably continue to assume that the object is still out of bounds and will repeat the translation of the object forever. This will lead to a scene where objects leave the scene and then cease to reappear again. Figure 11.12 shows a simple shaded box leaving the top of the scene and then reentering it from the bottom.

OK then, let's do it. The code for the *WrapTest* applet below allows the user to control a spaceship and wrap it around the scene bounds. Since the scene only contains one object, I did not implement a separate scene manager, but you may want to do so as you create more complex scenes. Try it out if the spirit moves you.

```java
import java.applet.*;
import java.awt.*;
import java.awt.event.*;

public class WrapTest extends Applet implements Runnable, KeyListener
{
    // a Thread for animation
    private Thread animation;

    private BufferedGraphics offscreen;

    // externally tracks the acceleration of the ship
    private Vector2D accel;
```

```java
    private final double MAX_ACCEL = 5.0f;

    // one degree of rotation
    private final double ONE_RADIAN =  Math.toRadians(1.0);

    // an actor to serve as our wrapped object
    private Actor2D ship;

    public void init()
    {
        // create the ship and its actor group
        StaticActorGroup group = new StaticActorGroup("ship.gif");
        group.init(this);

        ship = new StaticActor(group);
        addKeyListener(this);

        accel = new Vector2D.Double();

        offscreen = new VolatileGraphics(this);

        animation = new Thread(this);

        AnimationStrip.observer = this;

    }   // init


    public void start()
    {
        // start the animation thread
        animation.start();
    }

    public void stop()
    {
        animation = null;
    }

    public void run()
```

```
{
    Thread t = Thread.currentThread();
    while (t == animation)
    {
        repaint();

        try
        {
            Thread.sleep(10);
        }
        catch(InterruptedException e)
        {
            break;
        }
    }


}   // run

public void update(Graphics g)
{
    double accelX = accel.getX();
    double accelY = accel.getY();

    // accelerate the object by its separate x, y components, checking
    // against the maximum values
    if(accelX != 0)
    {
        ship.accelerate(accelX, 0);

        if(ship.getVel().getX() > MAX_ACCEL)
        {
            ship.getVel().setX(MAX_ACCEL);
        }
        else if(ship.getVel().getX() < -MAX_ACCEL)
        {
            ship.getVel().setX(-MAX_ACCEL);
        }
    }

    if(accelY != 0)
```

```
        {
             ship.accelerate(0, accelY);

             if(ship.getVel().getY() > MAX_ACCEL)
             {
                 ship.getVel().setY(MAX_ACCEL);
             }
             else if(ship.getVel().getY() < -MAX_ACCEL)
             {
                 ship.getVel().setY(-MAX_ACCEL);
             }
        }

        // slow the ship down if it is no longer accelerating
        if(! ship.getVel().equals(Vector2D.ZERO_VECTOR) &&
             accelX == 0 && accelY == 0)
        {
             Vector2D drag = ship.getVel();
             drag.normalize();
             ship.accelerate(-drag.getX(), -drag.getY());
        }

        // update the ship's position, wrapping as needed
        ship.update();

        int x = (int) ship.getX();
        int y = (int) ship.getY();
        int h = (int) ship.getHeight();
        int w = (int) ship.getWidth();

        if(x > getSize().width)
        {
             ship.setX(-w+1);
        }
        else if(x < -w)
        {
             ship.setX(getSize().width-1);
        }

        if(y > getSize().height)
```

```
        {
            ship.setY(-h+1);
        }
        else if(y < -h)
        {
            ship.setY(getSize().height-1);
        }

        // show the ship's stats on the status window
        showStatus(ship.getPos() + "      " +
                (int)Math.toDegrees(ship.getRot()) + "       " +
                ship.getVel());

        paint(g);
    }

    public void paint(Graphics g)
    {
        Graphics2D bg = (Graphics2D)offscreen.getValidGraphics();
        bg.setBackground(Color.BLACK);
        bg.clearRect(0, 0, getSize().width, getSize().height);

        // paint the ship
        ship.paint(bg);

        g.drawImage(offscreen.getBuffer(), 0, 0, this);
    }    // paint

public void keyTyped(KeyEvent e)
{

}

// monitors key presses and accelerates and rotates the ship as necessary
public void keyPressed(KeyEvent e)
{
    if(ship == null) return;

    switch(e.getKeyCode())
    {
```

```
// accelerate/decelerate the ship according to its 'forward'
// direction
case KeyEvent.VK_UP:
    accel.setX(Math.cos(ship.getRot()));
    accel.setY(Math.sin(ship.getRot()));
    accel.normalize();
    break;

case KeyEvent.VK_DOWN:
    accel.setX(-Math.cos(ship.getRot()));
    accel.setY(-Math.sin(ship.getRot()));
    accel.normalize();
    break;

// rotate the ship and update its forward acceleration
case KeyEvent.VK_LEFT:
    ship.rotate(-5*ONE_RADIAN);
    if(! ship.getVel().equals(Vector2D.ZERO_VECTOR))
    {
        accel.setX(Math.cos(ship.getRot()));
        accel.setY(Math.sin(ship.getRot()));
        accel.normalize();
    }
    break;

case KeyEvent.VK_RIGHT:
    ship.rotate(+5*ONE_RADIAN);
    if(! ship.getVel().equals(Vector2D.ZERO_VECTOR))
    {
        accel.setX(Math.cos(ship.getRot()));
        accel.setY(Math.sin(ship.getRot()));
        accel.normalize();
    }

    break;

default: break;
```

```
            }

        }

        public void keyReleased(KeyEvent e)
        {
            if(ship == null) return;

            switch(e.getKeyCode())
            {
                // cease acceleration once the up/down arrow keys are released
                case KeyEvent.VK_UP:
                case KeyEvent.VK_DOWN:
                    accel.setX(0.0);
                    accel.setY(0.0);
                    break;

                default: break;
            }
        }

    }   // WrapTest
```

Figure 11.13 depicts the spaceship from the *WrapTest* applet leaving the right side of the scene.

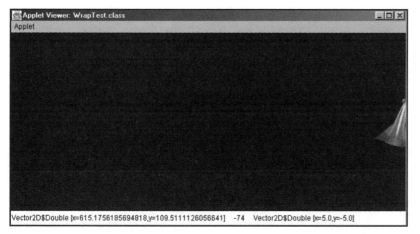

**Figure 11.13**

*The* WrapTest *applet*

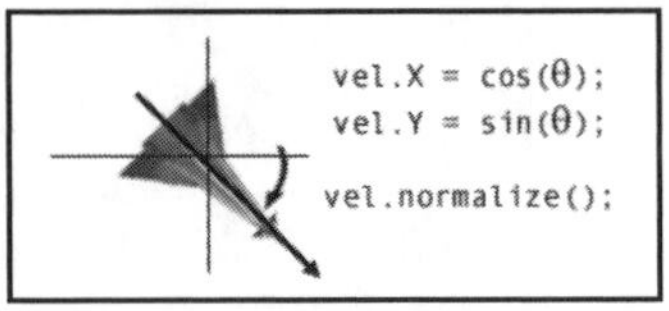

**Figure 11.14**

*Generating the forward vector*

Not bad. With wrapped scenes, you can keep the game play fresh yet simple. Wrapped scenes are a good alternative to just having the game objects bounce off the edges of the screen or, worse yet, losing the fleeing objects altogether.

If you tried the *WrapTest* applet already, you will have noticed that the ship accelerates in the direction that appears to be forward or backward. In the case of our ship, *forward* refers to the vector extending from the top of the plane. *Backward* refers to the same vector, just in the opposite direction. As you probably know, you can calculate the forward and backward vectors by taking the sine and cosine of the object's current rotation. After the vector components are defined, normalizing the vector will shorten (or expand) its size to unit length. One reason I created the `Vector2D` class was so that operations, such as normalization, could readily be available to us. Normalizing the vector is preferred because the distance moved each frame is guaranteed to be consistent. If you require your objects to move greater distances, you can then scale the vector using the `Vector2D scale` operation. Figure 11.14 shows one way to generate the forward vector of a moving object.

# Conclusion

I hope it's clear by now that using the proper scene management technique for the task can save you a lot of work. Unfortunately, it can be difficult to create a single general-purpose scene manager that works well for all games. For instance, parlor or casino games, such as poker or blackjack, probably won't need complex scene management components such as quad trees. On the other hand, a full-fledged top-view scroller probably won't go very far without a quad tree or other structure to manage collisions and rendering.

As always, feel free to make changes to the examples presented in this chapter. Of course, optimizations and customizations can always be made, so keep your eyes peeled for them. The following exercises contain several additional suggestions for improving and extending scene management. Try one today!

# Exercises

**11.1** One problem with trees in general is that they can take up a lot of unneeded memory when they are completed in full, especially when some nodes remain empty during the entire life cycle of the program. Alter the QuadNode and QuadTree classes so that nodes are only created as needed and are removed from the tree as they become empty.

**11.2** The LinkedList get method is fine for illustration but can be a costly operation as the list becomes large. Change the QuadNode and QuadTree classes so that they utilize ListIterator objects for traversing lists instead of using the get method. Try to quantify what, if any, benefits a ListIterator has over using the get method when processing entire lists of objects.

**11.3** Does the QuadNode class need to be declared as public? In other words, will you ever need to access a QuadNode from outside its package, or can all tree operations be carried out through the parent QuadTree object? Or doesn't it matter? If it adds to code clarity, try altering the visibility of the QuadNode class so that it is only directly available through the QuadTree class or within a specific package.

**11.4** You've seen how Actor2D objects contain their own internal list of collision objects. Develop a scheme for processing these collision lists within the Actor2D class. One way to identify what's what might be to impose a tagging mechanism, where each actor type receives its own integer tag. Another way to allow actors to identify themselves is through the instanceof operator. You can try one of these suggestions or come up with one of your own.

**11.5** Create a Choice object that allows the user to select from multiple screen resolutions before going into full-screen exclusive mode. Is it possible to determine beforehand which modes are full-screen compatible before they are added to the list? You can start by looking at the getScreenDevices method in the GraphicsEnvironment class.

**11.6** Change the *Fullscreen Test* applet to check for security permission to enter full-screen exclusive mode before actually attempting to do so. If it is not permitted, take appropriate action such as outputting a message or opening the program in windowed mode.

**11.7** Devise a mechanism that tiles small images and allows them to be scrolled within a scene. Your mechanism should be generic enough to be used with tiled scenes of different sizes and scrolling speeds. Figure 11.15 suggests how a tiled scrollable scene might look.

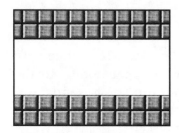

**Figure 11.15**

*Small scrollable tiles*

**11.8**  Alter the *IsoTest* applet so that the IsoMan cannot escape the bounds of the tile map yet can still walk on top of each tile. Also, the scene should stop scrolling before the void outside the tile map can be shown. This means the IsoMan character will need to actually move at times to reach remote tiles. I suggest maintaining an overall rectangle that represents the bounds of the scene, and one that represents the bounds of the display window. The IsoMan character should remain in the center of the display window rectangle. As you move the scene, update the window bounds as well. Once the window bounds intersect with the overall bounds, it's time to move your IsoMan character so that it remains in the middle of the view window rectangle.

**11.9**  Change the *IsoTest* applet to allow the user to use the mouse to move the IsoMan character à la games such as *Diablo* and *Ultima*. As you move the mouse around the scene and press down a mouse button, the IsoMan should appear to run toward the mouse cursor.

**11.10** Create a WrappedScene class that manages an entire scene of objects. Writing a game that introduces collision testing, such as an *Asteroids* clone, might be a good way to implement the WrappedScene class. You can also implement any additional scene management techniques you might need, such as a quad tree.

**11.11** Alter the *WrapTest* applet so that it wraps the visual image of objects as they leave the window bounds, much like the SceneScrollTest applet. You do not need to create a copy of the objects—just do a second paint to represent the wrapping of the image. Figure 11.16 shows how this applet might look in action.

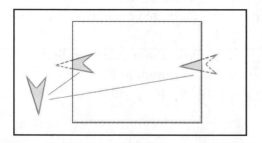

**Figure 11.16**

*Wrapping images as they leave the scene*

# CHAPTER 12

# CREATING CUSTOM VISUAL CONTROLS AND MENUS

In the quest to create extraordinary games, you know that it takes extraordinary graphics to keep your users engaged. Although the native Java AWT contains excellent components for communicating with the user, such as buttons, labels, and drop boxes, it would be nice to have a customizable set of components to use in your games. Customized components can give you complete control of how your games are presented to your users. In this chapter, we'll look at how you can implement a custom control and menu system in your games. We'll begin with the Component2D class, which will serve as the base class for all of your components. From there, we'll move on to creating customized labels, buttons, and radio buttons. We'll finish by looking at some container classes for holding your custom components, namely panels and menus.

Let's start by looking at some of the advantages (and disadvantages) of implementing a custom component system, then we'll dive right into some code.

# Why Reinvent the Wheel?

Before dedicating the time to creating your own custom components, it might be good to weigh the benefits versus the hindrances of doing so. As I mentioned above, the visual components of your games are extremely important as far as grabbing and keeping your user's attention. However, enhancing or rewriting what is already available to you can be risky.

- Creating a custom component system causes increased overhead in development.
- Custom components use too much memory.
- Custom components cause an increase in load time.
- Layout managers do a good enough job laying out native AWT components.

Complaints, complaints! That's the typical rhetoric you'll hear from those who are content with mediocre visual components. Now let's examine the benefits of the custom approach to game controls and menus:

- A custom component manager can give more exact placement of your components than does the native AWT.
- Custom components can give your programs their own customized look and feel.

**Figure 12.1**

*The native AWT versus
custom components:
Which would you choose?*

- The functionality of native AWT components can be easily emulated and extended.
- It's all about eye candy.
- Custom components just plain rule!

Figure 12.1 demonstrates exactly what I'm talking about. Using custom components will definitely give you and edge over the competition.

In all honesty, games are not famous for being conservative in their memory usage, so cheaping out on a few kilobytes worth of images in order to save memory and some loading time probably won't outweigh the benefits implementing a custom component system might bring. And yes, layout managers do provide a great way to automate component layout, but there's no reason you couldn't implement similar layout managers on your own. Also, since games are highly visual, being able to specify exact x, y coordinates in which to place your components will give you a lot more control over your scenes, not to mention a customized look and feel. A customized look and feel can especially come in handy when creating an entire suite of games or a promotion requiring a custom look.

If all that doesn't convince you, think of the bottom-line benefit of using customized controls: they just *look better.* Attractive components are good components, and in games that's what menu and control systems are all about. So if you can create components that properly function like the native AWT components do and they improve the look and feel of your games, I say go for it.

So now that you're convinced that a custom control mechanism is for you, let's look at an overview of the Component2D class and the subclasses that implement its functionality.

# Custom Control Overview

Now that we've discussed the benefits of creating a custom component system, let's look at how to actually implement it. Although our custom system is designed to override many of the already-existing AWT components, we're still going to need to

```
Object
├─Component2D
│ ├─Button2D
│ ├─Container2D
│ │├─Panel2D
│ │  └─Menu2D
│ ├─Label2D
│ ├─RadioButton2D
├─ImageGroup
│ └─ButtonImageGroup
└─RadioButtonGroup2D
```

**Figure 12.2**

*An overall look at the Component2D hierarchy*

use some of the existing AWT classes, such as the Graphics2D, Image, and Font classes from the java.awt package, as well as some of the various listener classes from the java.awt.event package. We'll also use some of the existing classes that have already been defined, such as the ImageGroup and AnimationStrip classes.

As you know, the root of the native AWT comes in the form of the Component class. (For a review of the Component class and its subclasses, refer back to Chapter 5.) We'll try to emulate the Component hierarchy as best as we can. Since we're creating a set of components using an existing set of rendering components, we obviously will not need to create a one-to-one correspondence between the two, but the overall correspondence should be pretty close.

The Component2D class will head our custom component system. Figure 12.2 represents an overall look at the Component2D class and its descendants. Compare it to figure 5.1 to see just how it correlates to the native Component class.

Now let's dig right into the meat of the Component2D hierarchy, starting with none other than the Component2D class.

# The Component2D Class

The Component2D class is an abstract class that serves as the base class for your custom components. It contains the fields and methods common to all of your visual components.

The Component2D class contains an ImageGroup for holding multiple images, as well as a copy of the image group's frame width and height. It also contains other common component attributes such as the position and bounds of the component, along with state information, such as those defining the enabled state and visibility.

The Component2D class also defines the methods for accessing information about it, along with a few incomplete methods for child classes to implement. Much like the Actor2D class, which was introduced in Chapter 10, Component2D classes are capable of updating and drawing themselves given a Graphics2D context.

Here's the code for the Component2D class. After glancing through the code listing, we'll look at some of its finer points.

```java
import java.awt.*;
import java.awt.geom.*;

// base class for creating custom visual components
public abstract class Component2D extends Object
{
    // the ImageGroup to hold component visuals
    protected ImageGroup group;

    // the size of the component
    protected int frameWidth;
    protected int frameHeight;

    // the position and bounds of the component, along with cached transform
    protected Vector2D pos;
    protected Rectangle2D bounds;
    protected AffineTransform xform;

    // flags for component visibility and use
    protected boolean enabled;
    protected boolean visible;

    // tracks the internal state of the component
    protected int state;

    // creates a new Component2D object with default attributes
    protected Component2D()
    {
        pos = new Vector2D.Double();
        xform = new AffineTransform();

        setEnabled(true);
```

```
            setVisible(true);

            bounds = new Rectangle2D.Double();
            frameWidth  = 0;
            frameHeight = 0;

            state = 0;
    }

    // paints the component using the sent Graphics2D context
    public abstract void paint(Graphics2D g2d);

    // paints the component at the sent offset coordinates
    public abstract void paint(Graphics2D g2d, double dx, double dy);

    // updates the internal transform of the component
    public void update()
    {
        xform.setToTranslation(pos.getX(), pos.getY());
    }

    // updates the bounding rectangle of the component
    public void updateBounds()
    {
        if(frameWidth <= 0 && group != null)
        {
            frameWidth = group.getFrameWidth();
        }
        if(frameHeight <= 0 && group != null)
        {
            frameHeight = group.getFrameHeight();
        }

        bounds.setRect(pos.getX(), pos.getY(), frameWidth, frameHeight);
    }

    // returns a String representation of the component
    public String toString()
    {
```

```
            // output the class name and current position
            return getClass().getName() + ": " + pos.toString();
    }


    // access methods for most attributes

    public void setEnabled(boolean e)
    {
        enabled = e;
    }

    public final boolean isEnabled()
    {
        return enabled;
    }

    public final void setVisible(boolean v)
    {
        visible = v;
    }

    public final boolean isVisible()
    {
        return visible;
    }

    public final void setX(double px)
    {
        pos.setX(px);
    }

    public final void setY(double py)
    {
        pos.setY(py);
    }

    public final double getX()
    {
        return pos.getX();
```

```
    }

    public final double getY()
    {
        return pos.getY();
    }

    public final void setPos(int x, int y)
    {
        pos.setX(x);
        pos.setY(y);
    }

    public final void setPos(double x, double y)
    {
        pos.setX(x);
        pos.setY(y);
    }

    public final void setPos(Vector2D v)
    {
        pos.setX(v.getX());
        pos.setY(v.getY());
    }

    public final Vector2D getPos()
    {
        return pos;
    }

    public Rectangle2D getBounds()
    {
        return bounds;
    }

}    // Component2D
```

As you can see, the Component2D class contains plenty of access and incomplete
methods, so it shouldn't seem too complex. Although this class is meant to emulate

the Component class, it does not subclass Component. And although it behaves much like the Actor2D class, it does not subclass it either. Why?

The reason for not extending the Component2D class from another base class varies. For the Component class, there really is no direct correlation between it and the Component2D class. The Component class contains a lot of low-level stuff you just don't need. Extending it would just create a lot of bulky overhead. In fact, the Component class fills up about 135 pages in my text editor, and most of it is stuff you don't need.

I also decided not to subclass Component2D from Actor2D, but for slightly different reasons. Although the Actor2D class is slightly bulkier than you need, it matches up pretty well with the Component2D class. However, I wanted to keep these two classes apart semantically. I don't feel that the custom components should be treated as regular scene objects. I think they should be treated separately by the applet. I also decided to keep the Component2D class independent of the Actor2D class so you will not be locked into maintaining my version of it. If you don't want to use the Actor2D class, or you modify it from its original form, you will not need to modify the Component2D class at all. I feel that a little extra code is worth the freedom to change it later.

Okay, now on to subclassing the Component2D class. We'll start with a noninteractive class I like to call Label2D.

# The Label2D Class

In Chapter 7 we took a rather extensive look into using the Font class to manipulate and render text. Using the Font class alongside the Graphics2D class gives you a lot of power over how text is rendered. For instance, you can translate, rotate, scale, and shear text strings, change their color, fill them with gradient and textured paints, control output quality, and a whole lot more.

However, one thing I always wanted was a container class that holds together the different properties needed to render a string of text. That's where the Label2D class comes in. With the Label2D class, you can contain attributes such as the text string, font, transformation, and color of the text you want to render all within one class.

I'll get off the soapbox and let you look at the code for the Label2D class. This class contains all of the features mentioned above plus a few extras you'll see in the test program.

```
import java.awt.*;
import java.awt.font.*;
```

```java
import java.awt.geom.*;
import java.util.*;

public class Label2D extends Component2D
{
    // the font to draw with
    protected Font font;

    // the actual text string to draw
    protected String text;

    // a Paint for both 'enabled' as well as 'disabled' states
    protected Paint paint;
    protected Paint disabledPaint;

    // default Paint if no other is specified
    protected final Paint DEFAULT_PAINT = Color.GRAY;

    // constructs a new Label2D with the given font, text, and paint
    public Label2D(Font f, String str, Paint p)
    {
        super();

        setFont(f);
        setText(str);
        setPaint(p);

        // set the disabled paint to the default paint
        setDisabledPaint(DEFAULT_PAINT);
    }

    // constructs a new Label2D with the given font, text, paint, and position
    public Label2D(Font f, String str, Paint p, Vector2D v)
    {
        super();

        setFont(f);
        setText(str);
        setPaint(p);
```

```
        setPos(v);

        // set the disabled paint to the default paint
        setDisabledPaint(DEFAULT_PAINT);
    }


// centers the label relative to the sent Rectangle2D object
public void centerOn(Rectangle2D r, Graphics2D g2d)
{
    // get the FontRenderContext for the Graphics2D context
    FontRenderContext frc = g2d.getFontRenderContext();

    // get the layout of our message and font
    TextLayout layout = new TextLayout(text, font, frc);

    // get the bounds of the layout
    Rectangle2D textBounds = layout.getBounds();

    // set the new position
    setX(r.getX() + (r.getWidth()/2) - (textBounds.getWidth()  / 2));
    setY(r.getY() + ((r.getHeight()  + textBounds.getHeight()) / 2));

    // update the overall bounding rectangle
    updateBounds(g2d);
}


// updates the bounds of the label using the layout of the current font
public void updateBounds(Graphics2D g2d)
{
    // get the FontRenderContext for the Graphics2D context
    FontRenderContext frc = g2d.getFontRenderContext();

    // get the layout of our message and font
    TextLayout layout = new TextLayout(text, font, frc);

    // get the bounds of the layout
    Rectangle2D textBounds = layout.getBounds();

    bounds.setRect(getX(), getY(),
```

```java
                                textBounds.getWidth(), textBounds.getHeight());
}

public void setFont(Font f)
{
    font = f;
}

public void setText(String str)
{
    text = str;
}

public String getText()
{
    return text;
}

public void setPaint(Paint p)
{
    paint = p;
}

public void setDisabledPaint(Paint p)
{
    disabledPaint = p;
}

// paints the label at its current position
public void paint(Graphics2D g2d)
{
    // only paint if visible
    if(isVisible())
    {
        // set the font
        g2d.setFont(font);

        // set the paint based on enabled state
        if(isEnabled())
```

```java
            {
                g2d.setPaint(paint);
            }
            else
            {
                g2d.setPaint(disabledPaint);
            }

            g2d.drawString(text, (int) pos.getX(), (int) pos.getY());
        }
    }

    // paints the label at the sent delta position
    public void paint(Graphics2D g2d, double dx, double dy)
    {
        // only paint if visible
        if(isVisible())
        {
            // set the font
            g2d.setFont(font);

            // set the paint based on enabled state
            if(isEnabled())
            {
                g2d.setPaint(paint);
            }
            else
            {
                g2d.setPaint(disabledPaint);
            }

            // paint the string, adding in the delta values
            g2d.drawString(text, (int) (pos.getX() + dx),
                                 (int) (pos.getY() + dy));
        }
    }

    // returns a String representation of the label
    public String toString()
```

```
        {
                // return the parent toString as well as the current text label
                return super.toString() + " " + text;
        }

    }    // Label2D
```

You'll probably remember some of the techniques used in the Label2D class from earlier chapters, such as retrieving font metrics as shown in the centerOn and updateBounds methods. Note that retrieving and working with font metrics can be costly operations, so these methods should not be called on a regular basis. Rather, they should be called only at construction time and when the label's state changes (such as its position, text string, etc.). If you need to update the label's position on a regular basis you can always call the paint method that takes x- and y-offset values as its parameters rather than changing the internal state of the label.

The following is a quick test of the Label2D class. It simply displays the names of five fonts from top to bottom. It uses TexturePaint objects to control how the labels are painted. It also toggles the enabled state of all of the labels every five seconds, so you get to see both states in action.

```java
import java.applet.*;
import java.awt.*;
import java.awt.image.*;
import java.awt.geom.*;
import java.util.*;

public class Label2DTest extends Applet implements Runnable
{
        // a Thread for animation
        private Thread animation;

        private BufferedGraphics offscreen;

        // an array of labels to draw
        private Label2D[] labels;

        // String descriptions of the various fonts we'll use
        private final String[] fonts =
```

```java
                    {"Helvetica", "Arial", "Courier", "Terminal", "Georgia"};

// utility class for easily creating TexturePaint objects
private TexturePaint createTexturePaint(String filename)
{
    MediaTracker mt = new MediaTracker(this);
    Image image = getImage(getCodeBase(), filename);
    mt.addImage(image, 0);
    try
    {    mt.waitForAll();
    }
    catch(InterruptedException e) { /* do nothing */ }

    // create a new BufferedImage with the image's width and height
    BufferedImage bi = new BufferedImage(
            image.getWidth(this), image.getHeight(this),
            BufferedImage.TYPE_INT_RGB);

    // get the Graphics2D context of the BufferedImage and render the
    // original image onto it
    ((Graphics2D)bi.getGraphics()).drawImage(image, new AffineTransform(),
                                        this);

    // create the bounding rectangle for the paint's image
    Rectangle bounds = new Rectangle(0, 0, bi.getWidth(), bi.getHeight());

    // create the Paint
    return new TexturePaint(bi, bounds);
}

public void init()
{
    labels = new Label2D[fonts.length];

    // create two TexturePaint objects to paint with--one for both the
    // "enabled" and "disabled" states
    TexturePaint tpEnabled  = createTexturePaint("label1.gif");
    TexturePaint tpDisabled = createTexturePaint("label2.gif");

    // create the labels
```

```java
        for(int i = 0; i < fonts.length; i++)
        {
            // create a new Label2D with the specified Font, Font name, and
            // enabled paint
            labels[i] = new Label2D(new Font(fonts[i], Font.PLAIN, 40),
                                    fonts[i], tpEnabled);

            // set the label's position
            labels[i].setPos(new Vector2D.Double(50, 50+(i*50)));

            // set the disabled paint for the label
            labels[i].setDisabledPaint(tpDisabled);
        }

        offscreen = new BufferedGraphics(this);

        AnimationStrip.observer = this;

    }   // init


    public void start()
    {
        // start the animation thread
        animation = new Thread(this);
        animation.start();
    }

    public void stop()
    {
        animation = null;
    }

    public void run()
    {
        long time = System.currentTimeMillis();

        Thread t = Thread.currentThread();
        while (t == animation)
```

```
        {
            repaint();

            try
            {
                Thread.sleep(10);
            }
            catch(InterruptedException e)
            {
                break;
            }

            // toggle the enabled state of the labels every few seconds
            if(System.currentTimeMillis() - time > 5000)
            {
                for(int i = 0; i < fonts.length; i++)
                {
                    labels[i].setEnabled(! labels[i].isEnabled());
                }

                time = System.currentTimeMillis();
            }
        }

}   // run


public void update(Graphics g)
{
    paint(g);
}

public void paint(Graphics g)
{
    Graphics2D bg = (Graphics2D)offscreen.getValidGraphics();
    bg.setPaint(Color.BLACK);
    bg.fillRect(0, 0, getSize().width, getSize().height);

    // paint the labels
```

```
                for(int i = 0; i < fonts.length; i++)
                {
                     labels[i].paint(bg);
                }

                g.drawImage(offscreen.getBuffer(), 0, 0, this);

        }     // paint

    }     // Label2Dtest
```

Figure 12.3 shows output from the *Label2DTest* applet. Notice that each label's text represents the font that was used to render it.

As you can see, with minimal code you can get very good control over text rendering in your games. Encapsulating font-rendering components within a single class sure beats using parallel arrays or some other "hacked" method. The Label2D class also beats the native Java Label class by a country mile. You can control not only the font used but also its exact position, size, and fill color. The Label class just doesn't compare!

In the *Label2DTest* applet, I used a TexturePaint object for controlling the paint of both the enabled as well as the disabled state of each label. You could just as easily use a GradientPaint or Color object as either the paint or disabled paint in your programs. Note that the default Color constant GRAY is used if no other color is specified for your paint attributes.

Now we'll look at a more complex class that uses Label2D objects for its rendering: the custom Button2D class.

**Figure 12.3**

*The* Label2DTest *applet*

# The Button2D Class

The Button2D class works like you would expect any other button to work—clicking it should generate some sort of action. The Button2D class also provides support for up to three frames of animation: one for the normal state, one for when the mouse hovers over the button, and one for when the button is actually being pushed. Figure 12.4 shows these three states in action.

Note how the buttons in Figure 12.4 use beveling to help convey the button's state. The first two states use the same beveling (just different colors) to convey that the button is in the "up" state. The button is depicted as being pressed, or in the "down" state, by flipping the bevel to the opposite edges of the button. Any good paint program with a bevel tool can generate these effects quite easily. Even if you don't have a program with a bevel tool, creating bevels is quite simple. A few light and dark lines around the sides, along with notches at the corners, should give you a reasonable bevel in little time.

Now on to how the Button2D class actually works. I took advantage of some of the native java.awt.event classes for this one. I gave each Button2D object an array of *ActionListener* objects. External objects that implement the *ActionListener* interface, like your typical Applet class, can register themselves for action events with the button by calling the addActionListener method and passing themselves (or any other action listener) as the parameter. The Button2D also implements the *MouseListener* and *MouseMotionListener* interfaces so that they can catch mouse events such as clicks and general movement. Button2D objects will need to be registered for mouse listening through a Component object; again, this will usually be an Applet object. While actions such as mouse movement can alter a button's internal state, pressing and then releasing a mouse button over the top of a Button2D will generate an action event. This event will then be passed to all of the objects contained in the button's actionListeners array. Figure 12.5 shows exactly how the buttons from Figure 12.4 will look in according to the various mouse states.

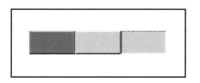

**Figure 12.4**

*The three visual states of a Button2D object*

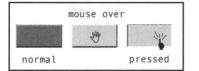

**Figure 12.5**

*A Button2D in its various mouse states*

Chapter 6 dealt with classes and interfaces contained within the java.awt.event package, such as the *ActionListener* interface. So check back there if you need a refresher or more help.

By now you should definitely see a pattern. We'll start with the code from the Button2D class, followed by an example. As always, I'll point out any rough spots along the way.

```java
import java.awt.*;
import java.awt.event.*;
import java.awt.geom.*;
import java.util.*;


public class Button2D extends Component2D implements MouseListener,
                                                      MouseMotionListener
{
    // an optional text label for the button
    protected Label2D label;

    // an array of listeners to receive action events
    protected ActionListener[] actionListeners;
    protected final int MAX_LISTENERS = 5;

    // the available states of the button, one for the normal, mouse over and
    // mouse pressed states
    public static final int BUTTON_NORMAL = 0;
    public static final int BUTTON_OVER   = 1;
    public static final int BUTTON_DOWN   = 2;

    // creates a new Button2D object with the given label, image group, and
    // position
    public Button2D(Label2D lbl, ImageGroup grp, Vector2D p)
    {
        super();
        label  = lbl;
        group  = grp;
        setPos(p);
        updateBounds();
```

```java
        update();

        // create an empty array of listeners to receive action events
        actionListeners = new ActionListener[MAX_LISTENERS];
        for(int i = 0; i < MAX_LISTENERS; i++)
        {
            actionListeners[i] = null;
        }
    }


    // creates a new Button2D object with the given image group and position
    public Button2D(ImageGroup grp, Vector2D p)
    {
        this(null, grp, p);
    }


    // creates a new Button2D object with the given label and image group
    public Button2D(Label2D lbl, ImageGroup grp)
    {
        this(lbl, grp, Vector2D.ZERO_VECTOR);
    }


    // attempts to add the sent listener to the array of ActionListener objects
    // this method fails if:
    //  1) l is null
    //  2) the array already contains MAX_LISTENERS elements
    public void addActionListener(ActionListener l)
    {
        if(l == null)
        {
            return;
        }

        for(int i = 0; i < MAX_LISTENERS; i++)
        {
            if(actionListeners[i] == null)
            {
                actionListeners[i] = l;
```

```java
            return;
        }
    }
}


// centers the button's label using the current button's bounding
// rectangle
public void centerLabel(Graphics2D g2d)
{
    if(label != null)
    {
        label.centerOn(this.getBounds(), g2d);
    }
}


// sets the enabled state of the button, updates its internal state, and
// updates the enabled state of its label, if necessary
public void setEnabled(boolean e)
{
    super.setEnabled(e);

    if(!isEnabled())
    {
        state = BUTTON_NORMAL;
    }
    if(label != null)
    {
        label.setEnabled(e);
    }
}



public void mouseClicked(MouseEvent e)
{
}

public void mouseEntered(MouseEvent e)
{
```

```
    }

public void mouseExited(MouseEvent e)
{
}

// sets the button to its "pressed" state if it is enabled and the click
// event took place over the button
public void mousePressed(MouseEvent e)
{
    if(isEnabled())
    {
        if(bounds.contains(e.getPoint()))
        {
            state = BUTTON_DOWN;
        }
    }
}

// simulates the "clicking" of a button by informing all action listeners
// that a click event took place.  if the mouse was released not while over
// the button, the button is returned to its normal state and no action is
// performed.
public void mouseReleased(MouseEvent e)
{
    // only process enabled components
    if(isEnabled())
    {
        // trigger the event only if the mouse is still over the button
        if(bounds.contains(e.getPoint()))
        {
            if(state == BUTTON_DOWN)
            {
                ActionEvent thisEvent = new ActionEvent(this,
                                  ActionEvent.ACTION_PERFORMED, "");

                // let all the listeners know something went down
                for(int i = 0; i < MAX_LISTENERS; i++)
                {
```

```
                                    if(actionListeners[i] != null)
                                    {
                                        actionListeners[i].actionPerformed(thisEvent);
                                    }
                            }
                    }

                    // restore the OVER state
                    state = BUTTON_OVER;
            }

            // return the button to normal if it wasn't released over the
            // button
            else
            {
                    state = BUTTON_NORMAL;
            }
        }
}


public void mouseDragged(MouseEvent e)
{
}

// updates the state of the button based on its current state and
// the position of the mouse
public void mouseMoved(MouseEvent e)
{
    if(isEnabled())
    {
        // don't do anything if the mouse is already down
        if(state == BUTTON_DOWN) return;

        // switch to the 'over' state if the
        if(bounds.contains(e.getPoint()))
        {
            state = BUTTON_OVER;
```

```java
                }

                // restore the state to normal in case the mouse pointer has just
                // left the button area
                else
                {
                    state = BUTTON_NORMAL;
                }
            }
        }


        // paints the button based on its current state
        public void paint(Graphics2D g2d)
        {
            // only paint visible components
            if(isVisible())
            {
                // draw the image first, if one exists
                if(group != null)
                {
                    g2d.drawImage(((ButtonImageGroup) group).getFrame(state),
                                xform, AnimationStrip.observer);
                }

                // draw the text label, if a valid one exists
                if(label != null)
                {
                    // if the button is down, augment the label a bit to make it
                    // look 'pressed'
                    if(state == BUTTON_DOWN)
                    {
                        label.paint(g2d, 2, 2);
                    }
                    // otherwise, just draw the label normally
                    else
                    {
                        label.paint(g2d);
                    }
                }
```

```java
            }
        }
    }

    // paints the button based on its current state and the sent delta x, y
    // values
    public void paint(Graphics2D g2d, double dx, double dy)
    {
        // only paint visible components
        if(isVisible())
        {
            // draw the image first, if one exists
            if(group != null)
            {
                g2d.drawImage(((ButtonImageGroup) group).getFrame(state),
                        AffineTransform.getTranslateInstance(pos.getX() + dx,
                                                             pos.getY() + dy),
                        AnimationStrip.observer);
            }

            // draw the label, if it exists
            if(label != null)
            {
                // if the button is down, augment the label a bit to make it
                // look 'pressed'
                if(state == BUTTON_DOWN)
                {
                    label.paint(g2d, dx+2, dx+2);
                }
                // otherwise, just draw the label normally
                else
                {
                    label.paint(g2d, dx, dx);
                }
            }
        }
    }

    // returns a String representation of this button
```

```
public String toString()
{
    // if the label is valid, return the parent's toString plus the label's
    // toString
    if(label != null)
    {
        return super.toString() + " " + label.toString();
    }

    // otherwise, just return the parent's toString
    return super.toString();
}

}   // Button2D
```

You should be able to track how the Button2D class tracks its internal state by looking at the various mouse action methods. Note that action events are still triggered if you hold the mouse button down over a button, leave the component, and then return before releasing the mouse button. Also note that by simulating clicking through separate mousePressed and mouseReleased methods, you can internally alter the state of the buttons more easily. This effect would not be possible if you only defined mouse action inside of the mouseClicked method.

Recall that Component2D objects contain their own ImageGroup to store image frames. Well, I decided to extend the ImageGroup class by creating the ButtonImageGroup class, which contains extra fields for the file name and number of objects the image file contains. So instead of extending the ImageGroup into separate classes each time you want to create a different button style, you can simply use this class and send it these parameters. When the ButtonImageGroup init method is called, all it needs to do is load the file and then chop it up into equal pieces. Figure 12.6 shows how you should lay out individual button images within a single image file.

Note that the image shown in Figure 12.6 is maintained all within a single row of cells. Also note that no cell padding or gridlines are marked. Button images should be added in a specific order; the normal state goes first, then the mouse over state,

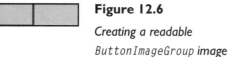

**Figure 12.6**

*Creating a readable*
*ButtonImageGroup image*

and then finally the mouse pressed state. Although you can add fewer frames, I generally feel that three will give you the best visual result.

And although the code for the ButtonImageGroup forces these constraints on button images, I feel that this makes things easier in the long run. With a few simple code changes, you can alter this class to behave in any way you want.

Briefly examine the code for the ButtonImageGroup class and think about how it extends the ImageGroup class. After you're done, I invite you to try out a test program that pulls everything together.

```java
import java.awt.*;

public class ButtonImageGroup extends ImageGroup
{
    // the image filename and number of frames it contains
    protected String filename;
    protected int numFrames;

    public ButtonImageGroup(int n, String str)
    {
        super();
        numFrames  = n;
        filename   = str;
        animations = new AnimationStrip[1];
    }

    // loads the animation strip and divides it into numFrames frames
    public void init(java.applet.Applet a)
    {
        ImageLoader loader;

        loader      = new ImageLoader(a, filename, true);

        // get the width and height of each frame; note it is assumed that all
        // images reside within a 1 x numFrames grid without any cell padding
        // or grid lines
        frameWidth  = loader.getImageWidth() / numFrames;
        frameHeight = loader.getImageHeight();

        animations[0] = new AnimationStrip();
```

```
                for(int i = 0; i < numFrames; i++)
                {
                        animations[0].addFrame(loader.extractCell(
                                        (i*frameWidth), 0, frameWidth, frameHeight));
                }
                animations[0].setAnimator(new Animator.Looped());
        }

        public Image getFrame(int frame)
        {
                animations[0].reset();
                for(int i = 0; i < frame; i++)
                {
                        animations[0].animate();
                }
                return animations[0].getCurrFrame();
        }

}    // ButtonImageGroup
```

Now let's put it all together and run through a small demo that allows the user to interact with some of our custom buttons. The following applet, *Button2DTest*, renders five buttons to the window and prints a simple message to the console every time one of them is pressed.

```
import java.applet.*;
import java.awt.*;
import java.awt.event.*;

public class Button2DTest extends Applet implements Runnable, ActionListener
{
        // a Thread for animation
        private Thread animation;

        private BufferedGraphics offscreen;

        // an array of Button2D objects to render
        private Button2D[] buttons;

        // an array of font names to use in rendering
```

```java
private final String[] fonts =
                  {"Helvetica", "Arial", "Courier", "Terminal", "Georgia"};
private final int NUM_BUTTONS = fonts.length;

public void init()
{
    // set up the ButtonImageGroup for our buttons to use
    ButtonImageGroup group = new ButtonImageGroup(3, "buttons.gif");
    group.init(this);

    // create the actual buttons
    buttons = new Button2D[NUM_BUTTONS];
    for(int i = 0; i < NUM_BUTTONS; i++)
    {
        // create a label that describes the font being used
        Label2D label = new Label2D(new Font(fonts[i], Font.PLAIN, 18),
                                    fonts[i], Color.BLACK);

        // create the button and center its label onto it
        buttons[i] = new Button2D(label, group,
                                    new Vector2D.Double(50, 10+(i*55)));
        label.centerOn(buttons[i].getBounds(), (Graphics2D)getGraphics());

        // register the button to receive mouse events
        addMouseListener(buttons[i]);
        addMouseMotionListener(buttons[i]);

        // let the button know the applet wants to receive action events
        // from it
        buttons[i].addActionListener(this);
    }

    offscreen = new BufferedGraphics(this);

    AnimationStrip.observer = this;

}   // init


public void start()
```

```java
{
    // start the animation thread
    animation = new Thread(this);
    animation.start();
}

public void stop()
{
    animation = null;
}

public void run()
{
    Thread t = Thread.currentThread();
    while (t == animation)
    {
        repaint();

        try
        {
            Thread.sleep(10);
        }
        catch(InterruptedException e)
        {
            break;
        }
    }
}   // run


public void update(Graphics g)
{
    paint(g);
}

public void paint(Graphics g)
{
    Graphics2D bg = (Graphics2D)offscreen.getValidGraphics();
    bg.setPaint(Color.BLUE.darker());
```

```
                bg.fillRect(0, 0, getSize().width, getSize().height);

                // paint the buttons
                for(int i = 0; i < NUM_BUTTONS; i++)
                {
                    buttons[i].paint(bg);
                }

                g.drawImage(offscreen.getBuffer(), 0, 0, this);

        }   // paint

        // when an action is sent from a Button2D object, just print the event to
        // the console
        public void actionPerformed(ActionEvent e)
        {
            System.out.println(e);
        }
    }   Button2DTest
```

Figure 12.7 shows the *Button2DTest* applet in action, with the button labeled "Terminal" in its pressed state.

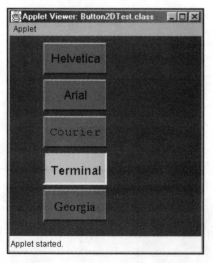

**Figure 12.7**

*The* Button2DTest *applet*

Not bad, eh? I think the buttons generated by the *Button2DTest* look just as good as (or even better than) anything the native AWT can give us. However, this is where some of the hindrances of the Component2D hierarchy come into play. First, Button2D objects take a bit more code to get up and running than does a standard Button object. Secondly, you must actively render your buttons in order to see them. Although this isn't a real big deal, it is still overhead you must not forget to include. But although there is a bit of work involved to get Button2D objects up and running, it's not really *that* much work. In all, I think it's well worth the extra effort.

Before I forget to mention it, note how the actionPerformed method is implemented. It merely echoes the ActionEvent sent back to the console. So, if you press the button labeled "Arial," the following should be printed to your console:

```
java.awt.event.ActionEvent[ACTION_PERFORMED,cmd=] on Button2D: Vector2D$Double
[x=50.0,y=65.0] Label2D: Vector2D$Double [x=81.1171875,y=95.5546875] Arial
```

I just thought I'd mention this in case you had your console window minimized or it was otherwise hidden.

We'll now revisit and rewrite an oldie but goodie component, the Checkbox component.

# The RadioButton2D Class

If you liked the Button2D class, you're sure to love the RadioButton2D class. The RadioButton2D mimics the Checkbox class in that it allows the user to distinguish between an "on" and "off" state for the button. It also allows you to associate several of them into groups so that only a single member of the group is guaranteed to be selected at any given time.

Surprisingly, the RadioButton2D class is simpler than the Button2D class. First, it only contains two states, on and off. You can also think of this as selected or not selected, whichever you prefer. In addition, RadioButton2D objects do not need to fire action events when they are pressed. Most applications actively seek the state of radio buttons rather than wait for the buttons to fire events. The RadioButton2D class still implements the *MouseListener* interface, but not the *MouseMotionListener* interface, since mouse-moved events are no longer applicable.

Enough jibber-jabber. Here's the code for the RadioButton2D class. Again, it's liberally commented to make it easy to follow along.

```
import java.awt.*;
import java.awt.event.*;
import java.awt.geom.*;
```

```java
import java.util.*;

public class RadioButton2D extends Component2D implements MouseListener
{
    // a label to display alongside the button
    protected Label2D label;

    // the group this button belongs to
    protected RadioButtonGroup rbGroup;

    // constants to tracking the state of the button
    public static final int BUTTON_OFF = 0;
    public static final int BUTTON_ON  = 1;

    // creates a new RadioButton2D with the sent label, image and button group,
    // and position
    public RadioButton2D(Label2D lbl, ImageGroup grp,
                         RadioButtonGroup rbg, Vector2D p
                         )
    {
        super();

        label   = lbl;
        group   = grp;
        rbGroup = rbg;

        if(rbGroup != null)
        {
            rbGroup.add(this);
        }

        setPos(p);
        updateBounds();
        update();
        setSelected(false);
    }

    // creates a new RadioButton2D with the sent image and button group and
    // position
    public RadioButton2D(ImageGroup grp, RadioButtonGroup rbg, Vector2D p)
```

```java
{
    this(null, grp, rbg, p);
}

// creates a new RadioButton2D with the sent label, image and button group
public RadioButton2D(Label2D lbl, ImageGroup grp, RadioButtonGroup rbg)
{
    this(lbl, grp, rbg, Vector2D.ZERO_VECTOR);
}

// creates a new RadioButton2D with the sent image group
public RadioButton2D(ImageGroup grp)
{
    this(null, grp, null, Vector2D.ZERO_VECTOR);
}

// returns whether the button is selected
public boolean isSelected()
{
    return (state == BUTTON_ON);
}

// sets the selected state of the button
public void setSelected(boolean selected)
{
    state = (selected) ? BUTTON_ON : BUTTON_OFF;
}

// returns the text description of the button, if any
public String getText()
{
    if(label != null)
    {
        return label.getText();
    }
    return "";
}

// sets the enabled state of the button and its label
public void setEnabled(boolean e)
```

```java
    {
        super.setEnabled(e);

        if(label != null)
        {
            label.setEnabled(e);
        }
    }


    // toggles the state of the button
    public void mousePressed(MouseEvent e)
    {
        if(!isEnabled() || !isVisible()) return;

        // no button group indicates that the button acts independently
        if(rbGroup == null)
        {
            if(bounds.contains(e.getPoint()))
            {
                setSelected(!isSelected());
            }
        }


        // otherwise, update the entire button group
        else
        {
            if(bounds.contains(e.getPoint()))
            {
                setSelected(true);
                rbGroup.updateGroup(this);
            }
        }

    }


    public void mouseEntered(MouseEvent e)
    {
```

```java
        }

        public void mouseExited(MouseEvent e)
        {
        }

        public void mouseClicked(MouseEvent e)
        {
        }

        public void mouseReleased(MouseEvent e)
        {
        }

        // draws the button at its current transform
        public void paint(Graphics2D g2d)
        {
            // only paint visible components
            if(isVisible())
            {
                g2d.drawImage(((ButtonImageGroup) group).getFrame(state), xform,
                            AnimationStrip.observer);

                // draw the label if it is valid
                if(label != null)
                {
                    label.paint(g2d);
                }
            }
        }

        // draws the button at the sent offset values
        public void paint(Graphics2D g2d, double dx, double dy)
        {
            // only paint visible components
            if(isVisible())
            {
                g2d.drawImage(((ButtonImageGroup) group).getFrame(state),
```

```
                                AffineTransform.getTranslateInstance(
                                        pos.getX() + dx,pos.getY() + dy),
                                AnimationStrip.observer
                                );

                // draw the label if it is valid
                if(label != null)
                {
                        label.paint(g2d, dx, dx);
                }
        }
}


// returns the String representation of this radio button
public String toString()
{
        if(label != null)
        {
                return super.toString() + " " + label.toString();
        }

        return super.toString();
}

}   // RadioButton2D
```

At first it may seem like the RadioButton2D class should extend the Button2D class. After all, a radio button can be thought of as a *type* of button. However, for the reasons mentioned above, the functionality of the custom radio button class is too different from the standard button class for it to be a direct subclass. RadioButton2D would be inheriting too much bulk it doesn't need, and no one wants that to happen. Additionally, there would be no advantage for a Button2D object to be morphed into a RadioButton2D object at run time by using the new operator. They simply represent different functional components.

One feature I thought the RadioButton2D class needed was to be grouped externally so that a single selection out of many can be made. The custom RadioButtonGroup class does just that. It contains a growable (and shrinkable) Vector object that will hold the buttons. This way, you do not need to know how many selections the group will have ahead of time. This class also contains methods for adding buttons to the group, fetching the currently selected button, setting attributes such as its enabled and visible states, as well as updating which button is selected and painting the buttons in the group. Try it—you just might like it.

```java
import java.awt.*;
import java.util.*;

// maintains a group of buttons so that only one can be selected at any given
// time
public class RadioButtonGroup extends Object
{
    // a dynamically growable Vector of radio buttons
    protected Vector buttons;

    // an enumeration for traversing the above Vector
    protected Enumeration e;

    // creates a new RadioButtonGroup object
    public RadioButtonGroup()
    {
        buttons = new Vector();
    }

    // adds the sent radio button to the vector
    public void add(RadioButton2D rb)
    {
        buttons.add(rb);
    }

    // gets the currently selected radio button, or null if no button
    // is selected
    public RadioButton2D getSelection()
    {
        for(e = buttons.elements(); e.hasMoreElements(); )
        {
            RadioButton2D rb = (RadioButton2D)e.nextElement();

            if(rb.isSelected())
            {
                return rb;
            }
```

```java
        }

        return null;
    }


    // enables/disables the entire group of buttons
    public void setEnabled(boolean b)
    {
        for(e = buttons.elements(); e.hasMoreElements(); )
        {
            ((RadioButton2D) e.nextElement()).setEnabled(b);
        }
    }


    // sets the visibility of the entire button group
    public void setVisible(boolean v)
    {
        for(e = buttons.elements(); e.hasMoreElements(); )
        {
            ((RadioButton2D) e.nextElement()).setVisible(v);
        }
    }


    // updates the group by un-selecting all but the sent buttons in the group
    public void updateGroup(RadioButton2D rb)
    {
        for(e = buttons.elements(); e.hasMoreElements(); )
        {
            Object o = e.nextElement();
            if(rb != o)
            {
                ((RadioButton2D) o).setSelected(false);
            }
        }
    }


    // paints each button in the radio group
    public void paint(Graphics2D g2d)
    {
```

```
                    for(e = buttons.elements(); e.hasMoreElements(); )
                    {
                        ((RadioButton2D)e.nextElement()).paint(g2d);
                    }
                }

                // paints each button in the group at the sent offset values
                public void paint(Graphics2D g2d, double dx, double dy)
                {
                    for(e = buttons.elements(); e.hasMoreElements(); )
                    {
                        ((RadioButton2D)e.nextElement()).paint(g2d, dx, dy);
                    }
                }

        }    // RadioButtonGroup
```

Clean, efficient: I like it. And what better way to illustrate both singular as well as groups of radio buttons than with a code example? The following applet, *RadioButton2DTest*, contains a button group that allows the user to select from a number of superpowers. It also contains a stand-alone button that is capable of enabling or disabling the button group containing the superpower selections. This demo is fun to play around with, so I suggest trying it out.

```
import java.applet.*;
import java.awt.*;

public class RadioButton2DTest extends Applet implements Runnable
{
    // a Thread for animation
    private Thread animation;

    private BufferedGraphics offscreen;

    // a radio button to enable or disable the list of available superpowers
    private RadioButton2D singleRB;

    // tracks whether or not superpowers are enabled
    private boolean powersEnabled;

    // a button group containing the list of superpowers available
```

```java
private RadioButtonGroup rbGroup;

// String descriptions of the available superpowers
private final String[] POWERS =
{ "Fireball", "Super Kick", "Acid Storm", "Razor Talons", "Electroshock" };

private final int NUM_BUTTONS = POWERS.length;

// a label that describes the selection status
private Label2D status;

public void init()
{
    // create a button group for our button imaging
    ButtonImageGroup group = new ButtonImageGroup(2, "radio.gif");
    group.init(this);

    Label2D label;
    Font font = new Font("Helvetica", Font.PLAIN, 18);

    // create the "single" radio button that toggles superpower abilities
    label = new Label2D(font, "Enable Superpowers", Color.WHITE);
    singleRB = new RadioButton2D(label, group, null,
                                 new Vector2D.Double(50, 50));
    label.centerOn(singleRB.getBounds(), (Graphics2D) getGraphics());
    label.setX(
        singleRB.getBounds().getX() + singleRB.getBounds().getWidth() + 5);
    singleRB.setSelected(true);
    powersEnabled = singleRB.isSelected();
    addMouseListener(singleRB);

    // create the radio button group containing the different powers
    RadioButton2D rb;
    rbGroup = new RadioButtonGroup();
    for(int i = 0; i < NUM_BUTTONS; i++)
    {
        label = new Label2D(font, POWERS[i], Color.WHITE);

        rb = new RadioButton2D(label, group, rbGroup,
```

```java
                                new Vector2D.Double(100, 100+(i*35))));
            label.centerOn(rb.getBounds(), (Graphics2D) getGraphics());
            label.setX(rb.getBounds().getX() + rb.getBounds().getWidth() + 5);
            addMouseListener(rb);

            // the 0th button should be selected by default
            if(i == 0) rb.setSelected(true);
        }

        // set up the status label with an initial blank string
        status = new Label2D(font, "", new Color(0, 255, 255));
        status.setPos(new Vector2D.Double(50, 325));

        offscreen = new BufferedGraphics(this);

        AnimationStrip.observer = this;

    }   // init


public void start()
{
    // start the animation thread
    animation = new Thread(this);
    animation.start();
}

public void stop()
{
    animation = null;
}

public void run()
{
    Thread t = Thread.currentThread();
    while (t == animation)
    {
        repaint();

        try
```

```java
            {
                Thread.sleep(10);
            }
            catch(InterruptedException e)
            {
                break;
            }
        }

    }    // run

    public void update(Graphics g)
    {
        // if the stand-alone selection changed, toggle the power selection
        // group
        if(powersEnabled != singleRB.isSelected())
        {
            powersEnabled = singleRB.isSelected();
            rbGroup.setVisible(powersEnabled);
        }


        // update the label description of what's going on
        if(powersEnabled == true && rbGroup.getSelection() != null)
        {
            status.setText("Selected superpower: " +
                            rbGroup.getSelection().getText());
        }
        else
        {
            status.setText("Superpowers disabled");
        }

        paint(g);
    }

    public void paint(Graphics g)
    {
        Graphics2D bg = (Graphics2D)offscreen.getValidGraphics();
        bg.setPaint(Color.BLACK);
```

```
        bg.fillRect(0, 0, getSize().width, getSize().height);

        // paint the stand-alone selection
        singleRB.paint(bg);

        // paint the button group
        rbGroup.paint(bg);

        // paint the status label
        status.paint(bg);

        g.drawImage(offscreen.getBuffer(), 0, 0, this);
    }     // paint

}     // RadioButton2DTest
```

Figure 12.8 shows two different states of the *RadioButton2DTest* applet: one with superpowers disabled and one with the "Razor Talons" superpower enabled.

As you can see, not all radio buttons need to belong to a group. Radio buttons not only can represent one selection out of many but can also serve as flags for attributes whose state can be one of two things. Radio buttons can enable or disable other buttons or menus, toggle the sound, control rendering quality, and so on. So if you're going to ask your users to make decisions, you might as well do it in style

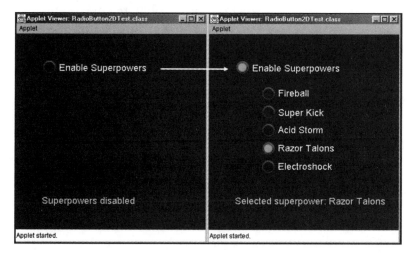

**Figure 12.8**

*The* RadioButton2DTest *applet*

and use my custom RadioButton2D class (or one that you design) along with some slick graphics of your own.

So far, I've shown you a few different custom components that you can put to work right away in your games. In the final sections of this chapter, we'll look at how to create custom containers, such as panels and menus, which are capable of containing other custom components, such as labels and buttons. We'll start by looking at the base class for holding components, the Container2D class.

# Creating the Container2D Class

Within the Java AWT, where there are visual components, there is often the need for classes that are capable of containing them. The Java Panel class is one good example of such a containment class. Classes such as Panel can contain visual components (even other containers) within their bounds, making them great for creating complex flow layouts, such as nested border layouts.

In this section, we'll continue our focus on creating a custom component system that parallels the native Component hierarchy by creating a class that mimics the Container class, called Container2D. If you'll recall, the Container class extends its functionality from Component. Likewise, the custom Container2D class extends its functionality from the Component2D class (refer back to Figure 12.2 if you need a refresher). Our goal for the Container2D class will be to emulate the functionality of the Container class as best as we can. I'll provide you with the skeleton for implementing this class and leave suggestions in the chapter exercises for you to make this class unbreakable.

Although container classes such as the Panel class hold other objects, they themselves may be visual as well. For instance, you can set the background color of a panel, window, or frame. We'll give the subclasses of Container2D, Panel2D, and Menu2D the ability to define a background image to render beneath their components. I'll leave the old standby of filling their backgrounds with Paint as a chapter exercise for you to do on your own.

For now, let's look at the code for the Container2D class. Notice that most methods are left incomplete, making it an abstract class.

```
import java.awt.*;
import java.util.*;


// defines a container capable of containing other components
public abstract class Container2D extends Component2D
```

```
{
    // a dynamic vector of components and an enumeration for traversing it
    protected Vector components;
    protected Enumeration e;

    // creates a new Container2D object with the sent background image and
    // position
    protected Container2D(Vector2D p)
    {
        super();

        components = new Vector();

        pos = p;
        if(pos == null)
        {
            pos = new Vector2D.Double();
        }

        updateBounds();
    }

    // adds the sent component to the container at the sent location
    public abstract void add(Component2D c, double x, double y);

    // updates the bounds of the container
    public abstract void updateBounds();

}    // Container2D
```

Although the Container2D class extends Component2D, I've decided to override the updateBounds method and re-declare it as abstract. Since subclasses will most likely be using Image objects as their background instead of an ImageGroup, they will need to define their bounds differently. Also note that I have not defined either of the Component2D paint methods either; therefore, Container2D subclasses will still be responsible for defining these two methods as well.

Before we get to the subclasses of the Container2D class, I'll point out again that components added to it should be added with respect to the container's origin, not the origin of the Applet or Window. And that's the whole point of the Container2D class: to physically keep its child components within its bounds. Figure 12.9 illustrates just that.

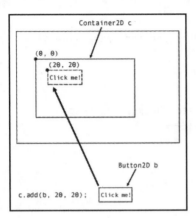

**Figure 12.9**

*Adding a component with respect to its parent container*

With that in mind, let's proceed to our first class that extends the Container2D class, Panel2D.

# The Panel2D Class

You saw way back in Chapter 5 that the Java Panel class is great for visually grouping related components. For instance, if your applet is using a BorderLayout for its layout management, panels can be added to the four ordinal directions as well as the center. Components added to these panels will be kept together according to their parent panel's own layout manager. Overall, each component is placed relative to its direct parent container.

Now that you have seen how to create the Container2D class to physically place components within a parent container, you are now ready to implement a class that actually implements the methods for adding and painting components. The first class we'll look at that does this is the Panel2D class. Like the Panel class, components that are added to a Panel2D object are kept within its bounds. The benefit of the Panel2D class is that components can be added at specific x, y locations, giving you added control over component placement.

Another benefit of the Panel2D class is that you can specify an Image that serves as the background of the panel. Logically, you should always render the background image before rendering its child components.

The following code listing is for the completed Panel2D class. It defines all incomplete methods declared by the Component2D and Container2D classes, making it a complete and usable class.

```java
import java.awt.*;
import java.awt.geom.*;
import java.util.*;

// defines a panel capable of containing other components
public class Panel2D extends Component2D
{
    // the background image of the Panel
    protected Image background;

    // a dynamic vector of components and an enumeration for traversing it
    protected Vector components;
    protected Enumeration e;

    // creates a new Panel2D object with the sent background image and position
    protected Panel2D(Image bgImage, Vector2D p)
    {
        super();

        background = bgImage;

        components = new Vector();

        pos = p;
        if(pos == null)
        {
            pos = new Vector2D.Double();
        }

        updateBounds();
    }

    // adds the sent component to the panel at the sent location
    // note the sent x, y values are relative to the origin (upper-left)
    // of the Panel
    public void add(Component2D c, double x, double y)
    {
        c.setX(getX() + x);
```

```java
            c.setY(getY() + y);

            // make sure the component fits within the bounds of the panel
            if(c.getX() + c.getBounds().getWidth() >
               getX() + getBounds().getWidth())
            {
                c.setX(getX() + getBounds().getWidth() - c.getBounds().getWidth());
            }

            if(c.getY() + c.getBounds().getHeight() >
               getY() + getBounds().getHeight())
            {
              c.setY(getY() + getBounds().getHeight() - c.getBounds().getHeight());
            }

            c.update();
            c.updateBounds();
            components.add(c);
    }

    // paints the panel and its components
    public void paint(Graphics2D g2d)
    {
            // draw the background
            if(background != null)
            {
                g2d.drawImage(background, (int) getX(), (int) getY(),
                            AnimationStrip.observer);
            }

            // paint the panel components
            for(e = components.elements(); e.hasMoreElements(); )
            {
                ((Component2D) e.nextElement()).paint(g2d);
            }
    }

    // paints the panel and its components at the given offset values
    public void paint(Graphics2D g2d, double dx, double dy)
    {
```

```
            if(background != null)
            {
                g2d.drawImage(background, (int)(getX() + dx), (int)(getY() + dy),
                            AnimationStrip.observer);
            }

            for(e = components.elements(); e.hasMoreElements(); )
            {
                ((Component2D)e.nextElement()).paint(g2d, dx, dy);
            }
        }

        // updates the bounds of the panel--if the panel has no image, no other
        // attempts will be made to calculate the panel's bounds
        public void updateBounds()
        {
            if(background != null)
            {
                frameWidth  = background.getWidth(AnimationStrip.observer);
                frameHeight = background.getHeight(AnimationStrip.observer);
            }
            else
            {
                frameWidth  = Integer.MAX_VALUE;
                frameHeight = Integer.MAX_VALUE;
            }

            bounds.setRect(pos.getX(), pos.getY(), frameWidth, frameHeight);
        }

    }    // Panel2D
```

Figure 12.10 illustrates how a Button2D object can be added to a custom panel.
As promised, components added to Panel2D objects are added with respect to the
panel's origin. So if a panel is located at (100, 100) and a button is added to a panel
at (20, 20), the button will actually be added at (120, 120). If the button's end
position places it outside of the panel, it will be replaced to fit within its bounds.
The exercises at the end of this chapter will ask you to make improvements to the
Container2D and Panel2D classes, such as keeping components relative to the panel
if its position is changed.

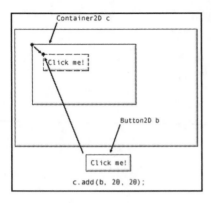

**Figure 12.10**

*Adding a component with respect to its parent container*

Notice that the `Panel2D` class makes use of the static `AnimationStrip observer` field when it needs to determine the size of the background image. So remember to always set this field in your applet's `init` method before calling methods that use the `observer` field.

Let's try a simple example. The *Panel2DTest* applet creates two panels and adds a few components to each at the same logical positions. You'll notice when you run the applet that the components will be placed with respect to its parent container.

```java
import java.applet.*;
import java.awt.*;

public class Panel2DTest extends Applet implements Runnable
{
    // a Thread for animation
    private Thread animation;

    private BufferedGraphics offscreen;

    // an array of Panel2D objects to contain other components
    private Panel2D[] panels;

    // the coordinates for placing the above Panel2D objects
    private Vector2D[] panelPos = { new Vector2D.Double( 10,  10),
                                    new Vector2D.Double(200, 100) };
    private final int NUM_PANELS = panelPos.length;

    public void init()
```

```java
    {
        // create an image group containing transparent buttons
        ButtonImageGroup biGroup = new ButtonImageGroup(3, "xpbuttons.gif");
        biGroup.init(this);

        // create an image group for some radio buttons
        ButtonImageGroup rbGroup = new ButtonImageGroup(2, "radio2.gif");
        rbGroup.init(this);

        // remember to set the observer field so panels can access its
        // background image's width and height
        AnimationStrip.observer = this;

        // a button, radio button, and label for creating components to add to
        // our panels
        Button2D button;
        RadioButton2D radioButton;
        Label2D label;

        Font font = new Font("Helvetica", Font.PLAIN, 16);

        // create the background image for the panels
        Image img = new ImageLoader(this, "panel.gif", true).getImage();

        // create the panels and add them to the scene
        panels = new Panel2D[NUM_PANELS];
        for(int i = 0; i < NUM_PANELS; i++)
        {
            // create a panel with the background image and indexed position
            panels[i] = new Panel2D(img, panelPos[i]);

            // add a radio button and two regular buttons to the panel
            radioButton = new RadioButton2D(null, rbGroup, null);
            panels[i].add(radioButton, 95, 95);
            radioButton.setSelected(true);
            addMouseListener(radioButton);

            label = new Label2D(font, "Java!", Color.WHITE);
            button = new Button2D(label, biGroup);
```

```java
                panels[i].add(button, 25, 25);
                label.centerOn(button.getBounds(), (Graphics2D) getGraphics());
                addMouseListener(button);
                addMouseMotionListener(button);

                label = new Label2D(font, "Java!", Color.WHITE);
                button = new Button2D(label, biGroup);
                panels[i].add(button, 130, 185);
                label.centerOn(button.getBounds(), (Graphics2D) getGraphics());
                addMouseListener(button);
                addMouseMotionListener(button);
        }

        offscreen = new BufferedGraphics(this);

    }   // init

    public void start()
    {
        // start the animation thread
        animation = new Thread(this);
        animation.start();
    }

    public void stop()
    {
        animation = null;
    }

    public void run()
    {
        Thread t = Thread.currentThread();
        while (t == animation)
        {
            repaint();

            try
            {
```

```
                    Thread.sleep(10);
            }
            catch(InterruptedException e)
            {
                break;
            }
        }

    }   // run


    public void update(Graphics g)
    {
        paint(g);
    }

    public void paint(Graphics g)
    {
        Graphics2D bg = (Graphics2D)offscreen.getValidGraphics();
        bg.setPaint(Color.BLACK);
        bg.fillRect(0, 0, getSize().width, getSize().height);

        // paint the panels
        for(int i = 0; i < NUM_PANELS; i++)
        {
            panels[i].paint(bg);
        }

        g.drawImage(offscreen.getBuffer(), 0, 0, this);
    }   // paint

}   // Panel2DTest
```

The *Panel2DTest* applet can be seen in Figure 12.11. Lovely, isn't it?

Pretty simple. The *Panel2DTest* applet uses the standard animation loop and actively updates and paints the panels. The panels, in turn, update and render their child components.

Let's look at one more Container2D class that extends the Panel2D class: the Menu2D class.

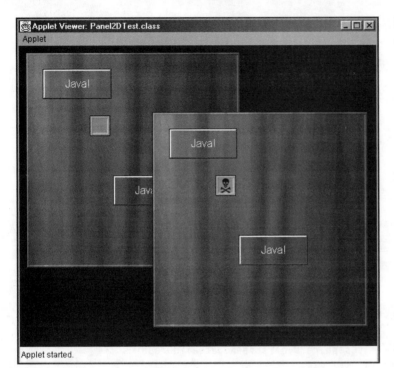

**Figure 12.11**

The Panel2DTest *applet*

# Creating Custom Menus with Menu2D

As your games become more complex and feature-rich, a custom menuing system will definitely come in handy. You already know how to use the native Java AWT components as well as custom components to communicate with the user. However, it helps to have a containment unit that is capable of holding components and displaying them only when they are needed.

Another important feature of menus is that once a menu is called, it generally should be given the entire user focus. For instance, when a menu is called, it should be the only active interface with the user; all other game action should be temporarily suspended. You'll need to keep this in mind when controlling menu updating and rendering.

For the custom menu system, I've decided to extend the Panel2D class and create the Menu2D class. Since the Panel2D class already contains the features for holding components within its bounds, as well as specifying its own background image, Menu2D should be simple to write.

At first glance, the `Panel2D` class seems like a sufficient class to use as a menu. However, I saw one big feature I wanted to add, and that is the *overlay* feature. If a particular menu is an overlay menu, then it will be rendered on top of the current scene. So if a menu is half the size of the scene, what's going on in the background will still be visible. On the other hand, if a menu is not an overlay menu, then it will be the only thing rendered as long as it is active and visible. This feature can come in handy when you don't want the user to be able to view the game action while a menu is being displayed. For instance, in a time-sensitive puzzle game, you probably don't want the user to pause the game by bringing up a menu when time is running out and plan out his or her next move while the timer is paused. Adding the overlay flag to the `Menu2D` class allows you to specify how menus are presented.

With that in mind, take a look at the code for the `Menu2D` class. This class is really simple, so if you're coding these classes as you go you won't have much typing to do.

```java
import java.awt.*;

// provides a simple menu class capable of overlaying the scene
public class Menu2D extends Panel2D
{
    // determines if the menu merely overlays the scene or if it dominates
    // the rendering loop
    protected boolean overlay;

    // constructs a new Menu2D object with the sent background image,
    // position, and overlay value
    protected Menu2D(Image bgImage, Vector2D p, boolean over)
    {
        super(bgImage, p);

        overlay  = over;
    }


    // returns if this menu is an overlay
    public final boolean isOverlay()
    {
        return overlay;
    }

}    // Menu2D
```

Another reason I decided to override the Panel2D class is because I wanted to maintain the naming mechanism that the Menu2D class provides. I think of a menu as a component that acts independently of the scene and is given focus while active. A panel, on the other hand, is a functional component that can coexist with the scene and does not pause game action. In short, a menu is a type of panel, but a panel is not a type of menu.

Now that you have a good idea of what a menu's responsibilities are, how do you actually implement a custom menuing system? Certainly you'll need a way to hop from one menu to another and remember where you've been in case you need to revisit a menu. I have found that a great way to manage menu transitions is by using what I call a *menu stack*. (Refer back to Chapter 4 if you need a refresher on how the Java Stack class works.) By using a menu stack, you can push menus onto the stack as they are called, then pop them back off as they are dismissed.

For instance, say you hit the Escape key to bring up the main menu. This will push the main menu onto the stack. From there, you click a button to call the options menu, which is in turn pushed onto the stack. The options menu contains a button that brings up a menu that allows you to control the volume and sound quality played during the game. This pushes a third menu onto the stack. After turning down the volume, you dismiss the sound options menu by pressing the Back button. This pops the sound menu from the stack. You do the same thing for both the main options menu as well as the main menu. This pops these menus from the stack as well. Once the menu stack is cleared, regular game play can then continue as normal.

That's how the menu stack works. If there are any menus on the stack, the menu on the top will be the one displayed to the user. Requesting a new menu will push it onto the stack; likewise, dismissing a menu will remove it from the stack. Figure 12.12 shows a menu stack in its active state, with a sound options menu at the top of the stack.

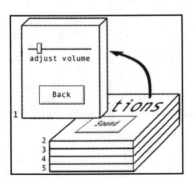

**Figure 12.12**

*Using a Stack for menu management*

When it comes down to painting the scene, I use the following algorithm to properly determine what to draw:

```
<clear the drawing surface>

if(<the menu stack is not empty>)
{
    if(<the top menu is an overlay menu>)
    {
        <paint the scene>
    }

    <paint the top menu>
}
else
{
    <paint the scene>
}
```

According to this routine, after clearing the drawing surface you must first check if the menu stack has anything on it. If it does, then check if the top menu is an overlay menu. If it is an overlay menu, then paint the scene before painting the menu. Otherwise, just paint the menu. If the menu stack ends up being empty, then just paint the scene as normal. A similar algorithm can be used in the update method as well. If the menu stack has at least one item on it, you would probably suppress any game processing for that frame and move right on to calling the paint method. Otherwise, you would update the scene as normal.

Let's solidify all of this and look at an applet that demonstrates the use of multiple menus. The following applet, *Menu2DTest*, contains three different menus, each of which reference the same three buttons. Each button allows you do bring up one of the three menus. The button that normally calls the currently active menu is disabled so that the same menu cannot redundantly call itself. Also, you can press the Escape key to dismiss the currently active menu or call the default menu if the stack is already empty. Since the code for the *Menu2DTest* is rather lengthy, you may want to copy it from the CD-ROM instead of typing it all in.

```
import java.applet.*;
import java.awt.*;
import java.awt.event.*;
```

```java
import java.util.*;

public class Menu2DTest extends Applet implements Runnable, KeyListener
{
    // a Thread for animation
    private Thread animation;

    private BufferedGraphics offscreen;

    // a couple of sample menus for the applet
    private Menu2D menuA;
    private Menu2D menuB;
    private Menu2D menuC;

    // buttons to be placed on the above menus
    private Button2D goToA;
    private Button2D goToB;
    private Button2D goToC;

    // a stack for holding menus
    private Stack menuStack;

    public void init()
    {
        AnimationStrip.observer = this;

        // get a Graphics2D context for centering labels
        Graphics2D g2d = (Graphics2D) getGraphics();

        // create an image group for the menu buttons
        ButtonImageGroup group = new ButtonImageGroup(3, "xpbuttons.gif");
        group.init(this);

        // setup navigation buttons
        Label2D label;
        Font font = new Font("Helvetica", Font.PLAIN, 18);

        label = new Label2D(font, "Menu A", Color.BLACK);
        label.setDisabledPaint(Color.WHITE);
        goToA = new Button2D(label, group);
```

```java
        label.centerOn(goToA.getBounds(), g2d);
        addMouseListener(goToA);
        addMouseMotionListener(goToA);

        label = new Label2D(font, "Menu B", Color.BLACK);
        label.setDisabledPaint(Color.WHITE);
        goToB = new Button2D(label, group);
        label.centerOn(goToB.getBounds(), g2d);
        addMouseListener(goToB);
        addMouseMotionListener(goToB);

        label = new Label2D(font, "Menu C", Color.BLACK);
        label.setDisabledPaint(Color.WHITE);
        goToC = new Button2D(label, group);
        label.centerOn(goToC.getBounds(), g2d);
        addMouseListener(goToC);
        addMouseMotionListener(goToC);

        // set up our listener class
        ActionListener listener = new ActionListener()
        {
            // push the proper menu onto the stack according to which
            // button was pressed
            public void actionPerformed(ActionEvent e)
            {
                if(goToA == e.getSource())
                {
                    // show menu 'A'
                    menuStack.push(menuA);
                    updateButtonSettings();
                }

                else if(goToB == e.getSource())
                {
                    // show menu 'B'
                    menuStack.push(menuB);
                    updateButtonSettings();
                }

                else if(goToC == e.getSource())
```

```
                    {
                        // show menu 'C'
                        menuStack.push(menuC);
                        updateButtonSettings();
                    }
            }
    };


    // register the applet to receive action events from our buttons
    goToA.addActionListener(listener);
    goToB.addActionListener(listener);
    goToC.addActionListener(listener);


    // set up custom menus
    Label2D header;
    final Vector2D pos = new Vector2D.Double(100, 50);


    menuA = new Menu2D(new ImageLoader(
                        this, "menuA.gif", true).getImage(), pos, false);
    header = new Label2D(font, "Menu A", Color.BLACK);
    menuA.add(header, 0, 0);
    header.centerOn(menuA.getBounds(), g2d);
    header.setY(menuA.getY() + header.getBounds().getHeight() + 5);
    menuA.add(goToA, 78, 50);
    menuA.add(goToB, 78, 120);
    menuA.add(goToC, 78, 190);


    menuB = new Menu2D(new ImageLoader(
                        this, "menuB.gif", true).getImage(), pos, true);
    header = new Label2D(font, "Menu B", Color.BLACK);
    menuB.add(header, 0, 0);
    header.centerOn(menuB.getBounds(), g2d);
    header.setY(menuB.getY() + header.getBounds().getHeight() + 5);
    menuB.add(goToA, 78, 50);
    menuB.add(goToB, 78, 120);
    menuB.add(goToC, 78, 190);


    menuC = new Menu2D(new ImageLoader(
                        this, "menuC.gif", true).getImage(), pos, false);
```

```java
        header = new Label2D(font, "Menu C", Color.BLACK);
        menuC.add(header, 0, 0);
        header.centerOn(menuC.getBounds(), g2d);
        header.setY(menuC.getY() + header.getBounds().getHeight() + 5);
        menuC.add(goToA, 78, 50);
        menuC.add(goToB, 78, 120);
        menuC.add(goToC, 78, 190);

        goToA.centerLabel(g2d);
        goToB.centerLabel(g2d);
        goToC.centerLabel(g2d);

        // set up our menu stack
        menuStack = new Stack();
        goToA.setEnabled(false);
        goToB.setEnabled(true);
        goToC.setEnabled(true);
        menuStack.push(menuA);

        // finish up normal applet initialization

        offscreen = new BufferedGraphics(this);

        addKeyListener(this);

    }   // init

    // disables buttons that would normally call the currently
    // active menu
    private void updateButtonSettings()
    {
        if(menuStack.empty()) return;

        Menu2D menu = (Menu2D) menuStack.peek();

        if(menuA == menu)
        {
            goToA.setEnabled(false);
            goToB.setEnabled(true);
```

```java
                    goToC.setEnabled(true);
        }

        else if(menuB == menu)
        {
            goToA.setEnabled(true);
            goToB.setEnabled(false);
            goToC.setEnabled(true);
        }

        else if(menuC == menu)
        {
            goToA.setEnabled(true);
            goToB.setEnabled(true);
            goToC.setEnabled(false);
        }
    }

    public void start()
    {
        // start the animation thread
        animation = new Thread(this);
        animation.start();
    }

    public void stop()
    {
        animation = null;
    }

    public void run()
    {
        Thread t = Thread.currentThread();
        while (t == animation)
        {
            repaint();

            try
            {
```

```java
                Thread.sleep(10);
            }
            catch(InterruptedException e)
            {
                break;
            }

        }

    }   // run

    public void update(Graphics g)
    {
        paint(g);
    }

    public void paint(Graphics g)
    {
        Graphics2D bg = (Graphics2D)offscreen.getValidGraphics();
        bg.setPaint(Color.BLACK);
        bg.fillRect(0, 0, getSize().width, getSize().height);

        // make sure our text looks sharp
        bg.setRenderingHint(RenderingHints.KEY_TEXT_ANTIALIASING,
                            RenderingHints.VALUE_TEXT_ANTIALIAS_ON);

        // if the stack is not empty, process the top menu
        if(! menuStack.empty())
        {
            // draw the scene only if the top menu is an overlay menu
            if( ((Menu2D)menuStack.peek()).isOverlay())
            {
                paintScene(bg);
            }

            // paint the menu after all other rendering is done
            ((Menu2D)menuStack.peek()).paint(bg);
        }
        // if the stack was empty, paint the scene as normal
```

```java
        else
        {
            paintScene(bg);
        }

        g.drawImage(offscreen.getBuffer(), 0, 0, this);

    }   // paint

public void paintScene(Graphics2D g2d)
{
    // render a gradient paint as a placeholder for an actual "scene"
    g2d.setPaint(new GradientPaint(0.0f, 0.0f, Color.BLACK,
        (float) getSize().width, (float) getSize().height, Color.WHITE));

    g2d.fillRect(0, 0, getSize().width, getSize().height);
}

public void keyPressed(KeyEvent e)
{

}

public void keyReleased(KeyEvent e)
{

}

// updates the flow of the menu stack
public void keyTyped(KeyEvent e)
{
    // the escape key will control menu flow
    if(e.getKeyChar() == KeyEvent.VK_ESCAPE)
    {
        // if the menu stack is not empty, remove its top item
        if(! menuStack.empty())
        {
            menuStack.pop();
            updateButtonSettings();
```

```
            }

            // otherwise, push menu 'A' onto the stack
            else
            {
                 menuStack.push(menuA);
                 updateButtonSettings();
            }
        }
    }

}      // Menu2DTest
```

Figure 12.13 shows output from our final applet for this chapter: the *Menu2DTest* applet.

As you can see, pressing the various buttons will push references to the menus onto the stack. Pressing the Escape key will unwind the stack. Therefore, you can press buttons to call the three different menus all day and night; you'll be able to back up through the menu system in the order in which it was created every time.

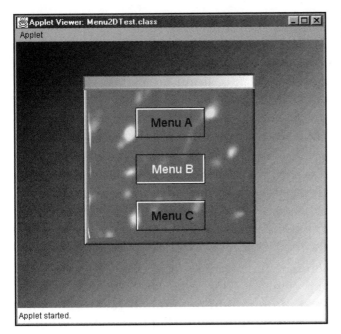

**Figure 12.13**

*The* Menu2DTest *applet*

Also note that menu B is the only menu of the three that is an overlay menu. To simulate a background scene I just used a `GradientPaint` object so you can see the difference between overlay and nonoverlay menus.

# Conclusion

Well, that's the end of my tirade on custom components and menuing systems. Although it doesn't parallel the native AWT exactly, it is good enough for the average AWT programmer to pick up and use rather quickly. Both the `Component2D` and the `Container2D` classes are key in the implementation of your custom component system. Allowing base classes to do most of the work allows you to create powerful base classes quickly and easily, as seen in the `Menu2D` class.

I purposely left out some features that could improve the functionality of your custom component system so that you can use your creative juices to improve it yourself. Several suggestions for improvement appear in the following exercises, which I hope you'll try. I had a lot of fun creating these custom components for you to look at, and I hope you'll have just as much fun using and improving them for your own purposes.

# Exercises

**12.1** We extended the `Component2D` to create custom button, radio button, and label classes, in addition to the custom `Container2D` classes. Extend the functionality of the `Component2D` class to create custom `Choice2D` and `TextField2D` classes. These classes should behave similarly to their related native AWT classes. For the `TextField2D` class, the Java AWT contains a host of font utilities for rendering text and placing a caret character in text strings. Also feel free to add any additional `Component2D` classes you feel you might use in your own endeavors.

**12.2** Add an additional field to the `Component2D` class called `parent`, which specifies which `Container2D` object is currently holding it. If the component does not have a parent, this field should be set to `null`. Be sure to update this field as components are added to their parent containers. When might it be useful for your program logic to know which object owns a particular component?

**12.3** Modify the `Container2D` class to update the positions of its child components automatically when its position is changed. This can most easily be done by calculating the change in position of the parent container before setting the new one and then moving each child component by that delta value. While you're at it, since you've already added the parent field to the Component2D class, force components to be moved with respect to their parent object's bounds whenever their position is moved as well. You'll find that by implementing these methods once up front, you'll save yourself the need to make these changes manually later. This will also solidify the contract that a Container2D object will always keep its child objects within its bounds at all times.

**12.4** Consider using a *Shape* object (for example, the Component2D bounds field) as a clipping area for painting components contained within a Container2D object, such as shown in Figure 12.14. This would allow you to change the add method to only force the origin of the added component to be within the bounding rectangle; the width and height can extend out of bounds. Any overhang of the added component will simply not be drawn.

**12.5** Create a dragging mechanism for Container2D objects so that containers can be moved around the window manually. This will require you to define a rectangular region, usually located at the north end of the container, which can catch mouse-pressed and mouse-dragged events. Remember that you'll need to update the position of the container's child objects as well. You should also create a boolean flag that determines whether a particular component is draggable or if it should remain in a fixed position.

**12.6** To alleviate the direct need for the applet to perform actions sent from components contained within a menu, try writing a menu adapter interface that supplies methods for performing actions when a menu triggers an event. These interfaces can be extended into inner classes or anonymous inner classes so they can use the existing fields already supplied by the applet.

**12.7** Create a second Label2D centerOn method that takes a Point2D object rather than a Rectangle2D object, such as the following prototype suggests:

```
public void centerOn(Rectangle2D r, Graphics2D g2d)
```

**12.8** Modify the Label2D class so that it prerenders itself to an Image object and uses that image for rendering. You can also try implementing a bitmapped font system so that labels will be rendered using predetermined font images. Remember that you'll need to repaint the image every time an internal field, such as its *Paint* or text string, is changed. Feel free to add any helper methods as needed. Will this method improve overall performance and why?

**Figure 12.14**

*Clipping a child component's overhang*

**12.9**   Modify the `Panel2D` class so that it permits several different background paint modes, namely

- a plain-vanilla background image, as you've seen already,
- a *Paint*, such as a `Color` or `GradientPaint`,
- an `Image` that is influenced by a *Paint* (such as a *TexturePaint* for image tiling), and
- no background rendering at all.

**12.10**   Try developing a few custom layout managers that will emulate the functionality of some of the more commonly used existing Java layout managers, such as `FlowLayout`, `GridLayout`, and `BorderLayout`. Be sure to supply the proper parameters to these classes as well, such as component spacing.

# CHAPTER 13

# CONNECTING WITH OTHERS! CREATING CLIENT-SERVER ARCHITECTURES

**W**hether it's with your boss, your spouse, your pet, or the person on the other end of the fast food drive-through intercom, communication can be a real pain. Computer communication is no exception.

Much like voice communication, communication between two or more computers requires some sort of medium to transmit the data. Usually network communication is carried out over a wire, but it can also be transmitted through the air.

The goal of this chapter is not to show you how packets are packed or how the actual bits of information are transmitted across the network, but to examine the broader strokes of network communication and see how they can be applied to game programming. It should come as no surprise that Java provides a highly abstracted networking toolkit built right in. We'll examine many of the classes contained in the `java.net` package and see how they can be applied to two different network paradigms: connection-oriented and connectionless networks.

# Overview of Networking in Java

Like anything else, different networking jobs require different networking tools. Jobs that require a true connection between two computers have different needs than jobs that deal with a single computer sending out broadcast messages to any number of computers. I'll refer to these tools as *protocols*. A protocol is simply an agreement of how two or more computers will communicate. Communication among computers includes knowing when the sending computer has completed transmitting data, having the receiving computer acknowledge received packets of information, and dealing with any errors that can happen along the way. Terms such as *handshaking* and *packet loss* are commonly used when talking about network protocols.

As mentioned above, we'll look at two types of network connection protocols: connection-oriented and connectionless protocols. Let's begin by taking a glance at the differences and similarities between these two protocols.

# Connection-Oriented Versus Connectionless Networks

Simply stated, a *connection-oriented* protocol involves a dedicated connection between a host and a client computer. Being connection-oriented means that there is a single specific path for data to travel from one computer to the other, as shown in Figure 13.1.

The advantage here is that data is guaranteed to arrive in the order in which it was sent, as each packet follows the same exact route. So if the packets shown in Figure 13.1 contain a single character each and are sent in the order "H", "E", "L", "L", "O", then the receiving computer is guaranteed to receive the packets in the same order.

TCP, or *Transmission Control Protocol,* is one type of networking protocol you've certainly heard of before. TCP uses a "windowing" system to transmit and acknowledge packets. Here, packets no larger than an agreed upon "window" size, such as 64 or 128 kilobytes, are sent. As packets are received, an acknowledgment is sent back to the original sender so it knows it's okay to send the next packet. If enough time goes by that the sender does not receive an acknowledgment, it can then assume that the packet never got there and resend the lost data. This is a simplified explanation of how TCP error-checking works. TCP is a connection-oriented protocol, so you know that packets arrive in the order in which they are sent. I make this distinction because, as you'll see, *connectionless protocols* make no guarantees as to the order in which packets are sent—or received!

Another protocol, called UDP, or *User Datagram Protocol,* is a commonly used connectionless protocol. Like TCP, UDP defines a protocol for how data is sent across a network. Unlike TCP, UDP does not specify any particular connection for data to flow, making it possible to broadcast data to an entire network of computers

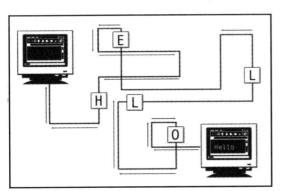

**Figure 13.1**

*A connection-oriented session*

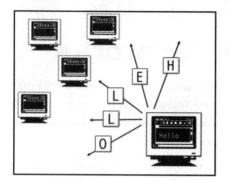

**Figure 13.2**

*A connectionless UDP session*

rather than a single connected computer. A simple UDP session might look like that depicted in Figure 13.2, above.

In Figure 13.2, the characters that make up the string 'HELLO' are sent in a specific order, but not through any specific route. It is up to the data packets themselves to find their way to their final destination. Therefore, they arrive in the order in which they get there, which is not necessarily the order in which they were sent. For instance, say the "H" packet takes a certain route to its destination computer. Halfway there, it gets bogged down in traffic and must be rerouted. Packets "E", "L", and "L" are then sent on their way as well. By the time the "O" packet is sent, traffic has cleared up on the original route taken by "H", and it has a clean trip to its destination. Immediately after "O" makes it to its destination, "E", "L", and "L" arrive. Finally, the leading "H" packet arrives, after being rerouted halfway across the world. The receiving computer can now reassemble the message into its original form. We don't need to get into how this is done, since it is taken care of automatically by the underlying hardware and software. What you will need to know is how the various network protocols can be established and used.

Note that data sent over a UDP connection will generally be faster, since data is free to find its own route to the destination. However, UDP is also less reliable since packets can be lost and are not acknowledged in any particular way.

Now that you know some of the protocols for establishing network connections, you need a way to actually address and deliver the data. Since we're dealing with networking within the Internet, it only makes sense to use what is called the *Internet Protocol,* or IP. IP specifies both the format for data to be sent as well as the addressing system. IP data packets are also referred to as *datagrams* and contain both the data to be sent as well as the destination address. Think of it in terms of the postal system—a piece of mail is a packet containing both data (the message) as well as the destination address (usually the name, street, city, state, and ZIP code of the receiver). Mail is then sent through a specific protocol, whether it's FedEx, UPS, or the good old-fashioned government mailing service.

You're already very familiar with the addressing scheme used by IP, whether you know it or not. IP uses both dotted quad as well as domain naming schemes to address data packets. Dotted quad notation contains 32 bits of information about the recipient and comes in the form *xxx.xxx.xxx.xxx*. Here, *xxx* refers to an eight-bit number ranging from 0 to 256. Therefore, 208.186.46.20 is one valid example of an address in dotted quad format. I won't get into what these numbers mean here; as long as you can get the current Internet address from the host computer, you'll have what you need to make the connection.

As I mentioned above, IP addressing also comes in a domain name flavor. The Internet address java.sun.com is one example of a domain name. Since it is generally easier for humans to remember words than numbers, domain names are used just as a convenience for people to remember. Domain names can be converted into machine-readable dotted quad form by a DNS, or *Domain Name System,* server. If one server does not know how to resolve an address, it will ask the next one, and so on until the address is resolved. So when you type "http://java.sun.com/" into your Web browser, the DNS will automatically convert it to "http://192.18.97.71/" for you. Try typing in both of these address formats in separate Web browsers; you'll find that they refer to the exact same place.

Now that you have some background on how basic networking schemes are used, let's dig in to some Java code that implements these network features.

## Implementing Connection-Oriented Networks Using TCP

In a connection-oriented society, the servers stand as the almighty pillars of communication. It is their job to sit and wait for connection requests from clients. For every connection made with a client, a service thread is generated so that the server can continue waiting for service requests. Once the client or server is finished with what it needs to do, the connection can then be terminated. This completes the cycle contained by the client-server connection model.

If you've ever implemented a client-server TCP network program in C, you've probably used the fork command to thread off the actual service. The approach in Java is similar but uses the Thread class to create a thread of execution, rather than forking off an entirely new process. You also may be familiar with using sockets in C

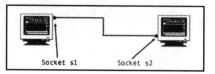

**Figure 13.3**

*Connecting two computers via the Socket class*

before. Java provides you with a Socket class, which creates a virtual endpoint of communication between two machines. Figure 13.3 shows two terminals, each with a Socket connection for transmitting data. Like all network-related Java classes we'll discuss in this chapter, the Socket class is found under the java.net package.

Possibly the easiest way to create a Socket object is by calling the constructor that takes two arguments: a String object that describes the host, and an integer that defines the port number. We've already discussed how the domain host mechanism works, but what is a port? A *port* simply refers to which service you are requesting on a particular computer. For instance, I could have a computer whose address is my.domain.com. On it, I could provide a number of different services, such as FTP, HTTP, or basic ping and time services. All the port specification does is tell the computer hosting the services which specific service is requested. For example, port 21 is the universal default port number for the FTP service; port 80 is used for HTTP services. You can define a port number for your own services as well. However, port numbers up to 1024 are reserved, so you should pick a higher number. Actually, the port number is specified by a 16-bit integer, so you have roughly 64,512 other port numbers to choose from. The following code creates a new Socket object named s:

```
Socket s = new Socket("localhost", 1234);
```

So that the examples shown in the chapter can be run on a single computer, I will always specify the host computer as "localhost." The "localhost" domain name always refers to the local computer in the network. This domain name always resolves to 127.0.0.1 in dotted quad format. Using this format will allow you to run both client and server programs all on one machine without the need to transfer programs to a remote server. I will also specify port 1234 as the default port for all services. Depending on your needs, you can always specify another port number to use. It's up to you.

Once two computers have established their socket connections, you can imagine a sort of "virtual cable" connecting the two. You don't know much about the physical connection that is made, but you don't really need to. All you need to know is how you can transmit and receive data from one computer to another.

Besides being able to open and close socket connections (which you'll see in a bit), you can also retrieve the input and output objects that send and receive data. All socket communication in Java is accomplished by using stream objects, namely those found under the `java.io` package. We examined these classes during the discussion on reading and writing data from and to the console in Part One. Network streams work much the same way. The input stream of a `Socket` object is specified as an `InputStream` object; similarly, an `OutputStream` object specifies the output stream of a `Socket`. But since we'll be dealing mostly with `String` objects rather than raw bytes, we should define the input stream as a `BufferedReader` and the output stream as a `PrintStream` at construction time, as in the following:

```
in  = new BufferedReader(new InputStreamReader(socket.getInputStream()));
out = new PrintStream(socket.getOutputStream());
```

To illustrate how socket connections can be used, I'll show you a technique that I have found quite useful in the past. Since we're on the topic of protocols, you can devise a set of protocols for your client-server programs to follow. This protocol can involve agreeing on how to parse a message into its component parts. For instance, say you have a weather and time service on the same port of your server. Connecting clients can request the current weather conditions in any state or country and the time in any time zone. Therefore, it would be handy to be able to parse a single incoming client message into the component parts of what it is requesting. An easy way to do this would be to specify which service (either weather or time) the client is requesting first, then appending the required parameter to the end of the message (either the state, country, or time zone). Of course, you will need to insert a delimiting string between the service name and the parameter so the server will know how to parse the message. Once the server receives the message, it will then be able to parse it and carry out the requested command, possibly sending back the requested data in a similar format. The server might also return an error message if the request could not be carried out, such as if the client specified a time zone for the weather service or if the service or parameter was not recognized. In all, the client and server must agree on the order in which message components are assembled, the service commands and parameters that are valid, and the text string that will separate the service name from the parameter.

Figure 13.4 shows an example of a request made by a client connected to the weather and time service. Here, the client is requesting the time service, denoted by string "TIME", along with the "Pacific" string, representing a request for the current time in the Pacific time zone. You can also see that the agreed upon delimiting string is "||". It is always a good idea to choose a delimiting string that normally

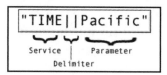

**Figure 13.4**

*Packing an entire service request into a single message*

would not appear anywhere else in the message, so that there will be no confusion as to where the message is separated

So how is the agreement for the valid parameters for the protocols made? One way would be to have both sides perform a handshaking routine at the time they connect. In the above scenario, the server can send out a list of all available services and parameters, as well as the delimiting character. This is a good method for when the options are dynamic and could not be known beforehand. It also allows you to put all of the constants in one place in your code. However, for our purposes, we will hard-code these values within our programs directly. This method will work fine as long as we are consistent and remember to change the code in both client and server code should anything change.

Now that you know the components that make up a TCP connection, and how messages are sent and received, let's look at a class that puts everything together into a single unit.

## The AbstractConnection Class

I wrote the AbstractConnection class as a means of wrapping common Socket operations, such as opening, closing, reading from, and writing to the Socket, into a single class. I also wanted to implement the message-parsing mechanism that I discussed earlier. Since you already know how to read from and write to I/O streams, there isn't much more for me to explain. So here's the code for the AbstractConnection class. Pay attention to the methods for opening and closing the connection, the methods for reading and writing to the socket, and the methods for parsing body and header parts from the unparsed message.

```
import java.io.*;
import java.net.*;
import java.util.*;

// this class defines all communications between client and server
public class AbstractConnection
{
```

```java
// the String that will separate the header from the message
public final String MSG_DELIM = "||";

// command to end the session
public static final String END_OF_TRANSMISSION = "EOT";

// a Socket for endpoint communication
protected Socket socket;

// the message received, including header, body, and delimiting string
protected String message;

// reader and writer for Socket I/O
protected BufferedReader  in;
protected PrintStream     out;

// creates an AbstractConnection object with no specified Socket
protected AbstractConnection()
{
    socket = null;
}

// creates an AbstractConnection object with the specified socket
public AbstractConnection(Socket clientSocket)
{
    socket = clientSocket;
}

// attempts to open the Socket for I/O
protected boolean open()
{
    // attempt to open the input and output streams
    try
    {
        in  = new BufferedReader(
                new InputStreamReader(socket.getInputStream()));
        out = new PrintStream(socket.getOutputStream());
    }
    catch(IOException e)
```

```java
            {
                System.err.println("Could not create socket streams; " +
                                   "closing connection.");
                // attempt to cleanly close the socket
                close(true);
                return false;
            }
            return true;
    }


    // attempts to close the socket
    protected final void close(
        boolean ioError     // true if connection is closing due to an I/O error
        )
    {

        // send an End Of Transmission first if an error occurred
        // this should hopefully terminate the service on the other end of the
        // connection
        if(! ioError)
        {
            send(END_OF_TRANSMISSION, "");
        }

        try
        {
            socket.close();
        }
        catch(IOException e)
        {
            System.err.println("Could not close socket connection.");
        }
    }


    // sends a command along with the specified message
    protected void send(String header, String msg)
    {
        // send the message only if the socket is connected
        if(socket.isConnected())
        {
            out.println(header + MSG_DELIM + msg);
```

```java
        }
        else
        {
            System.err.println("Socket not connected; terminating thread.");
        }
    }

// parses the header from the message
protected String parseHeader()
{
    if("".equals(message)) return "";

    StringTokenizer st = new StringTokenizer(message, MSG_DELIM);
    if(st.hasMoreTokens())
    {
        return st.nextToken();
    }
    return "";
}

// parses the message part from the overall message
protected String parseMessage()
{
    if("".equals(message)) return "";

    // create a StringTokenizer with the message and string delimiter
    StringTokenizer st = new StringTokenizer(message, MSG_DELIM);

    // advance one token, then return the second
    if(st.hasMoreTokens())
    {
        st.nextToken();

        if(st.hasMoreTokens())
        {
            return st.nextToken();
        }
    }

    return "";
```

```
        }

        // attempts to receive a message from the input stream
        protected void recv()
        {
            message = "";

            try
            {
                message = in.readLine();
            }
            catch(IOException e)
            {
                System.err.println("Unable to receive message; +
                                    "terminating connection.");
                close(true);
            }
        }

    }    // AbstractConnection
```

Let's break the AbstractConnection class down so you can see its component parts in more detail. First, I've defined the delimiting String as "||". This is the string that will serve as the delimiter between a message's header and body, as in the message shown in Figure 13.4. I have also defined the String "EOT" to represent the end-of-transmission message. As you'll soon see, when a client receives this message from another client it will know that the other client wants to terminate the session and will act appropriately.

The socket variable represents the Socket object that will logically keep the connection alive. Again, you don't need to know how this class works internally; all you need to know is how to read from and write to it and everything will work fine. That's where the in and out variables come in. Once an AbstractConnection object is created, a BufferedReader and PrintStream object can be created and wrapped around the socket's internal input and output streams. These objects will be assigned in and out, respectively. We'll then use the in and out variables to read from and write to the socket variable.

The AbstractConnection class contains a single constructor method. It takes a Socket object that will be passed from another object. As you'll se, when AbstractConnection objects are created, it will be calling objects that will actually create the Socket object for it to use. All the constructor has to do is copy the reference to the internal socket variable.

The open and close methods are pretty self-explanatory. The open method creates a BufferedReader (for input) object using the socket's getInputStream method. The BufferedReader class facilitates an excellent way to read character strings from a stream, perfect for our endeavors. The open method will similarly create the out variable by calling the socket variable's getOutputStream method.

As you would expect, the close method closes the socket and terminates the connection. I have provided an additional ioError parameter (a boolean) to flag any I/O errors that occurred. If any read or write errors occur, the AbstractConnection object will close the connection and send true to the close method. This will cause the socket to attempt to tell the other client that it has decided to terminate the connection. The other client will then know not to attempt to send or receive any more messages.

The send and recv methods are rather self-explanatory as well. The send method will attempt to send the sent message through the output stream only if the socket is connected. The println method from the out variable will send the message header and body, sandwiched around the delimiter string. So, according to the current definition of the delimiter string, if you pass "Feng" and "Shui" to the send method, the following text string will be sent:

```
"Feng||Shui"
```

Of course, the recv method does just the opposite as the send method. It stores the contents of the input stream into the message variable. The connection will be terminated if any I/O errors are caught.

Once a message has been received, it can be parsed into its header and body using the parseHeader and parseMessage methods, respectively. Both methods use a StringTokenizer object to extract the requested information from the message string. The parseHeader method extracts the first token from the message (everything before the delimiter string); the parseMessage method extracts the final token from the message (everything after the delimiter string). If you need a refresher on how the StringTokenizer class works, refer to Chapter 4.

As you can see, the AbstractConnection class contains a lot of preventative measures against various exceptions that may arise during your programs. Believe me, they're all necessary. Keep the AbstractConnection class in the back of your mind; pretty soon you'll be using it to communicate between a client and a remote service.

# The Server Class

The AbstractConnection class was written to connect clients with remote services. What you need now is a way to wait for incoming client requests and spawn these services. The following Server class does just that. The Server class defines a port number and ServerSocket object to listen for connections and implements the *Runnable* interface so that it can enter an infinite loop to listen for and create service connections. Check out the code below and we'll look at the details afterwards.

```java
import java.io.*;
import java.net.*;

// a simple server that sits and listens for remote connection requests
// the service request is then delegated to the createService method
public abstract class Server implements Runnable
{
    // the default port for server connections
    public static final int DEFAULT_PORT = 1234;

    // the port the service is located on
    protected int port;

    // a ServerSocket for listening for service requests
    protected ServerSocket listener;

    // a thread of execution for the server
    protected Thread exec;

    // exit with an error message when an exception occurs
    public static void fail(Exception e, String msg)
    {
        System.err.println(msg + ": " +  e);
        System.exit(1);
    }

    // creates a new Server object with the specified port
    public Server(int portNo)
    {
        // set the port, making sure it is non-negative and non-zero
```

```java
        port = (portNo <= 0) ? DEFAULT_PORT : portNo;

        try
        {
            listener = new ServerSocket(port);
        }
        catch (Exception e)
        {
            fail(e, "Exception occurred while creating server socket");
        }

        exec = new Thread(this);
    }

    // starts the execution thread
    public final void start()
    {
        exec.start();
    }

    // creates a service with the specified Socket
    protected abstract void createService(Socket socket);

    // the main workhorse of the server thread
    // listen for and accept connections from clients
    public void run()
    {
        System.out.println("Server: listening on port " + port);
        System.out.println("Server: use Ctrl-C to terminate service.");

        try
        {
            Thread thread = Thread.currentThread();
            while(exec == thread)
            {
                // listen for and accept the connection
                Socket clientSocket = listener.accept();

                // create the service using the accepted Socket
```

```
                createService(clientSocket);

                // print a connected message to the console
                System.out.println("\nConnected to " +
                                    clientSocket.getInetAddress() +
                                    " : " + clientSocket.getPort());

                try
                {
                    Thread.sleep(25);
                }
                catch(InterruptedException e)
                { }
            }
        }
        catch (IOException e)
        {
            fail(e, "Exception while listening for connections");
        }
    }

}   // Server
```

The Server constructor creates a new ServerSocket object at the specified port. The ServerSocket class listens to a specified port and returns a new Socket object for the service to use when a connection is requested from a client. After creating a Server object, you should then invoke its start method to begin the listening thread.

The Server class is declared as abstract in order to keep it as flexible and reusable as possible. Classes that extend the Server class will be responsible for overriding the createService method and spawning another Thread object for providing the actual service. This structure will allow the Server class to perform a single purpose, and that is to accept remote client connections. In the next section, you'll see an example of how the Server class can be extend to provide an actual service to remote clients.

The Server class contains no graphical features. Rather, it is run entirely from the command line instead. Since it runs in an infinite loop, you will need a way to terminate the program when you're finished using it. Like any console program, pressing Ctrl-C will terminate it and return you to the shell prompt.

Now let's look at an example program that extends the Server class and creates an actual service for clients to access remotely.

Ship returns to:

# THOMSON LEARNING
DISTRIBUTION CENTER
2360 PROGRESS DRIVE
HEBRON, KY 41048

The enclosed materials are compliments of
COURSE TECHNOLOGY, INC. 617 7577900

## SALES SUPPORT

SHIP TO:  LYNN GOLLEY
COURSE TECHNOLOGY INDIVIDUAL USE
C MILTON WRIGHT
BEL AIR MD 21015

## WAREHOUSE INSTRUCTIONS

SLA: 7    BOX: Staple

| LOCATION | QTY | ISBN | AUTHOR/TITLE |
|---|---|---|---|
| Y-12D-039-41 | 1 | 1-931841-07-1 | PETCHEL<br>JAVA 2 GAME PROGRAMMING |

INV# 48131676SM
PO# 34366978
DATE: 11/05/02
CARTON: 2 of 2
ID# 2927236

OFF_LINE
-SLSB

VIA: UP

PAGE 1 OF 1

BATCH: 1458839
003/003

## The EchoServer Program

With the AbstractConnection and Server classes under your belt, you can now start writing some killer services. Well, maybe not killer, but at least one that demonstrates how connection-oriented network programs are done. Thus far, we have created a client-server architecture like that shown in Figure 13.5.

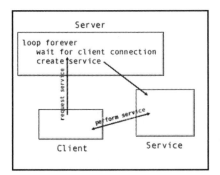

**Figure 13.5**

*Connecting a client to a TCP service*

Let's create a simple example that uses this architecture. We'll do it in two parts. First, we'll write a service class to communicate with a remote client, then we'll create a Server class that implements the createService method. The service class will extend the AbstractConnection class as well as implement the *Runnable* interface. Following is the code for the EchoService class, which will accept strings from the remote client and echo them back reversed:

```java
import java.io.*;
import java.net.*;

// the service routine provided by the server for echoing received text
class EchoService extends AbstractConnection implements Runnable
{
    // a thread of execution for the service
    private Thread exec;

    // creates a new EchoService object with the specified Socket
    public EchoService(Socket s)
    {
        super(s);

        exec = new Thread(this);
```

```java
        }

        // starts the thread of execution
        public void start()
        {
            exec.start();
        }

        // runs the execution thread
        public void run()
        {
            // open the connection
            if(! open())
            {
                System.out.println("Could not open connection.");
                return;
            }

            Thread t = Thread.currentThread();
            while(exec == t)
            {
                // wait for the next message
                recv();

                // get the message header
                String header = parseHeader();

                // quit if the client ended transmission
                if(header.equals(END_OF_TRANSMISSION))
                {
                    close(false);
                    return;
                }

                // if the header was "Reverse", reverse the message part of the
                // string and send it back to the client
                else if(header.equals("Reverse"))
                {
                    send("Echo",
```

```
                        new StringBuffer(parseMessage()).reverse().toString());
            }

            // otherwise, the response was not recognized
            else
            {
                System.err.println("Unrecognized header: " + header);
            }

            try
            {
                Thread.sleep(25);
            }
            catch(InterruptedException e)
            { }
        }
    }

} // EchoService
```

As you can see, the EchoService class implements the *Runnable* interface. Its run method will therefore communicate with the client until the end-of-transmission message is sent or an error occurs. After opening the connection, the run method will enter an infinite loop. Within this loop, strings will be read from the input stream and appropriate action will be taken. If the message header represents the end-of-transmission string, the connection will be terminated. If the header equals the String "Reverse," it will reverse the body of the incoming message and echo it back to the client. Finally, if the message header is not recognized, an error message is sent to the standard error stream. This is especially helpful when debugging your service applications.

You've seen the code for the Server class. Now let's look at how it can be extended to provide an actual service to remote clients.

```
    // a simple echo server for TCP connections
    public class EchoServer extends Server
    {
        // creates a new EchoServer with the specified port number
        public EchoServer(int portNo)
        {
            super(portNo);
```

```
    }

    // implements the Server createService method by creating a new EchoService
    // object to communicate with the client
    protected void createService(Socket socket)
    {
        new EchoService(socket).start();
    }

    // start the server up, listening on an optionally specified port
    public static void main(String[] args)
    {
        int port = 0;
        if(args.length == 1)
        {
            try
            {
                port = Integer.parseInt(args[0]);
            }
            catch(NumberFormatException e)
            {
                System.err.println("Invalid port specification; using " +
                                    "default port of " + DEFAULT_PORT);
                port = DEFAULT_PORT;
            }
        }

        // start the server
        Server s = new EchoServer(port);
        s.start();
    }

}    // EchoServer
```

The EchoServer class will be the starting point for the server side of the application. The EchoServer class looks much like the Server class, except that it also implements the main method as well as the createService method. The main method creates a new EchoServer object and lets it loose to create EchoService connections.

Try compiling and running the EchoServer program now. Better yet, try running it on a remote system if you have access to one. It will patiently sit there and wait for a client program to request a connection. The code for the EchoServer class can be found on the CD-ROM, under the \console_tcp directory in the Chapter 13 folder.

And now on to the client side of things. Like the EchoService class, the EchoClient class will extend the AbstractConnection class as well as implement *Runnable*. After a connection is made, it will initiate contact by first asking the user to input a string and then requesting the service to reverse the string. It will then output the reversed string response from the service and prompt the user for another string. This goes on until the user enters the sentinel value of "ZZZ." Check out the code, then we'll do a trial run.

```java
import java.io.*;
import java.net.*;

class EchoClient extends AbstractConnection implements Runnable
{
    // a Thread of execution for the client
    private Thread exec;

    // creates a new EchoClient with the specified Socket
    public EchoClient(Socket s)
    {
        super(s);

        exec = new Thread(this);
    }

    public void start()
    {
        exec.start();
    }

    public void run()
    {
        // open the connection
        if(! open())
        {
```

```java
        System.out.println("Could not open connection.");
        return;
    }

    // denotes end-of-input
    final String sentinel = "ZZZ";

    // create a BufferedReader for receiving user input
    BufferedReader reader = new BufferedReader(
                           new InputStreamReader(System.in));

    // a String to read from the user
    String input = "";

    while(true)
    {
        System.out.print("Enter a string, or '" + sentinel +
                         "' to quit: ");

        try
        {
            input = reader.readLine();
        }
        catch(IOException e)
        {
            System.err.println("General I/O error; client terminating.");
            close(true);
            return;
        }

        // send an EOT if the user enters the sentinel value
        if(sentinel.equals(input))
        {
            send(END_OF_TRANSMISSION, "");
            close(false);
            return;
        }

        // otherwise, request the reverse string service
        send("Reverse", input);
```

```java
                    recv();

                    // print the body of the service response
                    System.out.println(parseMessage());
            }
        }
    }    // EchoClient

// test program for TCP connections
public class TCPTest
{
    // the default port if no other is specified
    public final static int DEFAULT_PORT = 1234;

    public static void main(String[] args)
    {
        // assume the default port number until specified otherwise
        int port = DEFAULT_PORT;

        // make sure the user specified at least the host name to connect to
        if(args.length > 1)
        {
            // get the port number, if specified
            if(args.length >= 2)
            {
                try
                {
                    port = Integer.parseInt(args[1]);
                }

                catch(NumberFormatException e)
                {
                    System.err.println("Invalid port specification; using" +
                                        " default port of " + DEFAULT_PORT);
                    port = DEFAULT_PORT;
                }
            }

            // create the client
            try
```

```
                {
                        new EchoClient(new Socket(args[0], port)).start();
                }

                catch(Exception e)
                {
                        System.err.println("Could not create client socket!");
                }
            }

            // print an error message if the hostname was not specified
            else
            {
                System.out.println("Usage: java TCPTest <hostname> [<port>]");
                System.exit(0);
            }
        }    // main

    }    // TCPTest
```

The `TCPTest` class is the start-up point for the client side of the connection. It will look at the command line arguments and try to launch the client with the specified port and host name. If no port is specified, the default port is used. If no host name is specified, then the program will issue an error message and terminate.

Since I'm lazy, I just fired up the echo server and client programs on the same computer. I also used the default port number. Here's the output of the `EchoServer` program after having one connection:

```
java EchoServer
Server: listening on port 1234
Server: use Ctrl-C to terminate service.

Connected to /127.0.0.1 : 3709
```

Here's the output of a trial run I made with the `EchoClient` program as well:

```
java TCPTest localhost 1234
Enter a string, or 'ZZZ' to quit: lambchop
pohcbmal
Enter a string, or 'ZZZ' to quit: avaJ
Java
```

```
Enter a string, or 'ZZZ' to quit: hiccup
puccih
Enter a string, or 'ZZZ' to quit: redrum
murder
Enter a string, or 'ZZZ' to quit: bye
eyb
Enter a string, or 'ZZZ' to quit: ZZZ
```

There are a lot of different errors that could pop up, so testing even a simple program like this one can take some work. Try running the program with different parameters, invalid parameters, and no parameters at all. Also try running it without having an EchoServer running. A thorough program will ensure that all bases are covered in case bad or missing input is given. Also remember that the current implementation for the EchoClient class uses "ZZZ" to terminate the service, and is case-sensitive. You can change it to anything you want, and even disable case-sensitivity if necessary.

Now that you have a good understanding of how to write a TCP client-server program, let's embed one in a graphical user environment.

## The Visual GuessServer Applet

Let's focus our attention on creating a simple game (emphasis on *simple*) that uses what you've learned so far. The game we'll develop is a number-guessing game that comes in the form of a service.

For the GuessServer applet, all we need to do is wrap the server architecture we've already developed into a graphical interface. If we start by writing the server side of the game, we need to develop a visual server applet. The Server class already implements the *Runnable* interface, so all we need to specify is a component for receiving server messages. I have already written the GUIServer class for you (you can find it under the \guess_tcp directory on the CD-ROM). It uses a TextArea object for printing server messages. Other than that, it makes very few changes to the Server class, so I won't show the code here. If you're interested in looking at the GUIServer class, feel free to load it from the CD-ROM.

The following code is the workhorse for the server side of the guessing game applet. The first class is the actual GuessService class that processes the numbers sent from the client. It follows the same format as the EchoService class; only the specifics of the processing are different. Like before, you can try running this program before we look at the code for the client side of the program.

```java
import java.awt.*;
import java.applet.*;
import java.net.*;

// service for setting up a number guessing game with a client
class GuessService extends AbstractConnection implements Runnable
{
    // the target number to guess
    private int number;

    // the bounds of possible numbers to generate
    private final int LOW  = 1;
    private final int HIGH = 1000;

    // a few Strings to output when a correct guess is made
    private final String[] EXCLAIMS =
            { "Wow", "Cool", "Great", "Sweet", "Excellent", "Neat" };

    // a Thread of execution for the service
    private Thread exec;

    // creates a GuessService object with the specified Socket
    public GuessService(Socket clientSocket)
    {
        super(clientSocket);

        java.util.Random random = new java.util.Random();

        // generate a random number between LOW and HIGH
        do
        {
            number = Math.abs(random.nextInt());
        }   while(number < LOW || number > HIGH);

        // print the number to guess to the server console
        System.out.println("I'm thinking about " + number + "...");
    }

    // generates a random String from the EXCLAIMS array
```

```java
public String getRandomExclaim()
{
    java.util.Random r = new java.util.Random();
    int index = Math.abs(r.nextInt()%EXCLAIMS.length);
    return EXCLAIMS[index];
}

public void start()
{
    exec = new Thread(this);
    exec.start();
}

public void run()
{
    // open the connection
    if(! open())
    {
        System.out.println("Could not open connection.");
        return;
    }

    send("Prompt", "Enter a number between " + LOW + "and " + HIGH +
        ", or -1 to give up: ");

    // input from the client
    String str = "";

    // track the number of tries made
    int tries = 0;

    Thread t = Thread.currentThread();
    while(exec == t)
    {
        recv();

        str = parseHeader();

        // see if the user is making a guess
```

```java
if(str.equals("Guess"))
{
    int n = 0;   // the number guessed
    ++ tries;

    try
    {
        n = Integer.parseInt(parseMessage());
    }
    catch(NumberFormatException e)
    {
        // input was not a valid number
        send("Prompt",
            "Sorry, but you must guess a number! Try again: ");
    }

    // check if the user simply gave up
    if(n == -1)
    {
        send("Echo", "I'm sorry you gave up after " + tries +
            " tries! The number was " + number + "!");
    }

    // check if the guess was correct
    if(n == number)
    {
        send("Echo", getRandomExclaim() +
            "! You guessed correctly! And it only took you " +
            tries + " tries!");

        // wait a few seconds before terminating the service
        try
        {
            Thread.sleep(5000);
        }
        catch(InterruptedException e) { }

        break;
```

```
            }

            // otherwise, the number was either too high or too low

            else if(n < number)
            {
                send("Prompt", "Sorry, try guessing higher: ");
            }

            else if(n > number)
            {
                send("Prompt", "Sorry, try guessing lower: ");
            }
        }   // "Guess"

        // the client shouldn't throw any curve balls, so exit if an
        // invalid message header was sent
        else
        {
            send("Echo",
                "I don't know what you mean; terminating connection");
            return;
        }

        try
        {
            Thread.sleep(10);
        }
        catch(InterruptedException e) { }
    }

    // terminate the service
    send("Echo", "Thanks for playing!  Play again soon!");
    send(END_OF_TRANSMISSION, "");

    }   // run

}   // GuessService

// a simple server for TCP connections
```

```
public class GuessServer extends GUIServer
{
    // creates a new GuessService object
    protected void createService(Socket s)
    {
        new GuessService(s).start();
    }

}    // GuessServer
```

Be sure not to confuse the server with the service. Only the GuessServer class is visual; the GuessService class is not. GuessService threads run in the background and only communicate with the client.

Speaking of clients, it's about time we wrote a client to communicate with the guess server program. The following GuessClient program extends the Applet class and implements the *ActionListener* interface. Unlike the console client we looked at previously, the GuessClient class contains an instance of the AbstractConnection class rather than extending it. Also, since the client is running within an applet context, there is no need for a continuous input/feedback loop. Rather, it only needs to wait for input after a guess is submitted. Since the server side will sit and wait for input, you press the "Guess" button whenever you want, and the server will respond. Feedback from the server will be printed in the message field of the applet.

```
import java.awt.*;
import java.awt.event.*;
import java.applet.*;
import java.net.*;

public class GuessClient extends Applet implements ActionListener
{
    public final static int DEFAULT_PORT = 1234;

    // a TextField for user input
    private TextField textField;

    // Button for submitting guesses
    private Button button;

    // displays messages from the server
```

```java
private Label message;

// a connection for communicating with the server
private AbstractConnection client;

public void init()
{
    textField = new TextField("", 10);
    add(textField);

    button = new Button("Guess!");
    button.addActionListener(this);
    add(button);

    message = new Label();
    add(message);

    // get the port as an applet parameter
    int port = Integer.parseInt(getParameter("Port"));
    if (port == 0)
    {
        port = DEFAULT_PORT;
    }

    // get the host name as an applet parameter
    try
    {
        // create the client
        client = new AbstractConnection(new Socket(getParameter("Host"),
                                        port));

        // open the client connection
        if(! client.open())
        {
            message.setText("Could not open connection " +
                            getParameter("Host") + " : " + port);
        }
    }
    catch(Exception e)
```

```java
            {
                message.setText("Could not open connection " +
                            getParameter("Host") + " : " + port);
                disableControls();
                return;
            }
    }

    public void start()
    {
        String str = "";

        // wait for an initial service message
        client.recv();

        str = client.parseHeader();
        if(str.equals("Prompt"))
        {
            message.setText(client.parseMessage());
        }
        else
        {
            message.setText("Unrecognized server response");
            disableControls();
            return;
        }
    }

    private void disableControls()
    {
        textField.setEnabled(false);
        button.setEnabled(false);
    }

    public void actionPerformed(ActionEvent e)
    {
        // don't do anything if the text field is empty
        if(textField.getText().trim().equals("")) return;

        // temporarily disable the input button
```

```
    button.setEnabled(false);

    // send the guess to the server
    client.send("Guess", textField.getText().trim());

    // get the server response
    String str = "";
    client.recv();
    str = client.parseHeader();

    // the server will issue an echo command before terminating the service
    if(str.equals("Echo"))
    {
        // receive messages until EOT
        while(! str.equals(AbstractConnection.END_OF_TRANSMISSION))
        {
            message.setText(client.parseMessage());
            client.recv();
            str = client.parseHeader();
        }
        disableControls();
        return;
    }

    // set the message label text if the prompt command was issued
    else if(str.equals("Prompt"))
    {
        message.setText(client.parseMessage());
    }

    button.setEnabled(true);
    }

}    // GuessClient
```

Figure 13.6 shows the GuessClient and GuessServer applets being run from the same machine. Although it's a simple example, I suggest checking it out. If this is your first look at network programming, learning the fundamentals first will make writing more complex games much easier.

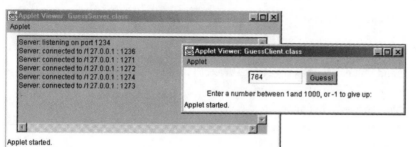

As you can see, the GuessClient is merely a graphical shell for an AbstractConnection object. Communication is done through TextField and Button objects. Once you have guessed correctly, or given up, the server and client will enter a final communication loop to say good-bye, and the service terminates. I'll leave it up to you to implement a replay option so multiple games can be played within the same session.

# Implementing Connectionless Networks Using UDP

Earlier in this chapter you learned the differences between connection-oriented and connectionless network connections. We used TCP as an example of a connection-oriented protocol and UDP as a connectionless protocol. I've already presented how TCP network connections are used in the form of the Socket class in Java. Next, you'll learn how to create a connectionless network client using the Java MulticastSocket class.

## The MulticastConnection Class

As you've seen, TCP connections are great for one-on-one communication between a client and server. Although TCP servers can thread off services for almost any number of incoming clients, all communication is confined to a two-way street. This works well for some games, such as a checkers or chess game where two people can play one another online. However, a vast number of games would require communication among a group of people rather than between two. Massively multiplayer online games are a good example of where group communication is needed. Games such as these, where thousands of people can convene at one time and that take place in a vast virtual universe, push the limits of current technology.

Group communication over a network can come in many forms. We'll focus on using what's called *multicasting* to meet the needs of a multiuser application. The term *multicasting* should not be confused with the term *broadcasting*. Broadcast clients transmit messages to everyone on the network, including those that may not be interested in receiving these messages. Multicast clients, however, narrow transmission to only those clients that belong to the same group.

A multicast environment can be thought of much like a classroom. As you know, classrooms are filled with attentive, eager students thirsty for knowledge. Communication in a classroom is kept only among those enrolled in the class. Each classroom can be thought of as a subnode of the entire network of classrooms. An announcement made over the loudspeaker piped into each classroom can be thought of as a broadcast message, since it is sent to all subnodes of the overall network. Since we're only interested in communication among members of a specific network group, transmitting packets through multicasting is the way to go.

To implement multicasting, Java provides the `MulticastSocket` class, which of course is contained under the `java.net` package. `MulticastSocket` objects are capable of connecting to groups containing other multicast clients on the Internet. The `MulticastSocket` class extends the `DatagramSocket` class, making it capable of sending IP packets in the form of datagrams.

The `MulticastSocket` class falls under what is known as *Class D* IP addressing. A Class D IP address is characterized by its first four bits. Class D addresses must contain a "1" bit in the first, second, and third bits of the address. A "0" bit must be placed as the fourth bit. The next 24 bits can be anything. The bit string for the first 8 bits of the lowest Class D address is `11100000`, which converts to 224 in decimal. The bit string for the first 8 bits of the highest Class D address is `11101111`, which is 239 in decimal. That makes the entire valid range of Class D addressing between 224.0.0.0 and 239.255.255.255, inclusive. However, keep in mind that 224.0.0.0 is reserved and 224.0.0.1 is used to send to all existing multicast hosts, so they should not be used. All other IP addresses are pretty much fair game.

I've already mentioned how multicast clients connect to a common IP address and port number. As always, the port number comes in the form of an `int`

> **NOTE**
>
> Remember, a multicast group address *must* be within the range of 224.0.0.1 through 239.255.255.255. A specified address that is not within this range will generate a `SocketException` when the multicast socket is created.

variable. Information about the IP address is encapsulated in the InetAddress class. The InetAddress class contains, among others, a static getByName method for converting a String into an IP address. An InetAddress object can therefore be created like the following:

```
InetAddress groupAddress = InetAddress.getByName("229.13.77.21");
```

I've also mentioned that the MulticastSocket class transmits and receives data in the form of IP, or datagram, packets. The DatagramPacket class is capable of containing all the information IP needs to carry a message. Remember, IP works like the mailing system; packets contain data as well as the address to which the data should be sent. Therefore, data packets can be sent like the following:

```
String msg = "Ich bin maroon";
DatagramPacket packet = new DatagramPacket(
                msg.getBytes(), msg.length(), groupAddress, port);
multicastSocket.send(packet);
```

If you've caught on to my cryptic message, then you'll know that I am indeed a sofa. Anyway, as you can see, the above packet contains the raw bytes that make up the message and its length, as well as the destination IP address and port number. Figure 13.7 shows what this structure would look like.

Receiving datagram packets is just as easy. First, you must set up a DatagramPacket with a byte array large enough to hold a message. Since you usually won't know how large the incoming message will be, you should make your byte array sufficiently large, but not too large. A one-kilobyte (1,024 byte) buffer should be good enough for most purposes. Once the packet is received, you can create a new String object that takes the bytes from the datagram packet as its parameter and print out the message, like the following:

```
byte[] data = new byte[1024];
dataPacket = new DatagramPacket(data, data.length);
multicastSocket.receive(dataPacket);
System.out.println(new String(dataPacket.getData()).trim());
```

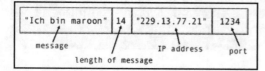

**Figure 13.7**

*Contents of a DatagramPacket*

With that in mind, here's the code for a class that encapsulates the methods for joining and leaving a multicast group, along with the methods for sending and receiving messages. We'll use the MulticastConnection class for making multicast group connections with a number of clients.

```java
import java.io.*;
import java.net.*;

public class MulticastConnection
{
    public static final int DEFAULT_PORT = 1234;

    // a multicast socket for connecting, sending, and receiving messages
    protected MulticastSocket mcSocket;

    // an IP address belonging to the multicast group
    protected InetAddress    groupAddress;

    // the port number we're connected to
    protected int            port;

    // a single IP packet for sending or receiving messages
    protected DatagramPacket dataPacket;

    // a byte array for receiving and sending data packets
    protected byte[]         data;

    // the maximum number of bytes a single packet can be
    protected final int PACKET_SIZE = 1024;

    // creates a new MulticastConnection with the specified address and port
    public MulticastConnection(String address, int portNo) throws Exception
    {
        // resolve the specified address into a valid IP address
        groupAddress = InetAddress.getByName(address);

        port = portNo;

        // make sure we connect to a valid port number
        mcSocket  = (port > 0) ? new MulticastSocket(port) :
```

```java
                                new MulticastSocket(DEFAULT_PORT);

        // link the socket to the group IP address
        mcSocket.joinGroup(groupAddress);

        data = null;
    }


    // attempts to disconnect from the group
    public void disconnect()
    {
        if(mcSocket == null) return;

        try
        {
            mcSocket.leaveGroup(groupAddress);
        }
        catch(IOException e)
        {
            // handle error message here...
        }
    }


    // attempts to receive a data packet from the group
    public String recv()
    {
        data = new byte[PACKET_SIZE];
        dataPacket = new DatagramPacket(data,data.length);

        try
        {
            mcSocket.receive(dataPacket);
        }
        catch(IOException e)
        {
            return "";
        }

        // convert the raw bytes of the packet into a valid String object
```

```
                    return new String(dataPacket.getData()).trim();
            }

            // attempts to send the specified String as an IP packet
            public boolean send(String msg)
            {
                dataPacket = new DatagramPacket(
                    msg.getBytes(), msg.length(), groupAddress, port);

                try
                {
                    mcSocket.send(dataPacket);
                }
                catch(IOException e)
                {
                    return false;
                }

                return true;
            }

    }    // MulticastConnection
```

Notice right away that the `MulticastConnection` class applies to both the server and client sides of an application. Actually, there really is no need to make the distinction between the two. A multicast group can consist completely of clients. As you'll see in the next section, a client can play the role as a server by performing tasks such as chat room moderation.

## Setting up a Simple Chat Room

A chat room is a really good example of a multicast group connection. In a way, your typical massively multiplayer role-playing game is just a glorified chat room wrapped within a visual universe. Although these games can take years to create, it all boils down to users communicating with one another within a common user environment.

Of course, you can add chat capabilities to your own games. Whether it's within a traditional mah-jongg game or a rock-'em sock-'em multiplayer deathmatch game, the ability to harass your opponents after a decisive defeat is always a nice option to have. In this section, you'll learn how to implement a simple chat service program using multicasting, such as shown in Figure 13.8.

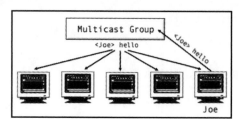

**Figure 13.8**

*Transmitting a message through a multicast group*

As I mentioned earlier, multicast connections require a host address and a port number. You can request this information from the user by asking for it to be either typed in directly or selected through another mechanism, such as a drop box containing several valid addresses. For simplicity, we'll just hard-code the values into the program.

To implement our simple chat program, I chose to create both server and client-side applications. The server's job will be only to announce a "welcome" message every minute or so for new users. The client side will be responsible for prompting the handle he or she wishes to use, then connecting to the group. It will then receive and display incoming messages, as well as send outgoing messages. We'll also implement an echoing system, so that users can choose not to display their own messages.

For a change of pace, we'll embed the chat client and server programs into a `Frame`, so that it can be run directly from the command line without the `appletviewer` utility. Here's the code for our `SimpleChatClient` program:

```java
import java.io.*;
import java.applet.*;
import java.awt.*;
import java.awt.event.*;
import java.net.*;
import java.util.*;

public class SimpleChatClient extends Applet implements ActionListener
{
    // an array of handles that are reserved by the server or any other chat
    // services
    public static final String[] reservedHandles = { "Server" };

    // the "handle", or nickname of the user
    protected String handle;

    // a MulticastConnection for communicating with a multicast group
```

```java
protected MulticastConnection client;

// text area to display incoming messages
protected TextArea textArea;

// field for typing outgoing messages
protected TextField input;

// button for sending messages
protected Button send;

// allows the client to toggle message echoing
protected Checkbox echo;

// address of the multicast group
protected String address;

// creates a new SimpleChatClient with the specified handle and address
public SimpleChatClient(String clientName, String addr) throws Exception
{
    address = addr;
    handle  = clientName;
}

public void init()
{
    // create the widgits for controlling I/O

    textArea = new TextArea("", 15, 80, TextArea.SCROLLBARS_VERTICAL_ONLY);
    textArea.setEditable(false);
    add(textArea);

    Panel p = new Panel();
    input = new TextField("", 80);
    // register the input box to send the message when the enter key is
    // typed
    input.addKeyListener(new KeyAdapter()
        {
                public void keyTyped(KeyEvent e)
```

```java
                {
                    if(e.getKeyChar() == '\n')
                    {
                        sendMessage(input.getText());
                        input.setText("");
                    }
                }
        } );

p.add(input);

send = new Button("Send");
send.addActionListener(this);
p.add(send);

add(p);

echo = new Checkbox("Echo responses", true);
add(echo);

// connect to the multicast group
try
{
    textArea.append("System Message: connecting to " + address + " : " +
                    MulticastConnection.DEFAULT_PORT + "...\n");

        client = new MulticastConnection(address,
                                        MulticastConnection.DEFAULT_PORT);

        textArea.append(
                "System Message: successfully connected to server!\n");
}
catch(Exception e)
{
    textArea.append("System Error: Could not connect to Chat Server! " +
                    e + "\n");
    send.setEnabled(false);
}
```

```
    }

    // receives incoming messages from the multicast group
    public void start()
    {
        // a received message
        String msg = "";

        // make sure we're still connected
        while(send.isEnabled())
        {
            msg = client.recv();

            // check if the client is allowing echoing
            if(echo.getState() == false)
            {
                // don't receive messages that we have sent
                if(! msg.startsWith("<" + handle + ">:"))
                {
                    textArea.append(msg+"\n");
                }
            }
            else
            {
                textArea.append(msg+"\n");
            }
        }

        textArea.append("System Message: disconnected from Chat Server!\n");
    }

    public void destroy()
    {
        // disconnect the client
        client.disconnect();
    }

    // attempts to send the specified message
```

```java
public void sendMessage(String msg)
{
    // don't send the message if it is only whitespace
    if(! "".equals(msg.trim()))
    {
        // send the user handle along with the message
        if(! client.send("<" + handle + ">: " + msg.trim()))
        {
            disconnect();
        }
    }
}

public void disconnect()
{
    client.disconnect();
    send.setEnabled(false);
}

public void actionPerformed(ActionEvent e)
{
    sendMessage(input.getText());
    input.setText("");
}

public static void main(String[] args) throws Exception
{
    // get the user's handle

    String name = "";
    BufferedReader reader = new BufferedReader(
                              new InputStreamReader(System.in));

    System.out.print("Enter your name: ");
    final String[] handles = SimpleChatClient.reservedHandles;
    name = reader.readLine();

    boolean usingReservedHandle = true;

    // make sure the user entered a non-reserved handle
```

```
            while(usingReservedHandle)
            {
                usingReservedHandle = false;
                for(int i = 0; i < handles.length; i++)
                {
                    if(name.equals(handles[i]))
                    {
                        usingReservedHandle = true;
                        System.out.print(name +
                                        " is a reserved handle; try another: ");
                        name = reader.readLine();
                        break;
                    }
                }
            }


            // create a new SimpleChatClient and add it to a Frame

            Applet a = new SimpleChatClient(name, "224.0.0.21");

            a.init();
            Frame f = new Frame("Java Chat Client - <" + name + ">");
            f.setSize(650, 400);
            f.addWindowListener(new WindowAdapter()
                {
                    public void windowClosing(WindowEvent e)
                    {
                        System.exit(0);
                    }
                } );

            f.add(a);
            f.show();
            a.start();
        }
    }    // SimpleChatClient
```

Notice that using the MulticastConnection class alleviates most of the work needed to perform basic networking tasks. The bulk of the program focuses on creating a user interface for sending and receiving messages.

The echo option is also available for those who don't want their own messages printed to the chat window. This works by filtering out messages that begin with that user's handle. Since all messages are transmitted in the following format:

```
<Joe>: hello
```

all the filter needs to do is see if the incoming message begins with "<Joe>:". If the user doesn't want to echo responses, then incoming messages such as these will simply be ignored. According to the code shown previously, the only way this mechanism can be broken is if more than one user is using the exact same handle, since only the message is checked and nothing else. Exercise 13.3 will ask you to implement a way in which all user handles are unique, making your filtering mechanism work correctly every time.

The code for the server end is very similar to that for the client end. The server does not allow any input from the user but will send a static message to welcome new users to the chat group. To do this, the server uses the TimerTask class to schedule a task to perform at a regular interval. The TimerTask class implements *Runnable*, allowing it to run as a separate thread. The following code schedules the task to send the welcome message after a one second pause, then every 60 seconds after that.

```
// create a timer to output the welcome message for new users once per minute
TimerTask task = new TimerTask()
{
        public void run()
        {
                synchronized(this)
                {
                        // have the MulticastConnection send the welcome message
                        service.send(WELCOME_MSG);
                }
        }
};

Timer msgTimer = new Timer(true);
msgTimer.scheduleAtFixedRate(task, 1000, 60000);
```

The Timer object schedules the actual scheduling of the task. You can also schedule the server to output other statements at regular intervals, such as the current time or a random quote.

To see the rest of the code for the SimpleChatServer class, check out the **CD-ROM** (under the \chat_udp directory). Notice that since the server and client applications

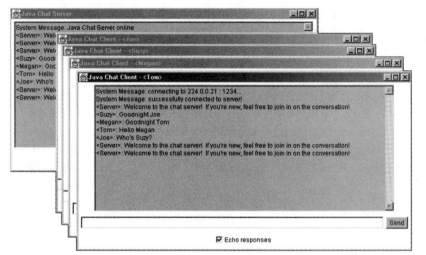

Figure 13.9

*A chat server running with several clients*

have no dependency on one another, you can have an entire chat session without a running server. I simply included it as a way to show how a server can provide services at regular intervals.

Figure 13.9 shows a rather disjointed conversation involving four clients and a central chat server.

It goes without saying that chat clients you incorporate into your games do not have to have the cookie-cutter look the one I have shown you does. By incorporating the custom components discussed in Chapter 12 you can make some real slick interfaces. A game that has chat capabilities does not have to use dedicated text boxes to display messages, either. You can allow typed messages to be drawn directly to the window using a Label2D object, for instance. Incoming messages can be placed in the upper-left corner of the applet window, away from the action. You can also have incoming messages fade in and out so they will not become a visual distraction for your users.

We'll wrap up basic networking in Java with one more example that uses the MulticastConnection class. Next, we'll create the skeleton features of a typical bingo program that provides a bingo server that broadcasts calls to listening clients.

## Creating the Visual Bingo Program: Grandma's Gone Hi-Tech

No longer is the game of bingo reserved for little old ladies in church basements on Friday nights. It's become much larger than that. In fact, there can be hundreds of people at a given time playing on any number of the various Internet bingo servers out there. Prizes for winning Internet bingo can be anything from money to prize tokens to absolutely nothing at all. Most people don't play Internet bingo to win—they play it because it's fun. The point is, the Internet has allowed developers to breathe life back into an old favorite.

Here's the skinny on implementing your own skeleton bingo application. On the server side, you could have the program join a specific multicast group and begin broadcasting bingo calls. Like any bingo game, each number should only be called once during each game. After all of the numbers are called, the server will broadcast a message for all listening clients to start over themselves, and the process starts all over again. Like the chat program, our BingoServer applet will run within a Frame. Here's the code:

```java
import java.applet.*;
import java.awt.*;
import java.awt.event.*;
import java.net.*;
import java.util.*;

public class BingoServer extends Applet
{
    // a multicast connection for broadcasting numbers
    protected MulticastConnection service;

    // area for placing internal server messages
    protected TextArea textArea;

    // holds the available bingo calls
    protected int[] numbers;

    // the number of bingo calls made this game
    protected int numbersCalled;

    // generates bingo calls
    protected Random random;

    // time to wait between calls
    protected final int CALL_PAUSE = 3000;

    public void init()
    {
```

```
        textArea = new TextArea("", 15, 60, TextArea.SCROLLBARS_VERTICAL_ONLY);
        textArea.setEditable(false);
        add(textArea);

        random = new Random();
        reset();

        // connect to the bingo group
        String address = "224.0.0.21";
        int port = 1234;
        try
        {
            service = new MulticastConnection(address, port);
            textArea.append("System Message: Java BINGO Server online\n");
        }
        catch(Exception e)
        {
            textArea.append("System Error: Could not create BINGO Server! " +
                            e + "\n");
        }
    }


// fills the array of valid bingo calls (1-75)
public void reset()
{
    numbers = new int[75];
    for(int i = 0; i < 75; i++)
    {
        numbers[i] = i+1;
    }
    numbersCalled = 0;

    // clear the text area
    textArea.setText("");
}


public void callNumber()
{
    // test if all of the numbers have been called
    if(numbersCalled == 75)
```

```java
        {
            reset();
            textArea.append("All numbers called!  Restarting game...\n");

            // broadcast the "Reset" action to the group
            service.send("Reset");

            // wait 10 seconds before starting a new game
            try
            {
                Thread.sleep(10000);
            }
            catch(InterruptedException e) {   }
        }

        // generate the next number to call
        int i = random.nextInt(75);
        while(numbers[i] == -1)
        {
            i = random.nextInt(75);
        }

        // save the next number and clear it from the array
        int n = numbers[i];
        numbers[i] = -1;

        // call the next number
        textArea.append("Calling " + n + "\n");
        service.send(""+n);
        ++ numbersCalled;
    }

    // start the server, calling bingo numbers forever
    public void start()
    {
        while(true)
        {
            callNumber();

            // pause before calling the next number
```

```
        try
        {
              Thread.sleep(CALL_PAUSE);
        }
        catch(InterruptedException e) {   }
    }
}

// creates a BingoServer applet and adds it to a Frame
public static void main(String[] args)
{
    Applet a = new BingoServer();

    a.init();
    Frame f = new Frame("Java BINGO Server");
    f.setSize(500, 320);
    f.addWindowListener(new WindowAdapter()
        {
              public void windowClosing(WindowEvent e)
              {
                  System.exit(0);
              }
        } );

    f.add(a);
    f.show();
    a.start();
}

}    // BingoServer
```

The client side is a bit more complex, but only because it should do a lot more rendering than the server program. After all, it is the client side of the program that your users will be seeing. I won't go through the process of writing the client here; you know enough about what's going on to write your own. Keep in mind the following when implementing your bingo client:

- The server can broadcast one of two different types of messages: either a restart message that tells the client to clear all calls and restart the game or a number between 1 and 75.

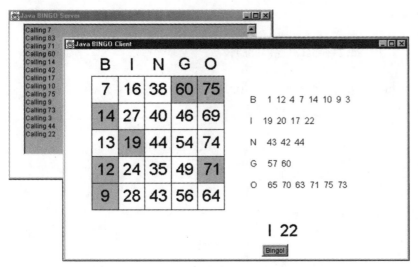

**Figure 13.10**

*Move over, Granny! The Internet bingo server and client programs*

- You should print out all of the numbers that the server has called during each game. Remember that numbers 1–15 fall under 'B', 16–30 fall under 'I', and so on. Given a number, you can algorithmically generate the column it falls under.

- Once a client calls "Bingo!" the client program should internally validate it against the numbers called. If the client does have a bingo, the client program should tell the server and the game should be restarted accordingly.

I created a quick sample client program for you to look at if you need help getting started. It is in no way a complete Bingo client; I left it for you to finish on your own. It's on the CD-ROM (under the \bingo_udp directory) along with the server program. Figure 13.10 shows the sample Bingo server and client programs in action.

Have fun writing the bingo client. It's a great way to test your skills and pull together most of the topics we've discussed throughout the book. It's also a great way to introduce those special seniors in your life to the wonderful world of Java and the Internet.

# Conclusion

The low-level details of network implementation are fascinating to me. The ideas and principles behind them are actually rather simple, but actually implementing a network system can be a major pain in the neck. Luckily, Java provides an assortment of classes that take most of the sting out of sending and receiving data over the Internet.

The classes I've developed and shown you, such as the `AbstractConnection` and `MulticastConnection` classes, wrap commonly used features associated with both connection-oriented as well as connectionless networks for you to use. Connecting to, disconnecting from, and sending and receiving messages are all frequently used network operations. Although you don't necessarily *need* to use the classes I've developed for you in this chapter, they will definitely save you work in the future. As always, feel free to add or change any features as you see necessary.

As a final thought, keep in mind that the current version of IP—IPv4 (as in IP *version 4*)—is slowly but surely becoming obsolete. Because of the limited address space it provides, the number of addresses available to new users is dwindling. A new version of IP, IPv6, will probably be the protocol to replace the current standard. Java 1.4 already contains some support for IPv6, so you know it will contain full-fledged support for it by the time it starts becoming more popular.

As always, I've come up with a batch of exercises for you. Just remember, the Java 2 documentation is also available if you need additional information on the `java.net` package.

# Exercises

**13.1**  For illustration, some example programs in this chapter simply hard-coded the server address and port specifications for the client programs to connect to. When possible, change these programs to use applet parameters or another way for the user to specify which address and port to connect to. If there is a way for the user to bypass entering this information, be sure to have a default address and port to which the program can connect.

**13.2**  Change the `GuessServer` and `GuessClient` programs so that they implement a replay option so that the user does not have to reconnect every time he or she wants to play again.

**13.3**  Implement a strategy for guaranteeing that each client in the `SimpleChatClient` program has a unique handle. For example, if a client named "Sally" has already joined the group, then every time another user named "Sally" attempts to join the group, she (or he, I suppose) will be prompted to enter another name. One way this can be done is to have each client make a separate TCP connection with a service that contains a table of used handles. The service should look up the requested handle against the table and either permit or deny access to the chat room. Only after receiving a thumbs-up response from the service should the client be allowed to join the multicast chat room. Similarly, when the user leaves the group, another TCP connection should be made to the service to remove his or her handle from the table so it will be free for someone else to use. Also, if the handle lookup service is unavailable, a "service unavailable" message should be output to the client window.

13.4 "Family-friendly" games and real-time chat often do not mix. Children and sensitive gamers should not have to deal with objectionable terms and language. Implement a filtering mechanism, such as the `SimpleChatClient` echo option, that prevents obscene language from reaching the chat window. To maintain at least some of this book's integrity, I won't mention which words you should filter—you've undoubtedly heard them all before. Questionable words can either be replaced with strings such as "#$%&" or they can be ignored altogether. Of course, allow the user to toggle this option in case he or she does not want incoming messages to be censored.

13.5 In the `SimpleChatClient` applet, associate different port numbers with various chat rooms that are available. For example, "Animals" can be on port 1000, "Games" can be on 1001, and so on.

13.6 Implement a `BingoClient` class to go along with the `BingoServer` class we've already seen. There's a lot that can be done with it, so make it as feature-rich as you'd like. One of the biggest problems you'll face is ending the game when a client has a bingo! For extra points, create a scoring system that gives clients points, or tokens, for each game won.

# CHAPTER 14

# A Look at the Nodez! Game

Hopefully, you're reading this chapter because you've read the previous 13 chapters and couldn't wait to see the grand finale. But if you just decided to open to a random page or are reading this book from back to front, that's okay too. It'll all make sense in the end.

In this chapter, we'll examine the Java game development engine that I have dubbed the *Magic* engine. The theory behind this engine isn't magic at all, however. Most of it makes use of concepts and code you have already become familiar with. The goal will be to wrap each component we've discussed in this book into a complete, succinct development system.

We'll then put the *Magic* game engine to use by implementing a small game that uses the concepts we've looked at thus far. From transparency to networking, we'll try to cover at least a little bit of everything. So, ladies and gentlemen, start your engines (no pun intended) and let's get moving!

# Captain Beefheart and His Magic Engine

Programmers have sought out the coveted "golden game engine" ever since creating large-scale games became possible. In fact, many hobbyist programmers spend so much time perfecting their own game engines, they never get the chance to actually create any games! By the time one engine is completed, many programmers seek to fix its flaws by starting on another one. Although this makes for better programmers and is a great learning experience, it is not necessarily the most productive use of a programmer's development time.

Many programmers also create game engines for the wrong reasons. Although creating an engine that can draw 1 billion polygons per second is nifty, it won't necessarily be useful for making games. Another engine might contain tons of features but boxes the developer into only a few different game genres to choose from. When it comes down to it, many games could have been written faster and more efficiently if the developer had just written the game from scratch and bypassed using an engine.

There are times, however, when creating a game engine *can* be useful. For instance, breaking down common programming tasks into small units can be a very useful asset to any game developer. The custom components we created in Chapter 12 are a good example of this. After you write the code to control things such as buttons and labels only once, instances of these components can be pumped out like an assembly line. This allows you to focus on game logic rather than reinventing the wheel every time you wish to add a character or other component to the game.

Having a hierarchy of components is another advantage to creating game engines. Imagine trying to control code that implements a spaceship, asteroids, power-ups, enemy crafts, terrain, weapons, and the animation techniques that control them without having a single base module to extend upon. It would make your programs very difficult to manage. This is where object-oriented programming can really bail you out. Java forces you to program abstractly because it is, for the most part, a purely object-oriented language. This helps curb bad programming habits and keeps the spaghetti out of your code.

There are several other considerations to make when designing a game engine. For instance, a 500-kilobyte or larger engine might seem impressive, but remember, your users will need to download your engine to use it. In other words, it should be feature-rich but not overly bloated. The compiled *Magic* engine code weighs in at a little more than 64 kilobytes. Also, a game engine needs to be useful. A good engine is one that can be used for any number of different game genres. Making a game engine more flexible can make it less useful, and vice versa. A polished game engine should therefore be flexible, but powerful enough to significantly shorten development time.

# Organization of the Magic Engine

By now, you've probably invoked the `import` statement enough times to drive yourself crazy. Now it's your chance to turn the tables by creating your *own* packages for others to import. Since packages help keep your classes organized, it makes sense to organize your game engine in this way. I organized the *Magic* engine into eight different packages. Some packages contain classes we've already examined; others will be completely new to you. Here's a rundown of what each package in the *Magic* engine consists of:

- **`magic.actor2d`.** Contains classes for setting up custom actors and scene components. This package contains those classes directly related to the actor management, namely `Actor2D`, `ActorGroup2D`, and *`Moveable`*. This package also contains the `StaticActor` and `StaticActorGroup` classes, which implement a specific subtype of `Actor2D`.

- **magic.awtex.** This is short for *AWT EX*tended. This package contains the classes for creating custom visual components like the ones we looked at in Chapter 12. The Component2D class leads off a host of visual and interactive components, including buttons, radio buttons, labels, and panels. This package also facilitates the custom menuing class, Menu2D. Use this package when the standard AWT just won't do.

- **magic.debug.** Contains a single class, Debugger, that is capable of sending warning and error messages to your end users. Message output can come in one of two forms: either stream output, such as to the console, or visual output to a Frame object. The exact method for displaying debugging output can be specified during the initialization phase of your games.

- **magic.gamelet.** This contains the beefed-up Applet class, appropriately named Gamelet. A *gamelet* works much like the name suggests; gamelets extend the functionality of an applet and are embedded within applet context, such as a Web browser. The Gamelet class provides a bunch of housekeeping services, such as a threaded animation loop, double buffering, framerate syncing, menu stacking, playing of audio clips, and of course, scene management. The Gamelet class is also an abstract class; therefore, you must extend it and implement any methods that have not yet been defined. This class saves you from writing the same code over and over and allows you to focus on the particular game at hand.

- **magic.graphics.** The graphics package in the *Magic* game engine provides a number of helper classes for providing graphics support. The ImageLoader class provides a way to load animation strips for actors and visual components. The ImageGroup, AnimationStrip, and Animator classes also provide support for actors and other visuals as well.

- **magic.net.** Contains classes for connectivity among computers on the Internet. Both Server and GUIServer are abstract classes for accepting TCP connections from remote clients. The AbstractConnection class gives you a way to allow connection-oriented services and clients to communicate with one another. Like the AbstractConnection class, the MulticastConnection class allows connectionless clients to send and receive multicast packets from a Class D IP address.

- **magic.scene.** Contains the abstract Scene class, which suggests a model for creating, updating, and painting a scene. Implementing a separate scene manager will remove some of the burden from your main applet class, plus it will help keep things organized. The QuadNode and QuadTree classes provide additional support for scenes that contain many objects or have extended interaction among objects.

- **magic.util.** Contains a single class, MagicUtils, which contains static utility methods for quickly accessing the sine, cosine, and tangent values for a given angle using lookup tables. This class can easily be added to for instances when additional utilities are needed. Appendix B contains an example of the benefits of using precalculated values, such as those contained within a trigonometry lookup table.

Remember, it is important to tag your classes with the package keyword. For instance, before any import statements are made, the Actor2D class should contain the following header at the top of the file:

```
package magic.actor2d;
```

Without the package tag, it would be difficult for classes outside the package to import the Actor2D class within their own implementation.

Figure 14.1 shows the entire *Magic* class hierarchy, organized by package name.

You've already seen many of the classes mentioned in the above package descriptions. Some of them you haven't, such as the Debugger, Gamelet, and MagicUtils classes. The Debugger and MagicUtils classes are pretty straightforward, but the Gamelet class should be of particular interest. As mentioned above, the Gamelet class extends the Applet class to provide common setup routines for your games. For instance, it automatically creates a double buffering mechanism as well as the standard animation loop. It also enforces framerate syncing. All your extended Gamelet class needs to do is provide the framerate value, and the rest is done for you.

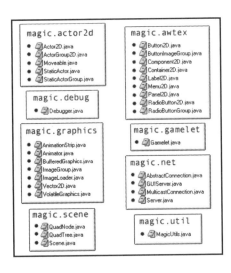

**Figure 14.1**

*Packages and classes available within the* Magic *game engine*

Remember to make the proper polymorphic calls when overriding `Gamelet` methods. One such example occurs with the `init` method. You'll usually want to perform custom initialization after the default parameters have been set. To do this, simply invoke the `init` method of the parent class, such as the following:

```
public class MyCustomGamelet extends Gamelet
{
    public void init()
    {
        // initialize the Gamelet
        super.init();

        // custom initialization here...
    }

    // other methods here as needed...
}
```

Much like how `this` references the calling object, `super` refers to the class from which the calling object directly inherits its functionality. Since Java supports only a single chain of inheritance, there is no question as to which parent method is to be called.

Rather than have you hunt down the implementation for each class separately, I have provided a complete source code listing for the *Magic* engine in Appendix G. Use it as a reference guide or as a walk-through for implementing your own game engine.

Next, we'll develop a small yet complete game that puts each of the *Magic* engine's components to good use.

# Assembling the *Nodez!* Game

In this section we'll assemble an easy-to-play puzzle game I named, aptly, *Nodez!* The game of *Nodez!* presents the player with a group of nodes connected by some type of circuitry. Any two nodes can be swapped by the user only if they are connected by a single straight section of circuitry. Each node is assigned a secret position within the overall circuitry. The nodes are then randomly placed throughout the circuitry. It will be the player's task to successfully rearrange the nodes so that they all end up in their correct positions. At any given time during the game, the user will know how many nodes are properly placed but won't be explicitly told which nodes are in the correct positions. Also, to better track their progress, users can visually flag nodes that they think are in their correct positions.

Once the user has successfully placed all of the nodes correctly in the scene, he or she will be taken to the next level, containing a more difficult circuitry layout.

As you've seen, the *Magic* game development engine pulls together most of what we've talked about throughout this book. However, its components are represented through generic structures. Our goal will be to extend and implement these structures into a more useful form. When complete, the *Nodez!* game will contain a multitude of features, including use of native shape drawing and filling, image rendering, audio playback, and basic chat capabilities over the Internet. To further whet your appetite, Figure 14.2 offers a glimpse at the finished *Nodez!* game.

To assemble the *Nodez!* game, we'll first look at an overview of each of its components and then follow up with its implementation using actual Java code.

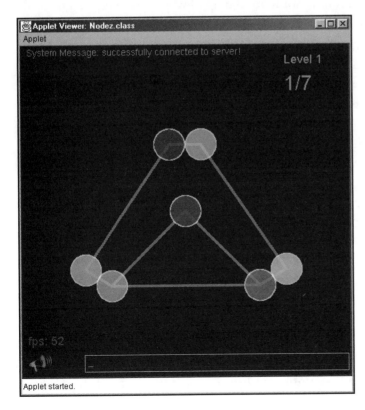

**Figure 14.2**

*A first look at the* Nodez! *game*

# Overview of the *Nodez!* Game

Like any piece of completed software, a completed game can be inherently complex. Each feature you add to a software package can potentially force another component to be changed. The resulting rippling effect on a product's code can be quite dramatic over its entire lifetime.

For example, if you wish to add a feature to your program that allows users to chat over a UDP connection, several code changes will be needed. Obviously, the first change would be the addition of code to connect to and send and receive messages. However, you would also need to provide areas within the rendering window to show incoming messages as well as display outgoing messages as they are typed. You might also want to provide a menu to allow the user to specify which chat server he or she would like to connect to. If the output window is already cluttered with too many things, or there is no available menuing system to work with, implementing new features can be more of an inconvenience than anything else.

Therefore, it is important to at least have some road map of where you want to go before venturing out on any programming endeavor. For our *Nodez!* game, I wanted to:

- Make use of a user interface within an applet context. This includes allowing `EventListener` classes to capture user input from both the mouse and the keyboard. Using an applet will also provide us with the rendering window on which to display the game.

- Rely less on static images loaded from file and more on the basic drawing and filling capabilities available with the Java 2-D packages. This will reduce network traffic and download times, as well as allow us to practice using what we learned in Chapters 7 and 8.

- Use each of the packages contained within the *Magic* development system. This includes classes related to scene management and actor creation.

- Implement simple chat capabilities using UDP. The `MulticastConnection` class contained in the `magic.net` package will make this relatively easy to do.

- Create a structure for containing level layout for the game. This structure should allow future maintainers of the game code to easily add or modify levels. A loading screen will also be used while the initial level is being loaded.

- Provide a simple mechanism for loading and playing various audio clips when certain events are generated.

Figure 14.3 offers a graphical representation of how component parts of the *Nodez!* game will fit together.

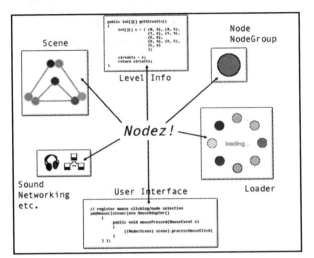

**Figure 14.3**

*Component parts of the
Nodez! game*

Now that you know a bit about how the *Nodez!* game will be played as well as the main features it will contain, let's dig right into the code required to implement it.

# Implementing the *Nodez!* Game

You've seen the components that make up the *Nodez!* game. Likewise, its implementation will come in various phases. We'll look at each of these phases along with the code, starting with creating the actual nodes themselves.

## Creating the Node and NodeGroup Classes

The driving force behind the *Nodez!* game is the actual nodes themselves. The nodes are the actors that define the state of the game. This presents us with the perfect opportunity to extend the Actor2D and ActorGroup2D classes from the magic.actor2d package. Naturally, the Node class will extend the Actor2D class, and the NodeGroup class will extend ActorGroup2D.

Let's begin by looking at the NodeGroup class, which defines the imaging and constant values for Node objects. Figure 14.2 showed that the nodes are merely circular objects filled with different colors and outlined in white. It would be a waste of memory and bandwidth to represent these objects through images accessed from disk. Therefore, we'll create our nodes the old-fashioned way: through the native drawing and filling operations contained in the Graphics2D class.

Node objects can have one of two animation states: normal or selected. Therefore, for each available node color, an AnimationStrip will be created containing these two states.

As you know, the heart of ActorGroup2D objects lies within their init methods. First of all, a NodeGroup object creates a circle within a Polygon object by using the sine and cosine values contained within the MagicUtils class. The circle geometry is then used for filling and outlining the circles. A second Polygon is created to represent the octagon shape that represented selected nodes. This shape is filled using a color on the opposite end of the Color array. Finally, the NodeGroup init method constructs the flag object for visually flagging correct nodes. Here's the code for the NodeGroup class:

```java
import java.applet.*;
import java.awt.*;
import java.awt.geom.*;
import java.awt.image.*;

import magic.actor2d.*;
import magic.graphics.*;
import magic.util.*;

public class NodeGroup extends ActorGroup2D
{
    // the target width and height of a node image
    public static final int NODE_WIDTH  = 48;
    public static final int NODE_HEIGHT = 48;

    // possible foreground node colors--this should be enough for most layouts
    public static final Color[] COLORS =
        {
        Color.BLUE, Color.CYAN, Color.DARK_GRAY, Color.LIGHT_GRAY,
        Color.GREEN, Color.MAGENTA, Color.ORANGE, Color.PINK, Color.RED,
        Color.YELLOW,
        Color.BLUE, Color.CYAN, Color.DARK_GRAY, Color.LIGHT_GRAY,
        Color.GREEN, Color.MAGENTA, Color.ORANGE, Color.PINK, Color.RED,
        Color.YELLOW
        };

    // the maximum number of nodez
```

```
public static final int NUM_NODES = COLORS.length;

// static Image for the 'flagged' nodes
public static BufferedImage flag;

public NodeGroup()
{
    super();

    animations = new AnimationStrip[NUM_NODES];
}

public void init(Applet a)
{
    MagicUtils.buildTrigTables();

    final Stroke outline = new BasicStroke(2.0f);

    // create the geometry for our nodes
    Polygon p = new Polygon();
    for(int angle = 0; angle <= 360; angle += 10)
    {
        p.addPoint((int) ((double)NODE_WIDTH/2 *MagicUtils.cos(angle)),
                   (int) ((double)NODE_HEIGHT/2*MagicUtils.sin(angle)));
    }

    // set the geometry for the Node class--this will help with things
    // such as mouse selection
    Node.geometry = p;

    // create the inner polygon that will 'highlight' selection
    Polygon hilite = new Polygon();
    for(int angle = 0; angle <= 360; angle += 45)
    {
        hilite.addPoint(
                (int) ((double)NODE_WIDTH/4 *MagicUtils.cos(angle)),
                (int) ((double)NODE_HEIGHT/4*MagicUtils.sin(angle)));
    }

    Graphics2D g2d;
```

```
// fill the node pool with one node for each color in the COLORS array
for(int i = 0; i < NUM_NODES; i++)
{
    // *** fill a node with solid color (frame 1)

    BufferedImage image = new BufferedImage(NODE_WIDTH, NODE_HEIGHT,
                                    BufferedImage.TYPE_INT_ARGB);
    g2d = image.createGraphics();

    // since images will be pre-rendered, make them look as good as
    // possible
    g2d.setRenderingHint(RenderingHints.KEY_STROKE_CONTROL,
                        RenderingHints.VALUE_STROKE_PURE);

    g2d.setPaint(COLORS[i]);
    g2d.translate(NODE_WIDTH/2, NODE_HEIGHT/2);
    g2d.fill(p);

    // draw the outline of the node
    g2d.setPaint(Color.WHITE);
    g2d.setStroke(outline);
    g2d.draw(p);

    // *** create a 'negative' of the image (frame 2)

    BufferedImage negative = new BufferedImage(
            NODE_WIDTH, NODE_HEIGHT, BufferedImage.TYPE_INT_ARGB);
    g2d = negative.createGraphics();

    g2d.setRenderingHint(RenderingHints.KEY_STROKE_CONTROL,
                        RenderingHints.VALUE_STROKE_PURE);

    g2d.setPaint(COLORS[i]);
    g2d.translate(NODE_WIDTH/2, NODE_HEIGHT/2);
    g2d.fill(p);

    g2d.setPaint(Color.WHITE);
    g2d.setStroke(outline);
```

```java
            g2d.draw(p);

            // fill the highlight geometry
            g2d.setPaint(COLORS[COLORS.length-1-i]);
            g2d.setTransform(AffineTransform.getTranslateInstance(
                            NODE_WIDTH/2.0, NODE_HEIGHT/2.0));
            g2d.fill(hilite);
            g2d.setPaint(Color.BLACK);
            g2d.draw(hilite);

            // add an animation strip containing both frames of our new node
            // image
            animations[i] = new AnimationStrip();
            animations[i].addFrame(image);
            animations[i].addFrame(negative);
            animations[i].setAnimator(new Animator.Looped());
        }

        // build the flag
        flag = new BufferedImage(NODE_WIDTH/4, NODE_HEIGHT/2,
                                BufferedImage.TYPE_INT_ARGB);
        g2d  = flag.createGraphics();

        Polygon triangle = new Polygon();
        triangle.addPoint(NODE_WIDTH/4, 0);
        triangle.addPoint(NODE_WIDTH/4, NODE_HEIGHT/8);
        triangle.addPoint(0, NODE_HEIGHT/8);

        g2d.setPaint(Color.WHITE);
        g2d.drawLine(NODE_WIDTH/4-1, 0, NODE_WIDTH/4-1, NODE_HEIGHT/2);

        g2d.setPaint(Color.RED);
        g2d.fill(triangle);
    }

} // NodeGroup
```

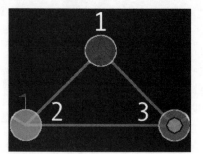

**Figure 14.4**

*Nodes in their*
*(1) normal state*
*(2) flagged state*
*(3) selected state*

You know how to use the Graphics2D class to draw and fill shapes, so I'll leave the details to you to examine for yourself. Figure 14.4 shows nodes in each of their three different states.

The NodeGroup class is no good without an Actor2D class that uses it. For the *Nodez!* game, it is the Node class that will use a NodeGroup object to get its animation frames for rendering. Since nodes can be swapped, each node will be given a destination vector for once they are set into motion. Nodes are also assigned an integer index to where they are placed within the circuitry as well as a destination index specifying the correct index position for the node to be in. This index value references a Vector2D object describing the current position of the node.

The Node class is pretty simple, so I won't beat it to death. I will, however, show you the source code here in case you don't have the CD-ROM handy or prefer your code printed out.

```
import java.awt.*;
import java.awt.geom.*;

import magic.graphics.*;

public class Node extends magic.actor2d.Actor2D
{
    // the destination vector for moving nodes
    private Vector2D dest;

    // current index of animation
    private int animIndex;

    // the index of the node within the circuitry
```

```
            private int circuitIndex;

            // the node's destination, or target, index
            private int circuitIndexDest;

            // determines if this node is flagged
            private boolean flagged;

            // node geometry for selection testing
            public static Polygon geometry = null;

            private final double ONE_RADIAN = Math.toRadians(1);

            // creates a new Node with the given ActorGroup2D object, index, and
            // position
            public Node(magic.actor2d.ActorGroup2D grp, int index, Vector2D p)
            {
                super(grp);

                animIndex = index;
                circuitIndex = index;
                circuitIndexDest = -1;

                setPos(p);
                dest = new Vector2D.Double();
                dest.setX(p.getX());
                dest.setY(p.getY());

                currAnimation = group.getAnimationStrip(animIndex);
                frameWidth    = currAnimation.getFrameWidth();
                frameHeight   = currAnimation.getFrameHeight();

                flagged = false;
            }


            // determines if a node is in its "correct" state
            public boolean isCorrect()
            {
                // a node is "correct" if its current index matches its target index
```

```java
        return (circuitIndex == circuitIndexDest);
    }

    // determines if this node contains the sent point
    public boolean contains(Point p)
    {
        // using the geometry centered on the origin, offset the point by the
        // node's position and see if it lands within the node's geometry
        return geometry.contains(new Point2D.Double(p.x - getX(),
                                                    p.y - getY()));
    }

    // swaps two nodes by their indices and destination position
    public static void swap(Node a, Node b)
    {
        int temp = a.circuitIndex;
        a.circuitIndex = b.circuitIndex;
        b.circuitIndex = temp;

        a.dest.setX(b.pos.getX());
        a.dest.setY(b.pos.getY());

        b.dest.setX(a.pos.getX());
        b.dest.setY(a.pos.getY());
    }

    // updates the node
    public void update()
    {
        if(isMoving())
        {
            // get the vector difference between the destination and position
            Vector2D oneStep = dest.minus(pos);

            // normalize the step to unit length
            oneStep.normalize();

            // scale the step so the node moves faster
```

```
                oneStep.scale(2.5);

                // now move by the step value
                pos.translate(oneStep);

                // rotate the node CW or CCW, depending on direction of travel
                if(oneStep.getX() > 0.0)
                {
                    rotation += ONE_RADIAN;
                }
                else
                {
                    rotation -= ONE_RADIAN;
                }

                // "settle" the node if it is within the tolerance of a single
                // step
                if(Math.abs(dest.getX()-pos.getX()) < oneStep.getX())
                {
                    pos.setX(dest.getX());
                }

                if(Math.abs(dest.getY()-pos.getY()) < oneStep.getY())
                {
                    pos.setY(dest.getY());
                }

                // if the node settled into its destination position, remove its
                // selected state and zero out its rotation
                if(! isMoving())
                {
                    setSelected(false);
                    rotation = 0;
                }
            }

            // center the node about its anchor point and set the transform
            xform.setToIdentity();
```

```
                    xform.translate(pos.getX(), pos.getY());
                    xform.rotate(rotation);
                    xform.translate(-frameWidth/2, -frameHeight/2);

                    updateBounds();
                    checkBounds();
              }

              public void paint(Graphics2D g2d)
              {
                    super.paint(g2d);

                    // draw the flag if needed
                    if(flagged && !isMoving())
                    {
                          g2d.drawImage(NodeGroup.flag,
                                AffineTransform.getTranslateInstance(
                                                      pos.getX()-NodeGroup.NODE_WIDTH/4,
                                                      pos.getY()-NodeGroup.NODE_HEIGHT),
                                AnimationStrip.observer);

                    }
              }

              // basic access methods

              public void setAnimIndex(int index)
              {
                    animIndex = index;
                    currAnimation = group.getAnimationStrip(animIndex);
              }

              public int getAnimIndex()
              {
                    return animIndex;
              }

              public void setCircuitIndex(int index)
              {
```

```java
        circuitIndex = index;
    }

    public int getCircuitIndex()
    {
        return circuitIndex;
    }

    public void setCircuitIndexDest(int index)
    {
        circuitIndexDest = index;
    }

    public int getCircuitIndexDest()
    {
        return circuitIndexDest;
    }

    // sets the proper frame of animation
    public void setSelected(boolean s)
    {
        currAnimation.reset();
        if(s)
        {
            animate();
        }
    }

    public boolean isMoving()
    {
        return(! pos.equals(dest));
    }

    public void toggleFlagged()
    {
        flagged = !flagged;
    }

    public boolean isFlagged()
```

```
        {

                return flagged;

        }


    }    // Node
```

One final thing I'll point out in the Node class is its update method. If the node is in motion, it needs to be kept along the circuit track. To accomplish this, I used the Vector2D methods for subtracting, normalizing, and scaling vectors. By normalizing and scaling the travel vector, the node is guaranteed to travel the same distance each frame regardless of the direction it is traveling in. The node is also rotated about its center point as it moves along the circuits.

## Creating the NodezScene Class

As you saw in Chapter 11, the Scene class allows you to offset much of the scene management of your games from the main Applet class to a dedicated scene module. Our NodezScene class contains a NodeGroup object as well as a Vector of Node objects for displaying the scene. It also contains a two-dimensional integer array describing how circuit nodes are connected. This works by matching up node indexes from column 0 with node indexes from column 1 for each row of the array, as shown in Figure 14.5.

As you can see, each node position is given an index value, starting with zero. Lines we want to connect are added to the array only once; that is, once node 0 is connected to node 2, then node 2 does not need to be connected back to node 0. It does not matter the order in which line segments are specified within the array. As a convenience, there is also an array of Line2D objects within the NodezScene class for rendering the circuit lines to the window. The original array is only kept for testing nodes for position swapping.

**Figure 14.5**

*Creating a circuit array*

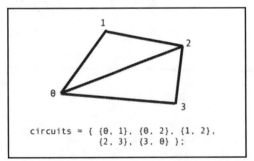

```
circuits = { {0, 1}, {0, 2}, {1, 2},
             {2, 3}, {3, 0} };
```

One final interesting thing that the NodezScene class provides is two additional references to Node objects, one for each user selection to swap. You'll see in the following code listing how these objects are used when the user clicks the left and right mouse buttons.

```java
import java.awt.*;
import java.awt.event.*;
import java.awt.geom.*;
import java.util.*;

import magic.gamelet.*;
import magic.actor2d.*;
import magic.debug.*;
import magic.scene.*;
import magic.graphics.*;

public class NodezScene extends Scene
{
    // an ActorGroup2D object for holding Node-related information
    private NodeGroup nodeGroup;

    // a Vector to contain the actual nodes
    private Vector nodes;

    // the color and stroke width of circuit lines connecting nodes
    private final Color  CIRCUIT_COLOR  = new Color(255, 50, 50);
    private final Stroke CIRCUIT_STROKE = new BasicStroke(4.0f);

    // 2-D array of indexes for drawing circuit lines
    // for example, { 2, 3 } would connect a line joining node indexes 2 and 3
    private int[][] circuits;

    // an array of lines connecting each circuit index pair in the above array
    private Line2D[] circuitLines;

    // the selections made by the user
    private Node selection1;
    private Node selection2;

    // creates a NodezScene object with the sent bounds and Applet reference
```

```java
public NodezScene(Rectangle2D r, java.applet.Applet a)
{
     super(r, r);

     // create and initialize a new NodezGroup for the Nodez
     nodeGroup = new NodeGroup();
     nodeGroup.init(a);

     // create the vector and initialize the selections
     nodes = new Vector();
     selection1 = null;
     selection2 = null;
}

// adds a node to the scene by adding it to the nodez vector
public void add(Actor2D a)
{
     nodes.add(a);
}

// loads the sent level into the scene
public void loadLevel(int level)
{
     // get a static NodezLevel structure with the specified level no.
     NodezLevel nodezLevel = NodezLevel.getLevel(level);

     // a return value of null means that no level data matched the level
     // number
     if(nodezLevel == null)
     {
          Debugger.reportError(Debugger.FATAL_ERROR,
                              "Invalid level specification",0);
          return;
     }

     // get 1) the positions of the nodes and 2) the circuit index arrays
     // from the level structure
     Vector2D[] nodePos  = nodezLevel.getNodePos();
```

```
circuits = nodezLevel.getCircuits();

// clear the Vector and selections
nodes.clear();
selection1 = null;
selection2 = null;

// nodes will be positioned relative to the center of the window so
// that they will fit in a window of varying sizes
double anchorX = getBounds().getWidth()  * 0.5f;
double anchorY = getBounds().getHeight() * 0.5f;

// create one Node for each position given in the level structure
for(int i = 0; i < nodePos.length; i++)
{
    // create a node with the specified NodeGroup, index, and position
    Node n = new Node(nodeGroup, i,
                new Vector2D.Double(anchorX + nodePos[i].getX(),
                                    anchorY + nodePos[i].getY()));

    add(n);
}

// create an array of indexes [0, nodes.length-1] and then randomize
// the array
// this randomized array will serve as the destination indices for the
// nodes

int[] indexDest = new int[nodes.size()];
for(int i = 0; i < indexDest.length; i++)
{
    indexDest[i] = i;
}

// keep randomizing and filling the destination indices until there are
// none that are initially correct
do
{
```

```
                    Random r = new Random();
                    for(int i = 0; i < indexDest.length; i++)
                    {
                         int temp = indexDest[i];
                         int rand = r.nextInt(indexDest.length);

                         indexDest[i] = indexDest[rand];
                         indexDest[rand] = temp;
                    }

                    int j = 0;
                    for(Enumeration e = nodes.elements(); e.hasMoreElements(); )
                    {
                         ((Node) e.nextElement()).setCircuitIndexDest(indexDest[j++]);
                    }

              }    while(getNumCorrect() > 0);


              // fill circuitry x,y line values
              Node node1;
              Node node2;
              circuitLines = new Line2D.Double[circuits.length];
              for(int i = 0; i < circuits.length; i++)
              {
                    // get nodes 0 and 1...
                    node1 = (Node)nodes.get(circuits[i][0]);
                    node2 = (Node)nodes.get(circuits[i][1]);

                    // ...and add their x, y values to the line array
                    circuitLines[i] = new Line2D.Double(node1.getX(), node1.getY(),
                                                     node2.getX(), node2.getY());

              }

        }

        // gets the NodeGroup for the scene
        public NodeGroup getNodeGroup()
        {
```

```
                return nodeGroup;
        }


        // returns the current number of nodes in play
        public int getNumNodes()
        {
                return nodes.size();
        }


        // returns the correct number of nodes
        public int getNumCorrect()
        {
                int numCorrect = 0;
                for(Enumeration e = nodes.elements(); e.hasMoreElements(); )
                {
                        if(((Node) e.nextElement()).isCorrect())
                        {
                                ++ numCorrect;
                        }
                }
                return numCorrect;
        }


        // processes a left-click action on the sent Node object
        private void processLeftClick(Node n)
        {
                // if the first selection is not set, set it now
                if(selection1 == null)
                {
                        selection1 = n;

                        // make sure nodez are selected in the order 1, 2
                        if(selection2 != null)
                        {
                                selection2.setSelected(false);
                        }
                        n.setSelected(true);

                        // play a sound that a selection was made
```

```java
        Gamelet.playSound(Nodez.NODE_SELECTED1, false);
        return;
    }

    // otherwise, select the second node and test for swapping
    else
    {
        selection2 = n;
        selection2.setSelected(true);

        // play a sound that the second selection was made
        Gamelet.playSound(Nodez.NODE_SELECTED2, false);

        // if the same node was selected twice, unselect it
        if(selection1 == selection2)
        {
            selection1.setSelected(false);

            selection1 = null;
            selection2 = null;
        }

        // otherwise, test for node swapping
        else if(canSwap(selection1.getCircuitIndex(),
                        selection2.getCircuitIndex()))
        {
            // swap the nodes
            Node.swap(selection1, selection2);

            // reset the selections
            selection1 = null;

             // test if the puzzle has been solved
            if(getNumCorrect() == getNumNodes())
            {
                Gamelet.playSound(Nodez.GAME_OVER, false);
            }
        }

        // no swap could be made; swap set selection 1 to selection 2 so
```

```
            // matches will be made in that order
            else
            {
                selection1.setSelected(false);
                selection1 = selection2;
            }
        }
    }    // processLeftClick

// processes a right-click event on a given node--this will toggle the
// flagged state of the node
private void processRightClick(Node n)
{
    n.toggleFlagged();

    // play a sound based on the flagged state
    if(n.isFlagged())
    {
        Gamelet.playSound(Nodez.TOGGLE_FLAG_ON, false);
    }
    else
    {
        Gamelet.playSound(Nodez.TOGGLE_FLAG_OFF, false);
    }
}

// processes a mouse click (either left or right) at the given point
public void processMouseClick(Point p, int button)
{
    // see which node contains the sent point, if any
    Node n;
    for(Enumeration e = nodes.elements(); e.hasMoreElements(); )
    {
        n = (Node) e.nextElement();

        // only "still" nodes can be selected
        if(! n.isMoving())
        {
            // if the node contains the point, perform action on it
            if(n.contains(p))
```

```java
                    {
                            if(button == MouseEvent.BUTTON1)
                            {
                                    processLeftClick(n);
                            }
                            else if(button == MouseEvent.BUTTON3)
                            {
                                    processRightClick(n);
                            }

                            return;
                    }
            }
        }
    }

    // tests for game over--the game is over when all nodes are correctly
    // placed in the scene
    public boolean gameOver()
    {
        return (getNumCorrect() == getNumNodes());
    }

    // determines if the scene is "settled"; that is, if there are any nodes
    // that are still moving
    public boolean isSettled()
    {
        for(Enumeration e = nodes.elements(); e.hasMoreElements(); )
        {
            if(((Node) e.nextElement()).isMoving())
            {
                return false;
            }
        }

        return true;
    }

    // determines if two nodes can be swapped; that is, if they are connected
    // by a common circuit line
```

```java
private boolean canSwap(
    int x,    // index of first  node
    int y     // index of second node
    )
{

    // don't swap a Node with itself
    if(x == y)
    {
        return false;
    }


    // this test can be tricky to understand.
    // if x = 2 and y = 3, then we will need to find a circuit whose first
    // value is either 2 or 3 and its second value is also either 2 or 3

    int len = circuits.length;
    for(int i = 0; i < len; i++)
    {
        if( (circuits[i][0] == x || circuits[i][0] == y) &&
            (circuits[i][1] == x || circuits[i][1] == y))
        {
            return true;
        }
    }

    return false;
}

// updates the Vector of node elements
public void update()
{
    for(Enumeration e = nodes.elements(); e.hasMoreElements(); )
    {
        ((Node) e.nextElement()).update();
    }
}

// paints the scene
public void paint(Graphics2D g2d)
{
```

```
                    // paint the node circuitry first
                    g2d.setPaint(CIRCUIT_COLOR);
                    g2d.setStroke(CIRCUIT_STROKE);
                    for(int i = 0; i < circuitLines.length; i++)
                    {
                        g2d.draw(circuitLines[i]);
                    }

                    // create a composite set to be 25% transparent
                    g2d.setComposite(AlphaComposite.getInstance(
                                            AlphaComposite.SRC_OVER, 0.75f));

                    // draw the nodes
                    for(Enumeration e = nodes.elements(); e.hasMoreElements(); )
                    {
                        ((Node) e.nextElement()).paint(g2d);
                    }
                }

        }    // NodezScene
```

The canSwap method is an interesting method that the NodezScene class provides. As you've seen, the Node class contains an index value corresponding to the node positions as shown in Figure 14.5. When the canSwap method is called, the indices of the two nodes the user wants to swap are sent as the x and y parameters. These values are compared against all of the values in the circuits array. If the sent values match both columns within any row of the array, then the nodes can be swapped. For instance, if 0 and 2 are sent as parameters to the canSwap method, then the nodes will be swapped along the diagonal of the circuitry. However, if 1 and 3 are sent as parameters, the method will return false and no swapping will be performed.

Two other important methods provided by the NodezScene class are the processLeftClick and processRightClick methods. When the user clicks a mouse button, the NodezScene processMouseClick is called, taking the mouse position and the button clicked as parameters. If this method determines that a Node object has been clicked, then the appropriate process*XClick method is called, sending the Node for further processing. Generally, left clicking selects or deselects nodes and right clicks toggle the flagged mode of a given node. I'll leave the details of these methods for you to explore.

Another responsibility of the NodezScene class is to load a level given a level number. We'll look at how this is done in the following section.

## Creating the NodezLevel Class

Perhaps the most complex NodezScene method is the loadLevel method. This method takes the level number to load and sets up the nodes as well as the circuit lines. It uses the static NodezLevel getLevel method to get the information for loading the level. The questions that remain are what is the NodezLevel class and how does it work?

The NodezLevel class is a simple container class that holds the vector positions of the nodes to be placed within the scene. It also contains the 2-D array for holding circuit segment connections, just like the one you saw in the preceding section. Again, this array references indices to Node objects' positions as they are placed in the scene.

So that our *Nodez!* game is not confined to specific applet size, node positions will be referenced with respect to the center of the applet window. Therefore, if a node position is specified as (50, 50), then it will actually be placed at 50 units to the right of and 50 units down from the center of the applet window, which will be determined at run time.

Since the NodezLevel class is declared as abstract, it will be up to its subclasses to define the actual positions of the nodes as well as the circuit indices. For this, the NodezLevel class contains several static subclasses that fully implement the methods for creating these fields. The static NodezLevel getLevel method returns a NodezLevel object based on the sent level number, as follows:

```
// returns a new NodezLevel object based on the sent level no.
public static NodezLevel getLevel(int n)
{
    switch(n)
    {
        case 1:
            return new NodezLevel1();

        case 2:
            return new NodezLevel2();

        case 3:
            return new NodezLevel3();

        default:
            return null;
    }
}
```

I won't go into the gory code to implement the NodezLevel subclasses. I suggest you look at this code for yourself and try to figure out how the NodezLevel class works. If you're having trouble figuring out the indexing scheme, try drawing it out on paper as well as running the applet to see the end layouts for yourself.

Now that the subfeatures of the *Nodez!* game have been covered, let's wrap things up by looking at the main Nodez class.

## Creating the Nodez Class

Since the Node and NodezScene classes contain most of the processing for the *Nodez!* game, the only thing left for us to do is create a user interface. The Nodez class extends the Gamelet class and will additionally provide an interface for allowing the user to toggle the audio on and off, connecting to the chat group, and catching keyboard and mouse events. It will also display the status of the game, namely the number of correctly placed nodes and the current level being played.

If you missed out on the Gamelet class description as mentioned earlier in the chapter, go back and reread it. This class is important since it controls the main processing for the game. Without it, you will need to rewrite the mechanisms for double buffering, framerate syncing, menu stacking, and scene management each time you create a new game. With the Gamelet class, these mechanisms will be automated for you.

For the most part, the contents of the Nodez class should come as no surprise: you've already learned about everything the class contains. One curveball I'll throw at you is the finalInit method. Since I wanted to implement a loading screen, I needed a way to postpone as much initialization as I could until this screen could be displayed. Since we don't have a valid Graphics2D context until the update method is called, I decided to create a flag for the first time the update method is called. When the update method is called for the first time, the sent Graphics2D context is passed to the finalInit method. This is where the loading screen is displayed while the rest of the applet is initialized.

The way the loading screen is used is simple yet worth mentioning. The NodezLoader implements the *Runnable* interface so it can provide an animated loading sequence as the applet is loaded in the background. The loading mechanism for the *Nodez!* class works something like the following:

1. Start the loading screen thread.
2. Perform last-minute applet initialization, such as loading up the audio, connecting to the chat group, loading the first level, and registering the keyboard and mouse to fire events back to the applet.
3. Terminate the loading screen thread once initialization has completed.

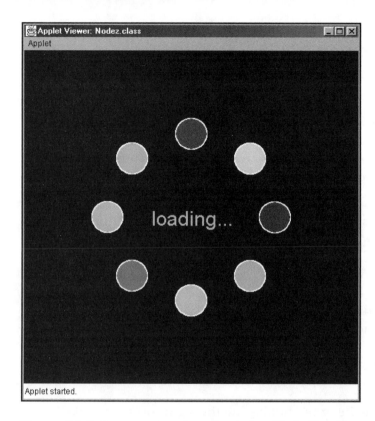

**Figure 14.6**

*The* Nodez! *loading screen*

Figure 14.6 shows a snapshot from the *Nodez!* loading screen.

It's a pretty easy mechanism to implement, and it gives the user something to look at while the applet initializes. Consider implementing a visual loader in each game you create on your own.

You can bring up the code for the Nodez class as well as the NodezLoader class from the CD-ROM if you like. If you're having trouble figuring out anything that's going on, the answer can probably be found in one of the previous chapters. With that in mind, let's finish things up and create the final published *Nodez!* game.

## Creating the Finished Product

Now that you've completed a Java game, it is time to publish it so others can play it. In general, you should use the following steps (taken from my experience) to create a complete Java game from start to finish:

1. Set any security permissions you will need with the policytool utility.
2. Write and test Java code using appletviewer.

3. Archive your game with the `jar` utility or another archive tool.

4. Sign the generated .jar file using the `jarsigner` utility.

5. Create a Java 2 compatible .html file using an .html conversion utility.

6. Enjoy distributing and playing your new Java game!

Indeed, archiving and signing your applets before distribution adds some work on your part, but these steps are necessary to deploy your games effectively. Not sure what a .jar file is or how to set security permissions? No problem. Just check out the appendices at the end of this book and you'll find out how to use the utilities mentioned above.

I insist on testing games with the `appletviewer` utility merely as a matter of convenience. Games can be viewed with the `appletviewer` without needing a converted .html file. I would also hold off on creating the signed .jar file until the end because it's not convenient to update your code archive every time you recompile. In all, just focus on the overall game play first and worry about a polished presentation when you're ready to distribute the finished game. Figure 14.7 shows the finalized *Nodez!* game as it will appear to the end user.

# Conclusion

Creating games can be quite challenging, but having the right tools can make it much easier and more enjoyable. Although Java comes with so many things at your disposal right out of the box, grouping them into focused units makes things even better. Creating a game development engine is one way you can meld native Java classes together so that the development process can run more smoothly.

It goes without saying that for any game engine to be successful, successful games must exist that use it. The *Nodez!* game is a simple example of how a game development engine can be deployed to create a complete Java game. And although it took some work to get the *Magic* game engine up and running, it only took me a few hours to develop the *Nodez!* game. Just imagine what could be done given a few talented programmers, a few weeks, and a whole lot of Mountain Dew!

I won't harass you with chapter exercises any more. Rather, you should now let your abilities run amok and start making some killer Java games. Try improving the *Magic* game engine or write your own from scratch. I have given you the tools to start creating just about any type of Web-enabled game that's popular today. It's now your job to use these tools to make your own games.

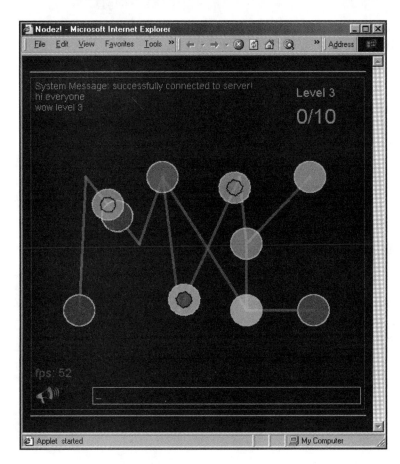

**Figure 14.7**

*The completed* Nodez!
*game as viewed through
Microsoft Internet Explorer*

# Where We Are
# and Where We're Going

I truly hope I have been able to present the wonderful world of game programming with the Java language in a clear and meaningful manner. I hope that we will all walk away from this as better programmers—not just as better game programmers or even better Java programmers, but as better programmers overall. If you've come to this book as a seasoned C++ developer, I hope this book gave you some perspective into expanding your object-oriented know-how into using Java for game development. If you are a novice programmer or have tried languages such as C or C++

and had limited success, you should be able to go back and use the object-oriented paradigm to start making those DirectX or OpenGL enabled games.

But why would you want to go back to C or C++ when you now have the fastest growing programming language at your disposal? Not only does Java have hundreds of classes ready for you to use, but it is also completely platform-compatible. Remember, "write once, run anywhere" is one of the ideals that has made Java the choice among software developers around the world.

By no means should you think that a good Java game can only be created by a Java expert, nor should you feel pressure to code at an expert level after reading this book. However, with a little bit of creativity and this book as your reference, anything is possible.

I'd like to take this final opportunity to thank you for reading *Java 2 Game Programming*. I hope you've enjoyed working through the sample programs and exercises as much as I did creating them. Armed with a solid understanding of how Java can be used for game development, there's no reason you won't be able to help change the face of online gaming, and that's the bottom line. So go ahead and start writing some killer games—'cause Stone Cold…SAID SO!

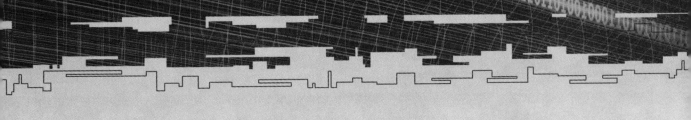

# Part Four

# Appendices

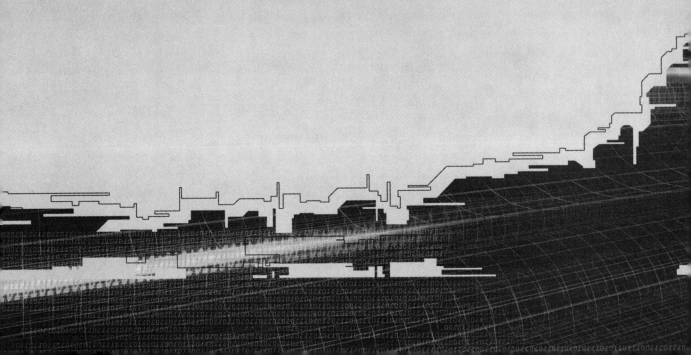

# APPENDIX A

# USING THE JAVADOC UTILITY

Y ou've probably noticed that the Standard Edition of the Java 2 platform comes with an obscene number of ready-to-use packages and classes right out of the box. This vast amount of resources would be practically unusable without some type of documentation that describes the purpose, use, and syntax of each package, class, and method available. Such documentation must also be accessible on any platform. For example, documentation written in Microsoft Word format wouldn't be of much use to someone working in a Solaris environment. Plain ASCII text files would work, but it wouldn't be convenient for the user to hunt down the specific information he or she needs from a pool of hundreds of different text files. There must be an easier way.

If you have used the Java 2 documentation before, then you know that this documentation is presented in the form of .html documents that can be loaded into any Web browser. This is the perfect solution, since these files can be viewed on any system containing Web browser software, plus these files have a wide range of capabilities such as hyperlink support, variable font display, and image support. Figure A.1 shows the documentation for the Applet class, if you haven't yet seen it for yourself.

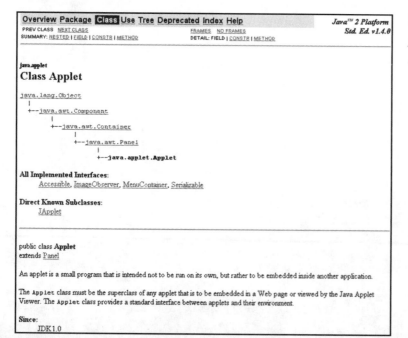

**Figure A.1**

*A portion of the Applet class documentation*

You've probably also noticed that the documentation for the Java 2 platform is actually quite pleasant looking. It contains frames, tables, and hyperlinks that link everything together. It would take a tremendous amount of time for the engineers at Sun to create documentation like this for the more than 2,500 available Java classes and interfaces. Therefore, it comes as no surprise that the process of documentation generation is a highly automated process.

In fact, the documentation for each Java class comes from each of their source files directly. You saw all the way back in Part One that javadoc comments are used not only for inline documentation but also for exporting code documentation to the javadoc utility. Remember that javadoc comments always come in the following form:

```
/**
 * This is a simple javadoc comment
 */
```

Notice that the first line begins with /**, which begins the comment, and the last line ends with */, which terminates the comment. Each line in between should start with its own asterisk as well.

Notice also that each documented class is separated into two parts: a *summary* section and a *detail* section. For each documented method or field, the first sentence of the comment is placed in the summary section, along with the method or field name. The entire javadoc comment block is placed in the detail part of the document. Therefore, the first sentence of any javadoc block should give a complete, yet concise, explanation of the functionality of the specified field or method.

In addition to generating plain-vanilla comments relating to Java code, you can also insert javadoc tags as well as .html tags that can perform a number of things. This tagging mechanism works like the following:

```
/**
 * comment line 1
 *
 * @tag   <tag parameters here>
 */
```

The javadoc utility recognizes a number of valid tags. Here are just a few you may find useful when commenting your code:

1. **@author.** Used to specify the author (or authors) of the class or interface being documented.
2. **@version.** Specifies the version of the tagged class or interface.
3. **@param.** Details parameters that are sent to a given method.

4. **@return.** Details the value returned by a nonvoid method.
5. **@throws.** Lists any occurrences when an exception may arise.
6. **@see.** Creates a link to a related class or method.
7. **@since.** Specifies the first version of Java under which the tagged code was implemented.
8. **@depreciated.** Specifies that the tagged code has been depreciated but is still included for backward compatibility.

When adding these tags to your code, you should add them in the order specified above. Notice that the `@author` and `@version` tags are only used with class or interface descriptions, and others, such as `@param`, `@return`, and `@throws`, are only used in conjunction with method and constructor details.

The following illustrates a few `javadoc` comment blocks for the `Actor2D` class. It contains a block for the class description, some field declarations, and one of the method descriptions.

```
package magic.actor2d;

import java.awt.*;
import java.awt.geom.*;
import java.util.*;

import magic.graphics.*;

/**
 * The <code>Actor2D</code> class is the base class for all actor objects
 * that can be added to a game scene.  Each <code>Actor2D</code> object
 * takes an <code>ActorGroup2D</code> object that specifies the global
 * properties of all actors.  Specific <code>Actor2D</code> instances specify
 * the specific state of the object, such as its position, velocity, and
 * animation state.
 *
 * @author   Thomas Petchel
 * @version  1.0
 *
 * @see      ActorGroup2D
 * @see      StaticActor
 * @see      Moveable
 * @since    1.4
```

```
*/

public abstract class Actor2D extends java.lang.Object implements Moveable
{
    /** The ALIVE state of an actor */
    public final int STATE_ALIVE = 1;

    /** The DYING state of an actor */
    public final int STATE_DYING = 2;

    /** The DEAD state of an actor */
    public final int STATE_DEAD  = 4;

    // more declarations here...

    /**
     * Creates a new Actor2D object belonging to the given ActorGroup2D
     *
     * @param grp the ActorGroup2D this actor belongs to
     */

    public Actor2D(ActorGroup2D grp)
    {
        // constructor code here...
    }

    /**
     * determines whether this actor has collided with another actor
     *
     * @param other the external Actor2D to test collision against
     * @return <code>true</code> if the sent actor has collided with this actor
     */

    // more methods here...

}    // Actor2D
```

Notice the use of the <code> tag. Using .html tags like this can offset important code so that it stands out. To generate the actual .html files containing inline documentation, simply run the javadoc utility, which on Win32 machines would typically be found under the \bin directory of the directory where you installed Java. After you have compiled a particular package, you can javadoc it like the following (again, using a Win32 path name):

```
javadoc -author C:\magic\actor2d\*.java
```

The -author parameter tells the javadoc utility to output any @author tags it comes across.

Figure A.2 illustrates the javadoc documentation for one of the classes found within the *Magic* game engine, the Actor2D class.

There are also a number of additional tags you can use to enhance your inline documentation, such as the {@link} tag. This tag allows you to provide a hyperlink inline with the comment block. It follows the format

```
{@link #name label}
```

where name refers to the actual code to link to (such as java.lang.Object#hashCode), and label specifies the actual code to display (such as hashCode}. Refer to the Java 2 documentation for more on this tag and any other tags I did not go over.

In all, javadoc comments should be used when needed, but not in excess. Of course, you don't have to javadoc code that you will keep privately. Use the javadoc utility when you wish to publish documentation alongside code you distribute, such as a game engine or the source listing to one of your games. Also, be sure to check Sun's Java Web site (http://www.java.sun.com) for any updates made to the javadoc utility, as it is frequently altered to fit the requests of Java developers.

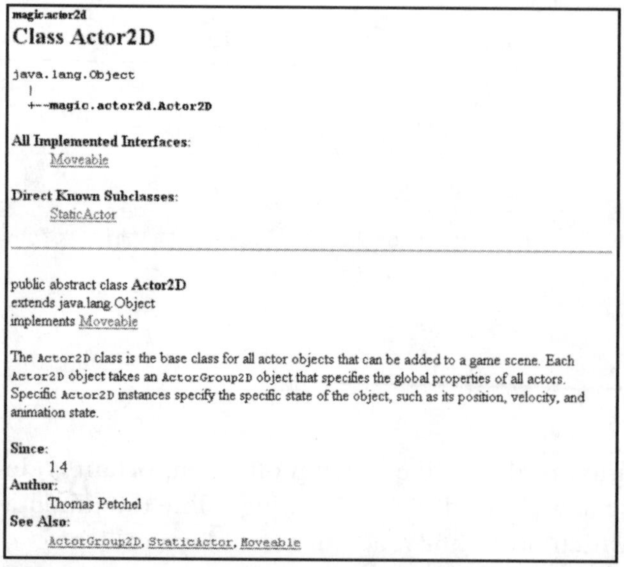

magic.actor2d

Class Actor2D

```
java.lang.Object
  |
  +--magic.actor2d.Actor2D
```

**All Implemented Interfaces:**
Moveable

**Direct Known Subclasses:**
StaticActor

public abstract class **Actor2D**
extends java.lang.Object
implements Moveable

The Actor2D class is the base class for all actor objects that can be added to a game scene. Each Actor2D object takes an ActorGroup2D object that specifies the global properties of all actors. Specific Actor2D instances specify the specific state of the object, such as its position, velocity, and animation state.

**Since:**
1.4
**Author:**
Thomas Petchel
**See Also:**
ActorGroup2D, StaticActor, Moveable

**Figure A.2**

*A peek at the documentation for the* Actor2D *class*

# APPENDIX B

# Some Common Java Do's and Don'ts

In your programming endeavors using Java, you'll come across instances where the code you write can either optimize or hinder the output of your programs. Here are just a few points you should consider when writing Java code. Some of them detail practices you should definitely incorporate into your code; others are things you should definitely avoid.

- ***Do* code abstractly, but not too abstractly.** The principle of abstraction is one of the cornerstones of object-oriented programming. Since Java is nearly 100 percent object-oriented, knowing when to abstract becomes even more important.

    For instance, the `Component2D` class we developed in Chapter 12 is a great example of when abstraction works to our advantage. With it, we can generically declare several `Component2D` instances and later define them each in completely different ways. For example, a `Component2D` array declared with nine members can later be defined as three `Button2D` objects, five `Label2D` objects, and one `Panel2D` object. These components can be redeclared as nine `Menu2D` objects, and everything will still work.

    So remember to use abstraction only when it will benefit or clarify your code. For example, do not implement separate `Kingdom`, `Phylum`, `Class`, `Order`, `Family`, `Genus`, and `Species` classes if you only need to define a single `K9` class that contains the name and age of a person's pet mutt.

- ***Don't* use Java reflection classes.** The `java.lang.reflect` package contains classes that allow Java classes to obtain information about themselves. Uses of this package include determining the run-time name of an object, along with any methods it contains. These classes are commonly used in the Java Virtual Machine itself, as well as external debuggers and profilers. If you come from a C++ background, you have probably used function pointers in your code. Since Java does not contain support for function (or method) pointers, it might seem tempting to send a `Method` object as a parameter to a function to simulate this functionality. I avoid using these classes whenever possible, especially for game programming. First, these classes can really bog down throughput of your applications, and as you know, speed is a critical component to any game. Reflection classes also blur the meaning of your code and can often be replaced by techniques that are more "organic" in nature.

So as a general rule, just say "no" to reflection and use preferred Java techniques such as anonymous inner classes, subclasses, or, if you need to, a good old-fashioned `switch` block, to discriminate among different routes of flow control.

- *Do* **try to incorporate code that optimizes both speed *and* size of your programs.** This includes incorporating things such as image strips into your projects, as well as eliminating the use of synchronization and exception handling when possible. Don't, however, blindly eliminate all of your exception-handling code; if catching an exception can save your program from completely bombing, by all means use it.

  Excessive use of threading can bog down your programs as well. Using a few threads in your games is usually necessary, but having 500 `Actor2D` objects each use their own threads may cause your machine to spend all of its time switching between threads, which will obviously slow things down way too much.

  Also, since machine memory has become, so available in the last few years, I would generally take speed over size if it comes down to choosing between the two. This includes prerendering drawing, filling, and text-rendering operations to a `BufferedImage` object instead of making the equivalent `Graphics2D` calls once per frame, which can become quite costly when high-quality metrics or compositing is needed.

- *Don't* **use Swing classes for games.** Although programmatically Java Swing is a very clean and robust way to create applications, I have generally found it to be too bloated for game development. Components such as `JApplet`, `JFrame`, `JButton`, etc., are based upon their lightweight AWT counterparts and contain the ability to take on a pluggable look and feel of any operating system. I feel that the benefits that Swing provides do not outweigh the speed hits that it makes on applications. Use Swing for that next productivity title you work on; less productive programs, such as games, can do without it.

- *Do* **think about minor code optimizations, but not too much.** Techniques such as loop unrolling and using register variables used to be very common among game programmers. However, with advances in processor speed, such as seen with today's 2 GHz bruisers, minor optimizations have become more of an afterthought. I suppose Donald Knuth (if you don't know who he is, look him up) put it best with this quote: "We should forget about small efficiencies, say about 97 percent of the time: premature optimization is the root of all evil." So if Mr. Knuth thinks it's bad to make small optimizations and efficiencies, then I do too.

- *Don't* **use sun.\* packages.** Java packages such as those contained under `java.*`, `javax.*`, and `org.*` are standard and are supported across all platforms, but classes under the sun.* package are not. Classes under sun.* packages are generally platform-specific and are known to change from version to version. For instance, say you have used the Image class to load and draw images from file. This is an abstract class, and it is programmed abstractly. On Win32 platforms, the Image class is implemented as the WImage class found under the sun.awt.windows package. Obviously, this package is not part of the standard Java 2 API. Furthermore, this class or its methods are not guaranteed to exist in further Java implementations. So even if you program your games exclusively for Windows, directly using the WImage class, or any other sun.* package class, is risky business.

■ **Don't calculate values more than once if possible.** It goes without saying that all program calculations take a finite processor time to execute. Therefore, the fewer calculations your game code makes, the faster it will run.

The sine, cosine, and tangent lookup tables implemented in the *Magic* MagicUtils class are one example of when precalculating values can greatly increase program throughput. Although methods such as Math sin calculate angular measurements quite quickly, continuous calls made frame after frame can actually start slowing things down. To illustrate this, try out the *UtilsTest* program found on the CD-ROM. It measures the time it takes to calculate the sine, cosine, and tangent of 10 million random numbers first using the Math class, and then calculates the same measurements using the same 10 million numbers using the values stored in the MagicUtils class. You'll see after running this program that the MagicUtils approach calculates the values considerably faster. To make things fair, the second measurement also incorporates the time it took to create the sine, cosine, and tangent lookup tables.

Referencing things such as string literals time after time can also slow down programs. For instance, referencing the string literal "All is well" over and over causes a new String object to be allocated each time. By creating String constants, you can eliminate the need to allocate memory when it is not necessary. For instance, consider making changes like the following in your code:

```
// a wasteful use of memory:
while(! input.equals("Finished"))
{
        // loop code here
}

// a better use of memory:
final String SENTINEL = "Finished";
```

```
while(! input.equals(SENTINEL))
{
        // loop code here
}
```

The reason I rarely follow this rule is that it can sometimes bloat example code. I feel that as far as example programs go, highlighting their purposes first should come before making any minor speed or size optimizations.

- *Don't* **attempt to optimize Java.** Here, I emphasize the word "attempt." Although you can sometimes find ways to rewrite standard C functions to perform faster or better, I wouldn't try to improve upon any standard Java class or method. Even if it looks like making an optimization to native Java code would be appropriate, it might not be due to considerations such as Java Virtual Machine issues or platform compatibility. So, if you think you have spotted an error in the native Java source, report it to Sun. If your optimization is indeed valid, it just might be included in a future edition of Java.

  Keep in mind that optimizing Java code doesn't mean that you shouldn't *extend* upon available Java classes. We've made hundreds of extensions to what's available in the standard Java library. My point is that if you feel as though you have developed a better `LinkedList` class (i.e., one that behaves *exactly* like the one provided) than the native one, you probably haven't.

There are hundreds more common do's and don'ts that are applicable to Java programming. However, I hope that these eight will make you think about some of the ways you can improve upon your own code so that your games will perform as quickly and efficiently as possible.

# APPENDIX C

# Using the JN1 to Create a Gamepad Reader

The object-oriented paradigm implemented in the Java language allows you to develop better programs in less time. However, if you have a large bank of code that you have already written in languages such as C or C++ and want to deploy it in Java, then you'll find yourself spending a lot of time rewriting your code. This process can be tough enough the way it is, but it gets even worse if your existing code uses low-level routines such as assembly language routines, which have no direct correlation in Java. Thankfully, Java provides a way to use existing code in your programs, by way of the Java Native Interface, or JNI. By using the JNI, you can speed up the overall development process as well as add power to your Java programs.

To illustrate how the JNI works, let's create a simple gamepad reader that can read the x- and y-axis of a gamepad as well as the two standard buttons that most gamepads contain.

The heart of the JNI lies in the use of native methods. A method declared as `native` tells the compiler that the method is actually implemented using a shared library written in some other language. Native methods are declared like the following:

```
public native void myMethod();
```

Of course, you can have a multitude of return types, as well as specify any number of method parameters. In general, you'll need to follow these steps to create native interface methods:

1. Write and compile Java code that contains any needed native methods, as well as the main method that will call them.
2. Generate a header file for your native methods by using the `javah` utility.
3. Tweak the source code that implements your native methods.
4. Compile your native source code into a shared library file, such as a .dll file under the Windows platform or a .so file under Solaris.
5. Enjoy your newly created native code!

I know, I know. It seems weird that the steps are backward. In essence, you must know the details about the native calls you will make before you write the code. But if you already have your native code lying around, you'll be ahead of the game.

As mentioned above, you need to write your Java code first. Doing so will provide the `javah` utility with the method names to export so your Java code and native code will match up. The following class sets up a simple gamepad reader that can access the state of the crosspad and two of its buttons.

```java
public class GamepadTest
{
    // masks for the gamepad buttons
    public static final int BUTTON_1 = 0x10;
    public static final int BUTTON_2 = 0x20;

    // the x and y axis of the crosspad
    public static final int GAMEPAD_AXIS_X = 1;
    public static final int GAMEPAD_AXIS_Y = 2;

    // the "centered" state of the crosspad
    public static int centerX;
    public static int centerY;

    // the max/min "bounds" of the crosspad
    public static int maxX;
    public static int minX;
    public static int maxY;
    public static int minY;

    // determines if the given button is being pressed
    public native int  gamepadButtonPressed(int button);

    // returns the position of the sent axis
    public native int  gamepadAxis(int axis);

    // load the shared library
    static
    {
        System.loadLibrary("GamepadImpl");
    }

    // creates a new GamepadTest object and calibrates the gamepad
    public GamepadTest()
    {
        calibrateGamepad();
```

```java
}


public void calibrateGamepad()
{
    System.out.println(
            "Swirl the gamepad around a bit then hit any button");

    // initialize the bounds to impossible values
    maxX = 0;
    maxY = 0;
    minX = 100000;
    minY = 100000;

    int x = 0;
    int y = 0;
    while(0 == gamepadButtonPressed(BUTTON_1 | BUTTON_2))
    {
        x = gamepadAxis(GAMEPAD_AXIS_X);
        y = gamepadAxis(GAMEPAD_AXIS_Y);

        // update the max/min values as the user swirls the crosspad
        maxX = Math.max(x, maxX);
        minX = Math.min(x, minX);
        maxY = Math.max(y, maxY);
        minY = Math.min(y, minY);
    }

    // user lets go of the crosspad; this must be our center position
    centerX = x;
    centerY = y;

    System.out.println(«Calibration complete!»);
    System.out.println("xmin: " + minX + " xcenter: " +
                        centerX + « xmax: « + maxX);
    System.out.println(«ymin: « + minY + « ycenter: « +
                        centerY + " ymax: " + maxY);
```

```java
        }

        public static void main(String args[])
        {
            GamepadTest test = new GamepadTest();

            int lastX = test.gamepadAxis(GAMEPAD_AXIS_X);
            int lastY = test.gamepadAxis(GAMEPAD_AXIS_Y);

            while(true)
            {
                // output any button-down states
                if(test.gamepadButtonPressed(BUTTON_1) != 0)
                {
                    System.out.println("Button 1 down!");
                }
                if(test.gamepadButtonPressed(BUTTON_2) != 0)
                {
                    System.out.println("Button 2 down!");
                }

                // output the crosspad states
                int x = test.gamepadAxis(GAMEPAD_AXIS_X);
                int y = test.gamepadAxis(GAMEPAD_AXIS_Y);

                if(x > centerX)
                {
                    System.out.println("+x");
                }
                else if(x < centerX)
                {
                    System.out.println("-x");
                }

                if(y > centerY)
                {
                    System.out.println("+y");
```

```
                    }
                    else if(y < centerY)
                    {
                            System.out.println("-y");
                    }


                }
            }
        }    // GamepadTest
```

Note the use of the native gamepadButtonPressed and gamepadAxis methods. These methods will be implemented in our native C code later. Compile the GamepadTest class with the javac utility and you'll be done with step 1. Also note the use of the System loadLibrary method. This will load the specified library at run time, implicitly adding the required suffix to the file name specified. So on a Solaris machine, the Virtual Machine will attempt to load the library file named GamepadImpl.so.

Step 2 will be a no-brainer. Simply run the javah utility with the –jni flag to generate a C-style header file containing the declarations for our native methods, like the following:

```
javah -jni GamepadTest
```

Here, GamepadTest refers to the .class file generated by the javac utility. It will generate a file named GamepadTest.h containing a body similar to the following:

```
/* DO NOT EDIT THIS FILE - it is machine generated */
#include <jni.h>
/* Header for class GamepadTest */

#ifndef _Included_GamepadTest
#define _Included_GamepadTest
#ifdef __cplusplus
extern "C" {
#endif
/*
 * Class:     GamepadTest
 * Method:    gamepadButtonPressed
 * Signature: (I)I
 */
JNIEXPORT jint JNICALL Java_GamepadTest_gamepadButtonPressed
```

```
    (JNIEnv *, jobject, jint);

/*
 * Class:     GamepadTest
 * Method:    gamepadAxis
 * Signature: (I)I
 */
JNIEXPORT jint JNICALL Java_GamepadTest_gamepadAxis
  (JNIEnv *, jobject, jint);

#ifdef __cplusplus
}
#endif
#endif
```

For Step 3, you must tweak your original source code file so that the method declarations match those found in the header file. The following code listing is a watered-down version of a gamepad reader I found in the book *Teach Yourself Game Programming in 21 Days,* written by none other than the Series Editor of this book, André LaMothe.

```c
#include <jni.h>
#include <conio.h>
#include "GamepadTest.h"

#define PORT 0x201

JNIEXPORT jint JNICALL Java_GamepadTest_gamepadButtonPressed
  (JNIEnv *env, jobject obj, jint button)
{
    _outp(PORT, 0);

    return (~_inp(PORT) & button);
}

JNIEXPORT jint JNICALL Java_GamepadTest_gamepadAxis
  (JNIEnv *env, jobject obj, jint stick)
{
    short ret_val;

    _asm
```

```
    {
        cli

        mov ah, byte ptr stick

        xor al, al
        xor cx, cx

        mov dx, PORT
        out dx, al

    discharge:

        in al, dx
        test al, ah
        loopne discharge

        sti
        xor ax, ax
        sub ax, cx

        mov ret_val, ax
    }

    return (int) ret_val;
}
```

Since we're focusing on using the JNI at the moment, I won't go into detail on how the above methods work. If you're good at assembly, then these methods shouldn't seem too hard to follow. The above code was saved in a file named GamepadImpl.c, which you can also find on the companion CD-ROM. Just keep in mind that all I had to do to convert the above source listing was change the header declarations to match those found in GamepadTest.h. Also remember that you have to include jni.h as well as GamepadTest.h in your source file so everything will compile and link correctly.

At this point, you'll need to compile the GamepadImpl.c file into a shared library file. Since the method for doing this varies from platform to platform, I won't go into details here. I'm currently on a Win32 machine, so I used Microsoft Visual C++ to create a new Win32 Dynamic-Link Library project with a Release build. I then copied the compiled .dll file to my project directory containing the original Java source.

You're now ready to start using your newly created native Java program! Making sure you have the compiled Java code as well as your shared library file in the same directory, go ahead and invoke the java utility as follows:

```
java GamepadTest
```

If you receive any run-time errors like an UnsatisfiedLinkError, then you'll need to go back and make sure you performed each step correctly. This error can pop up if you named the library file incorrectly, you placed it in the wrong directory, or it does not contain the methods that match the given declarations.

That's it for our simple gamepad reader. Of course, there's much more on the specifics of the JNI in the Java 2 documentation. Try writing a program that moves around an Actor2D object with a gamepad. Since you must implement a main method, it would be easiest to add your Applet class to a Frame object. You can also try writing a listener class that will continually poll the gamepad and automatically inform the main program that a gamepad event has occurred.

# APPENDIX D

# USING .JAR FILES TO DEPLOY JAVA APPLETS

O nce you have a completed game that you'd like to distribute over the Internet, you might want to consider archiving it into a single compressed file. Packaging applets or applications serves a dual purpose. First, since a package consists of a single file, the number of remote file requests from the server is always one. Instead of forcing a separate request for dozens or even hundreds of separate image, sound, and .class files, having only a single file request will surely save on the overall download time. Secondly, since the package file itself is compressed, the overall size of the download will be smaller, thus decreasing overall download time as well.

The preferred format for compressing Java applets and applications is the .jar format, which stands for *Java Ar*chive. The .jar format is based on the standard ZIP and ZLIB compression formats. Although you can generally use a commercial compression tool, such as PKZIP or WinZip, to archive your Java programs, Java provides a `jar` utility that will automate and optimize the process you.

There are three types of input specifications available to the jar utility: the actual files to be archived (image, sound, .class files), the .jar file to archive, and an optional manifest file. Flags can be specified to perform tasks such as creating a new archive, updating an archive, or extracting from an archive.

A .jar file can consist of any number of other .jar files. Therefore, it might make sense to first archive code you'll include in several distributions (such as a game engine) into its own .jar file. The following command packages the contents of the *Magic* engine into a single package named *magic.jar*:

```
jar cvf magic.jar actor2d awtex debug gamelet graphics net scene net
```

The above command creates a file named *magic.jar* and adds to it the contents of each of the specified directories. The *v* flag tells the `jar` utility to verbose output to the standard error stream.

Once you complete a game or application, you can package it for distribution as well. The following command archives the *Nodez!* game you saw in Chapter 14:

```
jar cvf nodez.jar *.class *.gif *.au -C magic magic.jar
```

Here, a file named *nodez.jar* is created containing all .class, .gif, and .au files contained in the current directory. The *-C* flag tells the jar utility to temporarily change directories and package the next argument. So the *magic.jar* file found in the /`magic` directory will also be added to the archive.

Starting with the 1.3 release of Java, an optional –*i* flag can be specified to more efficiently load files from a .jar package. This flag causes the `jar` utility to create an index file under the `/meta-inf` directory of the .jar package. In cases where several .jar files are embedded within a single package, the files needed to be extracted can be compared against the index so that only the necessary .jar files will be downloaded from the server.

If you want to add an index to a .jar package, simply run the `jar` utility a second time with the –*i* flag, like the following:

```
jar -i nodez.jar
```

Pretty simple. If you have created a .jar file containing applet code, then you now must specify this file in your .html code. The following code loads the *Nodez!* game by specifying *nodez.jar* as the file archive:

```
<APPLET CODE = Nodez.class ARCHIVE = nodez.jar WIDTH = 500 HEIGHT = 500></APPLET>
```

If your applet code requires security permissions to be made, you can do so by creating a signed .jar file. Refer to the Java Documentation for more on signing applets on your platform.

With just a few simple commands from the command-prompt you can create a compressed archive containing the files needed for your applet or application. This can significantly improve the download time required to receive remote applications. Once you have an .html file set up to display the applet, check out Appendix E for more on converting this document for use with the Java 2 plugin.

# APPENDIX E

# CORRECTLY RUNNING JAVA 2 APPLETS

You saw back in Part One how to code an .html file to read a Java applet. The following HTML code illustrates the use of the `<APPLET>` tag to load an applet named *MyGame*.

```
<html>
<head>
<title>My Game</title>
</head>
<body>
<APPLET CODE = MyGame.class WIDTH = 500 HEIGHT = 500> </APPLET>
</body>
</html>
```

This code works fine for pre-Java 2 applets or for use with the `appletviewer` utility. But if you want to view a Java 2 applet within a Web browser, the code will come up short, giving you only an empty gray box and some type of error message.

In the Web browser world, it basically comes down to two flavors: Netscape and Internet Explorer. No matter which browser you use, you will first need to install the Java 2 plugin for the current release before you can view Java 2 applets. The Java 2 plugin comes with the Java 2 SDK, and it can also be downloaded separately. Once the plugin is installed, you can view Java 2 applets after running a quick conversion utility.

The `HTMLConverter` utility essentially converts your .html files to a format readable by the Java 2 plugin. It leaves non-applet related code as it is, but adds additional tags for the Java 2 plugin to read. If your .html file contains content other than the applet itself, you might want to put the commands to run the converter into a batch or script file to save typing. Since Win32 platforms are most popular, here are the commands you might place within a batch (.bat) file to run the `HTMLConverter` utility:

```
PATH=.;C:\JDK1.4\bin;%PATH%
java -jar C:\JDK1.4\lib\htmlconverter.jar MyGame.html
```

Although there are several flags you can specify for additional options and logging, you can usually get away with the bare-bones command. The *–jar* flag tells the java program that the converter is contained within a .jar file; .jar files are discussed in more detail in Appendix *D*.

Take a look at the .html code after running the `HTMLConverter` utility. You'll notice that the applet tags look a bit mangled, but the applet can now be run within a standard Web browser. If you forgot to back up your original .html file, don't worry. The conversion utility backs up your original source, unless you specify for it not to. Running the conversion utility with no additional backup flags will create a backup folder with the same name as the current directory, but with a "_BAK" extension. If you ran the conversion utility to convert a file under the \Source\ Chapter14 folder, then the backup will automatically be placed under the folder named \Source\Chatper14_BAK.

As far as normal applet testing goes, I prefer to use an unconverted .html file and use the `appletviewer` utility, which allows me to quickly run the applet without any extra work. But for a finished product, creating a converted .html file is necessary to view the applet with the Java 2 browser plugin.

# APPENDIX F

# Source Code Listing for the Magic Game Engine

C hapter 14 culminated with a brief look at the *Magic* Java game development engine. Actually, there isn't much magic to it at all; just solid implementation of topics we had already covered. From graphics to networking, the *Magic* engine contains many classes to either guide you in the development of your own game engine, or to start using right away. For your convenience, here's a class-by-class listing of what the *Magic* engine contains, sorted by package. For more details on the layout or implementation of the *Magic* engine, refer to Chapter 14. With that in mind, let's start with the classes contained under the magic.actor2d package:

# The magic.actor2d Package

## The Actor2D Class

```
package magic.actor2d;

import java.awt.*;
import java.awt.geom.*;
import java.util.*;

import magic.graphics.*;

// contains general information for moving and rendering a 2-D game object
public abstract class Actor2D extends Object implements Moveable
{
    // some general states an actor might have
    public final int STATE_ALIVE = 1;
    public final int STATE_DYING = 2;
    public final int STATE_DEAD  = 4;

    // the state of this actor
    protected int state;

    // the actor group this actor belongs to
```

```java
    protected ActorGroup2D group;

    // position, velocity, and rotation of the actor, along with cached
    // transformation
    protected Vector2D pos;
    protected Vector2D vel;
    protected double    rotation;
    protected AffineTransform xform;

    protected final double TWO_PI = 2*Math.PI;

    // a bounding rectangle for things such as collision testing
    protected Rectangle2D bounds;

    // a list of actors this actor has collided with during one frame
    protected LinkedList collisionList;

    // width and height of this actor
    protected int frameWidth;
    protected int frameHeight;

    // reference to this actor's current animation strip
    protected AnimationStrip currAnimation;

    // number of frames to wait before animating the next frame, plus a wait
    // counter
    protected int animWait;
    protected int animCount;

    // creates a new Actor2D object belonging to the given ActorGroup
    public Actor2D(ActorGroup2D grp)
    {
        group = grp;

        bounds = new Rectangle2D.Double();
        collisionList = new LinkedList();

        state = 0;

        pos   = new Vector2D.Double();
```

```java
            vel    = new Vector2D.Double();
            rotation = 0;
            xform = new AffineTransform();

            currAnimation = null;
            animWait  = 0;
            animCount = 0;

            frameWidth  = 0;
            frameHeight = 0;
        }


        // animates the actor every animWait frames
        public void animate()
        {
            if(currAnimation != null)
            {
                if(++animCount >= animWait)
                {
                    currAnimation.getNextFrame();
                    animCount = 0;
                }
            }
        }


        // draws the actor using its native transformation
        public void paint(Graphics2D g2d)
        {
            if(currAnimation != null)
            {
                g2d.drawImage(currAnimation.getCurrFrame(), xform,
                            AnimationStrip.observer);
            }
        }


        // draws the actor at the sent x,y coordinates
        public void paint(Graphics2D g2d, double x, double y)
        {
            if(currAnimation != null)
```

```java
        {
            g2d.drawImage(currAnimation.getCurrFrame(),
                          AffineTransform.getTranslateInstance(x, y),
                          AnimationStrip.observer
                          );
        }
    }

    // simple bounding-box determination of whether this actor has collided with
    // the sent actor
    public boolean intersects(Actor2D other)
    {
        return bounds.intersects(other.getBounds());
    }

    // updates the bounding rectangle of this actor to meet its current x and y
    // positions
    public void updateBounds()
    {
        // make sure we know the correct width and height of the actor
        if(frameWidth <= 0 && currAnimation != null)
        {
            frameWidth = currAnimation.getFrameWidth();
        }
        if(frameHeight <= 0 && currAnimation != null)
        {
            frameHeight = currAnimation.getFrameHeight();
        }

        bounds.setRect(pos.getX(), pos.getY(), frameWidth, frameHeight);
    }

    // makes sure that the actor's bounds have not exceeded the bounds specified
    // by its actor group
    public void checkBounds()
    {
        if(group == null) return;

        if(bounds.getX() < group.MIN_X_POS)
```

```java
            {
                pos.setX(group.MIN_X_POS);
            }

            else if(bounds.getX() + frameWidth > group.MAX_X_POS)
            {
                pos.setX(group.MAX_X_POS - frameWidth);
            }

            if(bounds.getY() < group.MIN_Y_POS)
            {
                pos.setY(group.MIN_Y_POS);
            }

            else if(bounds.getY() + frameHeight > group.MAX_Y_POS)
            {
                pos.setY(group.MAX_Y_POS - frameHeight);
            }
    }

    // returns a String representation of this actor
    public String toString()
    {
        return super.toString();
    }

    // bitwise OR's the sent attribute state with the current attribute state
    public final void setState(int attr)
    {
        state |= attr;
    }

    // resets an attribute using the bitwise AND and NOT operators
    public final void resetState(int attr)
    {
        state &= ~attr;
    }

    public final int getState()
```

```java
{
    return state;
}

public final void clearState()
{
    state = 0;
}

// determines if the sent state attribute is contained in this actor's state
// attribute
public final boolean hasState(int attr)
{
    return ((state & attr) != 0);
}

// access methods for the velocity, position, and rotation of the actor

public final void setX(double px)
{
    pos.setX(px);
}

public final void setY(double py)
{
    pos.setY(py);
}

public final double getX()
{
    return pos.getX();
}

public final double getY()
{
    return pos.getY();
}

public final void setPos(int x, int y)
```

```java
{
    pos.setX(x);
    pos.setY(y);
}

public final void setPos(double x, double y)
{
    pos.setX(x);
    pos.setY(y);
}

public final void setPos(Vector2D v)
{
    pos.setX(v.getX());
    pos.setY(v.getY());
}

public final Vector2D getPos()
{
    return pos;
}

public final void setRot(double theta)
{
    rotation = theta;
}

public final double getRot()
{
    return rotation;
}

public final void rotate(double theta)
{
    rotation += theta;

    while(rotation > TWO_PI)
    {
```

```
            rotation -= TWO_PI;
        }
        while(rotation < -TWO_PI)
        {
            rotation += TWO_PI;
        }
    }

    public final void setVel(int x, int y)
    {
        vel.setX(x);
        vel.setY(y);
    }

    public final void setVel(Vector2D v)
    {
        vel.setX(v.getX());
        vel.setY(v.getY());
    }

    public final Vector2D getVel()
    {
        return vel;
    }

    public final void moveBy(double x, double y)
    {
        pos.translate(x, y);
    }

    public final void moveBy(int x, int y)
    {
        pos.translate(x, y);
    }

    public final void moveBy(Vector2D v)
    {
        pos.translate(v);
```

```java
        }

        public final void accelerate(double ax, double ay)
        {
            vel.setX(vel.getX() + ax);
            vel.setY(vel.getY() + ay);
        }

        public int getWidth()
        {
            return frameWidth;
        }

        public int getHeight()
        {
            return frameHeight;
        }

        // methods inherited from the Moveable interface

        public Rectangle2D getBounds()
        {
            return bounds;
        }

        // determines if a Moveable object has collided with this object
        public boolean collidesWith(Moveable other)
        {
            if(this == other)
            {
                return false;
            }

            return (bounds.contains(other.getBounds()) ||
                    other.getBounds().contains(bounds) ||
                    bounds.intersects(other.getBounds()));
        }
```

```java
// adds a collision object to this collision list
public void addCollision(Moveable other)
{
    if(collisionList == null)
    {
        collisionList = new LinkedList();
        collisionList.add(other);
        return;
    }

    if(! collisionList.contains(other))
    {
        collisionList.add(other);
    }
}

// stub method for processing collisions with those actors contained within
// the collisionsList this method is left empty, but not abstract
public void processCollisions()
{

}

// updates the object's position and bounding box, animates it, then updates
// the transformation
public void update()
{
    pos.translate(vel);

    updateBounds();
    checkBounds();

    animate();

    // subclasses which require the transformation to be centered about an
    // anchor point other than the position will need to override this
    // method
    if(rotation != 0)
```

```
            {
                xform.setToIdentity();
                xform.translate(pos.getX()+frameWidth/2,
                                pos.getY()+frameHeight/2);
                xform.rotate(rotation);
                xform.translate(-frameWidth/2, -frameHeight/2);
            }
            else
            {
                xform.setToTranslation(pos.getX(), pos.getY());
            }
        }

    }    // Actor2D
```

## The ActorGroup2D Class

```
    package magic.actor2d;

    import java.applet.*;

    import magic.graphics.*;

    // defines related attributes common to Actor2D objects
    public abstract class ActorGroup2D extends ImageGroup
    {
        // default min/max values for int's and float's

        protected static final int MAX_INT_UNBOUND = Integer.MAX_VALUE;
        protected static final int MIN_INT_UNBOUND = Integer.MIN_VALUE;

        protected static final double MAX_DBL_UNBOUND = Double.MAX_VALUE;
        protected static final double MIN_DBL_UNBOUND = Double.MIN_VALUE;

        // the maximum and minimum position and velocity an Actor2D can have
        // overriding classes can change these values at construction time or within
        // the init method

        public int MAX_X_POS = MAX_INT_UNBOUND;
```

```java
        public int MAX_Y_POS = MAX_INT_UNBOUND;

        public int MIN_X_POS = MIN_INT_UNBOUND;
        public int MIN_Y_POS = MIN_INT_UNBOUND;

        public int MAX_X_VEL = MAX_INT_UNBOUND;
        public int MAX_Y_VEL = MAX_INT_UNBOUND;

        public int MIN_X_VEL = MIN_INT_UNBOUND;
        public int MIN_Y_VEL = MIN_INT_UNBOUND;

        // constructs a new ActorGroup2D object
        protected ActorGroup2D()
        {
            super();
        }

        // initializes shared Actor2D attributes
        public abstract void init(Applet a);

    }   // ActorGroup2D
```

# The *Moveable* Interface

```java
    package magic.actor2d;

    import java.awt.geom.*;

    public interface Moveable
    {
        public Rectangle2D getBounds();
        public boolean collidesWith(Moveable other);
        public void addCollision(Moveable other);
        public void processCollisions();
        public void update();

    }   // Moveable
```

## The StaticActor Class

```
package magic.actor2d;

import java.awt.*;

import magic.graphics.*;

public class StaticActor extends Actor2D
{
    public StaticActor(ActorGroup2D grp)
    {
        super(grp);

        // just reference the Oth (and only) animation strip
        currAnimation = group.getAnimationStrip(0);

        frameWidth  = currAnimation.getFrameWidth();
        frameHeight = currAnimation.getFrameHeight();
    }

}    // StaticActor
```

## The StaticActorGroup Class

```
package magic.actor2d;

import java.applet.*;
import java.awt.*;

import magic.graphics.*;

public class StaticActorGroup extends ActorGroup2D
{
    private String filename;

    protected StaticActorGroup()
    {
        filename = null;
```

```
        }

        public StaticActorGroup(String fn)
        {
            filename = fn;
            animations = new AnimationStrip[1];
        }

        public void init(Applet a)
        {
            animations[0] = new AnimationStrip();
            Image image = a.getImage(a.getCodeBase(), filename);
            while(image.getWidth(a) < 0);
            animations[0].addFrame(image);
            animations[0].setAnimator(new Animator.Single());
        }

    }    // StaticActorGroup
```

# The magic.awtex Package
## The Button2D Class

```
    package magic.awtex;

    import java.awt.*;
    import java.awt.event.*;
    import java.awt.geom.*;
    import java.util.*;

    import magic.graphics.*;

    public class Button2D extends Component2D implements MouseListener,
                                                        MouseMotionListener
    {
        // an optional text label for the button
        protected Label2D label;

        // an array of listeners to receive action events
        protected ActionListener[] actionListeners;
```

```java
protected final int MAX_LISTENERS = 5;

// the available states of the button, one for the normal, mouse over and
// mouse pressed states
public static final int BUTTON_NORMAL = 0;
public static final int BUTTON_OVER   = 1;
public static final int BUTTON_DOWN   = 2;

// creates a new Button2D object with the given label, image group, and
// position
public Button2D(Label2D lbl, ImageGroup grp, Vector2D p)
{
    super();
    label  = lbl;
    group  = grp;
    setPos(p);
    updateBounds();
    update();

    // create an empty array of listeners to receive action events
    actionListeners = new ActionListener[MAX_LISTENERS];
    for(int i = 0; i < MAX_LISTENERS; i++)
    {
        actionListeners[i] = null;
    }
}

// creates a new Button2D object with the given image group and position
public Button2D(ImageGroup grp, Vector2D p)
{
    this(null, grp, p);
}

// creates a new Button2D object with the given label and image group
public Button2D(Label2D lbl, ImageGroup grp)
{
    this(lbl, grp, Vector2D.ZERO_VECTOR);
}

// attempts to add the sent listener to the array of ActionListener objects
```

```java
// this methods fails if:
//   1) l is null
//   2) the array already contains MAX_LISTENERS elements
public void addActionListener(ActionListener l)
{
    if(l == null)
    {
        return;
    }

    for(int i = 0; i < MAX_LISTENERS; i++)
    {
        if(actionListeners[i] == null)
        {
            actionListeners[i] = l;
            return;
        }
    }
}


// centers the button's label on itself using the current button's bounding
// rectangle
public void centerLabel(Graphics2D g2d)
{
    if(label != null)
    {
        label.centerOn(this.getBounds(), g2d);
    }
}


// sets the enabled state of the button, updates its internal state, and
// updates the enabled state of its label, if necessary
public void setEnabled(boolean e)
{
    super.setEnabled(e);

    if(!isEnabled())
    {
        state = BUTTON_NORMAL;
```

```java
        }
        if(label != null)
        {
            label.setEnabled(e);
        }
    }


    public void mouseClicked(MouseEvent e)
    {
    }

    public void mouseEntered(MouseEvent e)
    {
    }

    public void mouseExited(MouseEvent e)
    {
    }

    // sets the button to its "pressed" state if it is enabled and the click
    // event took place over the button
    public void mousePressed(MouseEvent e)
    {
        if(isEnabled())
        {
            if(bounds.contains(e.getPoint()))
            {
                state = BUTTON_DOWN;
            }
        }
    }

    // simulates the "clicking" of a button by informing all action listeners
    // that a click event took place.
    // if the mouse was released not while over the button, the button is
    // returned to its normal state and no action is performed.
    public void mouseReleased(MouseEvent e)
    {
```

```java
            // only process enabled components
            if(isEnabled())
            {
                // trigger the event only if the mouse is still over the button
                if(bounds.contains(e.getPoint()))
                {
                    if(state == BUTTON_DOWN)
                    {
                        ActionEvent thisEvent = new ActionEvent(this,
                                        ActionEvent.ACTION_PERFORMED, "");

                        // let all the listeners know something went down
                        for(int i = 0; i < MAX_LISTENERS; i++)
                        {
                            if(actionListeners[i] != null)
                            {
                                actionListeners[i].actionPerformed(thisEvent);
                            }
                        }
                    }

                    // restore the OVER state
                    state = BUTTON_OVER;
                }

                // return the button to normal if it wasn't released over the
                // button
                else
                {
                    state = BUTTON_NORMAL;
                }
            }
        }


    public void mouseDragged(MouseEvent e)
    {
    }

    // updates the state of the button based on its current state and
```

```java
        // the position of the mouse
        public void mouseMoved(MouseEvent e)
        {
            if(isEnabled())
            {
                // don't do anything if the mouse is already down
                if(state == BUTTON_DOWN) return;

                // switch to the 'over' state if the
                if(bounds.contains(e.getPoint()))
                {
                    state = BUTTON_OVER;
                }

                // restore the state to normal in case the mouse pointer has just
                // left the button area
                else
                {
                    state = BUTTON_NORMAL;
                }
            }
        }

        // paints the button based on its current state
        public void paint(Graphics2D g2d)
        {
            // only paint visible components
            if(isVisible())
            {
                // draw the image first, if one exists
                if(group != null)
                {
                    g2d.drawImage(((ButtonImageGroup) group).getFrame(state),
                                                xform, AnimationStrip.observer);
                }

                // draw the text label, if a valid one exists
                if(label != null)
                {
```

```
                    // if the button is down, augment the label a bit to make it
                    // look 'pressed'
                    if(state == BUTTON_DOWN)
                    {
                        label.paint(g2d, 2, 2);
                    }
                    // otherwise, just draw the label normally
                    else
                    {
                        label.paint(g2d);
                    }
                }
            }
        }


        // paints the button based on its current state and the sent delta x, y
        // values
        public void paint(Graphics2D g2d, double dx, double dy)
        {
            // only paint visible components
            if(isVisible())
            {
                // draw the image first, if one exists
                if(group != null)
                {
                    g2d.drawImage(((ButtonImageGroup) group).getFrame(state),
                        AffineTransform.getTranslateInstance(pos.getX() + dx,
                                                            pos.getY() + dy),
                                AnimationStrip.observer);
                }

                // draw the label, if it exists
                if(label != null)
                {
                    // if the button is down, augment the label a bit to make it
                    // look 'pressed'
                    if(state == BUTTON_DOWN)
                    {
                        label.paint(g2d, dx+2, dx+2);
```

```
                }
                // otherwise, just draw the label normally
                else
                {
                        label.paint(g2d, dx, dx);
                }
            }
        }
    }


    // returns a String representation of this button
    public String toString()
    {
        // if the label is valid, return the parent's toString plus the label's
        // toString
        if(label != null)
        {
            return super.toString() + " " + label.toString();
        }

        // otherwise, just return the parent's toString
        return super.toString();
    }

}    // Button2D
```

# The ButtonImageGroup Class

```
    package magic.awtex;

    import java.applet.*;
    import java.awt.*;

    import magic.graphics.*;

    public class ButtonImageGroup extends ImageGroup
    {
        protected String filename;
```

```java
    protected int numFrames;

    public ButtonImageGroup(int n, String str)
    {
        super();
        numFrames = n;
        filename = str;
        animations = new AnimationStrip[1];
    }

    public void init(Applet a)
    {
        ImageLoader loader;

        loader = new ImageLoader(a, filename, true);
        frameWidth  = loader.getImageWidth() / numFrames;
        frameHeight = loader.getImageHeight();

        animations[0] = new AnimationStrip();
        for(int i = 0; i < numFrames; i++)
        {
            animations[0].addFrame(
              loader.extractCell((i*frameWidth), 0, frameWidth, frameHeight));
        }
        animations[0].setAnimator(new Animator.Looped());
    }

    // if spec 1, 2, or 3 frames, will always work correctly
    public Image getFrame(int frame)
    {
        animations[0].reset();
        for(int i = 0; i < frame; i++)
        {
            animations[0].animate();
        }
        return animations[0].getCurrFrame();
    }

}    // ButtonImageGroup
```

# The Component2D Class

```java
package magic.awtex;

import java.awt.*;
import java.awt.geom.*;

import magic.graphics.*;

// base class for creating custom visual components
public abstract class Component2D extends Object
{
    // the ImageGroup to hold component visuals
    protected ImageGroup group;

    // the size of the component
    protected int frameWidth;
    protected int frameHeight;

    // the position and bounds of the component, along with cached transform
    protected Vector2D pos;
    protected Rectangle2D bounds;
    protected AffineTransform xform;

    // flags for component visibility and use
    protected boolean enabled;
    protected boolean visible;

    // tracks the internal state of the component
    protected int state;

    // creates a new Component2D object with default attributes
    protected Component2D()
    {
        pos = new Vector2D.Double();
        xform = new AffineTransform();

        setEnabled(true);
```

```java
        setVisible(true);

        bounds = new Rectangle2D.Double();
        frameWidth  = 0;
        frameHeight = 0;

        state = 0;
    }


// paints the component using the sent Graphics2D context
public abstract void paint(Graphics2D g2d);

// paints the component at the sent offset coordinates
public abstract void paint(Graphics2D g2d, double dx, double dy);

// updates the internal transform of the component
public void update()
{
    xform.setToTranslation(pos.getX(), pos.getY());
}


// updates the bounding rectangle of the component
public void updateBounds()
{
    if(frameWidth <= 0 && group != null)
    {
        frameWidth = group.getFrameWidth();
    }
    if(frameHeight <= 0 && group != null)
    {
        frameHeight = group.getFrameHeight();
    }

    bounds.setRect(pos.getX(), pos.getY(), frameWidth, frameHeight);
}


// returns a String representation of the component
public String toString()
```

```java
{
    // output the class name and current position
    return getClass().getName() + ": " + pos.toString();
}

// access methods for most attributes

public void setEnabled(boolean e)
{
    enabled = e;
}

public final boolean isEnabled()
{
    return enabled;
}

public final void setVisible(boolean v)
{
    visible = v;
}

public final boolean isVisible()
{
    return visible;
}

public final void setX(double px)
{
    pos.setX(px);
}

public final void setY(double py)
{
    pos.setY(py);
}

public final double getX()
```

```java
        {
            return pos.getX();
        }

        public final double getY()
        {
            return pos.getY();
        }

        public final void setPos(int x, int y)
        {
            pos.setX(x);
            pos.setY(y);
        }

        public final void setPos(double x, double y)
        {
            pos.setX(x);
            pos.setY(y);
        }

        public final void setPos(Vector2D v)
        {
            pos.setX(v.getX());
            pos.setY(v.getY());
        }

        public final Vector2D getPos()
        {
            return pos;
        }

        public Rectangle2D getBounds()
        {
            return bounds;
        }

    }   // Component2D
```

# The Container2D Class

```java
package magic.awtex;

import java.awt.*;
import java.awt.geom.*;
import java.util.*;

import magic.graphics.*;

// defines a container capable of containing other components
public abstract class Container2D extends Component2D
{
    // a dynamic vector of components and an enumeration for traversing it
    protected Vector components;
    protected Enumeration e;

    // creates a new Container2D object with the sent background image and
    // position
    protected Container2D(Vector2D p)
    {
        super();

        components = new Vector();

        pos = p;
        if(pos == null)
        {
            pos = new Vector2D.Double();
        }

        updateBounds();
    }

    // adds the sent component to the container at the sent location
    public abstract void add(Component2D c, double x, double y);

    // updates the bounds of the container
```

```
        public abstract void updateBounds();

}       // Container2D
```

# The Label2D class

```java
package magic.awtex;

import java.awt.*;
import java.awt.font.*;
import java.awt.geom.*;
import java.util.*;

import magic.graphics.*;

public class Label2D extends Component2D
{
    // the font to draw with
    protected Font font;

    // the actual text string to draw
    protected String text;

    // a Paint for both 'enabled' as well as 'disabled' states
    protected Paint paint;
    protected Paint disabledPaint;

    // default Paint if no other is specified
    protected final Paint DEFAULT_PAINT = Color.GRAY;

    // constructs a new Label2D with the given font, text, and paint
    public Label2D(Font f, String str, Paint p)
    {
        super();

        setFont(f);
        setText(str);
        setPaint(p);

        // set the disabled paint to the default paint
```

```java
        setDisabledPaint(DEFAULT_PAINT);
    }


    // constructs a new Label2D with the given font, text, paint, and position
    public Label2D(Font f, String str, Paint p, Vector2D v)
    {
        super();

        setFont(f);
        setText(str);
        setPaint(p);
        setPos(v);

        // set the disabled paint to the default paint
        setDisabledPaint(DEFAULT_PAINT);
    }


    // centers the label relative to the sent
    public void centerOn(Rectangle2D r, Graphics2D g2d)
    {
        // get the FontRenderContext for the Graphics2D context
        FontRenderContext frc = g2d.getFontRenderContext();

        // get the layout of our message and font
        TextLayout layout = new TextLayout(text, font, frc);

        // get the bounds of the layout
        Rectangle2D textBounds = layout.getBounds();

        // set the new position
        setX(r.getX() + (r.getWidth()/2) - (textBounds.getWidth()  / 2));
        setY(r.getY() + ((r.getHeight()  + textBounds.getHeight()) / 2));

        // update the overall bounding rectangle
        updateBounds(g2d);
    }


    // updates the bounds of the label using the layout of the current font
    public void updateBounds(Graphics2D g2d)
```

```java
    {
        // get the FontRenderContext for the Graphics2D context
        FontRenderContext frc = g2d.getFontRenderContext();

        // get the layout of our message and font
        TextLayout layout = new TextLayout(text, font, frc);

        // get the bounds of the layout
        Rectangle2D textBounds = layout.getBounds();

        bounds.setRect(getX(), getY(), textBounds.getWidth(),
                                        textBounds.getHeight());
    }

    public void setFont(Font f)
    {
        font = f;
    }

    public void setText(String str)
    {
        text = str;
    }

    public String getText()
    {
        return text;
    }

    public void setPaint(Paint p)
    {
        paint = p;
    }

    public void setDisabledPaint(Paint p)
    {
        disabledPaint = p;
    }

    // paints the label at its current position
```

```java
public void paint(Graphics2D g2d)
{
    // only paint if visible
    if(isVisible())
    {
        // set the font
        g2d.setFont(font);

        // set the paint based on enabled state
        if(isEnabled())
        {
            g2d.setPaint(paint);
        }
        else
        {
            g2d.setPaint(disabledPaint);
        }

        g2d.drawString(text, (int) pos.getX(), (int) pos.getY());
    }
}

// paints the label at the sent delta position
public void paint(Graphics2D g2d, double dx, double dy)
{
    // only paint if visible
    if(isVisible())
    {
        // set the font
        g2d.setFont(font);

        // set the paint based on enabled state
        if(isEnabled())
        {
            g2d.setPaint(paint);
        }
        else
        {
            g2d.setPaint(disabledPaint);
```

```
            }

            // paint the string, adding in the delta values
            g2d.drawString(text, (int) (pos.getX() + dx),
                                 (int) (pos.getY() + dy));
        }
    }

    // returns a String representation of the label
    public String toString()
    {
        // return the parent toString as well as the current text label
        return super.toString() + " " + text;
    }

}   // Label2D
```

## The Menu2D class

```
package magic.awtex;

import java.awt.*;

import magic.graphics.*;

// provides a simple menu class capable of overlaying the scene
public class Menu2D extends Panel2D
{
    // determines if the menu merely overlays the scene or if it dominates
    // the rendering loop
    protected boolean overlay;

    // constructs a new Menu2D object with the sent background image,
    // position, and overlay value
    protected Menu2D(Image bgImage, Vector2D p, boolean over)
    {
        super(bgImage, p);

        overlay  = over;
```

```
        }

        // returns if this menu is an overlay
        public final boolean isOverlay()
        {
            return overlay;
        }


}    // Menu2D
```

# The Panel2D class

```
package magic.awtex;

import java.awt.*;
import java.awt.geom.*;
import java.util.*;

import magic.graphics.*;

// defines a panel capable of containing other components
public class Panel2D extends Container2D
{
    // the background image of the Panel
    protected Image background;

    // creates a new Panel2D object with the sent background image and position
    protected Panel2D(Image bgImage, Vector2D p)
    {
        super(p);

        background = bgImage;
    }

    // adds the sent component to the panel at the sent location
    // note the sent x, y values are relative to the origin (upper-left) of the
    // Panel
    public void add(Component2D c, double x, double y)
```

```java
{
    c.setX(getX() + x);
    c.setY(getY() + y);

    // make sure the component fits within the bounds of the panel
    if(c.getX() + c.getBounds().getWidth() >
        getX() + getBounds().getWidth())
    {
        c.setX(getX() + getBounds().getWidth() -
                c.getBounds().getWidth());
    }

    if(c.getY() + c.getBounds().getHeight() >
        getY() + getBounds().getHeight())
    {
        c.setY(getY() + getBounds().getHeight() -
                c.getBounds().getHeight());
    }

    c.update();
    c.updateBounds();
    components.add(c);
}

// paints the panel and its components
public void paint(Graphics2D g2d)
{
    // draw the background
    if(background != null)
    {
        g2d.drawImage(background, (int) getX(), (int) getY(),
                    AnimationStrip.observer);
    }

    // paint the panel components
    for(e = components.elements(); e.hasMoreElements(); )
    {
        ((Component2D) e.nextElement()).paint(g2d);
```

```java
            }
        }

        // paints the panel and its components at the given offset values
        public void paint(Graphics2D g2d, double dx, double dy)
        {
            if(background != null)
            {
                g2d.drawImage(background, (int) (getX() + dx),
                                          (int) (getY() + dy),
                            AnimationStrip.observer);
            }

            for(e = components.elements(); e.hasMoreElements(); )
            {
                ((Component2D)e.nextElement()).paint(g2d, dx, dy);
            }
        }

        // updates the bounds of the panel-- if the panel has no image, no other
        // attempts will be made to calculate the panel's bounds
        public void updateBounds()
        {
            if(background != null)
            {
                frameWidth  = background.getWidth(AnimationStrip.observer);
                frameHeight = background.getHeight(AnimationStrip.observer);
            }
            else
            {
                frameWidth  = Integer.MAX_VALUE;
                frameHeight = Integer.MAX_VALUE;
            }

            bounds.setRect(pos.getX(), pos.getY(), frameWidth, frameHeight);
        }

    }    // Panel2D
```

# The RadioButton2D class

```
package magic.awtex;

import java.awt.*;
import java.awt.event.*;
import java.awt.geom.*;
import java.util.*;

import magic.graphics.*;

public class RadioButton2D extends Component2D implements MouseListener
{
    // a label to display alongside the button
    protected Label2D label;

    // the group this button belongs to
    protected RadioButtonGroup rbGroup;

    // constants to tracking the state of the button
    public static final int BUTTON_OFF = 0;
    public static final int BUTTON_ON  = 1;

    // creates a new RadioButton2D with the sent label, image and button group,
    // and position
    public RadioButton2D(Label2D lbl, ImageGroup grp,
                         RadioButtonGroup rbg, Vector2D p)
    {
        super();

        label   = lbl;
        group   = grp;
        rbGroup = rbg;

        if(rbGroup != null)
        {
            rbGroup.add(this);
        }

        setPos(p);
```

```java
        updateBounds();
        update();
        setSelected(false);
    }

    // creates a new RadioButton2D with the sent image and button group and
    // position
    public RadioButton2D(ImageGroup grp, RadioButtonGroup rbg, Vector2D p)
    {
        this(null, grp, rbg, p);
    }

    // creates a new RadioButton2D with the sent label, image and button group
    public RadioButton2D(Label2D lbl, ImageGroup grp, RadioButtonGroup rbg)
    {
        this(lbl, grp, rbg, Vector2D.ZERO_VECTOR);
    }

    // creates a new RadioButton2D with the sent image group
    public RadioButton2D(ImageGroup grp)
    {
        this(null, grp, null, Vector2D.ZERO_VECTOR);
    }

    // returns whether the button is selected
    public boolean isSelected()
    {
        return (state == BUTTON_ON);
    }

    // sets the selected state of the button
    public void setSelected(boolean selected)
    {
        state = (selected) ? BUTTON_ON : BUTTON_OFF;
    }

    // returns the text description of the button, if any
    public String getText()
    {
```

```java
        if(label != null)
        {
            return label.getText();
        }
        return "";
    }

    // sets the enabled state of the button and its label
    public void setEnabled(boolean e)
    {
        super.setEnabled(e);

        if(label != null)
        {
            label.setEnabled(e);
        }
    }

    // toggles the state of the button
    public void mousePressed(MouseEvent e)
    {
        if(!isEnabled() || !isVisible()) return;

        // no button group indicates that the button acts independently
        if(rbGroup == null)
        {
            if(bounds.contains(e.getPoint()))
            {
                setSelected(!isSelected());
            }
        }

        // otherwise, update the entire button group
        else
        {
            if(bounds.contains(e.getPoint()))
            {
                setSelected(true);
                rbGroup.updateGroup(this);
```

```java
                }
            }

        }

        public void mouseEntered(MouseEvent e)
        {           }

        public void mouseExited(MouseEvent e)
        {           }

        public void mouseClicked(MouseEvent e)
        {           }

        public void mouseReleased(MouseEvent e)
        {           }

        // draws the button at its current transform
        public void paint(Graphics2D g2d)
        {
            // only paint visible components
            if(isVisible())
            {
                g2d.drawImage(((ButtonImageGroup) group).getFrame(state), xform,
                            AnimationStrip.observer);

                // draw the label if it is valid
                if(label != null)
                {
                    label.paint(g2d);
                }
            }
        }

        // draws the button at the sent offset values
        public void paint(Graphics2D g2d, double dx, double dy)
        {
            // only paint visible components
            if(isVisible())
```

```
        {
            g2d.drawImage(((ButtonImageGroup) group).getFrame(state),
                    AffineTransform.getTranslateInstance(pos.getX() + dx,
                                                         pos.getY() + dy),
                        AnimationStrip.observer
                        );

            // draw the label if it is valid
            if(label != null)
            {
                label.paint(g2d, dx, dx);
            }
        }
    }

    // returns the String representation of this radio button
    public String toString()
    {
        if(label != null)
        {
            return super.toString() + " " + label.toString();
        }

        return super.toString();
    }

}    // RadioButton2D
```

# The RadioButtonGroup class

```
package magic.awtex;

import java.awt.*;
import java.awt.event.*;
import java.awt.geom.*;
import java.util.*;

// maintains a group of buttons so that only one can be selected at any given
// time
```

```java
public class RadioButtonGroup extends Object
{
    // a dynamically growable vector of radio buttons
    protected Vector buttons;

    // an enumeration for traversing the above Vector
    protected Enumeration e;

    // creates a new RadioButtonGroup object
    public RadioButtonGroup()
    {
        buttons = new Vector();
    }

    // adds the sent radio button to the vector
    public void add(RadioButton2D rb)
    {
        buttons.add(rb);
    }

    // gets the currently selected radio button, or null if no button
    // is selected
    public RadioButton2D getSelection()
    {
        for(e = buttons.elements(); e.hasMoreElements(); )
        {
            RadioButton2D rb = (RadioButton2D)e.nextElement();

            if(rb.isSelected())
            {
                return rb;
            }
        }

        return null;
    }

    // enables/disables the entire group of buttons
    public void setEnabled(boolean b)
```

```
{
     for(e = buttons.elements(); e.hasMoreElements(); )
     {
          ((RadioButton2D) e.nextElement()).setEnabled(b);
     }
}

// sets the visibility of the entire button group
public void setVisible(boolean v)
{
     for(e = buttons.elements(); e.hasMoreElements(); )
     {
          ((RadioButton2D) e.nextElement()).setVisible(v);
     }
}

// updates the group by un-selecting all but the sent buttons in the group
public void updateGroup(RadioButton2D rb)
{
     for(e = buttons.elements(); e.hasMoreElements(); )
     {
          Object o = e.nextElement();
          if(rb != o)
          {
               ((RadioButton2D) o).setSelected(false);
          }
     }
}

// paints each button in the radio group
public void paint(Graphics2D g2d)
{
     for(e = buttons.elements(); e.hasMoreElements(); )
     {
          ((RadioButton2D)e.nextElement()).paint(g2d);
     }
}

// paints each button in the group at the sent offset values
```

```java
    public void paint(Graphics2D g2d, double dx, double dy)
    {
        for(e = buttons.elements(); e.hasMoreElements(); )
        {
            ((RadioButton2D)e.nextElement()).paint(g2d, dx, dy);
        }
    }

} // RadioButtonGroup
```

# The magic.debug Package
## The Debugger Class

```java
package magic.debug;

import java.awt.*;
import java.awt.event.*;

// a frame for displaying debug messages
class DebuggingFrame extends Frame implements ActionListener
{
    private Label label;
    private Button button;

    private boolean active;

    public DebuggingFrame()
    {
        setLayout(new BorderLayout());

        label = new Label();
        add(label, BorderLayout.CENTER);

        Panel p = new Panel();
        button = new Button("Dismiss");
        p.add(button);
```

```java
        add(p, BorderLayout.SOUTH);

        active = false;

        button.addActionListener(this);
    }

    public boolean isActive()
    {
        return active;
    }

    public void show()
    {
        active = true;
        super.show();
    }

    public void hide()
    {
        active = false;
        super.hide();
    }

    public void setText(String text)
    {
        label.setText(text);
    }

    public void actionPerformed(ActionEvent e)
    {
        if(e.getSource() == button)
        {
            hide();
            active = false;
        }
    }
```

```java
        }

// accepts warning/error messages and sends them to the proper frame or output
// stream
public class Debugger extends Object
{
    public    static final int TYPE_FRAME_OUTPUT  = 0;
    public    static final int TYPE_STREAM_OUTPUT = 1;
    protected static int outputType = TYPE_STREAM_OUTPUT;

    public static final int FATAL_ERROR    = 0;
    public static final int NONFATAL_ERROR = 1;

    protected static DebuggingFrame frame = null;

    protected static boolean outputStreamAvailable = true;

    protected static boolean debuggingEnabled;

    public static void init(boolean enable, int output, boolean osAvail)
    {
        debuggingEnabled = enable;
        outputType = output;
        outputStreamAvailable = osAvail;

        if(outputType == TYPE_FRAME_OUTPUT)
        {
            frame = new DebuggingFrame();
            frame.setSize(300, 200);
            frame.addWindowListener(new WindowAdapter()
                {
                    public void windowClosing(WindowEvent e)
                    {
                        frame.hide();
                    }
                } );
            frame.pack();
```

```java
        }

        else
        {
            frame = null;
        }

        reportMessage("Debugger online.");
    }

    public static void reportError(int errorType, String desc, int code)
    {
        if(outputType == TYPE_FRAME_OUTPUT && frame != null)
        {
            if(errorType == FATAL_ERROR)
            {
                frame.setTitle("Fatal Error");
            }
            else
            {
                frame.setTitle("Applet Error");
            }
            frame.setText(desc + « (error code « + code + «).»);
            frame.pack();
            frame.show();
        }

        else if(outputType == TYPE_STREAM_OUTPUT)
        {
            if(errorType == FATAL_ERROR)
            {
                System.out.print("Fatal Error: ");
            }
            else
            {
                System.out.print("Applet Error: ");
            }
```

```
                    System.out.println(desc + " (error code " + code + ").");
            }
        }

        public static void reportWarning(String desc)
        {
            if(outputStreamAvailable)
            {
                System.out.println("Warning: " + desc);
            }
        }

        public static void reportMessage(String desc)
        {
            if(outputStreamAvailable)
            {
                System.out.println("<System Message>: " + desc);
            }
        }

        public static boolean isDisplayingOutput()
        {
            return (frame != null) ? frame.isActive() : false;
        }

    }    // Debugger
```

# The magic.gamelet Package
## The Gamelet Class

```
    package magic.gamelet;

    import java.applet.*;
    import java.awt.*;
    import java.awt.event.*;
    import java.awt.image.*;
```

```java
import java.awt.geom.*;
import java.util.*;

import magic.actor2d.*;
import magic.awtex.*;
import magic.debug.*;
import magic.graphics.*;
import magic.scene.*;

public abstract class Gamelet extends Applet implements Runnable
{
    /* private field declarations */

    // a Thread for animation
    private Thread animation;

    /* protected field declarations */

    protected BufferedGraphics offscreenGraphics;
    protected final int BUFFER_STYLE_NONE        = 0;
    protected final int BUFFER_STYLE_DOUBLE      = 1;
    protected final int BUFFER_STYLE_ACCELERATED = 2;
    protected final int BUFFER_STYLE_UNKNOWN     = 3;  // chain flipping, etc
    protected int bufferStyle;

    protected Stack menuStack;

    protected Scene scene;

    protected Color clearColor;
    protected final Color DEFAULT_CLEARCOLOR = Color.BLACK;

    protected int framerate;
    protected double reportedFramerate;
    protected final int DEFAULT_FRAMERATE = 1000/33;   // 33 fps, or 30ms/frame

    protected static AudioClip[] audioClips;
```

```java
        protected static boolean audioEnabled;

        /* methods inherited from java.Applet */

        public void init()
        {
            Debugger.init(true, Debugger.TYPE_FRAME_OUTPUT, true);

            AnimationStrip.observer = this;

            if(getGraphicsConfiguration().getImageCapabilities().isAccelerated())
            {
                createBufferStyle(BUFFER_STYLE_ACCELERATED);
            }
            else
            {
                createBufferStyle(BUFFER_STYLE_DOUBLE);
            }

            menuStack  = new Stack();
            scene      = null;
            clearColor = DEFAULT_CLEARCOLOR;
            animation  = new Thread(this);
            reportedFramerate = 0.0;
            setFramerate(DEFAULT_FRAMERATE);
            audioClips = null;
            audioEnabled = false;
        }   // init

        public void start()
        {
            // start the animation thread
            if(animation == null)
            {
                animation = new Thread(this);
            }
            animation.start();
```

```java
    }

    public void stop()
    {
        animation = null;
    }

    public void update(Graphics g)
    {
        if(Debugger.isDisplayingOutput())
        {
            return;
        }

        if(scene != null)
        {
            scene.update();
        }

        paint(g);
    }

    public void paint(Graphics g)
    {
        Graphics2D g2d = null;

        if(bufferStyle != BUFFER_STYLE_NONE &&
           bufferStyle != BUFFER_STYLE_UNKNOWN)
        {
            if(offscreenGraphics != null)
            {
                g2d = (Graphics2D)offscreenGraphics.getValidGraphics();
                g2d.setBackground(clearColor);
                g2d.clearRect(0, 0, getSize().width, getSize().height);
            }
            else
            {
                Debugger.reportWarning("Buffering style is double, " +
```

```java
                                "but graphics context references null");
                        g2d = (Graphics2D) g;
                    }
                }

                else
                {
                    g2d = (Graphics2D) g;
                }

                prepareGraphics(g2d);

                if(menuStack.size() > 0)
                {
                    if( ((Menu2D)menuStack.peek()).isOverlay())
                    {
                        paintScene(g2d);
                    }

                    ((Menu2D)menuStack.peek()).paint(g2d);
                }
                else
                {
                    paintScene(g2d);
                }

                g.drawImage(offscreenGraphics.getBuffer(), 0, 0, this);

        }    // paint

/* methods inherited from java.lang.Runnable */

public void run()
{
        long lastTime;
        long frameCount = 0;
        long elapsedTime;
```

```
long totalElapsedTime = 0;

Thread t = Thread.currentThread();
while (t == animation)
{
     lastTime = System.currentTimeMillis();

     repaint();

     elapsedTime = System.currentTimeMillis() - lastTime;

     try
     {
         if(elapsedTime < framerate)
         {
             Thread.sleep(framerate - elapsedTime);
         }
         else
         {
             // don't starve the garbage collector
             Thread.sleep(5);
         }
     }

     catch(InterruptedException e)
     {
         break;
     }

     ++ frameCount;
     totalElapsedTime += (System.currentTimeMillis() - lastTime);
     if(totalElapsedTime > 1000)
     {
         reportedFramerate = (double) frameCount /
                             (double) totalElapsedTime * 1000.0;
         frameCount = 0;
         totalElapsedTime = 0;
     }
```

```java
        }

    }    // run

    /* new methods for magic.Gamelet */

    public boolean isDoubleBuffered()
    {
        return (bufferStyle == BUFFER_STYLE_DOUBLE ||
                bufferStyle == BUFFER_STYLE_ACCELERATED
                );
    }

    protected void setFramerate(int fps)
    {
        framerate = fps;
    }

    protected void createBufferStyle(int style)
    {
        bufferStyle = style;

        switch(bufferStyle)
        {
            case BUFFER_STYLE_NONE:
                offscreenGraphics = null;
                return;

            case BUFFER_STYLE_DOUBLE:
                offscreenGraphics = new BufferedGraphics(this);
                return;

            case BUFFER_STYLE_ACCELERATED:
                offscreenGraphics = new VolatileGraphics(this);
                return;

            case BUFFER_STYLE_UNKNOWN:
                Debugger.reportWarning("Unknown buffer style (" +
```

```java
                                              style + ").");
                offscreenGraphics = null;
                return;
        }
    }

    protected void prepareGraphics(Graphics2D g2d)
    {

    }

    protected void paintScene(Graphics2D g2d)
    {
        if(scene != null)
        {
            scene.paint(g2d);
        }
    }

    public static void playSound(int index, boolean loop)
    {
        if(!audioEnabled)
        {
            return;
        }

        if(audioClips != null && index >= 0 &&
           index < audioClips.length && audioClips[index] != null)
        {
            if(loop)
            {
                audioClips[index].loop();
            }
            else
            {
                audioClips[index].play();
            }
        }
```

```
        }


        public static void stopSound(int index)
        {
            if(audioClips != null && index >= 0 &&
                index < audioClips.length && audioClips[index] != null)
            {
                audioClips[index].stop();
            }
        }


    }     // Gamelet
```

# The magic.graphics Package
## The AnimationStrip Class

```
    package magic.graphics;

    import java.awt.*;
    import java.awt.image.*;
    import java.util.*;

    // defines a dynamic list of Image frames that can be animated using a given
    // Animator object
    public class AnimationStrip extends Object
    {
        // observes drawing for external objects
        public static ImageObserver observer;

        // a linked list of Image frames, along with the size of the list
        protected LinkedList frames;
        protected int        numFrames;

        // the Animator responsible for animating frames
        protected Animator animator;

        // creates a new AnimationStrip object
```

```
public AnimationStrip()
{
    frames    = null;
    numFrames = 0;
    animator  = null;
}

public final void setAnimator(Animator anim)
{
    animator = anim;
    animator.setFrames(frames);
}

// adds an Image frame to the list
public void addFrame(Image i)
{
    if(frames == null)
    {
        frames = new LinkedList();
        numFrames = 0;
    }

    frames.add(i);
    numFrames++;
}

// returns the Animator's current frame
public Image getCurrFrame()
{
    if(frames != null)
    {
        return animator.getCurrFrame();
    }
    return null;
}

// allows the Animator to generate the next frame of animation
public void animate()
{
```

```java
            if(animator != null)
            {
                animator.nextFrame();
            }
    }

    // returns the Animator's next frame of animation
    public Image getNextFrame()
    {
        if(animator != null)
        {
            animator.nextFrame();
            return animator.getCurrFrame();
        }

        return null;
    }

    // returns the first frame of animation
    public Image getFirstFrame()
    {
        if(frames != null)
        {
            return (Image)frames.getFirst();
        }

        return null;
    }

    // returns the last frame of animation
    public Image getLastFrame()
    {
        if(frames != null)
        {
            return (Image)frames.getLast();
        }

        return null;
```

```
        }

        // resets the Animator's internal animation sequence
        public void reset()
        {
            if(animator != null)
            {
                animator.reset();
            }
        }

        // returns an animation frame's width
        public int getFrameWidth()
        {
            if(frames != null && !frames.isEmpty())
            {
                return getFirstFrame().getWidth(observer);
            }
            return 0;
        }

        // returns an animation frame's height
        public int getFrameHeight()
        {
            if(frames != null && !frames.isEmpty())
            {
                return getFirstFrame().getHeight(observer);
            }
            return 0;
        }

    }    // AnimationStrip
```

## The Animator Class

```
        package magic.graphics;

        import java.awt.*;
```

```java
import java.util.*;

// defines a custom way of animating a list of Image frames
public abstract class Animator extends Object
{
    // references a linked list of Image frames
    protected LinkedList frames;

    // the current index of animation
    protected int currIndex;

    // creates a new Animator object with a null-referenced set of frames
    protected Animator()
    {
        frames = null;
        currIndex = 0;
    }

    public final void setFrames(LinkedList list)
    {
        frames = list;
    }

    // resets this animation
    public void reset()
    {
        currIndex = 0;
    }

    // returns the current frame of animation
    public Image getCurrFrame()
    {
        if(frames != null)
        {
            return (Image)frames.get(currIndex);
        }
        return null;
    }

    // this method defines how frames are animated
```

```java
public abstract void nextFrame();

// animates frames based on a sent array of indices
public static class Indexed extends Animator
{
    protected int[] indices;
    protected int   arrayIndex;

    public Indexed()
    {
        super();
        arrayIndex = 0;
    }

    public Indexed(int[] idx)
    {
        indices = new int[idx.length];

        System.arraycopy(idx, 0, indices, 0, idx.length);
        arrayIndex = 0;
    }

    public void nextFrame()
    {
        if(frames != null)
        {
            // increments the index counter
            if(++arrayIndex >= indices.length)
            {
                arrayIndex = 0;
            }
            currIndex = indices[arrayIndex];
        }
    }

}   // Animator.Indexed

// iterates through the animation frames, looping back to the start when
// necessary
public static class Looped extends Animator
```

```
{
    public Looped()
    {
        super();
    }

    public void nextFrame()
    {
        if(frames != null)
        {
            if(++currIndex >= frames.size())
            {
                reset();
            }
        }
    }

}    // Animator.Looped

// iterates through the animation frames, but stops once it reaches the last
// frame
public static class OneShot extends Animator
{
    public OneShot()
    {
        super();
    }

    public void nextFrame()
    {
        if(frames != null)
        {
            if(++currIndex >= frames.size());
            {
                currIndex = frames.size()-1;
            }
        }
```

```java
        }

    }    // Animator.OneShot

    // generates a random animation frame during each call to nextFrame
    public static class Random extends Animator
    {
        private java.util.Random random;

        public Random()
        {
            super();

            random = new java.util.Random();
        }

        public void nextFrame()
        {
            if(frames != null)
            {
                currIndex = random.nextInt() % frames.size();
            }
        }

    }    // Animator.Random

    // represents an animation containing only one frame-- this class saves time
    // since it does no processing
    public static class Single extends Animator
    {
        public Single()
        {
            super();
        }

        public void nextFrame()
        {
            // do nothing...
```

```
            }

        }     // Animator.Single

    }     // Animator
```

# The BufferedGraphics Class

```java
package magic.graphics;

import java.applet.*;
import java.awt.*;

public class BufferedGraphics extends Object
{
    // the Component that will be drawing the offscreen image
    protected Component parent;

    // the offscreen rendering Image
    protected Image buffer;

    // creates a new BufferedGraphics object
    protected BufferedGraphics()
    {
        parent = null;
        buffer = null;
    }

    // creates a new BufferedGraphics object with the sent parent Component
    public BufferedGraphics(Component c)
    {
        parent = c;

        createBuffer();
    }

    public final Image getBuffer()
    {
        return buffer;
```

```java
}

// returns the buffer's Graphics context after the buffer has been validated
public Graphics getValidGraphics()
{
    if(! isValid())
    {
        createBuffer();
    }
    return buffer.getGraphics();
}

// creates an offscreen rendering image matching the parent's width and
// height
protected void createBuffer()
{
    Dimension size = parent.getSize();
    buffer = parent.createImage(size.width, size.height);
}

// validates the offscreen image against several criteria, namely against
// the null reference and the parent's width and height
protected boolean isValid()
{
    if(parent == null)
    {
        return false;
    }

    Dimension s = parent.getSize();

    if(buffer == null ||
       buffer.getWidth(null)  != s.width ||
       buffer.getHeight(null) != s.height)
    {
        return false;
    }

    return true;
```

```
        }

    }     // BufferedGraphics
```

# The ImageGroup Class

```java
package magic.graphics;

import java.applet.*;

// provides methods for creating and accessing AnimationStrip objects
public abstract class ImageGroup
{
    // an array of AnimationStrip objects that create our animation sequences as
    // a whole
    protected AnimationStrip[] animations;

    // the width and height of an individual image frame
    protected int frameWidth;
    protected int frameHeight;

    // creates a new ImageGroup object
    protected ImageGroup()
    {
        animations = null;
    }

    // initializes the ImageGroup using the sent Applet reference object
    public abstract void init(Applet a);

    public final int getFrameWidth()
    {
        return frameWidth;
    }

    public final int getFrameHeight()
    {
        return frameHeight;
```

```
        }

        // accesses the AnimationStrip at the given index
        public final AnimationStrip getAnimationStrip(int index)
        {
            if(animations != null)
            {
                try
                {
                    return animations[index];
                }
                catch(ArrayIndexOutOfBoundsException e)
                {
                    // send error to debugger or standard output...
                }
            }

            return null;
        }

    }   // ImageGroup
```

# The ImageLoader Class

```
    package magic.graphics;

    import java.applet.*;
    import java.awt.*;
    import java.awt.image.*;
    import java.util.*;

    public class ImageLoader extends Object
    {
        // an Applet to load and observe loading images
        protected Applet applet;

        // an Image, along with its width and height
        protected Image   image;
        protected int     imageWidth;
```

```java
    protected int     imageHeight;

    // a buffer to render images to immediately after they are loaded
    protected static BufferedImage buffer = new BufferedImage(200, 200,
                                            BufferedImage.TYPE_INT_RGB);

    public ImageLoader(
        Applet a,          // creates and observes loading images
        String filename,   // name of image to load on disk
        boolean wait       // if true, add to a MediaTracker object and wait to
                           // be loaded
        )
    {
        applet = a;

        image = applet.getImage(applet.getDocumentBase(), filename);

        if(wait)
        {
            // create a new MediaTracker object for this image
            MediaTracker mt = new MediaTracker(applet);

            // load the strip image
            mt.addImage(image, 0);
            try
            {
                // wait for our main image to load
                mt.waitForID(0);
            }
            catch(InterruptedException e) { /* do nothing */ }
        }

        // get the width and height of the image
        imageWidth = image.getWidth(applet);
        imageHeight = image.getHeight(applet);
    }


    public int getImageWidth()
    {
```

```java
        return imageWidth;
    }

    public int getImageHeight()
    {
        return imageHeight;
    }

    public Image getImage()
    {
        return image;
    }

    // extracts a cell from the image using an image filter
    public Image extractCell(int x, int y, int width, int height)
    {
        // get the ImageProducer source of our main image
        ImageProducer sourceProducer = image.getSource();

        Image cell = applet.createImage(new FilteredImageSource(sourceProducer,
                                new CropImageFilter(x, y, width, height)));

        // draw the cell to the off-screen buffer
        buffer.getGraphics().drawImage(cell, 0, 0, applet);

        return cell;
    }

    // extracts a cell from the image and scales it to the sent width and height
    public Image extractCellScaled(int x, int y, int width, int height,
                                int sw, int sh)
    {
        // get the ImageProducer source of our main image
        ImageProducer sourceProducer = image.getSource();

        Image cell = applet.createImage(new FilteredImageSource(sourceProducer,
                                new CropImageFilter(x, y, width, height)));

        // draw the cell to the off-screen buffer
```

```
                    buffer.getGraphics().drawImage(cell, 0, 0, applet);

                    return cell.getScaledInstance(sw, sh, Image.SCALE_SMOOTH);
            }

    }    // ImageLoader
```

## The Vector2D Class

```java
    package magic.graphics;

    public abstract class Vector2D extends Object
    {
        public static final Vector2D.Double ZERO_VECTOR = new Vector2D.Double(0, 0);

        public static class Double extends Vector2D
        {
            // the x and y components of this Vector2D.Double object
            public double x;
            public double y;

            // creates a default Vector2D with a value of (0,0)
            public Double()
            {
                this(0.0, 0.0);
            }

            // creates a Vector2D.Double object with the sent values
            public Double(double m, double n)
            {   setX(m);
                setY(n);
            }

            private Double(int m, int n)
            {   setX((double) m);
                setY((double) n);
```

```java
        }

        // get/set access methods for the x and y components

        public final void setX(double n)
        {    x = n;
        }

        public final void setY(double n)
        {    y = n;
        }

        public final double getX()
        {    return x;
        }

        public final double getY()
        {    return y;
        }

        // adds this vector to the sent vector
        public Vector2D plus(Vector2D v)
        {
            return new Double(getX() + v.getX(), getY() + v.getY());
        }

        // subtracts the sent vector from this vector
        public Vector2D minus(Vector2D v)
        {
            return new Double(getX() - v.getX(), getY() - v.getY());
        }

    }    // Double

public static class Integer extends Vector2D
{
        // the x and y components of this Vector2D.Integer object
        public int x;
```

```java
    public int y;

    // creates a default Vector2D with a value of (0,0)
    public Integer()
    {
        this(0, 0);
    }

    // creates a Vector2D.Integer object with the sent values
    public Integer(int m, int n)
    {   setX(m);
        setY(n);
    }

    private Integer(double m, double n)
    {   setX((int) m);
        setY((int) n);
    }

    // get/set access methods for the x and y components

    public final void setX(double n)
    {   x = (int) n;
    }

    public final void setY(double n)
    {   y = (int) n;
    }

    public final double getX()
    {   return (double) x;
    }

    public final double getY()
    {   return (double) y;
    }

    // adds this vector to the sent vector
    public Vector2D plus(Vector2D v)
```

```
        {
            return new Integer(getX() + v.getX(), getY() + v.getY());
        }

        // subtracts the sent vector from this vector
        public Vector2D minus(Vector2D v)
        {
            return new Integer(getX() - v.getX(), getY() - v.getY());
        }

    }    // Integer

    protected Vector2D()  {  }

    public abstract void setX(double n);

    public abstract void setY(double n);

    public abstract double getX();

    public abstract double getY();

    // adds this vector to the sent vector
    public abstract Vector2D plus(Vector2D v);

    // subtracts the sent vector from this vector
    public abstract Vector2D minus(Vector2D v);

    // determines if two vectors are equal
    public boolean equals(Vector2D other)
    {
        return (getX() == other.getX() && getY() == other.getY());
    }

    // normalizes this vector to unit length
    public void normalize()
    {
        double len = length();
        setX(getX() / len);
```

```java
        setY(getY() / len);
    }

    public void scale(double k)
    {
        setX(k * getX());
        setY(k * getY());
    }

    // translates the Vector2D by the sent value
    public void translate(double dx, double dy)
    {
        setX(getX() + dx);
        setY(getY() + dy);
    }

    // translates the Vector2D by the sent vector
    public void translate(Vector2D v)
    {
        setX(getX() + v.getX());
        setY(getY() + v.getY());
    }

    // calculates the dot (or inner) product of this and the sent vector
    public double dot(Vector2D v)
    {
        return getX()*v.getX() + getY()*v.getY();
    }

    // returns the length of this vector
    public double length()
    {
        return Math.sqrt(this.dot(this));
    }

    // returns the String representation of this Vector2D
    public String toString()
    {
        return getClass().getName() + " [x=" + getX() + ",y=" + getY() + "]";
```

```
        }

    }    // Vector2D
```

# The VolatileGraphics Class

```java
package magic.graphics;

import java.applet.*;
import java.awt.*;
import java.awt.image.*;

public class VolatileGraphics extends BufferedGraphics
{
    public VolatileGraphics(Component c)
    {
        super(c);
        createBuffer();
    }

    protected void createBuffer()
    {
        Dimension size = parent.getSize();
        buffer = parent.createVolatileImage(size.width, size.height);
    }

    protected boolean isValid()
    {
        if(! super.isValid()) return false;

        if(((VolatileImage)buffer).validate(parent.getGraphicsConfiguration()) ==
            VolatileImage.IMAGE_INCOMPATIBLE)
        {
            return false;
        }

        return true;
    }

}    // VolatileGraphics
```

# The magic.net Package
## The AbstractConnection Class

```java
package magic.net;

import java.io.*;
import java.net.*;
import java.util.*;

// this class defines all communications between client and server
public class AbstractConnection
{
    // the string that will separate the header from the message
    public final String MSG_DELIM = "||";

    // commond to end the session
    public static final String END_OF_TRANSMISSION = "EOT";

    // a Socket for endpoint communication
    protected Socket socket;

    // the message received, including header, body, and delimiting string
    protected String message;

    // reader and writer for Socket I/O
    protected BufferedReader  in;
    protected PrintStream     out;

    // creates an AbstractConnection object with no specified Socket
    protected AbstractConnection()
    {
        socket = null;
    }

    // creates an AbstractConnection object with the specified socket
    public AbstractConnection(Socket clientSocket)
    {
        socket = clientSocket;
```

```java
    }

    // attempts to open the Socket for I/O
    protected boolean open()
    {
        // attempt to open the input and output streams
        try
        {
            in  = new BufferedReader(
                    new InputStreamReader(socket.getInputStream()));
            out = new PrintStream(socket.getOutputStream());
        }
        catch(IOException e)
        {
            System.err.println("Could not create socket streams; " +
                               "closing connection.");
            // attempt to cleanly close the socket
            close(true);
            return false;
        }
        return true;
    }


    // attempts to close the socket
    protected final void close(
        boolean ioError    // true if connection is closing due to an I/O error
        )
    {
        // send an End Of Transmission first if an error occured
        // this should hopefully terminate the service on the other end of the
        // connection
        if(! ioError)
        {
            send(END_OF_TRANSMISSION, "");
        }

        try
        {
            socket.close();
```

```java
        }
        catch(IOException e)
        {
            System.err.println("Could not close socket connection.");
        }
    }


    // sends a command along with the specified message
    protected void send(String header, String msg)
    {
        // send the message only if the socket is connected
        if(socket.isConnected())
        {
            out.println(header + MSG_DELIM + msg);
        }
        else
        {
            System.err.println("Socket not connected; terminating thread.");
        }
    }


    // parses the header from the message
    protected String parseHeader()
    {
        if("".equals(message)) return "";

        StringTokenizer st = new StringTokenizer(message, MSG_DELIM);
        if(st.hasMoreTokens())
        {
            return st.nextToken();
        }
        return "";
    }


    // parses the message part from the overall message
    protected String parseMessage()
    {
        if("".equals(message)) return "";

        // create a StringTokenizer with the message and string delimiter
```

```
            StringTokenizer st = new StringTokenizer(message, MSG_DELIM);

            // advance one token, then return the second
            if(st.hasMoreTokens())
            {
                st.nextToken();

                if(st.hasMoreTokens())
                {
                    return st.nextToken();
                }
            }

            return "";
        }

        // attempts to receive a message from the input stream
        protected void recv()
        {
            message = "";

            try
            {
                message = in.readLine();
            }
            catch(IOException e)
            {
                System.err.println("Unable to receive message; terminating" +
                                " conection.");
                close(true);
            }
        }

    }    // AbstractConnection
```

# The GUIServer Class

```
    package magic.net;

    import java.io.*;
```

```java
import java.awt.*;
import java.applet.*;
import java.net.*;

// a simple graphical server for launching TCP connections
public abstract class GUIServer extends Applet implements Runnable
{
    // the default port for server connections
    public static final int DEFAULT_PORT = 1234;

    // the port the service is located on
    protected int port;

    // a ServerSocket for listening for service requests
    protected ServerSocket listener;

    // a thread of execution for the server
    protected Thread exec;

    // a TextArea for printing server messages
    protected TextArea textArea;


    public void log(String msg)
    {
        if(textArea != null)
        {
            textArea.append("Server: " + msg + "\n");
        }
    }

    // creates a ServerSocket to listen for connections
    public void init()
    {
        textArea = new TextArea();
        textArea.setEditable(false);
```

```java
        add(textArea);

        port = Integer.parseInt(getParameter(«Port»));

        if (port == 0)
        {
            port = DEFAULT_PORT;
        }

        try
        {
            listener = new ServerSocket(port);
        }
        catch (IOException e)
        {
            log("I/O exception creating server socket : " + e);
        }

        log(«listening on port « + port);
    }

    public void start()
    {
        exec = new Thread(this);
        exec.start();
    }

    public void stop()
    {
        exec = null;
    }

    protected abstract void createService(Socket s);

    public void run()
    {
        try
        {
            Thread thread = Thread.currentThread();
```

```
                        while(exec == thread)
                        {
                                Socket clientSocket = listener.accept();

                                log("connected to " + clientSocket.getInetAddress() +
                                    " : " + clientSocket.getPort());

                                createService(clientSocket);

                                try
                                {
                                    Thread.sleep(25);
                                }
                                catch(InterruptedException e)
                                { }
                        }
                }
                catch (IOException e)
                {
                        log("I/O exception raised while listening for connections : " +
                            e);
                }
        }

    }   // GUIServer
```

# The MulticastConnection Class

```
    package magic.net;

    import java.io.*;
    import java.net.*;

    public class MulticastConnection
    {
        public static final int DEFAULT_PORT = 1234;

        // a multicast socket for connecting, sending, and receiving messages
```

```java
protected MulticastSocket mcSocket;

// an IP address belonging to the multicast group
protected InetAddress     groupAddress;

// the port number we're connected to
protected int             port;

// a single IP packet for sending or receiving messages
protected DatagramPacket  dataPacket;

// a byte array for receiving and sending data packets
protected byte[]          data;

// the maximum number of bytes a single packet can be
protected final int PACKET_SIZE = 1024;

// creates a new MulticastConnection with the specified address and port
public MulticastConnection(String address, int portNo) throws Exception
{
    // resolve the specified address into a valid IP address
    groupAddress = InetAddress.getByName(address);

    port = portNo;

    // make sure we connect to a valid port number
    mcSocket  = (port > 0) ? new MulticastSocket(port) :
                             new MulticastSocket(DEFAULT_PORT);

    // link the socket to the group IP address
    mcSocket.joinGroup(groupAddress);

    data = null;
}

// attempts to disconnect from the group
public void disconnect()
{
```

```java
        if(mcSocket == null) return;

        try
        {
            mcSocket.leaveGroup(groupAddress);
        }
        catch(IOException e)
        {
            // handle error message here...
        }
    }

    // attempts to receive a data packet from the group
    public String recv()
    {
        data = new byte[PACKET_SIZE];
        dataPacket = new DatagramPacket(data,data.length);

        try
        {
            mcSocket.receive(dataPacket);
        }
        catch(IOException e)
        {
            return "";
        }

        // convert the raw bytes of the packet into a valid String object
        return new String(dataPacket.getData()).trim();
    }

    // attempts to send the specified String as an IP packet
    public boolean send(String msg)
    {
        dataPacket = new DatagramPacket(
            msg.getBytes(), msg.length(), groupAddress, port);

        try
        {
```

```
                mcSocket.send(dataPacket);
        }
        catch(IOException e)
        {
                return false;
        }

        return true;
    }

    }    // MulticastConnection
```

# The Server Class

```java
package magic.net;

import java.io.*;
import java.net.*;

// a simple server that sits and listens for remote connection requests
// the service request is then delegated to the createService method
public abstract class Server implements Runnable
{
    // the default port for server connections
    public static final int DEFAULT_PORT = 1234;

    // the port the service is located on
    protected int port;

    // a ServerSocket for listening for service requests
    protected ServerSocket listener;

    // a thread of execution for the server
    protected Thread exec;

    // exit with an error message, when an exception occurs.
    public static void fail(Exception e, String msg)
    {
        System.err.println(msg + ": " +  e);
```

```java
            System.exit(1);
        }

        // creates a new Server object with the specified port
        public Server(int portNo)
        {
            // set the port, making sure it is non-negative and non-zero
            port = (portNo <= 0) ? DEFAULT_PORT : portNo;

            //
            try
            {
                listener = new ServerSocket(port);
            }
            catch (Exception e)
            {
                fail(e, "Exception occurred while creating server socket");
            }

            exec = new Thread(this);
        }

        // starts the execution thread
        public final void start()
        {
            exec.start();
        }

        // creates a service with the specified Socket
        protected abstract void createService(Socket socket);

        // the main workhorse of the server thread.  listen for and
        // accept connections from clients.
        public void run()
        {
            System.out.println("Server: listening on port " + port);
            System.out.println("Server: use Ctrl-C to terminate service.");

            try
```

```java
        {
            Thread thread = Thread.currentThread();
            while(exec == thread)
            {
                // listen for and accept the connection
                Socket clientSocket = listener.accept();

                // create the service using the accepted Socket
                createService(clientSocket);

                // print a conected message to the console
                System.out.println("\nConnected to " +
                                    clientSocket.getInetAddress() +
                                    " : " + clientSocket.getPort());

                try
                {
                    Thread.sleep(25);
                }
                catch(InterruptedException e)
                { }
            }
        }
        catch (IOException e)
        {
            fail(e, "Exception while listening for connections");
        }
    }

}    // Server
```

# The magic.scene Package
## The QuadNode Class

```java
package magic.scene;

import java.awt.*;
import java.awt.geom.*;
```

```java
import java.util.*;

import magic.actor2d.*;

// represents a single node within a QuadTree structure
public class QuadNode extends Object
{
    // the next unique id to assign a node
    protected static int UNIQUE_ID = 0;

    // a unique integer to identify this node
    protected int id;

    // the parent that contains this node
    protected QuadNode parent;

    // an array of child nodes for this QuadNode
    protected QuadNode[] nodes;

    // true if this node is a leaf node (has no children)
    protected boolean leaf;

    // a linked-list of objects this node contains
    protected LinkedList objects;

    // the bounds of the node
    protected Rectangle2D bounds;

    // default constructor
    private QuadNode()
    {
        id = -1;
        parent  = null;
        nodes   = null;
        leaf    = true;
        objects = null;
        bounds  = null;
    }

    // constructs a QuadNode with the given parent, depth, and bounds
```

```java
public QuadNode(QuadNode p, int depth, Rectangle2D r)
{
    parent = p;
    bounds = r;

    id = UNIQUE_ID++;

    // this node is a leaf if the remaining depth is zero
    if(depth == 0)
    {
        leaf = true;
        objects = new LinkedList();
        nodes = null;

        QuadTree.addLeaf(this);
    }

    // otherwise, this node contains 4 child nodes
    else
    {
        leaf = false;
        objects = null;

        nodes = new QuadNode[4];
        double x = bounds.getX();
        double y = bounds.getY();
        double w = bounds.getWidth();
        double h = bounds.getHeight();

        // create the children
        nodes[0] = new QuadNode(this, depth - 1,
                    new Rectangle2D.Double(x, y + h/2, w/2, h/2));
        nodes[1] = new QuadNode(this, depth - 1,
                    new Rectangle2D.Double(x + w/2, y + h/2, w/2, h/2));
        nodes[2] = new QuadNode(this, depth - 1,
                    new Rectangle2D.Double(x + w/2, y, w/2, h/2));
        nodes[3] = new QuadNode(this, depth - 1,
                    new Rectangle2D.Double(x, y, w/2, h/2));
    }
```

```java
        }


        // returns true if this node is a leaf node
        public final boolean isLeaf()
        {
            return leaf;
        }


        // attempts to insert the sent object into this node
        public void insert(
            Moveable c,        // the Moveable object to insert
            boolean propagate  // if true, propagate upward if c does not fit within
                               // this node's bounds
            )
        {
            // try to insert the node
            if(bounds.contains(c.getBounds()) || bounds.intersects(c.getBounds()))
            {
                // if this node is a leaf node, insert the object into the list
                if(isLeaf())
                {
                    if(objects == null)
                    {
                        objects = new LinkedList();
                    }
                    if(! objects.contains(c))
                    {
                        objects.add(c);
                    }
                }

                // if this node is not a leaf, try to insert downward
                else
                {
                    for(int i = 0; i < 4; i++)
                    {
                        if(nodes[i] != null)
                        {
                            nodes[i].insert(c, false);
```

```
                    }
                }
            }
        }

        // otherwise, insert the object upward if propagation is allowed
        else
        {
            if(propagate)
            {
                if(parent != null)
                {
                    parent.insert(c, true);
                }
            }
        }
    }
}


// translates all of the objects this node contains by x, y
public void moveAll(double x, double y)
{
    if(objects == null || objects.isEmpty()) return;

    Actor2D a;
    for(int i = 0; i < objects.size(); i++)
    {
        a = (Actor2D) objects.get(i);
        a.moveBy(x, y);
    }
}


public void update()
{
    if(objects == null || objects.isEmpty()) return;

    // update the list, then remove objects that are no longer in this node
    Moveable m;
    for(int i = 0; i < objects.size(); i++)
    {
```

```java
            m = (Moveable)objects.get(i);
            m.update();

            // test if the object left the node; if so, insert upward
            if(!bounds.contains(m.getBounds()) &&
               !bounds.intersects(m.getBounds())) // might propagate upward
            {
                insert((Moveable)objects.remove(i), true);
            }
        }

        // get the updated size since some objects may have been removed
        int size = objects.size();

        // test each object for collision against each other object in this
        // node
        for(int i = 0; i < size-1; i++)
        {
            Moveable a = (Moveable)objects.get(i);

            for(int j = i+1; j < size; j++)
            {
                Moveable b = (Moveable)objects.get(j);

                if(a.collidesWith(b))
                {
                    a.addCollision(b);
                    b.addCollision(a);
                }
            }
        }
    }

    public void paintBounds(Graphics2D g2d, Color c)
    {
        if(c == null) c = Color.RED;
        g2d.setPaint(c);
        g2d.draw(bounds);
```

```
        }

    }    // QuadNode
```

# The QuadTree Class

```java
package magic.scene;

import java.awt.*;
import java.awt.geom.*;
import java.util.*;

import magic.actor2d.*;

// the root node for QuadTree management
public class QuadTree extends QuadNode
{
    // the overall depth of the tree
    protected int globalDepth;

    // a global linked list of leaf nodes
    public static LinkedList leaves = new LinkedList();

    // global linked list of objects that will be painted
    public static LinkedList paintList = new LinkedList();

    // creates a QuadTree with the sent depth, overall bounds, and viewable
    // screen bounds
    public QuadTree(int depth, Rectangle2D r)
    {
        super(null, depth, r);

        // global depth must be greater than zero
        if(depth <= 0)
        {
            throw new IllegalArgumentException(
                        "depth must be greater than zero");
```

```
        }

        globalDepth = depth;

        // initialize the overflow list
        objects = new LinkedList();
    }

    // adds a leaf node to the global leaf list
    public static void addLeaf(QuadNode node)
    {
        if(! leaves.contains(node))
        {
            leaves.add(node);
        }
    }

    // adds a Moveable object to the global paint list
    public static void addToPaintList(Moveable m)
    {
        if(! paintList.contains(m))
        {
            paintList.add(m);
        }
    }

    // QuadTree must override insert method to deal with objects that are not
    // within scene bounds
    public void insert(Moveable c)
    {
        // if the object is not within scene bounds, add it to the heap
        if(! bounds.contains(c.getBounds()) &&
           ! bounds.intersects(c.getBounds()))
        {
            if(! objects.contains(c))
            {
                objects.add(c);
            }
            return;
```

```
        }

        // add the object to the global paint list
        addToPaintList(c);

        // try adding the object to all child nodes
        for(int i = 0; i < 4; i++)
        {
            if(nodes[i] != null)
            {
                nodes[i].insert(c, false);
            }
        }
    }

    public void update()
    {
        // update the heap list
        if(objects != null && !objects.isEmpty())
        {
            for(int i = 0; i < objects.size(); i++)
            {
                Moveable a = (Moveable) objects.get(i);
                a.update();

                // test if the object entered the tree; if so, insert it and
                // remove it from the heap
                if(bounds.contains(a.getBounds()) ||
                   bounds.intersects(a.getBounds()))
                {
                    insert((Moveable) objects.remove(i), false);
                }
            }
        }

        //  update all leaf nodes for collisions and frame movement
        for(int i = 0; i < leaves.size(); i++)
        {
            ((QuadNode) leaves.get(i)).update();
        }
```

```
        }

        // paints all objects in the global paint list
        public void paint(Graphics2D g2d)
        {
            Actor2D a;
            for(int i = 0; i < paintList.size(); i++)
            {
                a = (Actor2D) paintList.get(i);
                // only paint the object if it is in bounds
                if(bounds.contains(a.getBounds()) ||
                    bounds.intersects(a.getBounds()))
                {
                    a.paint(g2d);
                }
            }
        }


        // paints gridlines showing the bounds of each leaf node
        public void paintBounds(Graphics2D g2d, Color color)
        {
            // paint all leaf nodes
            for(int i = 0; i < leaves.size(); i++)
            {
                ((QuadNode)leaves.get(i)).paintBounds(g2d, color);
            }
        }

    }    // QuadTree
```

## The Scene Class

```
package magic.scene;

import java.awt.*;
import java.awt.geom.*;

import magic.actor2d.*;

// skeleton class for providing scene management
```

```java
public abstract class Scene
{
    // the overall bounds of the scene
    protected Rectangle2D bounds;

    // the part of the scene that is viewable; usually this is the size of the
    // Applet window
    protected Rectangle2D viewable;

    // creates a new Scene object with the sent bounds and viewable area
    public Scene(Rectangle2D v, Rectangle2D b)
    {
        setViewable(v);
        setBounds(b);
    }

    // adds an Actor to the scene, subclasses that use Actor2D objects should
    // override this method
    public void add(Actor2D a)
    {

    }

    public final void setViewable(Rectangle2D r)
    {
        viewable = new Rectangle2D.Double(r.getX(), r.getY(),
                                          r.getWidth(), r.getHeight());
    }

    public final Rectangle2D getViewable()
    {
        return viewable;
    }

    public final void setBounds(Rectangle2D r)
    {
        bounds   = new Rectangle2D.Double(r.getX(), r.getY(),
                                          r.getWidth(), r.getHeight());
```

```
            }

            public final Rectangle2D getBounds()
            {
                return bounds;
            }

            // updates the scene
            public abstract void update();

            // paints the scene to the sent Graphics2D context
            public abstract void paint(Graphics2D g2d);

    }       // Scene
```

# The magic.util Package
## The MagicUtils Class

```
        package magic.util;

        import magic.debug.*;

        public class MagicUtils extends Object
        {
            // pre-calculated values for sin, cos, and tan values

            static double[] sinTable = null;
            static double[] cosTable = null;
            static double[] tanTable = null;

            // builds the three trig lookup tables
            public static void buildTrigTables()
            {
                Debugger.reportMessage(
                    "Building trig tables (MagicUtils.buildTrigTables)...");

                sinTable = new double[360];
                cosTable = new double[360];
```

```java
        tanTable = new double[360];

        double radians;
        for(int i = 0; i < 360; i++)
        {
            radians = Math.toRadians(i);
            sinTable[i] = Math.sin(radians);
            cosTable[i] = Math.cos(radians);
            tanTable[i] = Math.tan(radians);
        }

    }

    public static double sin(int degrees)
    {
        if(degrees < 0)
        {
            degrees = 360 + degrees%360;
        }
        if(degrees >= 360)
        {
            degrees %= 360;
        }

        try
        {
            return sinTable[degrees];
        }
        catch(NullPointerException e)
        {
            buildTrigTables();
            return sin(degrees);
        }
    }

    public static double cos(int degrees)
    {
        if(degrees < 0)
        {
            degrees = 360 + degrees%360;
```

```
        }
        if(degrees >= 360)
        {
            degrees %= 360;
        }

        try
        {
            return cosTable[degrees];
        }
        catch(NullPointerException e)
        {
            buildTrigTables();
            return cos(degrees);
        }
    }

    public static double tan(int degrees)
    {
        if(degrees < 0)
        {
            degrees = 360 + degrees%360;
        }
        if(degrees >= 360)
        {
            degrees %= 360;
        }

        try
        {
            return tanTable[degrees];
        }
        catch(NullPointerException e)
        {
            buildTrigTables();
            return tan(degrees);
        }
    }

}    // MagicUtils
```

# APPENDIX G

# MORE RESOURCES

There's a ton of places on the Internet you can go for more information on Java and on game programming in general. Here's a list of some of the places I've found to be great sources of additional resources in my game development endeavors:

- **http://www.java.sun.com.** This is Sun's main Java Website, chock full of development tools, white papers, and tutorials on the Java language. Visit this site often to get the latest on what's going on in the Java development industry or to check out the newest Java development releases.

- **http://www.javagaming.org.** This site is maintained by several Sun engineers who serve as evangelists for the use of Java for games. This site hosts a really nice message board, as well as tutorials and additional resources covering the latest advances in the Java language.

- **http://www.xgames3d.com.** This is the Xtreme Games LLC Web site. If you've ever read any of the books written by André LaMothe, then you've definitely been here before. In addition to publishing opportunities, the Xtreme Games Web site contains a killer bulletin board where you can talk about anything from newbie topics to advanced AI. There's also a place for general-discussion if you want to just hang out and talk about news, games, or anything else—even cannibalism.

- **http://www.gamejug.org.** This is the Game Developers Java Users Group (GameJUG). This site contains several discussion group lists concerning the latest news and advances within the Java gamed development network.

- **http://www.gameDev.net.** This is truly an awesome resource for anyone serious about game development. GameDev.net has been around for a number of years, so it has a great repository of tutorials—everything from the basics to the advanced. It also contains a discussion area for you to post your questions or talk about industry news.

- **http://www.gamasutra.com.** An excellent game development site, loaded with tons of industry news as well as whitepapers, tutorials, and how-to's. You can even post your resume when you're ready to join the "big boys" (and girls) of the game development industry.

# APPENDIX H

# WHAT'S ON THE CD-ROM?

In case you decided to sabotage the enclosed CD-ROM by placing it in the microwave or some other destructive device, here's the skinny on what you're missing.

- **Java Productivity Software**. Although this book focuses on the Java 2 SDK, version 1.4, it is still in its public beta stage at the time of this book's release. Therefore, I was unable to provide it on the CD-ROM. However, the Java 2 SDK, version 1.3.1, *is* provided, so that you can get started with Java programming right away. I also provided a copy of the Java 3-D API, version 1.2.1. I'm sad to say that the official documentation for the Java 2 platform is not available for redistribution either. Nonetheless, feel free to use the software provided on the CD-ROM, but remember that downloading the latest development and documentation packages from the Sun website (http://www.java.sun.com) is a necessity for any serious Java developer. Refer to Appendix G for more on game development resources.

- **Shareware/Freeware Utilities**. These include *Forte' for Java*, version 3.0, *WinZip* for Windows 8.0, *Paint Shot Pro*, version 7.0, and *Sound Forge 5.0* by Sonic Foundry.

- **Java 2 Example Source Code**. For those lazy cut-and-paste moments, or when you just want to take a quick glance at any of the example programs presented in this book, all of the source code is available on the CD-ROM. This includes a full source listing for the *Magic* game development engine. The fun begins in the \Source directory on the CD-ROM.

- **Xtreme Web Games**. These are just a few sample games I wrote for a talk I gave at the 2000 Xtreme Games Developer's Conference (XGDC). They were written with a preliminary version of the *Magic* game engine. Feel free to modify or improve on these in any way you like.

# Index

# License Agreement/Notice of Limited Warranty

By opening the sealed disc container in this book, you agree to the following terms and conditions. If, upon reading the following license agreement and notice of limited warranty, you cannot agree to the terms and conditions set forth, return the unused book with unopened disc to the place where you purchased it for a refund.

**License:**

The enclosed software is copyrighted by the copyright holder(s) indicated on the software disc. You are licensed to copy the software onto a single computer for use by a single user and to a backup disc. You may not reproduce, make copies, or distribute copies or rent or lease the software in whole or in part, except with written permission of the copyright holder(s). You may transfer the enclosed disc only together with this license, and only if you destroy all other copies of the software and the transferee agrees to the terms of the license. You may not decompile, reverse assemble, or reverse engineer the software.

**Notice of Limited Warranty:**

The enclosed disc is warranted by Premier Press, Inc. to be free of physical defects in materials and workmanship for a period of sixty (60) days from end user's purchase of the book/disc combination. During the sixty-day term of the limited warranty, Premier Press will provide a replacement disc upon the return of a defective disc.

**Limited Liability:**

THE SOLE REMEDY FOR BREACH OF THIS LIMITED WARRANTY SHALL CONSIST ENTIRELY OF REPLACEMENT OF THE DEFECTIVE DISC. IN NO EVENT SHALL PREMIER PRESS OR THE AUTHORS BE LIABLE FOR ANY OTHER DAMAGES, INCLUDING LOSS OR CORRUPTION OF DATA, CHANGES IN THE FUNCTIONAL CHARACTERISTICS OF THE HARDWARE OR OPERATING SYSTEM, DELETERIOUS INTERACTION WITH OTHER SOFTWARE, OR ANY OTHER SPECIAL, INCIDENTAL, OR CONSEQUENTIAL DAMAGES THAT MAY ARISE, EVEN IF PREMIER AND/OR THE AUTHORS HAVE PREVIOUSLY BEEN NOTIFIED THAT THE POSSIBILITY OF SUCH DAMAGES EXISTS.

**Disclaimer of Warranties:**

PREMIER AND THE AUTHORS SPECIFICALLY DISCLAIM ANY AND ALL OTHER WARRANTIES, EITHER EXPRESS OR IMPLIED, INCLUDING WARRANTIES OF MERCHANTABILITY, SUITABILITY TO A PARTICULAR TASK OR PURPOSE, OR FREEDOM FROM ERRORS. SOME STATES DO NOT ALLOW FOR EXCLUSION OF IMPLIED WARRANTIES OR LIMITATION OF INCIDENTAL OR CONSEQUENTIAL DAMAGES, SO THESE LIMITATIONS MIGHT NOT APPLY TO YOU.

**Other:**

This Agreement is governed by the laws of the State of Indiana without regard to choice of law principles. The United Convention of Contracts for the International Sale of Goods is specifically disclaimed. This Agreement constitutes the entire agreement between you and Premier Press regarding use of the software.